THE VALUES OF BUREAUCRACY

THE VALUES OF BUREAUCRACY

Edited by Paul du Gay

OXFORD
UNIVERSITY PRESS

OXFORD
UNIVERSITY PRESS

Great Clarendon Street, Oxford ox2 6DP

Oxford University Press is a department of the University of Oxford.
It furthers the University's objective of excellence in research, scholarship,
and education by publishing worldwide in

Oxford New York

Auckland Cape Town Dar es Salaam Hong Kong Karachi
Kuala Lumpur Madrid Melbourne Mexico City Nairobi
New Delhi Shanghai Taipei Toronto

With offices in

Argentina Austria Brazil Chile Czech Republic France Greece
Guatemala Hungary Italy Japan South Korea Poland Portugal
Singapore Switzerland Thailand Turkey Ukraine Vietnam

Oxford is a registered trade mark of Oxford University Press
in the UK and in certain other countries

Published in the United States
by Oxford University Press Inc., New York

© Oxford University Press 2005

The moral rights of the author have been asserted
Database right Oxford University Press (maker)

First published 2005

British Library Cataloguing in Publication Data
Data available

Library of Congress Cataloging in Publication Data

The values of bureaucracy / edited by Paul du Gay.
    p. cm.
Includes bibliographical references.
ISBN 0-19-927545-9 (alk. paper)—ISBN 0-19-927546-7 (pbk. : alk. paper) 1.
Bureaucracy. 2. Organizational change. I. Du Gay, Paul.
  HM 806.V35 2005
  302.3'5—dc22

ISBN 0-19-927545-9 (hbk.)
ISBN 0-19-927546-7 (pbk.)

1 3 5 7 9 10 8 6 4 2

Typeset by Newgen Imaging Systems (P) Ltd., Chennai, India
Printed in Great Britain
on acid-free paper by
Biddles Ltd., King's Lynn, Norfolk

Acknowledgements

The chapters in this volume derive from a workshop on 'Defending Bureaucracy' held at St. Hugh's College, Oxford, in March, 2003. I would like to thank everyone who participated in the workshop and to offer my considerable gratitude to Pamela Walker and Karen Ho, who helped organize the event and ensured its smooth running. The workshop would not have been possible without the generous financial support of the Pavis Centre for Social and Cultural Research at the Open University. The preparation of this volume was greatly facilitated by the support of the Department of Organization and Work Sociology (IOA) at the Copenhagen Business School where the editor spent some time as a Visiting Scholar in 2003. Finally, a word of gratitude to David Musson for commissioning the volume and to Matthew Derbyshire for editorial guidance, to the chapter authors who have borne stoically the successive rounds of alterations and amendments, and to Denise Janes, of the Centre for Citizenship, Identities and Governance at the Open University, for her exceptional administrative and secretarial support.

Contents

Contents

Part 4: Bureaucracy and Civil Society

List of Figures

List of Tables

Notes on Contributors

Mats Alvesson works at the Department of Business Administration, Lund University. His research interests include critical theory, reflexive methodology, organizational culture, and knowledge-intensive firms. His most recent books include *Reflexive Methodology* (Sage 2000, with Kaj Sköldberg), *Understanding Organizational Culture* (Sage 2002), and *Knowledge Work and Knowledge-Intensive Firms* (Oxford University Press 2004).

Thomas Armbrüster is an Assistant Professor of organizational behaviour at the University of Mannheim, Germany. He holds a Ph.D. from the London School of Economics and Political Science and his research interests comprise the management consulting business, cross-national comparisons of management, and a liberal approach to management and organization theory.

John Clarke is Professor of Social Policy at the Open University. His research has evolved around questions about the politics, ideologies and discourses at stake in the remaking of welfare states and in the shifting governance of public services. He is currently working with colleagues on a research project called 'Creating Citizen-Consumers: changing identifications and relationships' and his most recent book, *Changing Welfare, Changing States: new directions in social policy*, was published by Sage in 2004.

Paul du Gay is Professor of Sociology and Organization Studies, and Co-Director of the Centre for Citizenship, Identities and Governance, in the Faculty of Social Sciences at the Open University. His research is located in the sociology of organizational life and cultural studies. His recent publications include, *In Praise of Bureaucracy* (2000) and *Cultural Economy* (ed. with M. Pryke, 2002). *Culture, Person and Organization: Essays in Cultural Economy* will be published by Sage in 2006.

Yvonne Due Billing is Associate Professor of Sociology at the Department of Sociology at the University of Copenhagen in Denmark. She holds a Ph.D. from the University of Lund, Sweden and from CBS, Denmark. She has published on gender and organizations in several journals and her books on the subject include *Gender, Managers, and Organizations* (de Gruyter 1994) and *Understanding Gender and Organizations* (Sage 1997). Her research interests include studies of organizational cultures and power, 'cross-overs' (men in women's jobs and vice versa), organizational identities and the conceptualization of meanings of gender in organizations.

Charles T. Goodsell is Professor Emeritus of Public Administration at the Centre for Public Administration and Policy of Virginia Polytechnic Institute and State University. He is author of *The Case for Bureaucracy: A Public Administration Polemic*, now in its 4th edition (CQ Press, 2004). His other books include *The American Statehouse, Public Administration Illuminated*, and *Inspired by the Arts, The Social Meaning of Civic Space, American Corporations and Peruvian Politics*, and *Administration of A Revolution*. His current research is centred on the agency mission as a belief structure in public governance.

Paul Hoggett is Professor of Politics and Director of the Centre for Psycho-Social Studies at the University of the West of England, Bristol. Recent publications include *Emotional Life and the Politics of Welfare* (Palgrave 2000) and, with Robin Hambleton and Danny Burns, *The Politics of Decentralisation* (Macmillan 1994). He is currently undertaking an ESRC funded project entitled 'Negotiating Ethical Dilemmas in Contested Communities'. He co-edits the journal *Organisational and Social Dynamics*.

Janet Newman is Professor of Social Policy at the Open University. She has published widely on changing state forms and their impact on public services, drawing extensively on the experience of those working in the public sector. Publications include *Remaking Governance: Politics, Policy and the Public Realm* (Policy Press, 2005); *Modernising Governance: New Labour, Policy and Society* (Sage 2001) and *The Managerial State: Power, Politics and Ideology in the Remaking of Social Welfare* (with John Clarke: Sage 1997).

Dr Antonino Palumbo is ricercatore (lecturer) in Political Philosophy at Palermo University, Italy. His main research interests are: contemporary theories of social justice, rights, and democracy; modern social and political theory; analytical theories of the state and public choice. His more recent publications are: 'Weber, Durkheim and the Sociology of the Modern State', with Alan Scott, in R. Bellamy and T. Ball (eds.),

Cambridge History of Twentieth Century Political Thought (Cambridge University Press, 2003) and 'Liberalism', in R. Axmann (ed.), *Understanding Democratic Politics* (Sage, 2003).

Michael Reed is Professor of Organizational Analysis and Deputy Director (Research), Human Resource Management Section, Cardiff University Business School. Previously, he was Professor of Organization Theory and Associate Dean (Research) at Lancaster University Management School. Currently, he is 'lead editor' of the journal *Organization* published by Sage. His research interests are located in the general field of organization theory and analysis with particular reference to theory development, expert work, control, and public sector service organizations. Recent publications include 'The Agency/Structure Dilemma' in the *Oxford Handbook of Organisation Theory* and *The Manager-Academic and Technologies of Management in Universities*, also published by Oxford University Press.

Graeme Salaman is Professor of Organization Studies at The Open University Business School. He has written over fifty books and articles in the areas of Human Resource Management, Organizational Change, and Organizational Capability. Recent books include *Human Resource Management: A Strategic Introduction* (Blackwell 1998), *Strategy and Capability* (Blackwell 2003) and *How to Innovate—What Managers Think* (Blackwell 2004). Recent research projects include a study of innovation (ESRC) and currently a study of knowledge management (ESRC). He edits a series of books for the Open University Press (now McGraw Hill) on the management of work and organization. He has worked with and for the Government of Ethiopia for many years on a number of projects. He is currently working on the restructuring of the Ethiopian Ministry of Foreign Affairs funded by the Foreign and Commonwealth Office and designing and installing a performance management system for Addis Ababa City Authority funded by the British Council. He is the director of a project funded by the World Bank to develop a distance learning facility in the Ethiopian Civil Service College.

Mike Savage is Professor of Sociology and Director of the ESRC Centre for Research on Socio-Cultural Change (CRESC) at the University of Manchester. His interests are in social stratification, historical sociology, and urban sociology. Recent books include: *Globalisation and Belonging* (with Gaynor Bagnall and Brian Longhurst; Sage 2004).

Alan Scott is Professor of Sociology at the University of Innsbruck. Current research includes a project within the New Orientations for Democracy in Europe programme (http://www.node-research.at/englisch/index.php), and work on university organization. Relevant publications: 'Bureaucratic Revolutions and Free Market Utopias in *Economy and Society*, 25/1, 1996; 'Capitalism, Weber and Democracy' in *Max Weber Studies* 1/1, 2000 and, as co-author, 'Between Two Laws: University Reform in Austria,' in *Governance*, forthcoming.

Paul Thompson is Professor of Organizational Analysis and Vice Dean (Research) in the Business School at the University of Strathclyde. His latest publication is *The Handbook of Work and Organization* for Oxford University Press (co-edited with Stephen Ackroyd, Pam Tolbert and Rose Batt). He is co-organizer of the International Labour Process Conference; co-edits the Palgrave Series *Management, Work and Organisation, and Critical Perspectives on Work and Organization*, and is on the board of *Organization Studies*.

The Values of Bureaucracy: An Introduction

Paul du Gay

The demise of bureaucracy has been anticipated, and demanded, many times throughout the history of management thought, as well as in modern social and political theory. However, despite the scorn regularly heaped upon it, bureaucracy, both as an organizational ideal and as a diversely formatted organizational device, has proven remarkably resilient. Reports of its death have turned out to be somewhat premature.

Despite the dramatic claims of certain prominent contemporary management gurus and social theorists that the end of the bureau is once again nigh (Castells 2000; Giddens 1998; Heckscher and Donnellon 1994; Leadbeater 1999; Peters 1989), there remain plenty of reasons to be cautious. As even the fulsomely anti-bureaucratic *The Economist* noted in its review edition 'The World in 2003', despite the claims made in much management theory, representations of and practical prescriptions for, reforming organizational life bear witness to a 'partial return to values we thought were gone forever' (2002:118). In the wake of the corporate scandals at Enron, Worldcom et al., *The Economist*'s reviewers noted that the that the cult of 'the charismatic leader' is being 'cast aside' and in its place they espied an increased value being placed upon dull (but once again worthy) management skills such as 'attention to detail and the capacity to follow through' (2002:118). Linked to this, they noted the emergence of 'a version of command and control, though no one would ever dare to call it that'

(2002:118). In part, they concluded, this renewed concern with hierarchical forms of management followed from a recognition of the personnel problems deriving from a lack of clear guidelines and structure. 'People', they suggested, 'like to know to whom they are reporting. This will start to be built into company structures. Gently, the middle manager will stage something of a comeback' (2002:118). Taken together these developments pointed to a return of that which dare not utter its name: 'Bureaucracy, after many years of decline, will be on the rise again' (2002:118). While *The Economist* baulked somewhat at its own conclusions, stating that this 'trend has nothing at all to commend it', the logic of its analysis indicated all too clearly that contemporary attempts to de-bureaucratize organizational life in modern societies had clear practical limits. Bureaucracy, like the proverbial elephant in the living room could not be positively acknowledged nor could it be ignored, or magically spirited away.

Despite its evident utility for the conduct of any number of the activities we take for granted—in politics, business, social welfare and cultural production, for example—somehow bureaucracy remains morally and politically suspect and indefensible (Parker 1993; du Gay 2000; Goodsell 2004). Given the prevailing political and moral atmosphere, it seems almost unimaginable for a politician, say, to stand for re-election on a pro-bureaucracy ticket. Likewise, as B. G. Peters (2003), for instance has argued, contemporary public administrators find it very difficult to give voice to the values of Weberian public bureaucracy without appearing to be old-fashioned, anachronistic and irrelevant. It would seem then that the more one learns to appreciate the values of bureaucracy, the more difficult it is to give them a positive public airing.

In contrast to what we might term the seemingly 'permanent structure' of anti-bureaucratic thought, the present collection sets out to articulate explicitly some of the values of bureaucracy and to reassert their importance for the production of responsible and effective governance in a variety of organizational contexts.

At its heart, this collection seeks to interrogate and criticize contemporary anti-bureaucratic sentiment as it has appeared in a wide range of discourses—*inter alia*, the New Public Management, 'epochal' varieties of social and cultural theory, 'post-bureaucratic' organizational theory and 'Third-Way' political ideology—and across a diverse number of organizational sites. Its aim is twofold. First, to show how and why bureaucratic forms of organization have played, and continue to play, a vital and productive role in ordering existence in a number of domains—public and private, governmental and voluntary. A crucial aspect of this task involves indicating the extent to which bureaucracy, contrary to the views of many of its detractors, is alive, well, proliferating and hybridizing, rather than simply disappearing or decaying (Alvesson and Thompson 2004). Secondly, to describe and analyse the impact—political, ethical, social and cultural—of contemporary attempts to de-bureaucratize organizational life in those domains. The collection therefore seeks to highlight the values of bureaucracy and at the same time to indicate why distinctively bureaucratic forms of organization should continue to be valued.

This emphasis on the 'values' of bureaucracy suggests two further points. First, that bureaucracy is not—as many critics assume—a simple singularity. Rather whatever singularity it is deemed to possess is multiple not monolithic (Minson 1993; Osborne 1994; Adler and Borys 1996). To be more specific, bureaucracy has turned out to be less a hard and fast trans-historical model, but rather what we might describe as a many-sided, evolving, diversified organizational device (du Gay 2000; Courpasson 2000; Kallinikos 2004). Different states, for instance, with varying constitutional arrangements, have all produced recognizably 'bureaucratic' administrative apparatuses; but state bureaucracies in the plural, in the sense that they are distinctive and non-reducible. The idea, often propagated in the more dramatic of New Public Management texts, of a single, universal (and now obsolete) bureaucratic regime of public administration is as implausible as the solution proffered to this illusory problem: a global recipe which will deliver a form of 'post-bureaucratic', 'entrepreneurial' government that is always and everywhere 'best in world' (Osborne and Gaebler 1992; Osborne and Plastrik 1997)

This in turn suggests, secondly, that an abstract celebration or denunciation of 'bureaucracy' makes little sense. To defend or criticize bureaucracy, for instance, requires one to be quite precise about which bureaucratic ethics, capacities and comportments one is seeking to criticise or defend in relation to what specific purposes. Indeed, seen in context, what contemporary anti-bureaucrats represent as the inherently indefensible features of 'bureaucracy' per se—whether morally or in terms of practical outcomes—can potentially assume a much more positive character. For instance, the plurality and non-reducibility of state bureaux noted above, is also matched by the plurality of obligation and comportment within them. A senior public administrator working in the institutional milieu of British Central

Government, for instance, has traditionally, at least, needed to be, *inter alia*, something of an expert in the ways of the constitution, a bit of a politician, a stickler for procedure and a stoic able to accept disappointments with equanimity (Chapman 1988; Bogdanor 2001). As an institution of government, the public administration in Britain therefore reflects and performs not simply bureaucracy but also politics, diplomacy, and indeed certain forms of enterprise (clearly, an institution that in the immediate aftermath of the Second World War, under extraordinarily difficult circumstances, succeeded in establishing the National Health Service, a new social security system, the expansion of education at all levels and the nationalization of the major public utilities could hardly be considered to lack the qualities of managerial initiative and enterprise). However, reduction to any one of these various ethical capacities and comportments alone would undoubtedly damage the purposes the public administrator is charged with fulfilling. Such reductionism is not impossible but its costs are apt to be high. The point is that there are limits; limits, that is, to the extent to which the complex oscillations and balances between different ethical capacities within a given bureaucratic life order can be pushed in one direction towards any single vision of ordering without significant, perhaps pyrrhic, costs attaching to such an endeavour: whether that push is framed in terms of the demands of 'audit', 'modernization', 'governance' or 'managerialism' (du Gay 2000; Strathern 2001). Indeed, the more 'grey, meticulous and patiently documentary' one's descriptive and analytic practice is—to borrow Foucault's (1986) phrase—the more difficult it is to maintain a general, critical opposition to 'bureaucracy' *tout court* and the easier it should become to delineate the values of any particular bureaucratic organization of existence (due Billing 1994). In the field of public administration, for instance, this can be undertaken by describing the practical ways in which actually existing bureaucratic practices function as the institutional manifestation of a continuous effort to create responsible, accountable government by ensuring that discretion is not abused, that due process is the norm not the exception, and that undue risks are not taken that undermine the integrity of the political system (Kaufman 1977; Uhr 1999). In this way, free and easy slogans about eliminating red tape, freeing up enterprise and letting managers manage that have characterised the New Public Management movement and its offspring can be gently corrected.

Similarly, the dramatic dichotomies between simplicity and complexity, rigidity and flexibility, that regularly accompany political as well as social theoretical debates about the reform of public and private bureaux could also be one of the first casualties of such a contextualist approach to identifying 'the values of bureaucracy'. 'Complexity', for instance, is a term that has flattered many vanities in organization studies, political science, and social theory in recent years (Thrift 1999). In the field of public management, for instance, its deployment has often served, much like other forms of epochalist over-dramatization, to evacuate the field of its determinate content. For some advocates of 'network governance', for instance, recourse to 'complexity' functions both as a stick with which to spank modern states and the politics they practise, and as a 'roadmap' to constructing a new form of political ordering (Rhodes 1996; 2000). Yet, as any number of analyses testify, modern political life was never uncomplicated. Rather its complexities and inconsistencies were simply clarified and made more or less manageable by the order that modern political institutions, including, of course, centralized, bureaucratic state apparatuses, have been able to bestow on them (Holmes and Sunstein, 1999). In this respect, the world pictured by 'network governance' can sometimes seem less like a world of complexity and more like a universe in which no one has yet been able to work out a way of dealing with complexity (Runciman 2002).

To return to the main point, though, as Weber indicated long ago, an abstract celebration or denunciation of 'bureaucracy' makes little sense, for as he insisted, the mere fact of bureaucratization tells us comparatively little about the concrete directions in which it operates in any given context. Instead as Weber (1978 ii: 990–1) suggested, 'one must in every individual historical case analyse in which . . . directions bureaucratization has there developed'. In other words, it is pointless to apply global moral judgements to bureaucratic conduct *tout court*: to praise it for its impartiality or condemn it for its conservatism; to approve its efficiency or damn its amorality; to find its exemplar in Sir Warren Fisher on the one hand, or Adolf Eichmann on the other. Indeed, as their polyvalent and conflictual character testifies, such judgements do not really concern bureaucratic ethics at all but rather the forms in which they impact upon other conducts of life or departments of existence (Hunter 1994). Most especially, as many of the chapters in this collection testify, such global judgements refer—if a fever can be said to refer to a disease—to the relationship between bureaucracy and another quite distinct life-order, that of political leadership.

The structure of the book

The collection is divided into four thematic sections, each of which engages with a particular form of contemporary anti-bureaucratic or post-bureaucratic critique. In Part 1, 'The Politics of Bureaucracy', Charles Goodsell, Paul du Gay and Thomas Armbruster focus, in particular, on politically expressivist[1] or romantic critiques of bureaucracy as these have infected and inflected debates about institutional design and organizational reform in the spheres of public and private sector management. In Chapter 1, Charles Goodsell examines certain critiques of US public bureaucracies and seeks to show how empirically unsubstantiated such criticisms are, and to indicate that public bureaucracies in advanced industrial societies are far more efficient and effective than critics admit. More importantly, though, Goodsell, argues that the bureau, or administrative arm of government, is integral to the entire process of governance. The value of the bureau then lies not simply in its efficiency and effectiveness but in its capacity to support and develop responsible governance. For Goodsell rather than appearing as an old-fashioned organizational device whose time is up, the bureau may well become 'increasingly indispensable as an institutional node of potent, professional, and accountable authority that weaves together the strands of dispersed public action into coherent policy' (Chapter 1, p. 25). In Chapter 2, Paul du Gay takes a tour through some of the sites where anti-bureaucratic sentiment has been and continues to be most enthusiastically expressed, exploring, in particular, the foundational oppositions between bureaucracy and liberty that these anti-bureaucrats deploy. He argues that in government and business alike, bureaucracy has become a condition of freedom. He suggests that despite representing themselves as champions of individual rights and liberties, contemporary political expressivist critics of bureaucracy—whether libertarian, communitarian or neo-liberal in orientation—cannot be effective or consistent defenders of these precisely because rights and freedoms are an enforced uniformity, rarely guaranteed without the presence of large, centralized bureaucracies capable of creating and enforcing them. In Chapter 3, Thomas Armbrüster frames his discussion of the values of bureaucracy in relationship to debates in political philosophy about liberal interventionism and non-interventionism. He focuses particular attention on the various approaches to bureaucratic management evidenced in liberal non-interventionist thought (classical liberalism and contemporary libertarianism), liberal interventionism (contemporary liberalism or liberal egalitarianism), and communitarianism (or civic republicanism). He argues that contemporary anti-bureaucratic political culture, in the USA, and in other Western societies, combines particular elements of communitarianism and liberal non-interventionism and can be characterized as 'moralist non-interventionism' or 'moralist libertarianism'. Armbrüster concludes his chapter by drawing attention to the practical consequences of this form of 'anti-bureaucraticism' through a discussion of the recent upsurge of corporate scandals in the United States.

As indicated earlier, the end of bureaucracy has been anticipated many times. On both the right and left of the ideological spectrum, bureaucratic organization has been generally viewed as a necessary evil that will inevitably fade away as a particular dynamic inherent in historical change imposes itself upon the logic and trajectory of social development. Thus, as Mike Reed indicates in his contribution to the volume, 'a neo-liberal management theorist such as Bennis, a neo-liberalist economist such as Schumpeter, a social democrat such as Schumacher, a neo-corporatist such as Elias, a technological determinist such as Bell or Castells, and a theorist of radical participatory democracy such as Illich, can all agree that the underlying currents of history will, eventually, make bureaucracy an obsolete form of administrative power and organization' (Chapter 5, pp. 101–2). In this respect 'post-bureaucratic' thinking—whether framed in terms of 'network' forms of organization, marketization or corporate culture—that dominates much contemporary organizational analysis, is the latest manifestation of what can often appear to be an almost 'permanent structure' of anti-bureaucratic thought. In Part 2, 'The End Of Bureaucracy?', Paul Thompson, Mats Alvesson, Mike Reed, and Graeme Salaman, explore the claims of recent social, organizational and management theory that we are living through the final days of a bureaucratic era and entering an age of 'post-bureaucracy' and 'network governance'.

In Chapter 4, Paul Thompson and Mats Alvesson argue that there has been a shift in the grounds of critique of bureaucracy, away from the limits and dysfunctions of a 'permanent' logic of structure and action, to a claim of systemic dysfunctionality—that bureaucracy simply no longer works in contemporary economy and society. After critically examining the concepts and claims of post-bureaucratic theorists, Thompson and Alvesson carefully examine the evidence of contemporary changes in work, employment, and decision rules. They conclude that organizational researchers need to move away from sweeping, value-laden and undifferentiated claims about organizational change. Bureaucracy, they contend, has never been a single or static phenomenon. Contemporary organizational changes are not in the main 'post-bureaucratic', but rather tend towards a re-configuration or 'hybridization' of bureaucratic forms. In Chapter 5, Mike Reed focuses attention on the particular forms of post-bureaucratic thinking exemplified in the various forms of 'network theory' currently popular in organizational analysis. Reed assesses what he calls the 'post-bureaucratic/network thesis' in the context of the particular tradition of socio-political theorizing in which it is embedded. He suggests that this latest phase of 'anti-bureaucratic' theorizing and analysis embodies all the strengths and weaknesses of its intellectual forebears—both in its sensitivity to key features of contemporary change, and its incorrigible naivety in dealing with the consequences of those changes. In Chapter 6, Graeme Salaman considers the critiques of bureaucracy informing the development of management competency and leadership programmes. Salaman argues that despite their avowed opposition to, and claimed transcendence of, bureaucracy both programmes of reform depend upon bureaucratic mechanisms and techniques for the production of the conducts they define as 'post-bureaucratic'. For Salaman, the mechanisms of monitoring, definition, assessment and control that frame 'competency' systems represent a novel and more insidious form of control, one combining bureaucratic with communitarian and entrepreneurial norms and techniques in a heady but frequently debilitating brew.

Some of the most vehement criticisms of bureaucracy have arisen in the context of on-going attempts to 're-invent' or 'modernize' public sector organizations in accordance with the dictates of the New Public Management or Entrepreneurial Governance. The traditional 'Weberian' public bureaucracy has, it is generally agreed, been subject to continuous assault by proponents of radical managerial reform, although the character of the emergent rationality of institutional governance is not always clear. In Part 3, these on-going managerial reforms are themselves subject to critical examination and the values supported by traditional public bureaucracies are reviewed, and some of the virtues of bureaucratic public administration are highlighted. The logic of restoring some of the values of bureaucratic organization is proposed but not simply as a reflex resistance to current programmes of organizational change per se, but rather because those values were functional for maintaining public administration in both a politically responsible and effective manner. In Chapter 7, Paul Hoggett argues that public bureaucracies in their traditional forms are one of the few places where questions of technique ('what works') and questions of value stand a chance of being integrated. He argues that in embracing the tenets of the New Public Management in a wholehearted and largely uncritical manner, the British state, more than any equivalent formation, has suppressed the ethical and moral foundations of public service. He claims that in the UK 'efficacy rules' and that a consequent demoralization of public office has brought about a deep-seated demoralization of the public service workforce. In Chapter 8, Janet Newman focuses upon the relations between public bureaucracy and the 'new governance' around which public services are, in part, being reshaped. She argues that the dispersal of power across multiple tiers and spheres of governance raises significant questions about the power, agency, and accountability of public bureaucrats, especially in the context of a new emphasis on the importance of 'transformational leadership' in the public sector. In particular, she seeks to assess the extent to which key features of the Weberian state bureau are being subordinated within new governance regimes, or, alternatively, how they are being articulated with other meaning systems (leadership, entrepreneurship) in new logics of legitimation that bend, rather than fundamentally break, the ethos of bureaucratic office. In Chapter 9, John Clarke explores the role of audit, evaluation, and inspection in the governance of public institutions. The chapter focuses upon the issue of performance management and asks the question: what is being performed and for what audiences? Clarke argues that one of the key dimensions is that of 'performing the state'. But other performances are lodged—and not always comfortably— within this drama. Performing achievement and success is a prerequisite for different forms of organizational survival. Situated in shifting and uncertain formations of the public, the quest for 'success' creates a spiral of performances that are both in tension, and mutually reinforcing. However, their reinforcement may pose problems for the public-as-audience. In particular, how long will this audience 'suspend disbelief' when confronted by spiralling claims about effectiveness, success, innovation, and improvement? The chapter concludes with some observations concerning the relations between traditional bureaucratic forms of public administration and the governmental rationality of 'audit culture'. In Chapter 10, Daniel Miller offers an anthropological account of an ethnographic encounter with the Best Value audit of British local government services. Miller is concerned with the implications of the terms 'Best Value' as the name of this audit and what this says more generally about current concerns with the concept of 'value' in public services. In particular, the chapter examines the discrepancies this brings out between the values associated with audit and the values associated with traditional public bureaucracy.

Miller's wide-ranging discussion of value sets the scene for the final section of the book. As has already been argued, the devaluing of bureaucracy takes many forms. It presents itself in historical mode in the argument that bureaucracy is an anachronistic organizational form, the product of a bygone era, out of step with the economic, political, and cultural temper of the times. It presents itself in moral form, in the cataloguing of the many substantive values that an instrumental form of bureaucratic organization has undermined or otherwise corrupted. In this latter strain of anti-bureaucratic argument, the bureau is routinely conceived of a one sided expression of an 'instrumental rationality' which can sustain its identity only through repressing and marginalizing its 'other'—the emotional, the communal, the sexual and so forth (MacIntyre 1981; Ferguson 1984; Bauman 1989). From this perspective, 'bureaucratic culture' is assumed to be based upon a series of 'foundational exclusions'—between reason and emotion, public and private—whose 'absent presence' erupts onto the surface of organizational life in the form of cumulatively disabling dysfunctions. In this understanding of the matter, 'morality' can only be returned to organizational life once these separations are transcended, when official and citizenly commitments, for instance, are once again aligned. In Part 4, 'Bureaucracy and Civil Society', such devaluing is questioned and the ethical and moral bases of bureaucratic conduct reasserted through an examination of the substantive values that bureaucracy can give rise to and support. In Chapter 11, Yvonne due Billing questions the arguments of radical feminists that bureaucracy is an inherently masculinist form of organization. Looking at the meanings of bureaucracy, and the meanings of gender equity, due Billing compares and contrasts bureaucratic and non-bureaucratic theories and programmes of gender equity. She argues that the outcome of bureaucratic gender equity projects has been largely positive and that non-bureaucratic projects in this area often slide into wishful thinking and political romanticism. In Chapter 12, Antonino Palumbo and Alan Scott, take issue with two particular versions of anti-bureaucratic thought: that derived from public choice theory which sees public bureaux as inherently inefficient and recommends their replacement by more businesslike entrepreneurial organizational forms; and that derived from political romantic representations of civil society as unamenable to bureaucratic management. They argue that both are mistaken and go on to offer a partial defence of bureaucracy both as a necessary protector of the commons and as a precondition for the working of market institutions.

In Chapter 13, the final chapter of the book, Mike Savage focuses upon the relations between voluntary associations, social capital, and bureaucracy. He suggests that rather than being an alternative mode of organizing to the 'bureaucratic'—as some representations of 'civil society' and 'social capital' suggest—voluntary associations usually conform to most of the elements of Weber's ideal type of bureaucracy. Unlike work organizations, though, people usually volunteer to join such associations, and therefore they suggest a rather different angle to our understanding of the popular values of bureaucratic forms. Drawing on a wide range of original empirical material, Savage shows that bureaucratic forms are not simple impositions from above, but resonate in various ways with popular cultures and values.

Notes

1. By 'expressivism' I am referring to those critics who require a political order or institutional regime to express certain moral ideals—such as an all pervading spirit of community or an inalienable right to personal autonomy.

Such critics assume that these domains should express the highest ideals of its members, and thus refuse to envision the possibility that the political and institutional realms and other areas of life 'may heed different priorities' (Larmore 1987: 93).

References

Adler, P., and Borys, B. (1996). 'Two types of bureaucracy: enabling and coercive'. *Administrative Science Quarterly*. 41; 61–89.

Alvesson, M., and Thompson, P. (2004). 'Post-bureaucracy?', in S. Ackroyd, R. Batt, P. Thompson and P. Tolbert (eds), *A Handbook of Work and Organisation*. Oxford: Oxford University Press.

Bauman, Z. (1989). *Modernity and the Holocaust*. Cambridge: Cambridge University Press.

Bogdanor, V. (2001). 'Civil service reform: a critique'. *The Political Quarterly*. 71/3; 291–9.

Castells, M. (2000). *The Rise of the Network Society* (2nd edn). Oxford: Oxford University Press.

Chapman, R. A. (1988). *Ethics in the British Civil Service*. London: Routledge.

Courpasson, D. (2000). 'Managerial strategies of domination: power in soft bureaucracies'. *Organisation Studies*. 21/1; 141–61.

Due Billing, Y. (1994). 'Gender and bureaucracies: a critique of Ferguson's "The Feminist Case Against Bureaucracy" '. *Gender, Work and Organisation*. 1/4; 179–94.

du Gay, P. (2000). *In Praise of Bureaucracy: Weber/Organization/Ethics*. London: Sage.

The Economist (2002). *The World in 2003*. London: The Economist.

Ferguson, K. (1984). *The Feminist Case Against Bureaucracy*. Philadelphia: Temple University Press.

Foucault, M. (1986). 'Nietzsche, genealogy, history', in P. Rabinow (ed.), *The Foucault Reader*. Harmondsworth: Penguin.

Giddens, A. (1998). *The Third Way*. Cambridge: Polity Press.

Goodsell, C. (2004). *The Case for Bureaucracy* (4th edn). Washington, DC: CQ Press.

Heckscher, C., and Donnellon, A. (eds) (1994). *The Post-Bureaucratic Organisation: New Perspectives on Organisational Change*. London: Sage.

Holmes, S. and Sunstein, C. (1999). *The Cost of Rights*. New York: W. W. Norton.

Hunter, I. (1994). *Rethinking the School*. Sydney: Allen and Unwin.

Kallinikos, Y. (2004). 'The social foundations of the bureaucratic order'. *Organization*. 11/1; 13–36.

Kaufman, H. (1977). *Red Tape: Its Origins, Uses and Abuses*. Washington: Brookings Institution.

Larmore, C. (1987). *Patterns of Moral Complexity*. Cambridge: Cambridge University Press.

Leadbeater, C. (1999). *Living on Thin Air: The New Economy*. Harmondsworth: Viking.

MacIntyre, A. (1981). *After Virtue*. London: Ducksworth.

Minson, J. (1993). *Questions of Conduct*. Basingstoke: Macmillan.

Osborne, T. (1994). 'Bureaucracy as a vocation: governmentality and administration in nineteenth century Britain. *Journal of Historical Sociology*. 7/3; 289–313.

Osborne, D. and Gaebler, T. (1992). *Reinventing Government: How the Entrepreneurial Spirit Is Transforming the Public Sector*. Reading, Mass.: Addison-Wesley.

Osborne, D. and Plastrik, P. (1997). *Banishing Bureaucracy: The Five Strategies for Reinventing Government* Reading, Mass.: Addison-Wesley.

Parker, R. S. (1993). *The Administrative Vocation*. Sydney: Hale and Iremonger.

Peters, B. G. (2003). 'Dismantling and Rebuilding the Weberian State', in J. Hayward and A. Menon (eds), *Governing Europe*. Oxford: Oxford University Press.

Peters, T. (1989). *Thriving on Chaos*. London: Pan Books.

Rhodes, R. (1996). 'The new governance: governing without government'. *Political Studies*. XLIV; 652–67.

Rhodes, R. (2000). 'Governance and public administration', in J. Pierre (ed.), *Understanding Governance*. Oxford: Oxford University Press.

Runciman, D. (2002). 'The garden, the park and the meadow'. *London Review of Books*. 24/11.

Strathern, M. (ed.) (2001). *Audit Cultures*. London: Routledge.

Thrift, N. (1999). 'The place of complexity'. *Theory, Culture & Society*. 16/1; 31–69.

Uhr, J. (1999). 'Institutions of integrity'. *Public Integrity*. Winter; 94–106.

Weber, M. (1978). *Economy & Society* (2 vols.). Los Angeles: University of California Press.

PART 1
The Politics of Bureaucracy

1

The Bureau as Unit of Governance

Charles T. Goodsell

The bureau, or administrative department of government, is stereotypically thought of as not engaging in 'governance' writ large. It is seen as confined to implementation in the purely instrumental sense. Its work is regarded as carrying out the laws, policies, and instructions handed down by elected officials or issued by the regime as a whole—thus characterizing it a crucial but dependent link in the governing process.

In the following pages I question this view. I ask that we reconsider the bureau as performing a central and multifaceted role in modern democratic governance. I present the bureau not as performer of one aspect of governance but as integral to the entire process. Hence it is analysed as a 'unit' rather than a 'part' of governance. The purpose of this word choice is to reject the traditional public administration dichotomies of politics versus administration and policymaking versus policy implementation, since they conceive of the bureau as involved in only the second half of each distinction. The value of the bureau is that it contributes greatly to governance as a whole, a point that can be made only by employing other distinctions than the usual. In fact, compared to other governing institutions the bureau's contributions may be uniquely broad.

Before proceeding, some definitions are in order. By 'bureau' I refer to all ministries, departments, or subunits of the public sector which are charged with administrative responsibilities and operated at public expense. They can be at headquarters or in the field and situated in the executive, legislative, or judicial components of government. Furthermore they may be thought of as consisting of individual agencies or unified administrative jurisdictions like those of local government. While most bureaux probably answer in general to the classic Weberian characteristics of graded hierarchy, formal rules, specialized tasks, written files, and full-time, trained, salaried, career employees, this exact profile need not always be in effect. Bureaux vary in their make-up of course, although some kind of vertical line of authority is at their core, so as to assure external control and accountability in the use of sovereign power.

The meaning of 'governance' is somewhat uncertain in present discourse and needs to be clarified for our purposes here. Most contemporary scholars define the word very generally because they wish to incorporate within it actions of the civil society and international arena as well as the state. To illustrate, Robert Keohane and Joseph Nye call it 'the processes and institutions, both formal and informal, that guide and restrain the collective activities of a group' (Keohane and Nye 2000: 12).

I propose that we be more specific. Governance should be thought of as consisting of two fundamental, and in some ways opposing activities, (a) *Rule* and (b) *Response*. In one of his classic works, Carl Friedrich defined Rule as 'institutionalized political power', that is stabilized and structured use of legitimized authority (1963: 180). It is the side of government that unilaterally gives direction to those subject to its authority. In a constitutional republic, Rule is temporarily in authorized hands and heavily circumscribed by law, with respect to both content and process. Response, by contrast, is the source of democratic influence on Rule. Its essence is external reaction, as when government 'responds to an outside determinant', to quote Friedrich again (1963: 310). In democratic systems Response operates both *to* government, as when acts of Rule lead to popular outcry in the populace, and *by* government, as when unpopular Rule leads to a turnover election that places a new regime in power.

Although the Rule aspect of governance denotes collective control while Response contemplates counter-control, in democratic practice the two activities operate hand in hand. Rule imposes the collective order that makes democracy possible and Response assures the continuous readjustments to that order that are essential to democracy's fulfilment. In short, the rulership of the state coexists with the responsiveness of democracy. Moreover, often identical institutions—both public and private—are involved in each.

The central question being asked in this chapter is, then, in modern democratic polities such as Great Britain and the United States, 'What functions does the bureau perform with respect to Rule on the one hand and Response on the other?' In seeking to answer this question we consider, in turn, three matters: the bureau's *capabilities* for governance, its *contributions* to governance, and its *challenges* in governance.

The Bureau's Capabilities for Governance

Considering the bureau's governance capability in abstract isolation would be difficult and perhaps meaningless, even on a purely deductive basis. To make the exercise more tangible, I make a systematic comparison between the bureau and other units of governance along ten specific sources of capability. Five of these relate to Rule: endowment with political power, possession of financial and other resources, being conferred with legal authority, having technical (i.e. teachable) skills, and being privy to professional (or institutional) knowledge. The other five capabilities, relating to Response are: linkage to elections, incorporating public representation, being externally accountable, being open to change, and engaging citizens directly in governance. Table 1.1 summarizes my analysis. In it, cells containing an upper-case X are considered to possess 'much' of the feature and those with a lower-case x are evaluated as having 'some' of it. When entries are divided by a slash, the one on the left refers to the United Kingdom and the one on the right to the United States. An empty cell means little or no presence of the attribute.

With respect to the Rule side of governance, all eight governance actors, including bureaux, are deemed as possessing an essential prerequisite for significant involvement, the possession of significant political power. Yet there are some differences of emphasis between the United Kingdom and United States The disciplined nature of

Table 1.1 Comparative capability for democratic governance

	Elected bodies	Political parties	Advocacy groups	Mass media	Bureaux	Quangos, hybrids	Contractors	Non-profits
For rule								
Political power	X	X/x	x/X	X	X	X/x	X	x
Resource availability	x	x	x/X	x	X	X/x	X	x
Legal authority	X	x			X	X		
Technical skills					X	X	X	X
Professional knowledge			x	x	X	X	X	X
For response								
Election linked	X	X			X			
Representative	X	X/			X	x		
Externally accountable	X	X/			X	x		
Open to change	x	x		x	x		x	x
Participative	x	x	x		x			X

Notes: X = much, x = some, no entry = little; when slash, left is UK, right US.

British political parties (and parliamentary government itself) makes them more coherent and influential than America's loose, federated organizations. Contrariwise, special interest or advocacy groups have more room to manoeuvre under America's separation of powers than in Britain's unitary system. Quangos (quasi-non-governmental organizations, called hybrids in America) are agencies created by government for public purposes but privately owned and operated. These are particularly important in Britain, especially at the local level.

As for financial and other resources, again all actors, including bureaux, are sufficiently endowed to make their mark on the governance process. Material resources are, quite naturally, a frequent complement to political power. For government entities, funds come from appropriations and fees. Political parties, advocacy groups, and non-profit organizations depend on voluntary contributions. The media, hybrids, and contractors receive business income. Again in the context of the American separation of powers, advocacy groups are rated higher on this element than in Britain; meanwhile in the United Kingdom the relative importance of quangos seems to justify an upper-case X. Bureaux in both countries are similarly rated because of the power of their national governments to levy taxes, appropriate funds, enter into debt, and distribute revenues to sub-national governments.

With respect to the remaining more formal attributes that affect Rule capability, considerable variation exists among actors. By their very nature, elected executives and legislatures call upon relatively open realms of constitutional and statutory authority. Specific grants of legal authority are meanwhile given to parties, bureaux, and quangos, with the last two the locus of statute-based administrative programmes. Wholly private institutions like interest groups, the press, government contractors, and non-profit organizations, are protected by the law but use political influence rather than law to affect Rule. With respect to technical expertise, this is largely in the hands of administrative organizations in and out of government, including government contractors and non-profit organizations that carry out government programmes. The same is basically true for professional knowledge in policy subjects, although long-term lobbyists and journalists possess it as well.

Turning to the Response side of governance, elected bodies and political parties are themselves products of the ballot box. In that sense they consciously represent their constituencies and are accountable to them when re-election time rolls round. As for bureaux, the civil service concept removes them from electoral politics to a degree, but they are nonetheless subject to supervision by elected government ministers, as in London, or politically appointed executives, as in Washington. At the state and local levels in the United States some bureaux are themselves headed by elected commissioners. The remaining governance actors are not directly linked to elections.

On the matter of representation, elected bodies and parties represent voting constituencies, while advocacy groups and non-profit organizations speak for various interests or causes. As individual institutions, bureaux and quangos support their governmental and quasi-governmental missions and allied constituencies. In addition, as the representative bureaucracy literature points out, the demographic composition of the civil service as a whole may mirror to some extent that of the general population. Because of the more exclusive membership of legislatures and courts, these bodies are demographically less representative. A related point is that civil servants may or may not mirror the general public with respect to political and policy preferences.

As for external accountability, the elected institutions of governance are definitely held accountable by voters, the most drastic means being failure to re-elect. In Britain—but not America—party leadership is accountable to its rank-and-file membership. With respect to bureaux, they are subject to external reviews by many mechanisms: the budget process, audit reports, programme evaluations, performance reviews, inspector general reports, ongoing legislative oversight, individual legislative investigations, and cases heard by the courts. All elements of the government are in general open to press investigations and media exposure, and in the United States freedom-of-information laws facilitate such inquiry. Quangos and hybrids, however, tend to operate more independently and confidentially than bureaux.

An assumption of the Response aspect of governance is that institutions are receptive to change when confronted by shifting political and cultural winds, technological innovation, or specific programme demands. Also, it goes without saying, policy and operating flexibility is on the whole an asset in both Rule and Response. Although it is difficult to generalize, most governance actors seem to deserve a 'some' evaluation on this score. As established institutions they have a stake in the status quo, but also show evidence of a readiness to accept new ideas and developments. Legislators and candidates look for new ideas by which they can get attention. The mass media are attracted to recent trends because they are newsworthy. Bureaus, while often condemned as inherently inflexible, have a penchant for seizing the latest management reform fads to demonstrate they are *au courant*. Contractors are always ready to negotiate profitable change orders, and non-profit organizations look for new ways to appeal for grants.

On public participation, elected officials and political parties, because of their need for campaign volunteers, involve the public extensively at lower levels of importance. Some, but not all, advocacy groups support active membership participation, but again not at a high level. Bureaux quite often deliberately involve citizens and groups in their decision-making and operations, as do community-based non-profit organizations.

To sum up this broad survey of the comparative capability for governance on the part of eight governance actors, institutions associated directly with elections have extensive capacities for Rule and Response, with the exception of expertise and specialized knowledge. Actors such as interest groups and the media are well equipped with power, resources, and public insights, but lack authority, skills, and external accountability. Quangos, contractors, and non-profits are, for the most part, well equipped for Rule but not Response. This leaves the bureaux. They possess in abundance all capabilities for Rule and, to mixed degrees, those for Response as well. Hence, *as an actor in a democratic system the bureau stands apart with respect to the uniquely sweeping nature of its governing capability*. In what ways is this capability used? It is to this question that we now turn.

The Bureau's Contributions to Governance: Rule

Given the bureau's attributes, it is not surprising to discover that it makes numerous and wide-ranging contributions to Rule. We survey these contributions by describing several concrete examples, from which we later draw conclusions.

Birth of the Information Age

The dawn of the so-called information age can be placed at the midpoint of the last century. Its birthplace was a series of bureaux of the American federal government. In 1950, the National Bureau of Standards constructed the first all-diode logic machine that did not use vacuum tubes. Another computer it built that year was the first to be able to store programs. In that same year, private industry produced its first commercially available computer, under contract to the US Navy. In the following year the famous UNIVAC computer, occupying 943 ft^3, was delivered to the Bureau of the Census by Remington Rand to process census data. Thus the bureau was both a pioneer experimenter with and key sponsor of this revolutionary machine.

Later computers became linked by the Internet, and the bureau was a central actor here too. The basic concept for the Internet originated with J. C. R. Licklider of the Massachusetts Institute of Technology, who became head of the Defense Advanced Research Projects Agency, or DARPA, in 1962. During the 1960s and early 1970s this bureau spearheaded development of packet-switching and the open-architecture network, technologies that made practical development of the Internet possible. Around the same time it and the National Science Foundation sponsored creation of early cross-country computer networks that linked several universities. Later the Department of Energy and National Aeronautics and Space Administration constructed their own networks of researchers. In 1985, the National Science Foundation formed NSFNET, which involved the entire higher education community. The stage was now set for a transformation in the way the world communicates (Leiner et al. 2003).

Bill Teams in Whitehall

The way in which Acts of Parliament get written in Great Britain has been studied by Edward Page. He conducted numerous interviews in Whitehall to discover how this was done for four statutes passed in 2002. These concerned electronic land registration, the confiscation of criminal assets, adoption reform, and pro-family work rules. Page's conclusion was that small groups of civil servants, known as bill teams, performed the crucial tasks of developing and drafting legislation and briefing the relevant minister. Composed of three to ten relatively junior civil servants (at the lowest rank of the Senior Civil Service and below), these individuals came from the affected departments and in some cases had been involved in earlier studies and negotiations on the subject.

The larger point Page makes is that these teams actually made policy in every sense of the word. They not only worked out all the details of the legislation, but also helped to conceive the bill's purposes and design programmes. In some instances team members got the matter placed on the political agenda, even before 10 Downing Street took it up or the Labour Party adopted it for inclusion in its manifesto. Also the teams managed the parliamentary process, for example handling the back-and-forth process of minister consultation, securing parliamentary time, and negotiating later amendments.

Page concludes that civil servants do not merely process in a technical way the policy decisions of politicians, but routinely participate in the making of policy itself, in every sense of the word. Yet, at the same time, they obey all legitimate political signals received and bend over backward to accommodate the policy aspirations of the Government. Hence, according to Page, the supposed division of labour between politicians making policy and civil servants implementing it simply does not describe what goes on in Whitehall. He concedes that a distinction could be made between abstract and applied policy work, but even here civil servants do both (Page 2003).

September 11, 2001

Minutes after the first plane hit the World Trade Center (WTC) in Manhattan on the morning of September 11, 2001, the Director of Emergency Management for New York City activated an Emergency Operations Center on the 23rd floor of 7 WTC. There, without consulting the mayor, he closed all streets below Canal, as well as all tunnels and bridges around Manhattan. Suddenly his centre's offices were hit by flying debris, so the director moved the emergency command centre to a WTC lobby. From there he arranged for the Coast Guard to seal New York's harbour and the Defense Department to block its city's airspace. He also communicated to the NYPD that from that moment on police helicopters should crash their craft into any additional planes that were attempting to hit the city.

Meanwhile several other city agency heads took action, also on their own. The deputy Fire Commissioner evacuated the entire WTC area. The director of the Emergency Service Unit sent teams with rescue harnesses and hydraulic tools up the stairways of the North Tower. The Transportation Commissioner, her phones to city hall cut off, rerouted buses and ferries to remove people from Manhattan. The director and trainmaster of the commuter train to New Jersey, standing on the concourse beneath the WTC, ordered a loaded incoming train to skip the WTC stop and return to New Jersey. Another train waiting in New Jersey was instructed to unload and return to Manhattan for evacuation purposes. In the opening hours of this tragic day upwards of 3,000 people were safely removed from the scene of this historic disaster (Cohen, Eimicke, and Horan 2002).

The CIA and its WMD

As we know, the pre-emptive war on Iraq quickly secured 'regime change' in that country, although the military occupation following was much more difficult than anticipated. The principal reason given for removing Saddam Hussein in the first place was his supposed holdings of, and intent to use, 'weapons of mass destruction' (WMD). A year after the initial phase of the war was over, however, President Bush and Prime Minister Blair were politically embarrassed when no evidence of these weapons turned up. The prime rationale given for the invasion was invalidated.

Although other intelligence organizations were involved in both countries, the Central Intelligence Agency (CIA) became the centre of later recriminations over the giant WMD mistake. Several aspects of the CIA's situation in this matter are germane to consideration of the bureau as a unit of governance. First, Bush, and then Blair, was told the WMD existed, based on intelligence reports. They then based their invasion rhetoric on the reports. Second, the CIA, by misreading of the WMD danger, did seem to commit a colossal blunder of great importance. Third, although high Bush administration officials had long wanted to go to war against Iraq anyway, the WMD intelligence estimate gave them their excuse. Fourth, hawks in the administration exacerbated the situation by taking pains to overstress the immediacy of the WMD threat, leading the CIA director to deny publicly that its intelligence had characterized the threat as imminent. Fifth, in the months following the debacle the CIA itself took steps to improve its analytical processes so as to avoid this kind of error in the future, such as not retaining initial assumptions too long and keeping analysts in the dark about the sources of individual pieces of intelligence (*Washington Post* 6 and 12 February 2004).

Welfare Office Routines

The final example of bureau Rule is not a single case but a category of organizations. These are local welfare offices. These illustrate how the bureau's contribution to Rule includes direct interaction with citizens, in this case those at the bottom of society. More than 1,800 local welfare offices exist in America, half of which employ less than twenty workers. In order to find out what these places are like physically, over a period of months I entered twenty-eight of them as if I were a first-time client. What struck me was the range of differences among them. Some were crowded, with labyrinthine hallways, degrading signs, and armed guards. Others were spacious, efficient and colourful. Later, three students and I examined welfare application forms used by different states. Again great diversity was encountered: in one state it began with a warning of imprisonment for giving false information, while in another the applicant was asked how many adults and children needed help (Goodsell 2004: 44, 45, 113).

Interested in how clients viewed their experience in welfare offices, I conducted an 'exit poll' in the parking lots of welfare offices in four cities, identifying myself as a teacher doing research. When welfare recipients emerged from the building I asked them if they had achieved what they came for. Three-quarters said yes. Moreover two-thirds said the person assigned to them was courteous, listened to what they had to say, and 'really tried' to help (Goodsell 1994: 33, 35; 2004: 44–5, 113).

In 1996, Congress passed the Personality Responsibility and Work Opportunity Act, or 'welfare reform'. Among other aims, the law sought to shift clients from cash assistance to a job or training programme. Three years later researchers from the Rockefeller Institute of Government visited several welfare offices in five states to find out what changes had actually occurred in the field. They concluded, much to their astonishment, pervasive institutional change—the culture of the staff had changed radically. 'We now have permission to "be real" with clients, to make them understand they have an obligation to work', one county welfare administrator said. A case manager stated, 'This is what I was trained to do. Now I have some leverage. I love it' (Nathan and Gais 1999).

Observations on Rule

Two principal insights seem to emerge from these five examples. The first is that *the bureau participates fully in the direction-giving function of Rule*, at all levels of generality. Low-visibility science bureaux of the federal government set the stage for development work that gave birth to a new communications medium. Bill teams in Whitehall originated policy initiatives in some cases and in all instances translated them into minister briefings and statutory language. When disaster struck Manhattan on September 11, the professionals of New York City government acted immediately, on their own, to deal with the emergency. The CIA's intelligence verdict on WMD supported the decision to invade Iraq and helped change the course of events in the Middle East; when it was found to be wrong, the agency admitted its mistake, took corrective action, and stated publicly that it never said the threat was imminent. These were not dependent acts of implementation or simple exercises of administrative discretion. They consisted of projecting a vision, writing new policy, exceeding authority, and rationalizing a war.

The second insight gained from these examples is that *the bureau is an important source for creation of Rule's meaning*, probably the crucial source. By its function of implementing law, the bureau brings the intentions and implications of Rule alive. Just as court cases translate generic principles of the law into practical meanings for litigants and lawyers, the daily routines of bureaux do so for governance. This is accomplished in two senses.

First, from an objectivist standpoint, the goals of legislators and other lawgivers remain as abstract plans and intentions until they are translated into concrete action. Only then are actual impacts achieved and knowable. This point is illustrated by welfare reform, where the outcomes of work-training requirements were unknown and subject to scepticism until they were actually tried. The same was true with the aspirations of Whitehall bill teams.

Second, from a subjectivist standpoint, the formal actions of governance, no matter how clearly described to the public, mean little more than platitudes to individual citizens until they actually affect their own lives. Until that point they are not socially 'real'. Only when the detailed and diverse phenomenology of the impact is personally encountered, such as the physical character of welfare rooms, the phraseology of application forms, and the closure of streets, tunnels and bridges, does the act of Rule become truly felt and hence 'realized' in a literal sense. It is at that moment that the social meaning of governance is created.

The Bureau's Contributions to Governance: Response

We turn now to examples of bureau's contribution to the Response aspect of governance. How does the bureau assist the citizenry and groups of the civil society to influence the actions of Rule? And to wish to do so? As with Rule, I offer five empirical cases to consider.

Representative Government

We recall that members of Whitehall bill teams were careful to incorporate in their work the wishes of pertinent ministers as well as 10 Downing Street. This is a key point. Bureaux that accept the aims of a newly elected regime or the spirit of a final legislative consensus advance Response, while those that defy these democratic conclusions undermine it.

A number of researchers have investigated whether bureaux in Washington obey or ignore their political masters. In a study of the behavioural nuances of bureau policy-making, Cornell Hooten found that while individual bureaucrats certainly harbour personal preferences on policy, for the most part they work consciously and regularly to fulfil the goals of political appointees who head their organizations. At the same time, civil servants are not blindly obedient when taking action on new policy initiatives, but judiciously weigh such factors as existing agency capacity and political feasibility (Hooten 1992). In an examination of how career professionals reacted to the incoming administration of President Ronald Reagan, Marissa Martino Golden learned that while the bureaucrats often disputed the desirability of the Reaganites' rightward policy shifts, they tended at least passively to accept them in the end. She uncovered very few careerists who resigned on principle or attempted to sabotage the changes (Golden 2000). Dan Wood and Richard Waterman analysed the readiness of federal regulatory agencies to comply in their administrative actions to policy signals from several sources: the presidency, Congress, courts, and the larger political environment. They conclude that although responses to the signals took place, and often very fast, they tended to be an amalgamation of several external sets of preferences, plus the regulators' own interpretation of public preferences registered in the past (Wood and Waterman 1994). In short, bureaux are responsive and at least passively loyal to election returns, but are sensitive also to practical feasibility and competing expressions of democratic sentiment.

Representative Bureaucracy

As mentioned above, a form of representation in government which complements that achieved by popular election is the demographic composition of career employees. At issue is whether certain groups are disproportionately included in the workforce, such as men rather than women, or excluded, for example minorities as compared to whites. Of particular importance is proportionality at top levels, because that is where the greatest pay, power, and prestige reside. Far from a merely academic question, in a social climate where diversity and equity are heavily stressed by feminists and civil rights groups, the matter becomes a major cause. In addition, these advocates regard their share of representation as reflective of their share of power.

How representative is the bureau? The data on demographics present the following picture. While American bureaucracy, especially at the upper levels, seems more representative than that found in several other nations, it is by no means complete. White males are still disproportionate and sometimes dominant. Yet departures from the ideal have significantly decreased over time. Between 1990 and 2000 the minority portion of federal employment grew from 27 to 30 per cent, with African Americans, Hispanics, Asians, and Native Americans all benefiting. In the same time period the percentage of female employees, a mere 24 per cent following the Second World War, grew from 43 to 45 per cent. At senior pay levels these percentages are numerically lower, but the *rate* of improvement is higher. Between 1990 and 2000 the minority percentage of upper-level civil servants almost doubled, from 8 to 14 per cent. The proportion of upper-level women more than doubled, from 11 to 24 per cent. Comparable gains were not made in the private sector during these years (Goodsell 2004: 90–3).

In addition to their demographic characteristics, the personal values and attitudes of bureaucrats could conceivably mirror those of the general population as well. Gregory Lewis set out specifically to test whether bureaucrats are or are not like other Americans in their policy, political, and social views. In general he discovered a quite remarkable degree of mirroring. Within a point or two, public employees and the citizenry were identical in their concerns about crime, drugs, the environment, welfare, the condition of the cities, school busing, capital punishment, and premarital sex (Lewis 1990). Other researchers have found that while government employees are somewhat more liberal in their voting habits than other Americans, the difference is not great.

Public-Sector Innovation

The propensity to innovate among government employees has also been a topic for research. While many observers of the bureau assume it is not fertile ground for innovative change, many researchers have come to a different conclusion. One classic sociological study discovered that bureaucrats are less resistant to change than factory workers, and another found that they are more receptive to change than those who work in non-bureaucratic organizations. A researcher who studied innovation in the Coast Guard concluded that it's several examples of mission-succession and adoption of new technologies over the years suggests that the bureau functions in an environment that demands continuous change, something akin to a competitive market (Goodsell 2004: 55–6, 97–8).

For some years government innovation awards have been given out in a programme funded by the Ford Foundation and administered by the Kennedy School at Harvard. The winning and runner-up projects have been analysed to uncover patterns of public-sector innovation. One, by Sanford Borins (1998), found to the author's surprise that the most frequent sources of innovative ideas were the mid-level managers and front-line staff. They far out-paced elected officials and agency heads in this regard. In another study, by John Donahue (1999), it was concluded that the main factor that made the innovations succeed was professional pride on the part of bureaucrats.

Civic Values

In addition to a propensity for innovation, the values of public servants seem to stand apart in one other respect. These are attitudes towards democratic participation and civic life. Gregory Lewis (1990: 223) found that government employees are more tolerant of free speech. When asked if they would allow public speech in their own community by a gay man or against all churches and religions, they answered yes by a range of 10–12 percentage points above the general public. For professionals and managers the difference was nearly twice that amount. In a study that sought to compare government employees to the general public on commitment to democratic values, William Blair and James Garand (1995) concluded that bureaucrats are more likely to support the rights of political and social minorities as well as gender and racial equality. Likewise, Gene Brewer and Sally Seldon (1998) have noted that government employees are more likely than other citizens to belong to civic, social, and community groups. They are also more likely to vote, support a candidate, and become involved in a political organization. In a later research report, Brewer (2003: 14–16) observed that public employees, compared to the general population, score higher on indices of social trust, social altruism, equality, diversity, and humanitarian concern for others. On still another dimension of civic-mindedness, the Internal Revenue Service has reported that government employees are more inclined than other taxpayers to pay their federal income tax on time (*Washington Post* 19 March 1996, 24 March 2002).

Also the bureau's own administrative programmes may contribute to the civic-mindedness of the general population. Publicly financed schools, for example, cannot help but direct interest on the part of students to the outside world and community matters. A side effect of military service is to socialize recruits to public values such as patriotism. The Peace Corps has long noted that its volunteer alumni tend to engage in volunteer work when they return home.

Such linkages have been investigated empirically. Christopher Simon, studying the domestic volunteer programmes of AmeriCorps, found that members are more involved in community groups and more likely to express public-oriented values after the experience than before, regardless of gender or race (Simon 2002). In studying the consequences of receiving G. I. Bill educational assistance after the Second World War, Suzanne Mettler noticed a tendency for recipients to be especially active in civic organizations and partisan politics. She theorizes that, in addition to the upward social mobility obtained by the educational experience itself, the veterans felt they should 'pay back' society for the help they received (Mettler 2002).

Public Participation

For many years bureaux have employed a variety of institutional techniques to engage the public directly in their planning, management, operations, and decision-making activities. These include advisory groups, citizen boards, town meetings, neighbourhood meetings, community workshops, community scorecards, focus groups, planning forums, citizen policy panels, agenda-formation exercises, citizen coordinating councils, and volunteer activities. In addition to these face-to-face and often locally oriented tools of citizen participation, a number of jurisdictions are experimenting with use of information technology for this purpose. Roza Tsagarousianou and associates, who have compiled descriptions of a number of these experiments, point out that hundreds of cities in the United State and Europe have created civic networks that are being used to enrich the democratic process. Using a combination of digital technology, the Internet, audio and visual interactive telecommunications, and other technologies, ways are being found to connect government and the citizenry in unprecedented ways. These relate to information distribution, tailored service delivery, citizen preference measurement, and the development of agendas for change (Tsagarousianou 1998). While enormous procedural, equity, and consensus-formation problems lie in the path of digitalizing government, bureaux are major players in the fast-moving field of 'e-democracy'.

Observations on Response

What insights emerge from these studies of bureau contribution to Response? First, with respect to the electoral process, evidence indicates that the bureau generally supports and does not operate contrary to the proposals and wishes of elected officials and political appointees. While the bureau itself is well endowed with power and resources, and civil servants are by no means subservient to their political masters, the bureaucracy is by no means a runaway train on democracy's tracks. Importantly, it is prepared and even eager to follow the policy direction of a new administration, a crucial factor in making the outcome of elections meaningful.

Second, the bureau engages actively in direct popular democracy in the sense of receiving policy influences directly from groups in the civil society and from individual citizens in the community. Indeed, by means of many types of institutional linkage set up for this purpose, influence on the bureau is frequently bottom-up via citizens as well as top-down via elections. Moreover the continuous emergence of new information technologies opens up novel opportunities for this to happen.

The third insight is that the bureau is not only directly immersed in external influences from above and below but also it indirectly affects the likelihood of their production. An advancing extent of proportionate representation of minorities and women in government allays feelings of resentment and alienation from government that could otherwise exist. Although bureaucrats tend to vote somewhat to the left of citizens, the absence of a gulf of opinion between the two on basic social and political questions similarly avoids a divisiveness that would make reaching a consensus difficult. The absence of a severe stand-pat attitude on the part of government managers and their willingness to initiate innovations in their own organizations enhances the compatibility of the bureau with its authentically dynamic political environment. Finally, the bureaucrats' commitment to civic values and the bureaux' own contributions to civic engagement support generally an effective fulfilment of the Response function.

Summary and Future Challenges

In this chapter, I have argued that the bureau possesses unique capabilities for being involved in governance and makes indispensable contributions to it. This view of the bureau's role departs from the traditional public administration image of the bureau as subservient to and dependent on elected officials, with its role confined largely to implementation of policy.

My revised view conceives of governance as consisting of a duality of intertwined functions, Rule and Response. Within each function, the bureau is capable of making crucial and essential contributions. Its contribution to Rule is to provide informed direction at many levels and to confer practical and social meaning on policy. As for Response, the bureau fulfils the electorate's assumption that the ballot box can effect change, and at the same time promotes direct citizen input and augments a capacity for constructive dialogue and civic vitality. These contributions to both aspects of governance transcend the separation of politics and administration and provide a more realistic understanding of the bureau's role. Figure 1.1 emphasizes this point by rotating the governance framework ninety degrees in relation to the traditional model, thus depicting how the bureau's Rule and Response activities embrace both politics and administration.

Looking ahead, what uses might this revised view of governance have for its future? We conclude the chapter by noting two major challenges for the bureau that lie ahead. These concern its role at the national level of dispersed governance and the international level of global collective action.

Donald Kettl thoughtfully addresses both challenges. In effect he contends that the bureau, conceived in terms of hierarchy, authority, clear jurisdictional and national boundaries, and top-down control by elected officials, does not fit the realities of today. Two great shifts of our times cause this: the wholesale transfer of administrative responsibilities to private parties on the one hand and the extension of national governance to the global realm on the other. These twin forces of devolution and globalism require a new theory for the field, Kettl believes. He advances an agenda for rebuilding public administration doctrine that contemplates, among other things, more attention to network management, enhancement of inter-organizational processes, extended bottom-up public participation, and full use of information technology and performance management (Kettl 2002).

Jon Pierre and Guy Peters offer a parallel critique, although their focus is not public administration doctrine but the nature of governance and its relation to the state. They argue that governance is now best thought of not as a state steering but a system of interaction among varied governmental and non-governmental organizations

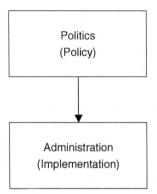

The politics–administration dichotomy
(The bureau is instrumental in function
and wholly subservient to elected officials)

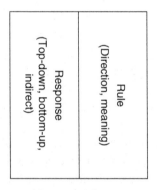

Proposed framework for governance
(The bureau is an integral part of
and indispensable to all of governance)

Fig. 1.1 Frameworks for conceiving the bureau's relation to governance

Note: The lower diagram's coordinates are rotated 90° from the upper diagram to show its cross-cutting relationship to it.

that pursue public purposes. This extra-state interaction already exists within nations, they say, but has now become even more critical at the global level. In today's world, they point out, the state is merely one actor among other state and non-state actors, requiring unified governance to be replaced by a capacity to deal in a decentralized, negotiated manner with multiple autonomous centres of power. At the same time, however, the system of global governance must be strong enough to stand up to the political power of international capital.

Transformation of the system is especially necessary at the present historical moment, the authors argue, because of the innate rigidities of hierarchical arrangements, the financial crises facing most national governments, and a worldwide ideological shift against direct state action and in favour of the private sector (Pierre and Peters 2000).

Both analyses correctly highlight a set of vast changes that have occurred in recent decades in the environment of governance, all over the world. No one can dispute that a vast dispersion has occurred of public action from in-house government to public–private hybrid organizations, government contractors and subcontractors, non-profit organizations, universities, research institutes, non-governmental organizations, partnerships, networks, and private organizations. Moreover, despite a plentitude of evidence that this enormous attenuation of the public realm has greatly complicated administration, and despite little evidence that it has saved money or increased efficiency, reversal of the phenomenon is not before us as an alternative.

The same is true with globalization. Contrary to simplistic visions of 'world government' or 'a global economy', the complex forces of technology, science, trade, finance, production, war, terrorism, and cultural transmission and conflict, among others, are causing great numbers of public and private organizations of all kinds to interact more fully on a daily basis. Increasingly, the exigencies of military intervention, intelligence gathering, international diplomacy, nation-building, economic regulation, law enforcement, space exploration, mass immigration, and worldwide epidemics have focused the nation state outward as much as inward, leading to enormous new challenges for governments as they deal with a proliferation of other governments, international agencies, and private global actors.

What does this all mean for the bureau? Kettl says the overriding need is to achieve adequate coordination. Mechanisms must be found to maintain coherence amidst the growing and spreading dispersion of collective action. I would add to this requirement the need to assure more completely the accountability of institutional actors and their leaders. The democratic idea, whose keystone is adequate accountability, must not be allowed to erode while tendencies to outsource government and decentre the state continue. This being the case, methods must be found to link plans, share information, create dialogue, join forces, and retain responsibility in given policy areas without creating massive, centralized organizations that suffer from the rigidities to which Pierre and Peters refer. Relationships must be formed but not too tightly. Many would argue that this is precisely why governance must now be transformed. The time has come, they say, for governance to be conducted not by bureau, but by contracts, markets, networks, partnerships, agreements, incentives, and information on outputs and outcomes. Hierarchy, centralization, control, stovepipes, jurisdictions, and rules are no longer up to the tasks of the contemporary world. The era of the bureau is over.

Allow me to enter a dissent, along the following lines. First, all of the bureau's capabilities for democratic governance listed in the table above, including power, resources, expertise, accountability, openness to change, and public participation, are still going to be needed. Second, the bureau, while wedded to basic principles of democratic control, clear authority, and public funding, does not need to be paralysed by an excess of central clearances, multiple layers of authority, detailed manuals of rules, or obsessions with turf. Theoretical excesses imagined by the sceptics of bureaucracy seldom need be taken seriously.

Third, it would be nothing new to the bureau to be asked to coordinate its work with that of other actors. They do so now, constantly. Bureaucrats know all about joint task forces, collaborative programmes, partnerships, information networks, meetings of principals, memos of understanding, shared training facilities and—above all—intergovernmental grants as the backbone of thousands of government programmes. Moreover, at the international level, multiple bureau participation is commonplace in bodies that regulate aviation, track icebergs, protect heritage sites, sponsor big science, attack HIV-AIDS, and conduct military expeditions.

Fourth, absent the state, and its handmaiden the bureau, from collective public and international action, it would be extremely difficult if not impossible to maintain systems of accountability that are sophisticated, possess inherent integrity, pose independent checks, and are faithful to the institution's intended goals. If delegations of politicians or networks of private parties are solely in charge, secrecy and self-serving could be harder to avoid; Pierre and Peters' concern for standing up to the power of international capital might turn out to be justified.

True, the bureau as a unit of governance need not always have a significant presence in collective action on behalf of the public.

Conceivably situations may become increasingly common where its capabilities for Rule and Response can be forgone. It is also possible, however, that *the bureau may become increasingly indispensable as an institutional node of potent, professional, and accountable authority that weaves together the strands of dispersed public action into coherent policy.* No other institution seems able to do that. Ironically, this simple realization may be the best response to Kettl's call for a new theory of public administration. For from being a dinosaur, the bureau may become more important than ever over the course of the twenty-first century.

References

Blair, W. and Garand, J. C. (1995). 'Are Bureaucrats Different? Democratic Values, Political Tolerance, and Support for the Political System among Government Employees and Other Citizens, 1982–1992', Paper delivered to annual meeting of American Political Science Association, September.

Borins, S. (1998). *Innovating with Integrity: How Local Heroes Are Transforming American Government.* Washington, DC: Georgetown University Press.

Brewer, G. A. (2003). 'Building social capital: civic attitudes and behavior of public servants'. *Journal of Public Administration Research and Theory.* 13/1; 5–26.

Brewer, G. A. and Selden, S. C. (1998). 'The Promise of Active Citizenship: Does Participation Increase Trust in Government?', Paper delivered to annual meeting of American Political Science Association, September).

Cohen, S., Eimicke, W., and Horan, J. (2002). 'Catastrophe and the public service: a case study of the government response to the destruction of the World Trade Centre'. *Public Administration Review.* 62; 24–32.

Donahue, J. D. (1999). *Making Washington Work: Tales of Innovation in the Federal Sector.* Washington, DC: Brookings Institution Press.

Friedrich, C. J. (1963). *Man and His Government: An Empirical Theory of Politics.* New York: McGraw-Hill.

Golden, M. M. (2000). *What Motivates Bureaucrats? Politics and Administration During the Reagan Years.* New York: Columbia University Press.

Goodsell, C. T. (1994). *The Case for Bureaucracy: A Public Administration Polemic,* 3rd edn. Chatham, NJ: Chatham House Publishers.

Goodsell, C. T. (2004). *The Case for Bureaucracy: A Public Administration Polemic,* 4th edn. Washington, DC: CQ Press.

Hooten, C. (1992). *Executive Governance: Presidential Administrations and Policy Change in the Bureaucracy.* Armonk, NY: M.E. Sharpe.

Kettl, D. F. (2002). *The Transformation of Governance: Public Administration for Twenty-First Century America*. Baltimore, MD: Johns Hopkins University Press.

Koehane, R. O. and Nye, J. (2000). 'Introduction', in R. O. Koehane and J. D. Donahue (eds), *Governance in A Globalizing World*, Washington, DC: Brookings Institution Press, 12.

Leiner, B. M., Cerf, V. G., Clark, D. D., Kahn, R. E., Kleinrock, L., Lynch, D. C., Postel, J., Roberts, G., and Wolff, S. (2003). 'A Brief History of the Internet' www.isoc.org/internet/history/brief.shtm.

Lewis, G. B. (1990). 'In search of the Machiavellian milquetoasts: comparing attitudes of bureaucrats and ordinary people'. *Public Administration Review*. 50/2; 220–7.

Mettler, S. (2002) 'Bringing the state back into civic engagement: policy feedback effects of the G.I. Bill for World War II veterans'. *American Political Science Review*. 96/3; 527–46.

Nathan, R. P. and Gais, T. L. (1999). 'A surprising look'. *Public Administration Times*. 22/6 (June); 1–2.

Page, E. C. (2003). 'The civil servant as legislator: law making in British Administration'. *Public Administration*. 81/4; 651–79.

Pierre, J. and Peters, B. G. (2000). *Governance, Politics, and the State*. New York: St. Martin's Press.

Simon, C. A. (2002). 'Testing for bias in the impact of AmericCorps service on volunteer participants: evidence of success in achieving a neutrality program objective'. *Public Administration Review*. 62/6; 670–8.

Tsagarousianou, R. (1998). *Cyberdemocracy: Technology, Cities and Civic Networks*. London: Routledge.

Wood, B. D. and Waterman, R. W. (1994). *Bureaucratic Dynamics: The Role of Bureaucracy in a Democracy*. Boulder, CO.: Westview Press.

2

Bureaucracy and Liberty: State, Authority, and Freedom

Paul du Gay

Introduction

Opposition to the idea of 'the state', and to 'bureaucracy', has long been a feature of a wide variety of political discourses. Over the last thirty years or so, however, it has enjoyed a remarkable resurgence in popularity. One of the most prominent of the many recent criticisms directed at the 'cold monsters' of state and bureaucracy concerns their presumed negative consequences for personal liberty.[1] Whether couched in predominantly economistic terms—states and their bureaucracies hinder the unique virtue and efficacy of a capitalistic organization of production—or in relation to populist criteria of political right—only governments that are responsive to, and thus accurately and sensitively express, the opinions and judgements of their own citizens can be fully entitled to their obedience—states and bureaucracies are seen as undermining freedom.

Underlying the first of these conceptions, we might contend, is the assumption that economic freedom, and the efficiency of governmental policy, is a function of the state's subordination to the laws of the 'free' markets. For the second, the guiding assumption is that the justness of governmental policy is directly related to the degree of the bureaucracy's subordination to the popular will. In this chapter, I seek to reassess and reassert the political and ethical basis of the authority of state and bureaucracy. In so doing, I seek to indicate the myriad ways in which personal liberty is dependent upon the liberal institutions of state and bureaucracy and not antithetical to them. What libertarians, neo-liberals, communitarians, and other, what I term 'expressivist',[2] critics of state and bureaucracy commonly represent as 'natural' independence is in fact profound dependence on the powers of sovereign states and their public bureaux.

The Authority of the State

As Quentin Skinner (1989; 2002), among many others, has argued, the idea of the modern state was developed slowly and with some difficulty to facilitate the construction of a single integrated system of authoritative political and legal decision-making over a given territory and subject-population, and to offset the continuing subversive or anarchistic potential of the long-standing viewpoint that derived political authority, in one way or another, from the people over whom it was exercised. At the centre of this novel idea was the concept of sovereignty, of ultimate worldly authority over people and territory, and its firm location within specific institutions and decisions: the right to be obeyed without challenge. 'The entity in which that right inhered', as John Dunn (2000: 80) indicates, was no longer envisaged as a particular human being

> . . . but as a continuing structure of government, decision-making, legal interpretation and enforcement, which was sharply distinct from its current human incumbents. Such a structure could take in or lose subjects or territory without altering its identity. It could change its system of rule or legal adjudication almost beyond recognition, and yet remain intractably itself.

These arguments for the modern state find their classic expression in the work of Hobbes (though by no means only Hobbes). While there have always been those who see the germs of totalitarianism in

Hobbes' idea of 'sovereign authority', nothing could be further from the truth (Kriegel 1995). For, without being a liberal himself, Hobbes 'had in him', as Oakeshott (1975: 67) put it, 'more of the philosophy of liberalism than most of its professed defenders'. So how could such an authoritarian also be a great precursor of modern 'liberalism'? It is worth, briefly, outlining some of the key features of Hobbes' argument in *Leviathan*, as these are still crucial to understanding the mutually constitutive relationship of liberty and authority in most modern liberal polities.

As is well known, Hobbes is fundamentally concerned with outlining and justifying the mechanisms necessary for the establishment of a 'constant and lasting' social peace in the context of the enduring civil strife of his own time. For Hobbes, both states, and the forms of political authority unique to them, are imperfect remedies for the threat of civil chaos and violent death. Hobbes (1991: II: 94), like all good liberals, accepts the fact of pluralism. 'All men', he writes, 'are by nature provided by notable multiplying glasses (that is their Passions and Selfe-Love)'. Moreover, because 'Nature hath made men so equall' in both 'ability' and right, from this 'ariseth equality of hope in the attainment of our Ends' (1991: I: 61). However, these ends may not be the same, or even if they are, they may be such that they cannot be attained equally by both parties, and so, in the absence of an arbiter 'to keep them quiet', they 'become enemies' (1991: I: 61–2). For Hobbes, then, pluralism and equality, rather than being conditions that argue for our freedom from government, are, in fact, conditions demanding governmental authority. If society is to endure and perpetual conflict be curtailed there arises the need for 'a common Power to keep them all in awe' (1991: I: 62).

Famously, Hobbes (1991: II: 87) argues that the only way to erect such a Common Power is for 'men' [*sic*]

. . . to conferre all their power and strength upon one Man, or upon one assembly of men, that may reduce all their Wills, by plurality of voices, unto one Will: which is as much as to say, to appoint one Man, or Assembly of men, to beare their Person: and every one to owne, and acknowledge himself to be Author of whatsoever he that so beareth their Person, shall Act, or cause to be Acted, in those things that concern the Common Peace and Safetie; and therein to submit their Wills, every one to his Will, and their Judgements, to his Judgement . . . And he that carryeth this Person, is called SOVERAIGNE, and said to have *soveraigne Power*.

Because 'the plurality of voices', if left to its own devices, can result in discord or anarchy, and because there is simply no mechanism in nature to harmonize them, an artificial mechanism—a pacifying reason of state—must be established and fastidiously maintained.

In the truly autonomous realm, beyond government, there can be no a priori guarantees. Therefore, it 'is very absurd for men to clamor as they doe' for such 'absolute Libertie', Hobbes (1991: II: 109) argues, because the proper 'Liberty of a Subject' depends on the presence not absence of an absolute authority (see also Skinner 2002: chap. 6). Thus, the idea that 'every man has an absolute Propriety in his Goods', Hobbes (1991: II: 169) continues, 'tendeth to the Dissolution of a Commonwealth'.

Every man has indeed a Propriety that excludes the Right of every other Subject: And he has it onely from the Soveraign Power; without the protection whereof, every man should have equall Right to the same. But if the Right of the Soveraign also be excluded, he cannot perform the office they have put him into; which is, to defend them both from forraign enemies, and from the injuries of one another; and consequently there is no longer a commonwealth.

It is hardly surprising that Hobbes' *modus-vivendi* authoritarianism appears illiberal when benchmarked against the standards of contemporary 'expressivist' liberal (and communitarian) thought. Hobbes is negatively coded in the eyes of contemporary expressivist liberals, for example, because he refuses to affirm from the doctrines of pluralism and equality the *positive* values—autonomy, free choice, free association, individual self-realization—that inform much modern liberal thought. As Fish (1999: 180) has argued,

For Locke, Kant, Mills and Rawls (in their different ways), the equality of men and the values they invariably espouse points to the rejection of any form of absolutism: if no one's view can be demonstrated to be absolutely right, no one should occupy the position of absolute authority. For Hobbes the same insight into the pluralism of values and the unavailability of a mechanism for sorting them out implies exactly the reverse: because no one's view can be demonstrated to be absolutely right (and also because every one prefers his own view and believes it to be true), someone *must* occupy the position of absolute authority. (Fish 1999: 180)

In other words, weak-state or no-state pluralism is not a prescription for liberal freedoms but rather a recipe for deadly antagonism and anarchism (Holmes and Sunstein 1999). As Michael Ignatieff (2001: 35), for instance, argues in his perceptive critique of contemporary anti-statist human rights discourse:

Today . . . the chief threat to Human Rights comes from civil war and anarchy. Hence we are discovering the necessity of state order as a guarantee of rights . . . It is utopian to look forward to an era beyond state sovereignty. Instead of regarding state sovereignty as an outdated principle, destined to pass away in an era of globalization, we need to appreciate the extent to which sovereignty is the basis of order in the international system.

Clearly, then, sovereignty, regardless of form, 'so far from being inimical to liberty, is a necessary condition for it. Liberty of the natural state is intolerable and, in its proper signification, almost meaningless as a ubiquitous feature of existence' (Condren 2002: 71). Thus, the standard tropes of modern liberal thought—individual rights, for example—do not function as transcendental limits on state action but are rather the product of action by sovereign states. As Holmes (1994: 605) puts it, 'statelessness means rightlessness. Stateless people, in practice, have no rights'. Inhabitants of weak or poor states tend to have few or laxly enforced rights. Without centralized and bureaucratic state capacities, there is no possibility of forging 'a single and impartial legal system—the rule of law—on the population of a large nation. Without a well-organized political and legal system, exclusive loyalties and passions' are difficult to control (Holmes 1994: 605).

In expressivist accounts of liberalism, where self-organization, free association, limited government, and so on are seen to emerge from a 'critique of state reason' and function as elements of a moral ideal—a particular practice—religious toleration, say—is tied to a profound moral principle—a Kantian respect for the autonomy of free agents, for example. As we have seen, though, not all liberalism is expressivist. Under Hobbesian 'authoritarian liberalism', toleration is enacted from fear of civil chaos and as a means to peaceful coexistence. It does not function as a moral ideal. 'Nothing in Hobbes', argues John Gray (2000: 3), 'suggests he favoured toleration as a pathway to the true faith. For him, toleration was a strategy of peace'.

Hobbes saw that, in its capacity to guarantee social peace, the sovereign state had no need for 'higher' religious or philosophical justifications. The state's indifference to the transcendent beliefs of the rival communities over which it ruled was based neither on an ideal of individual liberty or free agency nor on a commitment to a shared moral consensus amongst its citizens.

> The emergent ethical autonomy of the state meant that the 'citizen' (whose public obedience to the law was a condition of social peace) could no longer be thought of as identical with the 'man' (who might freely follow the light of his conscience as long as this did not interfere with his public duty to the law). (Hunter, 1994: 41)

The state's indifference to the personal beliefs of those over whom it ruled was therefore grounded in an 'art of separation', to use Walzer's (1984) term, which was opposed to the idea of society as an organic 'whole', and the associated conception of the human being as a unified moral personality. A pacified civil society required a conception of the human being as the bearer of a differentiated set of *personae* (Saunders 2002). The persona of the citizen as inhabitant of the sovereign state, and the persona of the practitioner of religious (or other forms of communal) self-governance, now represented two distinct and autonomous modes of comportment, housed in two distinct realms, of 'public' and 'private' conduct. For Hobbes, religious toleration, or the state's indifference to moral identities and transcendent truth claims, was a crucial element in the state's elevation to sovereignty in the political arena, which in turn was the precondition for social pacification.

What is still so contentious about Hobbes' position, and what most frequently generates the accusation of 'totalitarianism', is his resolute insistence that the state cannot hope to be able to undertake its core functions unless it can decide for itself 'without internal impediment just what opinions may be publicly expressed and just who can own what and why' (Dunn 2000: 84). Neither of these views is well regarded in any Western society at the present moment. But, both are deeply implicated in the idea of the modern state and in the practical activities of many existing states.

When a state sees no obvious danger in its subjects expressing their opinions freely, or in the patterns of property-holding and the use to which they believe they are entitled, 'Hobbes does not, of course, recommend that it interfere in either area. To do so would be perverse and inequitable' (Dunn 2000: 87). But that does not undercut the state's main responsibility, which is to judge this degree of jeopardy in every case. The state carries (and must carry) the authority of its own subject's will and choice to make that judgement on their behalf, and to act decisively upon it (Oakeshott 1975; Dunn 2000: 87–8). Indeed, as we saw earlier, each subject has a right against every other subject that it should do just this. The authority of the state is thus binding and content-independent—it forms a premise for the subject's action without that subject considering the merits of what it requires (Green 1988: 19).

As I suggested, this has often been taken to be a licence for the destruction of personal liberty and yet, as Oakeshott (1975: 66) remarked, the *Leviathan* is not

. . . a designed destruction of the individual; it is in fact the *minimum* condition of any settled association among individuals. The Sovereign is absolute in two respects only and neither of them is destructive of individuality: first, the surrender of natural right to him is absolute and his authorization is permanent and exclusive; and secondly, there is no appeal from the legitimacy of his command . . . For the rest, Hobbes conceives the Sovereign as a law-maker and his rule, not arbitrary, but the rule of law . . . [T]hat law as the command of the sovereign holds within itself a freedom absent from law as Reason or custom; it is reason not Authority that is destructive of individuality. And of course, the silence of the law is a further freedom; when the law does not speak the individual is sovereign over himself. What, indeed, is excluded from Hobbes's *civitas* is not the freedom of the individual but the independent rights of spurious authorities and of collections of individuals such as churches, which he saw as the source of the civil strife of his time.

For Hobbes, then, unlike so many liberals of today, the development of a sovereign state heralds an increase in, not a decrease or rescission of, individual freedom. If Hobbes' reconstruction of political authority makes the state effectively absolute in the political arena, it also simultaneously gives birth to a 'liberal' domain of extra-political rights and freedoms. Those commentators who view Hobbes as the apostle of despotism are therefore considerably wide of the mark. Hobbes' secularizing of politics is accompanied by a liberating separation of public and private conduct. For just as the uncoupling of civil governance from transcendent morality renders the state absolute in the political domain, it simultaneously precludes the exercise of political power in the moral domain (unless of course, the state judges the issues in conduct threaten the peace whereupon they cease to be 'purely' moral).

The Neutrality of the State

In sharp contrast to many contemporary liberal theorists, Hobbes is not interested in the ideal of rational consensus. Instead, he is concerned with the practical problem of peaceful coexistence. These are not two sides of the same coin, but rather rival projects. The Hobbesian project of *modus vivendi* is not based on the vain hope that human beings will cease to make universal claims for their own specific ways of life. Rather, it regards these claims with *indifference*—except of course where they endanger peaceful coexistence. As John Gray (2000: 25) puts it, 'A Hobbesian state extends to private belief the radical tolerance of indifference. Hobbes is thereby the progenitor of a tradition of liberal thought in which *modus vivendi* is central'. In this tradition, the distinctive liberal notion is that of the *neutrality* of the state.

Clearly, in practice the entities we call states can come to be seen as pure structures of domination by some of those subject to their rule. For one thing, what states do, the decisions they make, and the policies they pursue generally benefit some people more than others, and so certain practices and conceptions will inevitably fare better than others. This, though, is neither surprising nor avoidable. Ways of life that depend, for instance, upon close and exclusive bonds of language and custom may lose, within a liberal association also tolerating different ways of life, some of the authority and cohesion they would have had if they were allowed to form complete societies unto themselves. This may well be the price of toleration. But this does not mean that the liberal state is not neutral. For its neutrality is not meant to be one of *outcome*, but one of *procedure*. That is because, as Charles Larmore (1988: 44) suggests, 'political neutrality consists in a constraint upon the factors that can be invoked to justify a political decision'. Thus, to describe the liberal state as 'neutral' in these terms is not to suggest that there is a natural, universal condition of association that we can call 'neutral' to which the actions of a state should approximate. The state's neutrality should not be seen as a vain attempt to acquire a general capacity to take, in the English moral philosopher Henry Sedgwick's phrase, 'the point of view of the Universe'. Rather, neutrality, understood procedurally, leaves open to a large extent the goals that any particular liberal state can pursue—except where these endanger peaceful coexistence. Clearly, this sits uneasily with the contemporary obsession with 'situatedness', where any claim to 'neutrality' is quickly represented and castigated as a 'God trick', an attempt by one party to get its own way under the mantle of a universal viewpoint. Here, 'neutrality' is thought of as being an impossible mode of conduct and hence as offering loose cover for a range of oppressive interests whether these be racist, patriarchal, or classist in orientation. Thus, the principal objection being articulated here is that because the state cannot practically achieve the heights of neutrality it aspires to, it must therefore forfeit any claims to special authority. There are at least two problems with this argument. First, as Michael Seidler (2002: 247) has pointed out, there is a simple retort to the charge of 'imperfection': 'other collectivities are still less neutral and do not provide even an imperfect forum for the peaceful resolution of differences. Or, if they do, it is merely a happy coincidence. The liberal state at least aims explicitly at such a goal; most other collectivities do not even pretend to it'. The second problem for this argument revolves around precisely how one would then describe the role of the state if one were to deprive it of any claim to procedural neutrality, however imperfectly it might be realized in practice. In being practically stripped of its claims to 'neutrality' and being re-embedded 'in society' along with everything else, the state becomes something different from what it is in its own terms. It stops being a state.

After all, it is a perfectly simple academic move to indicate how the state is a (social) construct—sociologists, political scientists, and critical legal scholars have been doing so for years—but that is not something a state itself can be expected to take cognisance of and act upon and still remain operative as a state. The achievements of sovereign 'stateness'—social pacification, individual rights, religious toleration, and so forth—flow from the assumption and performance of independence from society and ultimate authority over it. To take an academic insight into the state's reliance on some other—extra-statist—structure of concern in its own self-constitution and then try to make the operations of the state transparently accord with this insight is a recipe for confusion, if not worse. For example, were the state to deploy its procedures in the company of an analysis of their roots in extra-state discourses and techniques, it would not be exercising, but rather dismantling, its authority; in short, it would no longer be acting like a state, but rather engaging in some sort of academic enterprise (Fish 1994). Rather than producing the authority it retroactively invokes, the state would be in the business of continually calling into question the basis of its authority, and hence producing uncertainty, one of the very things it was instituted to avoid.

To actively attempt to de-autonomize the state, under the aegis of its status as a social 'construct', or the imperatives of moral expressivism, is effectively to re-theologize it (Hunter 1998). One needs only to point to the rise of democratic and nationalist movements in the nineteenth century armed with similar expressivist concerns to indicate the dangers such re-theologization poses to social pacification, the rule of law and the practice of religious toleration. Bodin (quoted in Holmes, 1995: 129) made this point elegantly and forcefully when he argued that the state could only serve as an umpire between religious factions if it refused to identify itself too closely with the spiritual aspirations of any single sect. As Holmes (1995: 129) puts it, '[t]he peacekeeping regime is necessarily unresponsive'.

Neutral, indifferent, unresponsive. It is difficult to think of a set of conducts more inimical to those—whether communitarians, expressivist liberals or neo-liberals—seeking, for one reason or another, and in one way or another, to make a political order express certain moral ideals; and to replace the grim world of state power and bureaucratic compulsion with, for instance, the jaunty realm of economic voluntarism or the all embracing cuddliness of community. Yet, these conducts are fundamental to the state's *raison d'être*, and, as such, are crucial constitutive features of the status-conduct of the state's legal and administrative agencies.

Bureaucracy as a Non-Sectarian Comportment of the Person

The representation of the agencies of the state, most particularly, but not exclusively, state bureaucracies, as 'unresponsive' features regularly in a wide range of political discourses, and never positively. The 'unresponsiveness' of which so many democrats complain, for instance, often appears to be based on the assumption that it is impossible to justify substantial governing power being allotted to unelected officials. Thus, the ceaseless demands for 'modernization' and 'reinvention' of state bureaux made on behalf of advocates of enhanced democratic rule, are based on the belief that bureaucracies should be more 'responsive' to the wishes of their political masters and to the people they serve. And yet, the role accorded to state bureaux in many polities has been deliberately devised to isolate officials from the electoral process, thus institutionalizing the very 'unresponsiveness' which so many people decry. And, it has been so organized for positive political purposes—to help preserve a modicum of stability, consistency, and continuity in the face of the vagaries and experimental enthusiasms of partisan politicians (e.g. Rohr 1998; du Gay 2000).

The non-sectarian bureaucratic comportment of the person, against which so many critics have railed, can therefore be seen as a positive ethical and political achievement rather than its opposite. Max Weber was simply among the earliest and most eloquent of human scientists to draw attention to the ethical discipline and rigour required by the conduct of bureaucratic office. More than this, Weber (1978) indicated how the construction of a Hobbesian 'buffer' between *homme et citoyen*—between civic virtues and personal principles—would not have been possible without the emergence of a particular *lebens-führung*: that of the bureau and the bureaucrat. Hobbes was no doubt correct to insist that civil law defined the rights and duties of the individual as citizen. The law alone, however, was not enough to detach political administration from 'personal' ideals and loyalties. As Weber's work indicates, it was the bureau that emerged to perform this difficult task.

According to Weber (1978: 958 ff.) the bureau comprises the social and cultural conditions of a distinctive and independent comportment of the person, one that is basically non-sectarian in character. Among the most important of these conditions is that the office constitutes a 'vocation' (*Beruf*)—a focus of ethical commitment and duty, autonomous of and superior to the holder's extra-official ties to kith, kin, class, or conscience. For Weber, this marks out the bureau as a specific *lebensordung* or 'life-order', and they provide the bureaucrat with a distinctive ethical bearing and status-conduct. Unlike other forms of office holding, the privileges of modern bureaucratic office are not personal possessions to be bargained or traded:

Rather, entrance into an office . . . is considered an acceptance of a specific duty of fealty to the purpose of the office (*Amstreue*) in return for the grant of a secure existence. It is decisive for the modern loyalty to an office that . . . it does not establish a relation to a *person*, like the vassal's or disciple's faith under feudal or patrimonial authority, but rather is devoted to *impersonal* . . . purposes. (Weber 1978: 959)

For Weber, the ethical attributes of the good bureaucrat—strict adherence to procedure, acceptance of sub- and superordination, *esprit de corps*, abnegation of personal moral enthusiasms, commitment to the purposes of the office—are to be seen as a positive moral achievement requiring the mastery of definite ethical techniques and routines—declaring one's 'personal' interest, developing appropriate professional relations with one's colleagues, subordinating one's 'self' to the dictates of procedural decision-making—through which individuals come to acquire the disposition and ability to conduct themselves according to the ethos of bureaucratic office. As Hobbes realized, it is the duty of citizens not to allow their spiritual zeal to overpower their civic demeanour; and as Weber points out, it is the honour of bureaucrats not to allow their 'personal' commitments to determine the manner in which they perform the administrative duties of their office. And this very 'impersonality' is the source of many freedoms. Weber, for instance, describes the formalistic impersonality of bureaucratic administration—its blindness to inherited differences in status and prestige—as producing a democratic, equalizing effect: 'the dominant norms are concepts of straightforward duty without regard to personal considerations. Everyone is subject to formal equality of treatment'.

Weber (1994: 330) famously described the ethos of bureaucratic office as requiring an official to conduct him- or herself *'sine ira et studio'*, without passion or prejudice. He went on to argue that state bureaucrats, unlike politicians, should not be seen as, or encouraged to become, partisan party political animals. Certainly, the governmental life-order within which bureaucrats found themselves was distinctively 'political', and official bureaucratic actions could have political ramifications, but this did not mean that bureaucrats were, of themselves, partisan political beasts. Rather, the ethos governing the conduct of officials required them to avoid 'fighting'.

Partisanship, fighting, passion—*ira et studium*—all this is the very element in which the politician, and above all the political leader, thrives. His actions are subject to a quite different principle of responsibility, one diametrically opposed to that of the official. When, despite the arguments advanced by an official, his superior insists on the execution of an instruction which the official regards as mistaken, the official's honour consists in being able to carry out that instruction, on the responsibility of the man issuing it, conscientiously and precisely in the same way as if it corresponded to his own convictions. Without this supremely ethical discipline and self-denial the whole apparatus would disintegrate. (Weber 1994: 330)

The key to this self-denial is the official's trained indifference to party or partisan creed combined with an attachment to the authority of the state, political order, or regime. In other words, official 'indifference' means not being committed, by convictions guiding one's official actions, to the creed and platform of a current political party, while being able without a crisis of conscience to further the policies of any current party (Parker 1993: 138). State bureaucrats are thus likely to greet the panaceas and enthusiasms of all political parties with caution. That is part of their job and in performing that role they may be seen as servants of the state. This, of course is one of the main reasons for maintaining party political neutrality as a key feature of bureaucratic state service, and thus for keeping the vast majority of its membership independent of party control. This does not, of course, preclude a political officer of state—a minister, say—from having political advisers, but it certainly has costs in the form of a less enthusiastic official embrace of party programmes—especially programmes of radical change— than party enthusiasts might wish. Yet, to give into the partisan political urge for more 'responsiveness' and less 'indifference' carries its own costs—creeping politicization of the state service, with all the dangers this can pose to established political and personal liberties, for instance.[3] Seen in this light, the unresponsivness and impersonality of bureaucratic conduct, which critics represent as fundamentally illiberal, becomes instead 'a condition of freedom' (Larmore 1987: 42).

The Freedom of Bureaucratic Constraint: Some Concluding Comments

Formalities and procedures were the wisdom of human organization and were in themselves civilizing instruments. She knew that now. When she was younger she'd opposed all red tape. Not any more. Red tape was often just a way of causing a pause in the impatience of things so that everything could be properly checked and considered. She realized that when enthusiasm and dedication had been expended, an organization had to leave in their place a bureaucracy' (Frank Moorhouse 1993, *Grand Days*).

Given the popularity and political reach of common sense assumptions about the negative relations between state authority and personal freedom, and bureaucracy and personal liberty, it is hardly surprising that 'constraint' is a term frequently negatively coded by many enthusiasts for the radical reform of state institutions. Constraint suggests limits to the scope for spontaneous action and possibilities of transformation. Worse it can imply a necessary conservatism as well as a status of subordination. These are not qualities that naturally appeal to those categories of person—critical intellectuals, management gurus, policy wonks—keen to advocate radical reform of the public administration as a bureaucratic institution of state. These are persons who indeed embody the very 'impatience of things'. It is unsurprising then that these persons would regard the idea of 'constraint' as a defining feature of bureaucratic conduct as *inter alia*—an excuse for inaction and inefficiency, a nefarious way of exercising a dubious political power, a strategy of social exclusion, and so on and so forth. All these and much else besides have been levelled at the public administration as a bureaucratic institution of government. Yet despite the moral outrage that critics both express and seek to engender it nonetheless remains the case that the very uniqueness of the public administration as a form of governmental institution lies in the extent of bureaucratic constraints permeating it. These constraints are intrinsic to the practice of liberal state administration. They are not by-products that can be removed at will to produce fresher, cleaner, faster, shinier public sector management.[4] For instance, values of formal equality of treatment for citizens and due process considerations means that the public administration is constrained in its ability to act 'fast and loose'. It cannot drop the nuisance client (or 'marginal customer') for the sake of administrative convenience. For the public bureau, the client is everyone who meets (politically and frequently legally) pre-established criteria for service. The point is that once a clientele is described with operational specificity, all individuals meeting that criteria of personhood have a claim on the administered service. Similarly, the preservation of due process obliges officials to give people affected by governmental action a fair chance to get their views on official decisions registered so that their interests are not overlooked or arbitrarily overridden. This naturally is an extremely time consuming and administratively burdensome way of operating. Due process considerations add to the practices and constraints generally regarded as 'red tape' or 'bureaucracy'. Yet, are they inefficient? Only, if efficiency is judged in simple quantitative terms. When the value-laden expectations of government are born in mind a different judgement presents itself (see Goodsell, Chapter 1, this volume).

Similarly, allegations of 'inefficiency' and 'red-tape' are frequently associated with financial controls in government. The public administration as an institution of government operates within a political context in which principles governing the use of public money are minutely detailed and where the use of such funds is rigorously monitored. There is nothing surprising about this. Public funds possess a unique status, in large part because abusing them is held to eat away at the foundations of government. Rigid criteria for deployment and use of public funds—the 'excessive "red tape"' and bureaucracy beloved of critics—is a price that the political system is prepared to pay to safeguard its own integrity. For instance, exceedingly tight and 'bureaucratic' controls are in place to keep the political system from turning into an instrumentality of private profit for those in its employ. After all, the temptations facing officials can be enormous (see the recent uproar about 'celebrity browsing' by Inland Revenue staff in the United Kingdom). Through the use of elaborate procedural safeguards—as well as formal training and learning by example—corruption and other forms of malpractice have been inhibited and gradually squeezed out of the system. For years, though, the cry has been heard that prevention costs more than the ailment itself. And yet, government has its own specific purposes and 'regime values' (Rohr 1998). Businesses may be tempted to ditch costly bureaucratic procedures whose benefits are not easily weighted but government and hence public administration is different. Here, as Herbert Kaufman (1977: 53) put it, it is no contradiction at all to argue that governments should 'spend $20 to prevent the theft of $1'. In the constrained political environment that public administration operates highly value-laden matters of process—concerned with qualitative issues about the manner in which results are achieved—will always intermingle and frequently compete with the so-called 'bottom-line' issues of costs and quantities of outputs (Chapman 2000).

There are, in fact, any number of areas in which fashionable attempts to remove bureaucratic constraints are attempted on the basis of little to no understanding of the status and role of those constraints within the conduct of state service. For instance, in recent years, the issue of 'leadership' has once again emerged as a hot topic within the field of public management (see Salaman and Newman, Chapters 6 and 8 respectively, this volume). The British New Labour Government's White paper 'Modernising Government' (CM4310 1999) and its related policy documents (Cabinet Office 1999) places considerable emphasis upon the capacity of executive leadership to help change the culture of 'risk aversion' that it considers endemic to the British Civil Service. Thus, the White Paper states that officials must 'move away from the risk-averse culture inherent in government' and that this is to be achieved through removing 'unnecessary bureaucracy which prevents public servants from experimenting, innovating and delivering a better product'. As with a previous attempt to inculcate 'real qualities of leadership' among senior civil servants, the *Next Steps Report* (Efficiency Unit 1998: para. 35), explains quite what this means in the British constitutional context, where ministerial accountability is still assumed to be a crucial constitutional convention, is not at all clear. At one level, encouraging all senior civil servants to become leaders and to take individual personal responsibility for their decision-making would make the accountability trail more complicated. With so many leaders among politicians and civil servants, where would the buck stop, exactly?

The Australian author Frank Moorhouse indicates what can happen when there are too many people trying to be leaders within an organization. In his prize winning novels, *Grand Days* and *Dark Palace*, Moorhouse charts the career of an Australian woman employed at the League of Nations in Geneva during the interwar years. The story of Edith Campbell-Berry, a would-be ideal–typical bureaucrat, is told against the rise and fall of the fortunes of the League, which is itself, for Moorhouse, a model of the ideal–typical public organization.

Moorhouse's character Edith illustrates many of the problems of leadership and ethics in a bureaucratic organization. At an early point in *Grand Days*, soon after her arrival at the League, we see Edith stealing in and out of the office of the League's Secretary General.

Edith is not the official leader of the League but she is convinced that what she is doing, however covert, is ethical because it is in the cause of true leadership. Edith is, in fact, impersonating Sir Eric Drummond, the real Secretary General, by using his office, his letterhead and his forged signature to send out letters to groups around the world that Edith thinks deserve the official support of The League, of which she is, in fact, a recent and relatively junior recruit.

As John Uhr (2001) has argued, Edith is a model of the public-spirited and highly principled employee. Above all else, she wants her organization to be as ethical as she is. We see, in effect, Edith speaking on behalf of the League's ideals by impersonating what she considers to be its better nature. Her tactic is one that honours outsiders who will in turn regard the organization more highly as a result.

But at a critical point, one of Edith's colleagues, Florence, who is in on the whole escapade, asks Edith to turn the game around, to use her access to the Secretary General's office to send a message internally. Florence has none of Edith's high-minded zeal: she simply wants Edith to steal some of the Secretary General's embossed paper so that they can impress their colleagues with their wily skills. At this point, Edith begins to see the error of her ways. What if everyone took it upon themselves to be leader and, in effect, sought 'to pursue private policies by stealth' (Moorhouse 1993: 178)? How dangerous this could be. Edith suddenly sees the entire episode from the Secretary General's point of view. And from his perspective, she sees the import-ance of employees acting within the confines of their office, and of being on guard against the temptations of impetuosity and heart-led enthusiasms. In other words, she sees the importance of bureaucratic constraint (as the quote opening this section makes clear).

The pursuit of private policies by stealth to circumvent seemingly tiresome bureaucratic constraints and the dangers therein for account-ability and integrity has its counterpart in private sector organizations too. The cases of Enron, Anderson, WorldCom, et al. indicate all too clearly what can happen when the bureaucratic process is subverted or ignored (see Armbrüster, Chapter 3, this volume). Perhaps we shouldn't be surprised about such wanton and culpable conduct given the regularity and insistence with which private sector managers have been warned of the inherent evils of bureaucracy over the last two decades. Executive freedom has come to be seen as the product of an absence of bureaucratic constraints (remember Tom Peters' famous rallying cry 'I beg each and everyone of you to develop a passionate and public hatred of bureaucracy'). Perhaps it is time to return to some of the classics of management literature for a more nuanced and sensitive understanding of the conduct of management, and the positive role of bureaucracy.[5] In his classic, but now largely ignored, text *Exploration in Management* (1960) the businessman and organizational analyst Wilfred Brown outlined what he considered to be some of the errors of conventional views about 'executive freedom to act'.

Many managers feel that 'freedom' lies in the sort of situation where their superior says to them: 'There are not many regulations in this place. You will understand the job in a month or two and you make your own decisions. No red tape—you are expected to take command; make the decisions off your own bat as they arise. I am against a lot of rules or regulations, and we do not commit too much to paper'. In my experience a manager in such a situation has virtually no 'freedom to act' at all. He starts making decisions and his boss sends for him [*sic*] to say: 'Look here, Jones, I am sorry to tell you that you have made two rather serious mistakes in the course of reorganizing your work. You have promoted one man to supervisor who is not the next man due for promotion in the factory, and you have engaged five additional machinists, a decision you should have referred to me, because we have some surplus men in this category in an adjacent factory'. Now, Jones might well say: 'You said there were no regulations but, in fact, you have already mentioned the existence of two: one concerned with promotion and the other with increase in establishment. Please detail these regulations to me precisely, so that I can work to them in future, and let me know now of any further regulations which bear upon my work'.

In practice, Jones probably says nothing of the kind, because he does not think in this way; to him regulations are stumbling blocks in the path of those wishing to display initiative. He will proceed, over the years, to learn by making mistakes, of the whole array of regulations, which by the very nature of executive systems, do in fact exist.

It is much more efficient to delineate as precisely as possible to a new subordinate all of the regulations he [*sic*] must observe and then say: 'You must take all of the decisions that seem to you to be required, so long as you keep within the bounds of that policy. If, keeping within those bounds, you take decisions which I think you should have referred to me, then I cannot criticize; for such a happening implies that some part of the policy which I wish you to operate has not been disclosed to you. I must, then, formulate that policy and add it to the prescribed content of your job'. If, in addition, the manager can give his subordinate a rounded idea of the discretionary component of his job by stating the types of decision which he must make, then that subordinate is in a real position to act on his own initiative in the prescribed area . . . In fact, it is only by delineating the area of 'freedom' in this way that a subordinate knows when he can take decisions. (Brown 1960: 119–20)

Bureaucratic constraints, or limits, on executive freedom to act are therefore best understood as conditions for its existence rather than its rescission.

Notes

1. By 'person' I am not referring exclusively to human beings. Rather, in taking a common law approach to the status of personhood, I am using the term to refer to any entity, human or non-human (a corporation; an association) which is capable of being allotted rights or duties. In legal terms, persons are nothing but the subjects or substances of which rights and duties are the attributes. Thus, not only may non-humans be 'persons' but also not all humans will be 'persons' in all contexts and circumstances. See, for instance, the classic discussion in Cousins (1980).
2. By ' expressivism' I am referring to those critics of state and bureaucracy who require a political order to express certain moral ideals—such as an all pervading spirit of community or an inalienable right to personal autonomy. Such critics assume that the political domain should express the highest ideals of its members, and thus refuse to envision the possibility that the political realm and other areas of life 'may heed different priorities' (Larmore 1987: 93)
3. As I am not, by and large, a party political enthusiast, I feel certain that the costs of the alternative situation would be much greater.
4. As Herbert Kaufman (1977: 61) argued some time ago,'red tape is not the same as unwanted material by-products. The latter are easily distinguished from the desired products with which they are associated, and people by and large agree on what is product and what is waste, no matter how bitterly they may quarrel over the acceptable balance between the two. In the case of government requirements and restraints, both substantive and procedural, people disagree about what is valued output and what is dismal by-product . . . one person's red tape is another person's sacred protection'.
5. I am thinking here of Jaques (1990) on hierarchy, Barnard (1938) and Parker Follett (1980) on leadership and Vickers (1995) on judgement, for instance.

References

Barnard, C. (1938). *The Functions of the Executive*. Cambridge, MA: Harvard University Press.

Brown, W. (1960). *Exploration in Management*. Harmondsworth: Penguin.

Cabinet Office (1999). *Civil Service Reform*. London: Cabinet Office.

CM4310 (1999). *Modernising Government*. London: HMSO.

Chapman, R. A. (2000). 'Ethics in public service for the new millennium', in R. A. Chapman (ed.), *Ethics in Public Service for the New Millennium*. Aldershot: Ashgate.

Condren, C. (2002). '*Natura naturans*: Natural Law and the Sovereign in the writings of Thomas Hobbes', in I. Hunter and D. Saunders (eds), *Natural Law and Civil Sovereignty*. Basingstoke: Palgrave.

Cousins, M. (1980). '*Mens Rea*: a note on sexual difference, criminology and the law', in P. Carlen and M. Collison (eds), *Radical Issues in Criminology*. Oxford: Martin Robertson.

Du Gay, P. (2000). *In Praise of Bureaucracy*. London: Sage.

Dunn, J. (2000). *The Cunning of Unreason*. London: Harper-Collins.

Efficiency Unit (1988). *Improving Management in Government: The Next Steps*. London: HMSO.

Fish, S. (1994). *There's No Such Thing as Free Speech . . . and it's a Good Thing Too*. Oxford: Oxford University Press.

Fish, S. (1999). *The Trouble with Principle*. Cambridge, MA: Harvard University Press.

Follett, M. P. (1980). *Dynamic Administration*. New York: Hippocrene Books.

Gray, J. (2000). *The Two Faces of Liberalism*. Cambridge: Polity Press.

Green, L. (1988). *The Authority of the State*. Oxford: Clarendon Press.

Hobbes, T. (1991). *Leviathan*. Cambridge: Cambridge University Press.

Holmes, S. (1994). 'Liberalism for a world of ethnic passions and decaying states'. *Social Research*. 61/3; 599–610.

Holmes, S. (1995). *Passions and Constraint*. Chicago, IL: Chicago University Press.

Holmes, S., and Sunstein, C. (1999). *The Cost of Rights*. New York: W. W. Norton.

Hunter, I. (1994). *Re-Thinking the School*. Sydney: Allen & Unwin.

Hunter, I. (1998). 'Uncivil Society', in M. Dean and B. Hindess (eds), *Governing Australia*. Sydney: Cambridge University Press.

Hunter, I. (1999). 'Is Metaphysics a Threat to Liberal Democracy?', Paper Presented to a Colloquium on 'The End of Postmodernism?', Humanities Research Centre, Australian National University, August.

Hunter, I. (2001). *Rival Enlightenments*. Cambridge: Cambridge University Press.

Ignatieff, M. (2001). *Human Rights as Politics and Idolatry*. Princeton, NJ: Princeton University Press.

Jaques, E. (1990). 'In praise of hierarchy'. *Harvard Business Review.* Jan/Feb, 127–33.

Kaufman, H. (1977). *Red Tape: its Origins, Uses and Abuses.* Washington: Brookings Institution.

Kriegel, B. (1995). *The State and the Rule of Law* (trans. M. LePain and J. Cohen). Princeton, NJ: Princeton University Press.

Larmore, C. (1987). *Patterns of Moral Complexity.* Cambridge: Cambridge University Press.

Moorhouse, F. (1993). *Grand Days.* Sydney: Vintage.

Oakeshott, M. (1975). *Hobbes on Civil Association.* Indianapolis, IN: Liberty Fund.

Parker, R. (1993). *The Administrative Vocation.* Sydney: Hale & Iremonger.

Rohr, J. (1998). *Public Service, Ethics and Constitutional Practice.* Lawrence, KS: University of Kansas Press.

Saunders, D. (2002). 'Within the orbit of this life—Samuel Pufendorf and the autonomy of law'. *Cardozo Law Review.* 26/3; 101–24.

Seidler, M. J. (2002). 'Pufendorf and the politics of recognition', in I. Hunter and D. Saunders (eds), *Natural Law and Civil Sovereignty.* Basingstoke: Palgrave.

Skinner, Q. (1989). 'The state', in T. Ball, J. Farr, and R. L. Hanson (eds), *Political Innovation and Conceptual Change.* Cambridge: Cambridge University Press, 90–131.

Uhr, J. (2001). 'Whatever Happened to Leadership?', Plenary Paper Presented at the 'Governance and Justice' Conference, Griffith University, Brisbane, 10th July.

Vickers, G. (1995). *The Art of Judgement.* London: Sage.

Walzer, M. (1984). 'Liberalism and the art of separation'. *Political Theory.* 12/3; 315–30

Weber, M. (1978). *Economy and Society* (2 Vols.). Los Angeles, CA: University of California Press.

Weber, M. (1994). 'The profession and vocation of politics', in P. Lassman and R. Speirs (eds), *Weber: Political Writings.* Cambridge: Cambridge University Press.

3

Bureaucracy and the Controversy between Liberal Interventionism and Non-Interventionism

Thomas Armbrüster

Introduction

Critics of bureaucracy typically present a twofold argument for why public administration in democracies needs to be reduced. One part of the argument is economic; it says that public bureaux are inefficient and waste taxes. Private firms, contracted by higher authorities and ideally exposed to market forces, can conduct the work more efficiently and save taxpayers' money. The other part of the argument is political rather than economic. It says that state authorities represent unresponsive and unaccountable organizations, develop their own self-referential and opaque procedures, undermine the elected government's control over them, and limit the freedom of citizens. Based on these arguments, the quest for a privatization of state bureaucracies is associated with treating citizens as clients rather than as administrative subjects, and with applying market principles to the procedures of public bureaux. The most prominent books in this context, those by Osborne and Gaebler (1992) and Osborne and Plastrik (1997) are conceived as politically neutral. In the United States for instance, they were endorsed by the Clinton/Gore administration and both Democratic and Republican governors and mayors have followed their advice.

If the critique of bureaucracies were only economic, then political scientists and organizations theorists would not have much to worry about and could focus on efficiency issues such as benchmarking and optimizing bureaucratic procedures. However, the juxtaposition between bureaucracies and markets is not only based on efficiency concerns or technical and investment-related specifics as in transaction cost economics. Rather, in many cases the assumption is that market-based solutions are more democratic than public administrations. The attitude to bureaucracies is thus deeply affected by societal mores, implicit images, or explicit proclamations about enjoyable polities, good democracies, and the role of the state.

Hence this chapter tries to frame the debate on bureaucracy in terms of political philosophy. Liberal non-interventionism (classical liberalism and contemporary libertarianism), liberal interventionism (contemporary liberalism or liberal egalitarianism), and communitarianism (or civic republicanism as the contemporary version) associate state bureaucracy with different notions and ideals of democracy. Outlining the relation between bureaucracy critique and defence on the one hand and political philosophy on the other can make underlying assumptions about democracy explicit. Political theorists such as Rawls (1971; 1993) and Nozick (1974), for example, discuss the role of the state, but not the consequential role of state bureaucracies for their democratic ideals. While it is clear that Rawls's 'well-ordered society' cannot do without a significant quantity of ordering institutions, he seems to take the role of public administration for granted. To Nozick (1974), market forces are central to individual liberty even if they do not lead to an optimal allocation of resources. Thus his argument is political rather than economic. He seems to accept the role of bureaucracy for maintaining a liberal order if it is kept very slim, or he assumes that minimalist government does without bureaucracy.

Contemporary critics of bureaucracy typically assume that liberal non-interventionists are on their side. As I shall point out below, however, this assumption holds only partially. Liberal non-interventionists have in fact pointed out that bureaucracy has its place. Certainly, the concerns about bureaucracies as strengthening 'big government' are immense, and the belief in markets as spontaneous orders has led people such as Hayek (1944) to associate all kinds of interventionism with planned economies and totalitarianism. However, classical liberals also outline in great detail the principles of constitutionality for a liberal society, and even if they ignore the question of how much bureaucratic administration is needed, they implicitly assume a slim but strong and well-functioning state administration. Hence, as I will outline below, the prudent side of liberal non-interventionism does not support contemporary market populism.

After sketching the relation between state bureaucracy and certain political philosophies, I will argue that the current anti-bureaucratic political culture in the United States and other Western countries is not based on any one particular political philosophy, but draws on specific elements of libertarianism and communitarianism. A closer look at political philosophy thus explicates common and popular concerns about state bureaucracies. In its moralization of originally more prudent libertarianism, current market populists rely not only on elements of liberal non-interventionism but also on a component of communitarianism. As Kymlicka (1998) points out, in political practice in the United States, liberal non-interventionism has formed an alliance with non-liberal strands of political thought. The contemporary anti-bureaucratic culture is based on a combination of particular elements from different political philosophies, and this combination could be labelled 'moralist libertarianism' or 'moralist non-interventionism'.

An Economic Consideration of Bureaucracy

We shall begin with an economic consideration of the 'bureaucracy versus markets' debate. Williamson (1999), who is careful not to adopt any political position, applies the instruments of transaction cost economics to the question of whether sovereign transactions such as foreign affairs should be handled by a public agency, a private institution, or a hybrid form in the sense of a regulated private company. He is aware that contemplating the privatization of the State Department is mind-boggling, but he argues that it is instructive to assess extreme instances and to explicate the obvious in order to get cues for the non-obvious.[1] Williamson argues that, 'politics aside', an economic appreciation for the properties of alternative modes of governance is necessary. Denouncing public agencies because they have weaker incentives, more rules and regulations, and greater job security than private companies misses the point if those features have been deliberately crafted into the public bureau. Under particular consideration of the hazards of probity, that is the loyalty and rectitude necessary in foreign-affairs transactions, Williamson argues as follows.

The ideal type of bureaucracy described by Max Weber (and now widely scorned) actually meets many of the needs of foreign affairs: jurisdictional ordering by official rules and regulations; clearly established hierarchical authority and appeal through administrative due process; the separation of business assets from private wealth; deep knowledge of procedure; and a vocational commitment to include training and loyalty to the office . . . High-powered incentives, according to which individual (or groups of) agents appropriate streams of net receipts, are notably absent in the Weberian description of bureaucracy. That is because high-powered incentives place the fidelity of the system at risk.

To be sure, flat compensation comes at a cost, in that noncontingent compensation will induce some workers to shirk. Bureaucratic rules, regulations, standard operating procedures, and the like are thus partly explained by the fact that egregious shirking can be limited in this way. On the argument advanced here, however, the main purpose of administrative controls is to promote probity in mission, responsiveness, and communication respects. (Williamson 1999: 325)

In other words, in terms of the comparative institutional analysis between markets, hybrids, and bureaucracies, foreign affairs transactions score highest on bureaucracy—and this in terms of probity-hazard efficiency rather than simply on political grounds. Williamson extends these reflections to defence procurement, office supplies, income tax collection, and prisons. Under consideration of cost-control, asset specificity hazards, and probity hazards, he finds that only office supply offers an easy case for procuring in the market. The other institutions might under certain circumstances be eligible for a hybrid solution of regulated business, but many variables signal precaution (Williamson 1999: 338–9). Williamson concludes that at least in the context of foreign affairs transactions, practices that are widely condemned, such as low-powered incentives, convoluted bureaucratic procedures, and excesses of employment security, serve legitimate economizing purposes (see Goodsell, Chapter 1, for further instances).

Liberal Interventionism and Bureaucracy

If scholars such as Williamson argue that economic considerations lead to the legitimacy of bureaucracy, then there might still be political reasons to discard bureaucracies. We shall start with an outline of the relation between liberal interventionism and bureaucracy. As opposed to libertarianism and classical liberalism, liberal interventionism does not see a stark contrast between liberty and equality (Rawls 1971, 1993; Ackerman 1980; Sen 1992; Holmes 1995; Van Parijs 1995; Dworkin 2000; Holmes and Sunstein 2000). While freedom must always have priority over equality, since there cannot be any equality if there is no freedom, and full equality can never be achieved without abandoning freedom, liberating people not only from interference of state authorities but also from the pains of hunger, unemployment, ill-health, and miserable old-age, also renders them more equal. To employ Berlin's (1958) terms, the idea of freedom is not only a negative one (freedom from intrusion or interference of authorities, the state, other individuals, etc.) but also a positive one, that is, freedom to choose the kind of life that individuals have a reason to value. Positive freedom depends on capabilities such as physical characteristics and social opportunities and is thus connected to the sort of healthcare and education that enables individuals to develop these freedoms. Like classical liberalism, liberal interventionism is rooted in the work of John Stuart Mill (1859), since he was not only concerned that rulers may be powerless against their subordinate bureaucracies if the latter become too strong, but also about the role of the wage labourer; and he addressed not only protection from interference but also individual development as a feature of liberalism. Liberal interventionism is concerned with supplying and securing a certain degree of positive freedom for all citizens, and it endorses an institutional system to secure equal opportunities that is sensitive to citizens' ambitions and individual efforts, but insensitive to their natural endowments. Progressive taxation and (limited) wealth redistribution belong to the basic principles, since the wealthy would otherwise be able to dominate the poor and the freedom of many would diminish.

With regard to bureaucracy, liberal interventionists agree with classical liberals on a number of issues. Self-referential administration and organizational slack and inefficiency are under all circumstances to be avoided. Bureaucracies must be prevented from growing beyond their role subordinate to the executive and the standing laws. Moreover, the bureaucratic ethos of impartial conduct free from status, personal relations, social background, and party-political conviction must be secured (see du Gay, Chapter 2). This ethos must extend to a bureaucratic self-concept as servicing rather than patronizing citizens and to considering the state administration an instrument at the disposal of democratically legitimate governments rather than a power in itself. For liberal interventionists, therefore, neutral proceduralism is the central mechanism for achieving equal opportunities, equality before the law, and not favouring any particular conception of the good. Bureaucracies are considered central elements of a state that offers positive freedom to its citizens, and the commitment to the rule of law must not be diluted by an overweening commitment to efficiency.

In contrast to non-interventionists, interventionists consider government and regulation as positive instruments in themselves rather than as a necessary evil. From the interventionist viewpoint, the role of state bureaucracies is not only to defend property rights against force or fraud, but also to enforce the principles of positive freedom that have been agreed upon in democratic legislation. To this end, state bureaucracies must be responsive and function efficiently and effectively; otherwise they lose legitimacy in the eyes of the citizenry. Reforming state bureaucracies towards higher efficiency and effectiveness, therefore, is one of the main concerns of liberal interventionists, since this secures the acceptance of positive freedom and its enforcement in the population. Too slim a public administration may simply not guarantee the elements of positive freedom, and the transfer of public authority to market-based organizations may endanger a democratic order, since the commitment to impartial treatment, in bureaucracies based on a trained and neutral administrative workforce, may erode. For liberal interventionists, therefore, the main issue concerning bureaucracy is not its size, but the political and public control over it. Bureaucracies may grow and shrink according to the tasks the elected government gives them. Whether bureaucracies then develop their 'own logic' or become too powerful is a matter of institutional design and control rather than an inevitable development.

Liberal Non-Interventionism and the Demand for Slim but Strong Bureaucracies

Mostly associated with anti-bureaucratic political theory is, of course, classical liberalism. In terms of twentieth-century writers, classical liberalism is represented in the work of Friedrich von Hayek (1944; 1960 [1990]; 1982), Hayek's teacher Ludwig von Mises (1944; 1949), and Milton Friedman (1962). One of their assumptions is that market forces ensure a Pareto optimum that ultimately leads to the mutual advantage of all. The term 'social justice' is for them a contradiction in itself, since they assume that state intervention and redistribution precludes achieving the Pareto optimum. But they endorse market forces not only for economic but also for political reasons.

Undoubtedly, public administration and state bureaucracy is in many respects antithetic to the position of classical liberalism. While Mises, Hayek, and Friedman meticulously outline the role of the *Rechtsstaat* (constitutional state; rule of law) for both democracy and a functioning market economy, one of their main concerns is the overarching power of a central government, expressed in state bureaucracies. The following sentences by Hayek (1979 [1982]) summarize the classical-liberal fears about bureaucracy.

As little as the whole role of the growing para-government can I at this stage begin to discuss the threat created by the incessant growth of the government machinery, i.e. the bureaucracy. Democracy, at the same time at which it seems to become all-engulfing, becomes on the governmental level an impossibility. It is an illusion to believe that the people, or their elected representatives, can govern a complex society in detail. Government relying on the general support from a majority will of course still determine the major steps, so far as it is not merely driven to these by the momentum of its previous proceedings. But government is already becoming so complex that it is inevitable that its members, as heads of the various departments, are increasingly becoming puppets of the bureaucracy, to which they will still give 'general directions', but on the operation of which the execution of all the detail depends. It is not without reason that socialist governments want to politicize this bureaucracy, because it is by it and not in any democratic body that more and more of the crucial decisions are made. No totalitarian power can be achieved without this. (Hayek 1979 [1982]: 144–5)

The fears connected to bureaucracy are that democratic governments lose control over them, that bureaucracies pursue their own internal logic rather than democratically constituted purposes, and that they relentlessly grow and become all engulfing for civic life. As in Hayek's earlier book (1944), public administration and state intervention are seen in the context of overarching state power and even totalitarianism. They symbolize the obstruction of market forces, high taxation, and corporatism that hampers not only efficiency, creativity, and innovativeness, but also political freedom. Democracy is associated with the free interplay of market forces, and economic freedom, rather than public administration, is viewed as the foundation of political freedom.

This attitude led to popular perceptions of classical liberalism and libertarianism: a position that stands resolutely against bureaucracy and that emphasizes unfettered markets rather than public administration as the fundament of democracy. However, by reading Hayek the question emerges as to how constitutionality and the equal application of rules, which classical liberals fervently emphasize, can be administered if not by bureaucracies. For example, Hayek outlines his image of a democracy as follows.

I am the last person to deny that increased wealth and the increased density of population have enlarged the number of collective needs which government can and should satisfy. Such government services are entirely compatible with liberal principles so long as, *firstly*, government does not claim a monopoly and new methods of rendering services through the market (e.g. in some now covered by social insurance) are not prevented; *second*, the means are raised by taxation on uniform principles and taxation is not used as an instrument for the redistribution of income; and *thirdly*, the wants satisfied are collective wants of the community as a whole and not merely collective wants of particular groups. (Hayek 1973 [1991]: 389; emphasis in original)

Thus, while Hayek rejects that taxation be used for income redistribution, he admits that there is room for government intervention in the economy for the sake of what he calls 'collective needs' or 'collective wants', as long as this does not favour particular groups. Moreover, given that he embraces public services if this does not preclude private competitors, he seems to appreciate, for example, public health insurance if the citizen is also free to choose private health insurance. His main concern is the equal and completely predictable treatment of citizens. Public bureaucracy to guarantee positive freedom seems to be fine if there are also alternative market-based solutions.

Hayek lived long enough to read Rawls's *Theory of Justice* (1971). He acknowledged the importance of Rawls's contribution and—surprising as this may be for many—he did not disagree with much of it.

In one instance the feeling that I ought to justify my position vis-à-vis a major recent work has also contributed to delaying the completion of this volume. But after careful consideration I have *come to the conclusion that what I might have to say about John Rawls' Theory of* Justice (1972) would not assist in the pursuit of my immediate object because the differences between us seemed more verbal than substantial. (Hayek 1982: xvii)

While Hayek disagrees with Rawls about the use of the term and possibility of 'social justice', he agrees that principles of justice are the basis of institutional design and that law and government must act to keep markets competitive (Hayek 1976 [1982]: 100, 179, and 183). As Hayek argued earlier, it 'may be wise or unwise in the particular instance, but they [government regulations] do not conflict with liberal principles so long as they are intended to be permanent and are not used to favour or harm particular people' (Hayek, 1944: 60). Unfortunately, Hayek did not further explore—and indeed underestimated—the question of what this means in terms of public bureaucracy and its size.

If we look at the work of Ludwig von Mises (1944, 1949), Hayek's teacher in Austria and founding father of what is today called Austrian Economics, the non-interventionist mist on bureaucracy lifts a little. Mises set out to look at bureaucracy both as a measure of safeguarding individuals' rights and freedom and as a measure of executing the will of the supreme authority. He meticulously distinguished between bureaucratic and commercial management and argued that both have their due place in a democracy. Although his main concern was that bureaucratic management was unduly replacing commercial management in more and more areas in the United States (he referred to the New Deal era when he wrote his 1944 book on bureaucracy

while living in exile in New York), he defended the area in which
bureaucratic rather than commercial management is appropriate. For
example, he argued:

In public administration there is no connection between revenue and expenditure. The public services are spending money only . . . The revenue derived
from customs and taxes is not 'produced' by the administrative apparatus. Its
source is the law, not the activities of custom officers and tax collectors . . . In
public administration there is no market price for achievements. This makes
it indispensable to operate public offices according to principles entirely
different from those applied under the profit motive. (Mises 1944: 47)

Thus, one of the basic authors who equated the expansion of bureaucratic agencies with the rise of socialism, also defended bureaucratic
conduct in public administration. Mises, who as a young man before
the First World War quit his career as a civil servant in Austria's financial administration in disgust with bureaucracy (Hülsmann 2003),
went even further and criticized popular opinion against bureaucracy:

The plain citizen compares the operation of the bureaus with the working of
the profit system, which is more familiar to him. Then he discovers that
bureaucratic management is wasteful, inefficient, slow, and rolled up in
red tape. He simply cannot understand how reasonable people allow such a
mischievous system to endure. Why not adopt the well-tried methods of
private business?

However, such criticisms are not sensible. They misconstrue the features
peculiar to public administration. They are not aware of the fundamental difference between government and profit-seeking private enterprise. What they
call deficiencies and faults of the management of administrative agencies are
necessary properties. A bureau is not a profit-seeking enterprise . . . it has to
solve problems which are unknown to business management. (Mises 1944: 48)

The continuing timeliness of what Mises wrote sixty years ago
becomes even clearer at the following point:

It is vain to advocate a bureaucratic reform through the appointment of businessmen as heads of various departments . . . A former entrepreneur who is
given charge of a government bureau is in this capacity no longer a businessman but a bureaucrat. His objective can no longer be profit, but compliance
with the rules and regulations. As head of a bureau he may have the power
to alter some minor rules and some matters of internal procedure. But the

setting of the bureau's activities is determined by rules and regulations which are beyond his reach. It is a widespread illusion that the efficiency of government bureaus could be improved by management engineers and their methods of scientific management. However, such plans stem from a radical misconstruction of the objectives of civil government. (Mises 1944: 49)

One of the founding fathers of Austrian economics, therefore, did not only see a due place for bureaucracy in the execution of democratically legitimate rules, but went even further than common practice today when executives from the private sector are appointed heads of public bureaucracies and management consulting firms are employed to reform them. To Mises (1944), a clear separation of public administration and commercial conduct belongs to the fundament of democracy. He restated this in his later book:

Bureaucratic conduct of affairs is conduct bound to comply with detailed rules and regulations fixed by the authority of a superior body . . . Profit management is inapplicable in the pursuit of affairs which have no cash value on the market . . . Bureaucratic conduct of affairs is, as such, not an evil. It is the only appropriate method of handling governmental affairs, i.e., the social apparatus of compulsion and coercion. As government is necessary, bureaucratism is—in this field—no less necessary. Where economic calculation is unfeasible, bureaucratic methods are indispensable. (Mises 1949: 310–11)

Thus, what we have here is an introduction to and defence of bureaucracy. Classical liberalism is not, as many left-wing critics have argued, 'against' bureaucracy as such, but only against 'big government' in the sense of total government by administrative means. Indeed on occasion, classical liberals fervently defend bureaucratic against commercial conduct. Whether the role of bureaucracy is ignored as in the case of Nozick (1974), explicitly criticized but implicitly accepted as in the case of Hayek,[2] or explicitly embraced as in the case of Mises (1949: 310–11), liberal non-interventionism assumes that a clear separation is necessary between goods that have a cash value on the market and those that must be handled in bureaucratic ways.

We can now turn to the work of Milton Friedman. One of his most-often quoted sentences is, 'there is one and only one social responsibility of business—to use its resources and engage in activities designed to increase its profits so long as it stays within the rules of the game, which is to say, engages in open and free competition, without deception or fraud' (Friedman 1962: 133). To business ethicists and stakeholder theorists, this sounds outrageous, since Friedman's tenet supposedly comes close to 'anything goes in business'—corporations having the right to engage in all kinds of activities without any moral concerns. However, this is a misinterpretation or even misrepresentation of Friedman's (1962) creed, for it ignores the second part of the sentence. Friedman's point 'so long as it stays within the rules of the game . . . , without deception or fraud' is an expression of the legal-positivist assumption that morals are to be manifested in the law and that legislators rather than business executives are in charge of defining the rules of the game. Thus Friedman made a forceful case for a clear separation of economic and public management. He wrote, 'The existence of a free market does not of course eliminate the need for government. On the contrary, government is essential both as a forum for determining the "rules of the game" and as an umpire to interpret and enforce the rules decided on' (Friedman 1962: 15). In the tradition of classical liberalism, he elaborates on the role of government in upholding competition against cartels or monopoly businesses, defining and enforcing property rights and contracts, providing a monetary framework, etc. His assumption is that, if legislation succeeds in capturing ethics in the letters of the law, then business operates within the confines of ethics and social responsibility as long as it does not engage in illegal activity. Friedman believes, therefore, in legal positivism and the legitimacy of the power of government to rule. Thus he must believe in the power of public administration and the separation of the corporate and the public sphere. And indeed, he writes:

If businessmen do have a social responsibility other than making maximum profits for stockholders, how are they to know what it is? Can self-selected private individuals decide what the social interest is? Can they decide how great a burden they are justified in placing on themselves or their stockholders to serve that social interest? Is it tolerable that these public functions of taxation, expenditure, and control be exercised by the people who happen at the moment to be in charge of particular enterprises, chosen for those posts by strictly private groups? (Friedman 1962: 133–4)

Friedman thus points out that democratically legitimate officials, rather than business executives, should be in charge of public matters, and that it is the job of the legislative power to define the rules of the game, and of the executive power rather than economic actors to enforce them. In this way, Friedman outlines a state that is protected from business taking over or codetermining public matters.

From Prudent to Moralist Non-Interventionism

If even liberal non-interventionists offer qualified support for a strong public administration, then the question emerges as to why in the past two decades there has been a persistent and dramatic quest to 'de-bureaucratize' government? Half a century ago, Mises (1949: 310) suggested that there are many non-profit sectors that could be perfectly handled in a commercial way, and he named schools, hospitals, and the postal system as examples. Fifty-five years after Mises' publication, the postal system, telecommunications, utilities, and aviation have been privatized in most industrialized states, while the privatization of schools and hospitals have remained contested issues for which different countries pursue varying solutions. Why, then, does the trend towards implementing commercial principles go on, even in areas in which a cash value can hardly be determined? The current market populism seems at odds with prudent non-interventionism, since the latter seeks to dispassionately distinguish between those services for which a cash value in the market can be determined and those for which it cannot, and to fully apply commercial principles to the former and bureaucratic principles to the latter. We therefore need to look at the question of why today's anti-bureaucratic culture has departed from prudent non-interventionism. Are there elements of liberal non-interventionism or other political philosophies that lend themselves to today's market populism?

We can again start with Hayek. While the above-quoted elements of his thought acknowledge the need for slim but strong public administration, he failed to discuss the necessary size or the purpose of public administration as an institution of government. In order to ensure just, non-arbitrary, and predictable decisions, rules and regulations must be thoroughly checked beforehand and decisions must be protected against private economic interests or price-based compromising. But Hayek did not engage in a more specific discussion of what this means for public administration, other than it needs to be 'slim'. Moreover, his comparison between British interventionist policy in the 1930s and the totalitarian dictatorship in Nazi Germany (Hayek 1944), that is the amalgamation of interventionism and totalitarianism, was a clear category error. In his *Law, Legislation and Liberty* (1982), Hayek seems to acknowledge that Rawls, too, is a liberal. At that time he no longer put command economies and the provision of positive liberties into the same box. Nevertheless, his earlier amalgamation of these issues provided an intellectual predecessor of what could today be called market populism.

A similar critique can be levelled at Friedman (1962). I earlier pointed out that his most notorious quote on the social responsibility of business is in fact a plea for legal positivism and a strict separation between the economic and the rule-setting sphere. But there is another side to Friedman's thinking. First, rather than strengthening the law, at many points Friedman's (1962) doctrine de-legitimizes those elements of the legal framework that seek to guarantee equal freedom among the citizenry and prevent a domination of the wealthy over the poor. In this way he contradicts his ambition to prudently distinguish the economic from the public sphere. Second, his approach in general is characterized by a deep and almost irrational distrust of public administration, which emerges in the following, for instance.

When technical conditions make a monopoly the natural outcome of competitive market forces, there are only three alternatives that seem available: private monopoly, public monopoly, or public regulation. All three are bad so we must choose among evils. Henry Simons, observing public regulation of monopoly in the United States, found the results so distasteful that he concluded public monopoly would be a lesser evil. Walter Eucken, a noted German liberal, observing public monopoly in German railroads, found the results so distasteful that he concluded public regulation would be a lesser evil. Having learned from both, I reluctantly conclude that, if tolerable, private monopoly may be the least of evils. (Friedman 1962: 28)

Friedman thus has more trust in private monopolies than in public regulation of private businesses. His argument that this is because private monopolies are more responsive to societal and technical changes (Friedman 1962: 28–9) is not convincing because it ignores, for instance, the possibility for private monopolies charging high prices and the redistributive and political issues involved in administering natural monopolies. Third, the problem of Friedman's legal positivism is that in many instances the law is not refined enough to protect the broader frames of justice that it seeks to secure. As Regan (1998: 305) puts it, 'Law cannot anticipate every instance in which corporate actions may have broad social impacts. The cultivation of managerial judgment often may be the only assurance that corporations will take account of the externalities they impose'. In other words, law is always imperfect, and utilizing legal gaps for profit maximization may be economically understandable, but it has nothing to do with social responsibility. What renders Friedman a predecessor of contemporary market populism is his description of profit maximization as a social responsibility, and thus as a moral rather than prudent act. If Friedman had been familiar with the controversy between legal positivism and natural-law theory in philosophy of law (see, e.g. Bix 1999; Coleman and Leiter 1999), he might still have adopted the positivist position but probably not confused positivist lawfulness with moral responsibility.

Non-interventionist philosophy and economics, therefore, is characterized by two components: a prudent, dispassionate one, and a moralizing, passionate one. The prudent component of Mises (1944), Hayek (1944), and Friedman (1962) is their insistence on a clear separation of economic and public matters, on the protection of the public sphere from economic inequalities, and on the importance of predictable procedures and decisions by key bureaucratic institutions. The moral and passionate component involves representing profit maximization as a moral duty rather than as a prudent selling of services and products to those who value them most; the representation of liberal interventionism as equivalent to state socialism and totalitarianism; the argument that private monopolies are to be trusted more than public monopolies and public regulation; and the presentation of freedom as being in an eternal contradiction to, rather than just prior to, the demands of equality. Liberal non-interventionism thus lends itself partly, but only partly, to current market populism and does not alone explain the recent rise of anti-bureaucratic sentiment. The current political culture combines additional sources, and a critical look at communitarianism or civic republicanism and its relation to bureaucracy is instructive on a deeper understanding of contemporary anti-bureaucratic sentiment.

In the 1980s, communitarians criticized both liberals and libertarians for neglecting the development of civic virtues for a functioning democracy. More recently, Sandel (1996) blamed the rise of liberal state neutrality and the eclipse of civic-republican politics for not fostering virtues conducive to deliberative self-rule. He advocated a cultural change and a public philosophy that is more attuned to civic virtue. Communitarians and civic republicans suggest that public policy needs to foster a comprehensive public philosophy rather than execute only neutral proceduralism. To them, bureaucracy implies a different kind of suspicion than it does for liberal non-interventionists. Bureaucracy stands for neutral proceduralism rather than for coherent communal values and a commitment to civic virtue. The most explicit outline of communitarian economics has been delivered by Garfinkle (1997).

Social goals which involve putting economic policy to work as a means to the end of building a strong society include:
- To offer people strong economic incentives to strengthen community life, add to the vitality of our civil society, encourage volunteerism, and otherwise strengthen the bonds that link us together as a people sharing a genuine unity of purpose.
- To create an economic structure that simultaneously advances both individual freedom and social responsibility.
- To provide a safety net to prevent the poorest and neediest in society from suffering the worst consequences of poverty and disease.
- To sustain a sense of moral legitimacy for the economy such that average citizens perceive the economic system as fair and equitable as well as efficient. (Garfinkle 1997: 5)

Liberal interventionists certainly agree with communitarians about the importance of a social safety net, but they disagree about the communitarian creed that economic matters are supposed to strengthen 'community life' or 'the bonds that link us together as a people sharing a genuine unity of purpose'. To liberals, there is no such 'us' beyond an overlapping minimal consensus (Rawls 1993), and there is no unity of purpose either. Also, community life is for liberals no end in itself but just one conception of the good life. Demanding that the economy shall foster community life, therefore, overextends the purposes of economy. Communitarianism, however, prefers internal moral values of economic actors to external regulations, and associates the latter with 'corporatist oligopolistic economies' or a 'command economy'. Garfinkle (1997) formulates this creed as follows:

While it is unrealistic to hope for unlimited corporate altruism, it is reasonable to expect that inspired leadership and social encouragement can ensure that the profit motive will be tempered by concern for the common good. This would mean that corporations would avoid efforts to take unfair profits from the formation of monopolies or oligopolies which control prices, restrict consumer access to innovation and ultimately have a negative impact on the GDP. A corporatist oligopolistic economy, like a command economy, is too highly controlled to be productive for the larger society. Rather than rely solely on government regulation to combat unfair business collusion, social support for self-regulating initiatives can help to maintain energetic competition. (Garfinkle 1997: 19)

Communitarians thus seem to assume that moral behaviour of individual actors ('inspired leadership', 'social encouragement'), rather than rules and their enforcement, limit the external effects of profit-maximizing behaviour. This represents a far cry from the position of liberal interventionism, for which limiting external effects of profit-maximizing behaviour, and directing the fruits of wealth creation into channels of redistribution, is a matter of legislation and law enforcement—not of the economy itself. But communitarianism views regulation as the road to a 'corporatist oligopolistic economy', which comes close to the early Hayek's association of interventionism with totalitarianism. Communitarians seem to assume that voluntary moral behaviour of economic actors, and 'social support for self-regulating initiatives', maintain competition. One wonders whether communitarians still hold this belief today after prominent firms have been caught manipulating balance sheets.

The communitarian opposition to bureaucracy is also reflected at the level of management and organization studies. Rothschild (1979) and Rothschild and Whitt (1986) juxtapose 'collectivist–democratic organizations' to bureaucracies and thus put bureaucracy into an anti-democratic corner. As I have noted elsewhere (Armbrüster and Gebert 2002), Rothschild and Whitt criticize fixed and universalistic rules as detrimental to democratic management. Calculability, we are told, arises not on the basis of transparent rules and their predictable application, but on the basis of knowing the 'substantive ethics'. Rothschild and Whitt not only fall into what liberals call the 'community trap', but they also foster the impetus against proceduralism and promote a moralist rather than prudent approach to management and the economy.

The interesting point here is the convergence of communitarian beliefs and the moralist component of liberal non-interventionism. Both believe in the inherent goodness of the economy and in morality-based self-organization. Communitarians reject regulation because they think voluntary moral behaviour will do the job, and liberal non-interventionists reject regulation because they think it limits rather than enables competition. Both associate liberal interventionism and regulation with command economies. For the early Hayek, it represents the road to serfdom and totalitarianism; for communitarians, it represents the road to a corporatist–oligopolistic economy, which is, we are told, 'like a command economy, too highly controlled to be productive for the larger society' (see above). As Kymlicka (1998) has pointed out, in political practice liberal non-interventionism has formed an alliance with non-liberal strands of political thought. The amalgamation of the communitarian insistence on virtuousness and the moralist component of libertarianism can thus be described as 'moralist libertarianism' or 'moralist non-interventionism'. The market in itself is considered a moral institution. Rather than conceiving of it as a place to prudently exchange goods and services to those who value them most, we are told that there is a moral core in it. And since this is so, we are asked why we need the politico-legal framework, market regulations, accounting principles, consumer protection, etc. The economic sphere and its moral agency, we are told, sort out moral or public issues better than any regulatory body could ever do.

Certainly, as pointed out above, the law is often not powerful enough to anticipate all instances in which corporate action has external effects. In this sense, an ethos of legality is required in areas in which the law is not refined enough or that law enforcement cannot reach. But this does not take the responsibility from legislation and the state to render the law as biting as possible for securing the principles of justice and ensuring fair competition. From the viewpoint of liberal interventionism, bureaucracy and neutral proceduralism are required to deliver positive freedom and to secure competition and thus ensure negative freedom (freedom from intrusion of the economically more powerful). Self-organization or the voluntarily moral behaviour of economic actors will not do. Voluntary compliance is good, but not without regard for, or at the expense of, strengthening the politico-legal framework. Bureaucracies do need reform, but only so as to render them more efficient and effective and thus maintain their legitimacy in the public political culture. They do not need doing away with.

Conclusion

When think tanks such as The Objectivist Center (Kochhar, 2002), commented on corporate scandals, they argued that 'the market' has driven the fraudulent firms out of business. Not the state attorney, not the law and its enforcement, not public outrage or the investigations of the Securities and Exchange Commission—no, we are told, 'the market' has selected between fraud and legal behaviour. The market is considered an ontological entity with an own consciousness, indeed with a moral consciousness, rather than an abstract institution in which individual actors exchange goods and services. This quasi-religious image of the market goes so far as to attribute healing power to it. Some individuals or firms may at times behave illegally, but 'the market sorts it all out, don't you see it?'

No, I don't see it. Has not the public philosophy of moralist libertarianism, the belief in the inherent morality of markets, provided the politico-cultural basis for circumventing rules and thus for corporate fraud? To approach this question, we need to look at the link between moralist libertarianism as a political culture and its reflection in management.

Gary Hamel's (2000) 'revolutionary management' approach represents a manifestation of moralist libertarianism in management theory. Naming business guru Tom Peters as one of his heroes, Hamel argues that revolutionary rule-breaking, enthusiasm, and belief rather than reason are the basis of all entrepreneurship and innovativeness. Ironically, the example he uses most enthusiastically is Enron. He published his book about one year before the corporate fraud became public and wrote, 'Enron's chief executive, Kenneth Lay, deserves much of the credit for Enron's ability to innovate . . . But Lay dreams up few of Enron's rule-breaking business concepts. Instead, he has helped create an organization where thousands of people see themselves as revolutionaries.' (Hamel 2000: 212). If Hamel is right and Enron's corporate culture represented one of revolutionary rule-breaking, is it then so surprising that Enron's executives were not too concerned about the law? In their report about Enron's vision and values, admittedly journalistic rather than academic, Swartz and Watkins (2003) describe Enron's vision and values as follows:

In order to shape Enron's new identity—to figure out what it should be—a team from Enron's ad agency, Ogilvy & Mather, arrived from Manhattan to interview its employees and find out about what mattered to them. Ogilvy found Enron to be a company of 'believers'. Employees believed in Ken Lay and Jeff Skilling; they believed Enronians were the best and the brightest, and they believed they were doing good in the world by opening new markets and creating new products and services.

As a result, Enron and Ogilvy decided to hone its vision, and its new ad campaign, around a concept called 'What We Believe'. Those beliefs included 'the wisdom of open markets' and 'being a laboratory for innovation'. (Swartz and Watkins 2003: 103)

If Enron's corporate culture thus represented a corporate equivalent to moralist libertarianism, then not only energy market regulation but also accounting laws may appear as manifestations of an annoying, nanny-state bureaucracy. If a political culture influences the cognitive categories of managerial actors and shapes their attitude to market regulation, legislation, and law enforcement, then circumventing regulations may well be perceived as legitimate and appreciated by the social environment. But rather than seeing the connection between the quasi-religious belief in markets and corporate law transgression, we are still told that the market has sorted it all out and driven fraudulent firms out of business.

In this chapter, I have sought to explore attitudes to bureaucracy through the prism of political philosophy. Bureaucracy is one of the central links between the state and individuals, and the different political philosophies thus conceptualize it in different ways (see du Gay, Chapter 2, this volume). I have argued that the present anti-bureaucratic political culture represents a combination of a moralist component of libertarianism and a communitarian approach to the economy. From the viewpoint of liberal interventionism, by contrast, legislation and law enforcement—and not voluntary ethics or some assumed moral nature of markets—are the basic mechanisms that protect market participants, shareholders, and clients from fraud. While corporations are fully entitled to pursue profit maximization, public administration and thus bureaucracy must prevent corporations from externalizing the costs of pursuing material self-interest.

Notes

1. In view of recent developments, it seems that what Williamson considered obvious five years ago is no longer obvious now. According to the legislation approved by Congress in November 2002, civil service laws governing pay and promotions, job classification, collective bargaining, performance appraisals, discipline, and lay-offs will not apply to the 170,000 employees of the Homeland Security Department. Moreover, there are plans to privatize large parts of federal employee positions, including guarding prisoners, safeguarding borders and processing social security checks (see Suleiman 2003, 2).
2. Compare Hayek's critique of bureaucracies (Hayek 1979 [1982], 144–5) with his earlier appreciation of Mises' outline of bureaucracy (Hayek 1960 [1990], 124, 447).

References

Ackerman, B. (1980). *Social Justice in the Liberal State*. New Haven, CT: Yale University Press.

Armbrüster, T. and Gebert, D. (2002). 'Uncharted territories of organizational research: the case of Karl Popper's open society and its enemies'. *Organization Studies*. 23; 169–88.

Berlin, I. (1958). 'Two concepts of liberty', Inaugural Lecture to the University of Oxford, 31 October 1958. Reprinted in Berlin, I. (1969). *Four Essays on Liberty*. Oxford: Oxford University Press, 118–72.

Bix, B. (1999). 'Natural law theory', in D. Patterson (ed.), *A Companion to Philosophy of Law and Legal Theory*. Oxford: Blackwell, 223–40.

Coleman, J. L. and Leiter, B. (1999). 'Legal positivism', in D. Patterson (ed.), *A Companion to Philosophy of Law and Legal Theory*. Oxford: Blackwell, 241–60.

Dworkin, R. (2000). *Sovereign Virtue: The Theory and Practice of Equality*. Harvard: Harvard University Press.

Friedman, M. (1962). *Capitalism and Freedom*. Chicago, IL: University of Chicago Press.

Garfinkle, N. (1997). 'Communitarian economics'. *Journal of Socio-Economics*. 26/1; 1–24.

Hamel, G. (2000). *Leading the Revolution*. Boston, MA: Harvard Business School Press.

Hayek, F. A. von, (1944). *The Road to Serfdom*. Chicago, IL: University of Chicago Press.

Hayek, F. A. von, (1960 [1990]). *The Constitution of Liberty* (reprint 1990). London: Routledge.

Hayek, F. A. von, (1973 [1991]). 'Economic Freedom and Representative Government', The Fourth Wincott Memorial Lecture, published originally as IEA Occasional Paper No. 39 (1973); reprinted in F. A. von Hayek, (1991). *Economic Freedom*. Oxford: Blackwell, 383–97.

Hayek, F. A. von, (1976 [1982]). *The Mirage of Social Justice*. Volume 2 of *Law, Legislation and Liberty* (reprint in one volume, 1982). London: Routledge.

Hayek, F. A. von, (1979 [1982]). *The Political Order of a Free People*. Volume 3 of *Law, Legislation and Liberty* (reprint in one volume, 1982). London: Routledge.

Hayek, F. A. von, (1982). *Law, Legislation and Liberty*, Volumes 1–3. London: Routledge.

Holmes, S. (1995). *Passions and Constraint: On the Theory of Liberal Democracy*. Chicago, IL: University of Chicago Press.

Holmes, S. and Sunstein, C. R. (2000). *The Cost of Rights: Why Liberty Depends on Taxes*. New York: Norton.

Hülsmann, J. G. (2003). 'von Mises, Ludwig'; *American National Biography Online August 2003 Update*. www.anb.org/articles/14/14–01132.html; American Council of Learned Societies; published by Oxford University Press.

Kochhar, M. (2002). 'Capitalism and financial scandal'. *The Objectivist Center*, posted to the Web on 7/23/2002; www.objectivistcenter.org/articles/mkochhar_capitalism-financial-scandal.asp.

Kymlicka, W. (1998). 'Liberal egalitarianism and civic republicanism: friends or enemies?', in A. L. Allen and M. C. Regan, Jr. (eds), *Debating Democracy's Discontent: Essays on American Politics, Law, and Public Philosophy*. New York: Oxford University Press, 131–48.

Mill, J. S. (1859). *On Liberty* (1989 edn). Cambridge: Cambridge University Press.

Mises, L. von (1944). *Bureaucracy*. New Haven, CT: Yale University Press.

Mises, L. von (1949). *Human Action: A Treatise on Economics*, 3rd and revised edn 1963. New Haven, CT: Yale University Press.

Nozick, R. (1974). *Anarchy, State, and Utopia*. New York: Basic Books.

Osborne, D. and Gaebler, T. (1992). *Reinventing Government: How the Entrepreneurial Spirit is Transforming America*. Reading, MA: Addison-Wesley.

Osborne, D. and Plastrik, P. (1997). *Banishing Bureaucracies: The Five Strategies for Reinventing Government*. Reading, MA: Addison-Wesley.

Rawls, J. (1971). *A Theory of Justice*, revised edn 1999. Oxford: Oxford University Press.

Rawls, J. (1993). *Political Liberalism*, pbk edn 1996. New York: Columbia University Press.

Regan, Jr., M. C. (1998). 'Corporate speech and civic virtue', in A. L. Allen and M. C. Regan, Jr. (eds), *Debating Democracy's Discontent: Essays on American Politics, Law, and Public Philosophy*. Oxford: Oxford University Press, 289–306.

Rothschild, J. (1979). 'The collectivist organization: an alternative to rational-bureaucratic models', in F. Fischer and C. Sirianni (eds), *Critical Studies in Organization and Bureaucracy*. Philadelphia, PA: Temple University Press, 448–75.

Rothschild, J. and Whitt, J. A. (1986). *The Cooperative Workplace: Potentials and Dilemmas of Organizational Democracy and Participation*. Cambridge: Cambridge University Press.

Sandel, M. J. (1996). *Democracy's Discontent: America in Search of a Public Philosophy*. Cambridge, MA: Belknap Press.

Sen, A. (1992). *Inequality Reexamined*. Cambridge, MA: Harvard University Press.

Suleiman, E. (2003). *Dismantling Democratic States*. Princeton, NJ; Princeton University Press.

Swartz, M. and Watkins, S. (2003). *Power Failure: The Inside Story of the Collapse of Enron*. New York: Doubleday.

Van Parijs, P. (1995). *Real Freedom for All*. Oxford: Clarendon.

Williamson, O. E. (1999). 'Public and Private Bureaucracies: A Transaction Cost Economics Perspective'. *Journal of Law, Economics, and Organization*. 15/1; 306–42.

PART 2

The End of Bureaucracy?

4

Bureaucracy at Work: Misunderstandings and Mixed Blessings

Paul Thompson and Mats Alvesson

In its review of 'The World in 2003', *The Economist* proclaims that 'Bureaucracy, after many years of decline, will be on the rise again'. Apparently, empowerment and flexibility are out, and hierarchy, structure, and command and control are in. A more accurate take on this might be that after many years of decline in the management *literature*, bureaucracy is back. In the world of practice, it never went away, though in crucial respects it has changed in form and content. The purpose of this chapter is twofold. We subject the evidence on the extent and character of organizational change to critical scrutiny. Less conventionally, we try to explain how academics and other commentators could get it so wrong, arguing that the answer lies in part with the symbolic character of the post-bureaucratic project.

Some of the material in this chapter is drawn from a contribution, 'Post-bureaucracy?', in S. Ackroyd, R. Batt, P. Thompson, and P. Tolbert (eds) (2004) *A Handbook of Work and Organization*. Oxford: Oxford University Press.

Defending and Attacking Bureaucracy

The traditional commentary and critique of bureaucracy in the workplace is a well-trodden territory that is unnecessary to repeat in any detail here. Suffice to say that most academics writing about bureaucracy have operated within either or both of two sets of assumptions. First, that while bureaucratic rationalization is the dominant organizing logic of modernity, it produces degrees of inefficiency, dehumanization, and ritualism. Case studies (Merton 1949; Blau 1955) questioned whether the bureaucratic ideal type was fully rational and efficient, or developed typologies that emphasized different forms of bureaucracy appropriate to organizational context and type of work. Examples include the distinction between workflow and personnel bureaucracies in the Aston Studies (Pugh et al. 1969), and machine and professional bureaucracies (Mintzberg 1983).

Second, that while bureaucracy may be appropriate and indeed functional to particular economic or political environments, it does not 'fit' others, notably where there is a high degree of unpredictability and instability and innovation and situational adaptiveness are vital parts of work. This is the foundation of contingency and open systems theory, exemplified in Burns and Stalker's (1961) manufacturing case studies and mechanistic/organic model. Because there is an emphasis on a continuum of models suited to different environments, contingency theory moves away from alternative designs within a purely bureaucratic framework.

The central rationale of this chapter is that the focus of critique has changed from principle to contingency. In other words, from the limits and dysfunctions of a 'permanent' logic of structure and action, to a claim of systemic dysfunctionality—that bureaucracy simply no longer works in contemporary economy and society. It is now argued that a broad set of powerful economic, social, and technological changes—intensification of competition, globalization of production, rising rates of product innovation, new forms of knowledge and information technology, differentiated and rapidly changing customer preferences—have meant that the days of stable structures and fine-tuning of bureaucratic models are over. Like dinosaurs, mechanistic organizations are doomed and the days of post-bureaucracies have arrived.

Most influential social theories of the last two decades from post-Fordism, through to postmodernism and the knowledge economy, have invoked a break with bureaucracy as cause or consequence of change. In one of the most sustained attempts to explore new organizational forms, Heydebrand (1989: 349) argued that there is, an 'intrinsic elective affinity between postindustrialism and postbureaucratic forms'.

Such claims are flatly contradictory to the traditional defence of bureaucracy made from within organization theory by writers such as Perrow (1979) and Jaques, (1976, 1990). Jaques argues that criticisms of bureaucracy fail to understand the imperatives of both hierarchy and human nature. Bureaucracy is the best way of getting work done because it is the only form of organization that deals with size, complexity, and the need for accountability. Bureaucracy in other words is what works. Setting aside the issue of human nature, such views are vulnerable to post-bureaucratic claims that changes in the organizational environment mean that such arrangements are no longer functional or efficient. Framed in the language of universality, traditional perspectives have no other grounds on which to defend bureaucracy.

This is clearly not the case for many of the chapters in this volume in that bureaucracy is defended less on grounds of efficiency or instrumental rationality, but through claims of substantive rationality—that bureaucracies represent positive values, ethics, and practices: 'So far I have argued that state bureaucracies are necessarily contested, value saturated places in which ends are constantly being problematized' (Hoggett, Chapter 7, this volume). Such values as impartial conduct, due process, accountability to impersonal order rather than social persons, and a separation between the public and private are seen by many contributors to be under attack through the spread of entrepreneurial ideas and practices, new forms of audit and performance measurement, and attempts to re-enchant organizational life through corporate cultures and transformational leadership.

Bureaucracies may indeed possess many virtues, but this new defence of bureaucracy has limitations. First, there is a danger that practices are presented in a mirror image of the universalistic and idealized abstractions advanced by Jaques and others. What is to be understood by or supported with reference to bureaucratic values and modes of governance should only be approached through a concrete examination of the socially embedded character of particular bureaucracies. In other words, bureaucracy is constructed in highly different ways partly on the context. Once idealized accounts are abandoned, two things follow. Any discussion of the expansion or decline or virtues and shortcomings of bureaucracy must be sensitive to context and delimited in terms of what claims are meaningful to make. Second, it is necessary to evaluate explanations and attitudes in terms of the interplay between the ideologies, interests, and practices of different actors.

There are theoretical resources that avoid universalism and can help analyse bureaucracy in such terms. The development of Labour Process Theory (LPT) from the mid-1970s combined Marxian and radical Weberian perspectives that highlighted the interconnections between capitalism and bureaucratic organization (Clawson 1980; Littler 1982). Richard Edwards' (1979) account of bureaucratic control as the dominant management strategy of large firms in the post-war period became the best known of these. Bureaucracy is, however, not reduced simply to the class interests of capitalists. First, because rationalization is a pervasive tendency in complex organizations and societies that takes particular forms in different modes of production. Secondly, bureaucracy is seen under particular conditions also to benefit employees through internal labour markets, seniority and demarcation rules, grievance procedures, and other features of what Burawoy (1979) called the 'internal factory state'. Despite the benefits of mutually binding rules in constraining capital, LPT sees bureaucratic control as inherently precarious and contested; practices which imposed costs on labour and that employers would abandon if no longer appropriate to their interests.

Contributors to early labour process debates also emphasized that internal labour markets and career structures primarily benefited and were supported by male workers and their organizations (Rubery 1978; Crompton and Jones 1984). Such arguments prefigured later feminist perspectives that sought to reveal the gendered substructure that lay beneath the formal, instrumental rationality of bureaucratic organization (Acker 1992). Some feminists have taken this further to argue that bureaucratic rationality is inherently male (Ferguson 1984; Bologh 1990). Male rationality and social action is therefore embodied in authoritarian methods of control and hierarchical ways of decision-making. Rejecting bureaucracy in principle tends to result in downplaying the pursuit of female interests within existing structures in favour of ways of organizing dependent on emotional connection, nurturance, intimacy, and cooperation. For our purposes, such arguments are deficient at the level of structure and agency. What is important is the intersection of capitalism, patriarchy, and bureaucratic rationalization. Those interrelations are shaped by the agents who populate actual organizations and can interpret and contest existing practices and procedures (Halford, Savage and Witz 1997). Essentialist feminism is discussed and critiqued in more detail in Chapter 11 of this volume by Due Billing. Our commentary and critique focuses primarily on the management–employee relations in the private sector in a thorough, though inevitably compacted, assessment of the evidence on the existence and character of bureaucratic practices across key territories of change. This emphasis is a necessary corrective given that in this book the 'ethos of bureaucratic office' (du Gay, Chapter 2, this volume), is approached primarily through a conceptual and empirical focus on the public sector and the state.

The Scope of Post-Bureaucratic Perspectives

The territories covered by post-bureaucratic claims are huge and encompass virtually every change undertaken by organizations in the past two decades. In general terms, we can state that reversing formal rationality, a fixed hierarchy and the division of labour is associated with interrelated internal and external changes. Organizations are said to be changing both their internal organization and their external boundaries. This section outlines those projected changes in a little more detail and discusses what they imply for processes and mechanisms of coordination.

At the heart of projected internal change is functional decentralization of managerial structures. There are a variety of associated forms. For example, Heydebrand (1989: 330–1) argues that profit centres overcome the market–hierarchy dichotomy, reduce the need for CEO control, while encouraging direct negotiation among subunits. An emphasis on horizontal coordination is also applied to the increased use of project and other types of self-governance. Miles et al. (1997)

argue that more organizational members are expected to develop the ability to self-organize around operational, market, and partnering tasks. This 'cellular' organization allows employees to be more entrepreneurial and identify customer needs, as well as experience psychological ownership of particular clients, products, and services. While shop floor work teams are clearly not an alternative means of managerial coordination, they are seen as a central feature of decentralized decision-making and delayered structures.

A number of the most fashionable contemporary change programmes have been presented by business writers as an integral part of the anti-bureaucratic agenda. Both Total Quality Management (TQM) and Business Process Reengineering (BPR) have been seen as ways of introducing flatter structures and reduced hierarchy as employees take increased responsibility, conception and execution are reintegrated, and more complex jobs are created. Hierarchy is also reduced by a network of interdependencies arising from the necessity for employees to treat each other as internal 'customers'.

One interesting link to earlier comments is that a move towards less hierarchical, more network-based organization is seen by a number of commentators as linked to the spread of women managers and female styles of leadership. Some authors talk about a 'feminization of management' without this being recognized in this way—it is rarely coached in gendered language—or involving direct references to females (Fondas 1997). It is argued that there is a strong affinity between qualities such as collaboration, consensus, and soft skills such as teambuilding and the new structures and styles required as organizations move towards more informal, horizontal webs of relationships within and across national boundaries (Martin 1993; N. Adler 1994; Institute of Management 1994). On the policy front, such arguments have been paralleled by attacks on equal opportunities rule-based bureaucratic regulation and a move towards the more individualistic management of diversity.

Sometimes this de-masculinization of management and organization involves ideas about the shift from hierarchy to networks, which overlap with other (non-gendered) claims about loosening of organizational boundaries and an emphasis on collaboration and non-formal links. Organizations may not be boundaryless, but a case can be made for their external relations being increasingly shifting and permeable.

Post-bureaucratic claims on this terrain are summarized in the following quote:

If the old model of organization was the large hierarchical firm, the model of organization that is considered characteristic of the New Competition is a network, of lateral and horizontal interlinkages within and among firms. (Nohria 1992: 2)

Restructuring is associated with the process of disaggregation that transforms loose coupling into decoupling. This may take the form of dispersal of business functions to small firms, or outsourced to specialist units and franchises (Perrow 1992). At its most extreme, this may result in the growth of virtual forms of organization (Jackson 1999). The other primary manifestation of external restructuring is the growth of inter-organizational networks, whose fluidity and flexibility makes them suited to rapid change.

It is recognized that some of these internal and external changes may lead to problems, particularly on the human resource front. If hierarchies are reduced or eliminated, boundaries become more permeable and roles more flexible, it is difficult for firms to offer career paths and rewards for loyalty and conformity to standardized organizational obligations (Heckscher and Applegate 1994: 7). For some managerial writers, this circle is squared through concepts such the portfolio worker who, mobile and reliant on his/her own human capital and knowledge, exists largely outside corporate hierarchies, working either simultaneously or sequentially for a number of employers (Handy 1995; Knell 2000).

Whether a substantial group of employees exist outside such hierarchies is open to question, but it is clear that in the absence of conventional hierarchies, post-bureaucratic theorists have to conceptualize alternative means of holding organizations together. Many authors argue that cultural and other forms of indirect coordination replace the bureaucratic roles formerly carried out by a rapidly disappearing middle management (Heydebrand 1989: 347; Scarbrough and Burrell 1996). Such delayering is also facilitated by new, horizontal communication channels and devolution of responsibility to self-managing and project teams. Nevertheless, there is a further argument used about substitutes for bureaucratic coordination. Direct regulation is also being replaced by the simulation of market disciplines, units are compelled by new ownership and accounting mechanisms to be independent and treat each other as customers (Clegg 1990: 180).

The Territories of Change: Evaluating Claims and Empirical Work

The scope of claims made about post-bureaucracy is, unfortunately, not matched by a similar depth or scope of empirical support. It is one thing to indicate that most organizations have undergone change programmes or processes or that there has been a general increase in the pace of change, quite another to demonstrate necessary or specific outcomes. Too often it is simply assumed that by definition bureaucracy cannot adapt or evolve. Far too much of the discussion is speculative and insufficiently specified. Reliance on new organizational forms and inverted ideal types leads to a failure to be clear enough about the content of bureaucracy and therefore what post-bureaucracy should be evaluated against. In an attempt to move away from over-generalized explanations, we explore the nature and extent of change across three areas—work, employment, and decision practices.

In this section, we operate with the assumption that the central feature of bureaucracy at work is hierarchical authority, underpinned by rationalization and rule-governed behaviour. Bureaucratic structures and practices need not be antithetical to flexibility once roles as well as rules are considered. Kallinikos argues that the separation of role from person is the 'fundamental structural and behavioural element of modern formal organizing' (2004: 21). People join and participate based on their capacity to perform a role built of abstract operational requirements. A non-inclusive relationship between persons and organizations is seen as the foundation of bureaucratic organization. While this view perhaps underplays the significance of hierarchy and standardization, flexibility is facilitated as roles are easier to change and adjust than people and their personalities.

Work Practices

Work practices here refer to the aspects of work organization that are designed to control work behaviour, that is how specific jobs are being structured and steered. Important changes have taken place since the 1980s. Under the practical and theoretical impact of Japanese competition, employers began to move decisively against key aspects of traditional work rules. Benefits previously accruing to management under systems of bureaucratic control, such as capacity to specify job assignments and motivate workers through job ladders were outweighed by the associated rigidities in organization and performance. Changes made in the name of flexibility were directed largely at practices such as task demarcation and seniority rules governing job protection. Research into routine manufacturing work under conditions of lean production shows a consistent picture of functional flexibility, teamworking as the organizational form most appropriate to multitasking in the new technical division of labour, and task-centred participation in quality and continuous improvement.

However, increased flexibility does not necessarily mean either the elimination of Taylorism or fewer rules across the board. While demarcation rules have undoubtedly declined, most other work rules remain intact or have intensified. Extensive formal procedures have been shown to govern most US establishments (Marsden, Cook, and Knoke 1996). While teams undoubtedly provide a framework for functional flexibility and utilization of employee expertise, most remain based on fragmented and highly specified tasks (Findlay et al. 2000). Tasks themselves are still subject to high degrees of standardization, testament largely to the continuing use of Taylorist techniques for measuring, timing, and evaluating work (Slaughter 1987; Williams et al. 1992). Moreover, the benchmarking systems used to redesign work and drive continuous improvement, such as TQM and BPR, require a concern for standardized procedures and uniform, dependable practices (Wilkinson and Willmott 1994). New computer-based systems are also used to aid task specification and engineered work standards in areas such as warehousing (Wright and Lund 1998). With these processes in mind, Paul Adler's (1993) notion of 'learning bureaucracies' offer an appropriate term for work arrangements in advanced manufacturing.

The shift towards a service economy has long been associated with a post-industrial society, yet a powerful body of evidence has accumulated about the 'industrialization' of services. Evidence about the bureaucratization of service tasks is associated primarily with Ritzer's (1993) McDonaldization of society thesis. He and other writers have convincingly demonstrated that fast food and other retail, leisure, and media operations incorporate classic Weberian processes of calculability, predictability, and quantification. Other writers see the competitive requirement to meet more sophisticated customer needs as driving standards of service and work requirements upwards, at least in some sectors (Frenkel et al. 1999; Korczynski 2002). Yet, even they use the term 'customer-oriented bureaucracy' to describe the most common forms of interactive service work, such as those in the fast-growing number of call centres.

Work rules in call centres and settings such as hotel chains focus on the standardization of the service encounter. 'Quality' provision and consistency of product is maintained through mechanisms such as the scripting of language and behaviour. When reinforced by high-surveillance technology and procedurally based software, work tasks are routinized and service operatives experience 'an assembly line in the head' (Taylor and Bain 1998). There has also been a growth of output controls through non-technological monitoring based on 'control by customers', though there is an element of bureaucratization in this via report cards and surveys (Fuller and Smith 1991).

A further and well-documented facet of scripting focuses on feelings as well as behaviour. Originally identified through Hochschild's work (1983) on flight attendants and other employees involved in emotional labour, what might be described as 'feeling rules' have now been the subject of research in a variety of service settings from insurance, supermarkets, leisure parks, and again call centres. Scripted and standardized displays of feelings are achieved through 'smile factories', forced niceness and other forms of verbal interplay and body posture (Van Maanen 1991).

Finally, there are the trends in the sphere of 'knowledge' and knowledge management. The current focus on the importance of knowledge assets reinforces the long understood point that high levels of autonomy are effective preconditions for creative outcomes. Multifunctional projects teams, like their equivalents lower down the organizational hierarchy, help to break down bureaucratic hierarchies. Many advocates of knowledge management emphasize networks and the building of knowledge-sharing communities (Swan et al. 1999) and the cultivation of care within organizations (Von Krogh 1998). Yet the language of much knowledge management—codification, storing, and distribution—also remind us that this frequently takes the form of standardized, highly structured systems in areas such as software design or surveying as well as rules for the use of databases in order to recycle knowledge. Many initiatives involve efforts to develop measures to systematically codify knowledge and then let people follow particular procedures and work according to the associated templates and project metrics (Hansen et al. 1999), though the extent to which such measures are used to guide rather than constrain through rules will vary according to context (Alvesson and Kärreman 2001a).

As we have already noted recent public service reform has often been legitimized through attacks on bureaucracy. Yet the focus of reform has tended to be policies to break down producer control and make professionals more accountable to management, the state, funding bodies, or clients. Yet the price of a shift towards professional and performance management, plus enhanced output controls has been a significant growth of centralized audit and monitoring, with a consequent decline in trust and collegiality. While such measures have by no means eliminated professional autonomy and power, they do constitute 'new layers of bureaucracy' (Hoggett, quoted in Clarke and Newman 1997: 158). Among groups such as welfare and social workers, managerial specification of work rules also reflects the need to conform to increased legislation and to avoid costly litigation.

Employment Practices

Employment practices refer to issues such as the recruitment, reward, and representation of labour. There is consensus that considerable changes have taken place compared to post-war industrial relations, which at least in large manufacturing firms, were based on 'inflexible company policy, detailed contract language, legalistic procedures for dispute resolution, and bureaucratic union and management structures' (Fairris 1991: 133). To a large degree, work rules generated employment rules embedded in internal labour markets. Removing the former could, therefore, dispense with some of the need for the latter.

There is little doubt that a variety of measures have been directed towards increasing managerial flexibility in the employment sphere. These include, the use of contingent workers, outsourcing, and temporary contracts that allow firms to escape the obligations imposed by conventional employment rules; some shift away from career hierarchies towards personal 'employability'; and decentralized, market-driven or individualized reward systems. What is less obvious is the existence of powerful countervailing tendencies that reimpose other types of employment rules.

First, even with a reduction in the complexity or standardization of pay scales, contemporary performance management systems are grounded in highly bureaucratized metrics and measurement, in part as a product of the spread of international 'best practices'. For example, Ferner (2000) reports, based on case studies, that multinational corporations (MNCs) move towards more internationally homogeneous, integrated, and centralized approaches to a range of issues in production, marketing, and human resources management (HRM). This resulted in a pervasive bureaucratization of control, for example through standardized systems for appraising and rewarding senior managers and for identifying those of 'high potential'.

Second, employment rules and their expression in contracts, have moved away from enforcing tasks to wider forms of behaviour. For example, a combination of legislation, perceived best practice, and fear of litigation have led to a significant growth of codes of conduct to deal with a variety of 'inappropriate' behaviours (Ackroyd and Thompson 1999). Equal opportunity policies are probably the most well known, but many large firms have extended these into wide-ranging harassment codes, or others dealing with issues of health or even romantic liaisons. The public sector is frequently at the forefront of trends towards increased enforcement of wider behavioural norms or codes of conduct, given the prominence of human resources (HR) professionals and the concern for standardized and equitable employment criteria.

Decision and Coordination Practices

As we saw earlier, post-bureaucratic arguments rely heavily on notions of decentralization and networks as means of breaking with hierarchical authority. New arrangements are sometimes described as 'heterarchies' that rely instead on collaboration and cooperation (Solvell and Zandar 1995). There are different elements here: the relationship between headquarters (HQ) and other units, the distribution of decision rules within the operative unit, and the existence of alternative means of cultural or market rather than hierarchical coordination.

With respect to inter-organizational relations, neither surveys nor case studies give any significant support to the idea that 'pyramidal hierarchies are replaced by looser networks' (Sennett 1998: 85). In wide-ranging studies, Ruigrok et al. (1999) and Hill, Martin, and Harris (2000) found some structural indicators of post-bureaucratic organization (PBO), such as business units as profit centres, flattened hierarchies, a reliance on task forces and teams rather than rigid compartmentalization, and extensive use of IT and communication networks. But these results do not support often far-fetched claims about the rise of the new PBO. Hill, Martin, and Harris reported that decentralization is regulated and restricted by central control of the resource allocation process and target setting; a finding supported by a survey of the largest companies operating in the United Kingdom, 'headquarters exerts tight controls over business unit operations and profitability targets are not devolved' (Armstrong et al. 1998: 13).

More sophisticated IT systems facilitate rather than remove managerial power. This may once again be in the form of output controls rather than central direction, but increased capacity to financially monitor, control, and predict performance still constitutes hierarchical authority, even though it deviates from traditional forms of bureaucracy. Integrated computer-based models can be used to predict yield and return, and standardized central planning systems remain a core feature of business practice, retaining hierarchy, though degrees of autonomy may vary across functions (McKinlay 1999).

The most persuasive conceptualization of these developments is provided by Harrison's term 'concentration without centralization'. The very fact of spatial and functional diversity in networked large organizations or supply chains has led to concentrated economic power changing shape: 'production may be decentralized, while power finance, distribution, and control remain concentrated among the big firms' (1994: 20). Another way of describing companies such as Benetton, with its tightly integrated and specified outsourced production and franchised distribution is *extended hierarchy* (Thompson 1993). In other words, hierarchical relations extend and change their form as organizational boundaries become more permeable. A good example is provided in Pulignano's (2002) account of modular production systems at Fiat, Renault, and Volkswagen. Many service and production units have been outsourced, but operate under the same roof and are regulated both through internal markets and highly specified formal rules for coordinating inter-unit transactions. In his extensive review of the evidence on network forms, Ackroyd (2002: 187) argues that 'The decentred firm is a special kind of network in which significant power is retained by the hub'. Such forms allow corporations to maintain or extend their spheres of interest and control while allowing for greater flexibility and disallowing full costs of ownership. In this sense, networks combine elements of hierarchy and market rather than constituting a separate means of coordination.

What about decision processes and hierarchies within units? Large organizations appear to have become increasingly reliant on cross-functional project teams for coordination and innovation. As with inter-organizational relations, the mistake made in some accounts of change is the notion that horizontal forms of coordination replace bureaucratic hierarchy. Intra-organizational developments, however, manifest not an extended but a parallel hierarchy. Horizontal forms of coordination are a kind of 'shadow division of labour', added to and existing alongside conventional hierarchies in order to per-form different activities (Warhurst and Thompson 1998: 19). Reed (Chapter 5, this volume) makes a similar point when referring to the 'variable geometry' of network organizing existing alongside a 'fixed geometry' of imperatively coordinated structures and stabilizing mechanisms.

One of the few studies to explicitly examine the 'internal network' argument strongly downplays the extent of change. Using cases from a variety of national and sectoral contexts, Hales argues that 'responsibility for unit performance continued to be vested in individual managers who were accountable vertically to identifiable "bosses" and who were judged on the basis of conformance with centrally-imposed rules about appropriate levels of performance' (2002: 61).

Finally, we need to assess parallel changes in the public sector. Despite the introduction of competition and quasi-markets, plus devolved managerial authority, the management of public services remains to a large extent dependent on external political authority and legitimacy. As one British National Health Service (NHS) man-ager observed in Schofield's study, 'There is a bureaucracy, all these hoops you have to jump through . . . They set the rules, we have to meet them' (2001: 86). Put another way, there are inherent constraints to the reconfiguring of decision and coordination rules—public and private organizations remain different in goals and operation, even in the United States (Scott and Falcone 1998). It is hardly surprising, therefore, that empirical studies show limited movement in the direction of post-bureaucracy. For example, studies of public sector change in Australia (Considine 1996; Parker and Bradley 2000) confirm Schofield's (2001) account of the United Kingdom: employees and managers report the continued saliency of central regulation, hierarchical authority, conformity to rules, and bureaucratic values.

Discussion: The Difficulties in Exploring Bureaucracy

As we have seen, many people seem to view the widespread existence and rapid expansion of PBO as a self-evident fact. But it is easy to identify a wealth of powerful counter-trends. To sum up, empirical studies of changes reveal relatively modest changes in structural terms, and where change has taken place in some spheres it is in the direction of more rules, hierarchy and centralization (Warhurst and Thompson 1998; Hill et al. 2000). Nor, contrary to some arguments (Heydebrand 1993: 324), are bureaucratic forms confined to a few residual institutional niches such as the public sector. Falls in the size of individual units and decentring of organizations may change the form of bureaucracy, but they do not necessarily diminish its impact. As Hales (2002) observes, 'bureaucracy-lite', with its reduced levels of hierarchy and shift to control over outcomes, may be more consistent with certain aspects of the impersonal, means–end calculations of bureaucratic rationalization.

This is not to deny that important changes, for example in the areas of decentralization and disaggregation are taking place, but they are not producing a fully fledged post-bureaucratic alternative. Internal forms of horizontal organization and external network-type relations can and do coexist with vertical hierarchies. Most organizations draw upon a spectrum of control forms: from output, bureaucratic, professional/occupational, and customer control to charismatic and authoritative leaders to corporate cultures and emotional control. To some extent this has always been true. But as environments and organizational structures become more complex, a diversification of types of controls and coordination ensues.

Noting the fact of durability in bureaucratic governance is not the same as explanation. Of course, one can stick to the traditional script that hierarchy is an indispensable mechanism for coordinating complex tasks and divided labour. It is true that most firms regard hierarchy and formalized procedures as essential tools for assuring efficiency, conformance quality, and timeliness. Machine bureaucracies efficiently producing inexpensive goods and services certainly play a major role. And as Reed (Chapter 5, this volume) argues, the view that network forms of governance are necessarily more efficient at such coordination in the contemporary political economy is highly questionable (see also Marchington et al. 2004).

However, it is not just business (or hierarchy) as usual. In general terms, we can identify a common search across manufacturing, private, and public services for more flexible, responsive ways of organizing, while maintaining a capacity for formalization and central control. Rather than the classic contingency argument of a fit between an organizational structure and its environment, it is better to see contemporary organizational forms as a series of hybrids, within which bureaucratic mechanisms normally remain dominant. As a number of other contributors to this volume also note, hybridization is the outcome of a requirement of more complex regimes of coordination and control than can attempt to reconcile the increased tensions between different functional requirements (e.g. flexibility and accountability) and interests (employers, employees, customers). Such tensions are captured in the vocabularies of contemporary research such as customer-oriented bureaucracies in the service sector (Frenkel et al. 1998; Bourgeois 2001) or soft bureaucracy in which decentralized responsibilities are combined with centralized decision-making (Courpasson, 2000).

So how, then, do we account for the huge discrepancy between the theory and practice of post-bureaucracy? A key ingredient in contemporary society is the idea of the outmoded, inefficient, and rigid bureaucracy, which makes it an easy target for politicians and policy-makers. Actors involved in or commenting on organizational change—consultants, academics, executives—are eager to emphasize the more progressive, fashionable, positive-sounding vocabulary in accounting for management and how the organization operates.

In relation to outcomes, a range of actors promote and benefit from bureaucratic measures. Not only top management and political elites, but unions and advocates of equal opportunity frequently favour formal rules to reduce uncertainty, give direction, and accomplish higher standards. But the academic and practitioner defenders of bureaucracy as form and practice are few in number and very seldom frame their values and actions in such terms. Bureaucracy as a term is so loaded with negative meaning for most people that it is mainly used as a negative rhetorical resource and it is difficult to make an explicit ideological case for bureaucracy. Often, policies are framed through other vocabularies, notably those of 'rights'. So, for example, enforcing the rights of PhD students typically leads to an expansion of specific rules and standards for the programmes. In sum, we can observe two tendencies. First, a framing–doing discrepancy that obscures the interests and actions of key economic and political actors. Second, PBO as an identity project through which actors draw upon particular entrepreneurial, network, and anti-hierarchy symbolism and rhetoric.

Aspects of the Normative Dimension

In this chapter we have focused more on 'what goes on here?' than what should go on? At one level this orientation tends to 'what may work best under specific circumstances?' But a focus on actors, ideologies, and interests also leads to the question 'works for whom?' There is a strong current running through this volume that sees bureaucracy as working in the public interest. Such arguments are often associated with the benefits of a distinctive bureaucratic ethos in the public sector. The continued existence of bureaucratic forms and values is used persuasively by du Gay (2000; Chapter 2, this volume) to support and reinvigorate Weber's arguments concerning the distinctive ethos and 'regime values' of bureaucratic public administration. A 'good bureaucrat' remains someone who adheres to particular standards of procedure, expertise, impersonality, and hierarchy. This, in turn, constitutes 'a positive moral and ethical achievement in its own right' (2000: 7) with respect to the public governance requirements to equitably treat citizens and employees. Across all sectors bureaucracy can act as a counterweight to arbitrariness and managerial power.

This emphasis is valuable, but somewhat one-sided. Producer interests focused on the defence of traditional work and employment rules can and do conflict with the needs of citizens for flexible, responsive services that treat the client as a whole person (see Palumbo and Scott, Chapter 12, this volume). While various chapters outline some of the negative effects of public sector reform, governments and citizens have a legitimate interest in enhancing accountability, transparency, and access.

Bureaucracy is here often a mixed blessing and the specific impact on the work lives of employees and the services of clients and the public probably vary and cannot be deduced a priori from the popular ideologies of either bureaucracy or anti-bureaucracy. This can be illustrated in the discussions among feminists about the merits and possibilities of bureaucracy versus idealized female-friendly organizational forms. While such debates are extensively covered by Billing (1994; Chapter 11, this volume), we can perhaps open this out to consider some of those mixed blessings underlying the demand for organizations to be flexible enough to allow 'work-life balance'.

Whatever advantages may accrue to some members of organizations in this context, one could equally argue that bureaucracy has two major advantages. One frequent observation is that formal emphasis on education and work expertise are viewed as central for employment and promotion. This helps to reduce the risk of personal preferences and prejudices—which arguably often harm women more than men—playing a significant role, thus creating more fairness in recruitment, rewards, and promotion. More controversially, it can be argued that bureaucracy protects other aspects of individual's lives from organizational regulation. As we indicated earlier, Kallinikos (2004) demonstrates that bureaucracy tends to be non-inclusive. For example, people are only relevant as far as they are carrying out roles and 'extra-role' issues are protected from managerial interference. He compares this with total institutions, where the individual disappears and is taken over by the organization. Indeed, there are no individuals—in the 'full' sense of the word—in this kind of organization. This non-inclusive quality in a sense characterizes almost the entirety of organizational life, with some exceptions including the military, some small business people, and free professionals who are married to their work/business.

One can, however, argue that bureaucracy represents one end of the spectrum of 'normal' organizations built around an employment contract—and that other versions are more inclusive, tending to downplay the role–person distinction and incorporating more of the full person at work. This is the case with many organizations emphasizing cultural values and/or positive social relations as a key element in the employment relation. Many social movements and collective organizations, including those celebrated by feminists, typically call for or want to encourage a deeper commitment and an interest in the organization going beyond the wage-earner or instrumental one (Ashcraft 2001). But also some contemporary profit-oriented businesses can be said to be high-inclusive: recruiting and encouraging people who fit in and have similar values and commitments. This is relatively typical within the knowledge-intensive sector, for example consultancy, advertising, and IT work (Alvesson 1995; Kunda 1992). Such organizations become a site for meaning and intimacy and occupy a larger significance in life than being just a place where one fulfils role requirements in line with an employment contract. In this sense, they are 'non-bureaucratic', at least in some of their practices.

Repressing the slight feeling of embarrassment for producing another four-fielder, we think that it is worth confronting the low-versus high-inclusive dimension with the possibility of different ways in which people can be subordinated to or protected from organizational demands that may be experienced as unwanted or stressful interference with private and domestic life (Figure 4.1).

	Bureaucracy/low-inclusive organizations	Non-bureaucracy/high-inclusive organizations
Strict priority to organization goals (rules or values focused on job role and performance)	rules given priority to job role	emphasis on job commitment
Compromise individual/organization goals (rules and values facilitating job/family balance)	rules restricting job role under certain conditions (e.g. small children)	values encouraging mutual adjustment person/organization

Fig 4.1 Low-inclusive (bureaucracy) versus high-inclusive (non-bureaucracy) organizations in relation to organization/employee goal compatibility

As we have said, some for-profit organizations combine high-inclusive and pro-family values, although restricted to certain conditions. For example, a major international management consultancy firm, normally expecting work far exceeding the 40-hour week, had generous conditions for employees during parental leave, thus balancing high demands and support. Most employees—of which about 30 per cent were female—lived in dual-career couples and there was a general expectation that women would also be engaged in career work after having had children, and the firm should adapt to this.

What is probably more common, in terms of organizations adapting to the needs of women balancing work/family obligations, are bureaucracies characterized by rule sets allowing employees to be on leave or work part-time, and thus to reduce work role to adapt to other commitments. This is very common in Sweden, where legislation, conventions within the public sector and also employee-friendly organizational-level policies leads to sets of rules that reduce the work role when desired by employees. The interest from employees in clear policies on parental leave and childcare therefore often acts as a driver of bureaucracy, to provide a guaranteed space for (temporary or permanent) positions allowing for low-inclusive roles. This is not to argue that there is a simple relationship between interests and bureaucracy: rules may simultaneously protect and constrain, act as a resource and a source of alienation.

Concluding Comments

To really understand the presence and significance of bureaucracy requires in-depth exploration of practices in different sectors and sections of organizations, thus escaping traditional analytical dichotomies such as mechanistic–organic and centralization–decentralization. Forms of control and coordination do not only interact, overlap with, or weaken one another; managers may comply with, reinforce, or circumscribe bureaucracy. For example, organizations may have extensive rules and procedures for HRM issues such as recruitment, compensation, training, development, and promotion, but studies are more sceptical about the extent to which managers follow them in practice (Jackall 1988; Alvesson and Kärreman 2001b). Caution is therefore required before ticking off bureaucratic or post-bureaucratic control forms without checking their meaning and impact carefully and in practice. Superficial studies are likely to register primarily formal arrangements and claims by fashion-conscious corporate actors eager to emphasize progressiveness and to comply with institutional norms (Meyer and Rowan 1977). In our case, this caution is particularly motivated by observation of the interests of many actors in locating themselves and their organizations in a fashionable anti-bureaucracy camp. Such reform frameworks look good and improve legitimacy, acting as identity construction projects in the private and public sectors.

Although most organizational practices—as our review clearly shows—score higher on bureaucracy than PBO, the latter phenomenon dominates the symbolic sphere. In 'defending' bureaucracy against the hollowness of post-bureaucratic claims, we should not exaggerate the benefits of bureaucracy to either efficiency or mutual gains among organizational participants. Arguments 'bending the stick back' against wholly negative views, should rather be seen as complementary to purely empirical questioning of undifferentiated and one-dimensional analyses of bureaucracy. Whether in theory or practice, as Reed argues in Chapter 5 of this volume, we need to be eternally vigilant about all forms of organization.

References

Acker, J. (1992). 'Gendering organizational theory', in A. J. Mills and P. Tancred (eds), *Gendering Organizational Analysis*. London: Sage.

Ackroyd, S. (2002). *The Organization of Business*. Oxford University Press.

Ackroyd, S. and Thompson, P. (1999). *Organizational Misbehaviour*. London: Sage.

Adler, N. (1994). 'Competitive frontiers: women managing across borders', in N. Adler and D. N. Izraeli (eds), *Competitive Frontiers: Women in a Global Economy*. Oxford: Blackwell.

Adler, P. S. (1993). 'Time-and-motion regained'. *Harvard Business Review*, 71/1; 97–107.

Alvesson, M. (1995). *Management of Knowledge-Intensive Companies*. Berlin/New York: de Gruyter.

Alvesson, M and Kärreman, D. (2001a). 'Odd couple: making sense of the curious concept of knowledge managment'. *Journal of Management Studies*, 38/7; 995–1018.

Alvesson, M. and Kärreman, D. (2001b). 'Perfection of Meritocracy or Ritual of Bureaucracy?—HRM in a Management Consultancy Firm', Paper Presented at 2nd International Conference on Critical Management Studies, Manchester, July.

Armstrong, P., Marginson, P., Edwards, P., and Purcell, J. (1998). 'Divisionalization in the UK: Diversity, size and the devolution of bargaining'. *Organization Studies*. 19; 1–22.

Ashcraft, K. L. (2001). 'Organized dissonance: feminist burreaucracy as hybrid form' *Academy of Management Journal*, 44/6; 1301–22.

Billing, Y. Due (1994). 'Gender and bureaucracies—a critique of Ferguson's "The feminist case against bureaucracy"'. *Gender, Work and Organization*, 1/4; 173–93.

Blau, P. M. (1955). *The Dynamics of Bureaucracy*. Chicago: University of Chicago Press.

Bologh, R. (1990). *Love or Greatness: Max Weber and Masculine Thinking—A Feminist Inquiry*. London: Unwin Hyman.

Bourgeois, D. (2001). 'Towards Customer-Oriented Neo-Bureaucracies', Paper to EGOS Conference.

Burawoy, M. (1979). *Manufacturing Consent: Changes in the Labour Process under Monopoly Capitalism*. Chicago, IL: Chicago University Press.

Burns, T. and Stalker, G. M. (1961). *The Management of Innovation*. London: Tavistock.

Clarke, J. and Newman, J. (1997). *The Managerial State: Power, Politics and Ideology in the Remaking of Social Welfare*. London: Sage.

Clawson, D. (1980). *Bureaucracy and the Labour Process: The Transformation of US Industry, 1860–1920*. New York: Monthly Review Press.

Clegg, S. (1990). *Modern Organizations: Organization Studies in the Post-Modern World*. London: Sage.

Considine, M. (1996). 'Market bureaucracy? exploring the contending rationalities of contemporary administrative regimes'. *Labour and Industry*. 7/1; 1–28.

Courpasson, D. (2000). 'Managerial strategies of domination. Power in soft bureaucracies'. *Organization Studies*. 21/1; 141–61.

Crompton, R. and Jones, G. (1984). *White Collar Proletariat*. London: Macmillan.

du Gay, P. (2000). *In Praise of Bureaucracy*. London: Sage.

Edwards, R. (1979). *Contested Terrain: The Transformation of the Workplace in the Twentieth Century*. London: Heinemann.

Fairris, D. (1991). 'The crisis in US shopfloor relations'. *International Contributions to Labour Studies*. 1: 133–56.

Ferguson, K. (1984). *The Feminist Case Against Bureaucracy*. Philadelphia, PA: Temple University Press.

Ferner, A. (2000). 'The underpinnings of "bureaucratic control" systems: HRM in European multinationals'. *Journal of Management Studies*. 37/4; 521–40.

Findlay, P., Marks, A., McKinlay, A., and Thompson, P. (2000). 'Flexible if it suits them: the use and abuse of teamwork skills', in F. Mueller and S. Proctor (eds), *Teamwork*. London: Macmillan.

Fondas, N. (1997). 'Feminization unveiled: management qualities in contemporary writings'. *Academy of Management Review*. 22/1; 257–82.

Frenkel, S., Korczynski, M., Shire, K., and Tam, M. (1999). *On the Front Line: Pattern of Work Organization in Three Advanced Societies*. Cornell, NY: Cornell University Press.

Fuller, L. and Smith, V. (1991). 'Consumers' reports: management by customers in a changing economy'. *Work, Employment and Society*. 5/1; 1–16.

Hales, C. (2002). ' "Bureaucracy-lite" and continuities in managerial work'. *British Journal of Management*. 13; 51–66.

Halford, S., Savage, M., and Witz, A. (1997). *Gender, Careers and Organizations*. London: Macmillan.

Handy, C. (1995). *The Future of Work*. WH Smith Contemporary Papers 8.

Hansen, M. T., Norhia, N. and Tierney, T. (1999). 'What's your strategy for managing knowledge?' *Harvard Business Review*, March–April; 106–16.

Harrison, B. (1994). *Lean and Mean: The Changing Landscape of Corporate Power in the Age of Flexibility*. New York: Basic Books.

Heckscher, C. and Applegate, L. (1994). 'Introduction', in C. Heckscher and A. Donnellon (eds), *The Post-Bureaucratic Organization: New Perspectives on Organizational Change*. London: Sage.

Heydebrand, W. (1989). 'New Organizational Forms'. *Work and Occupations*. 16/3; 323–57.

Hill, S., Martin, R., and Harris, M. (2000). 'Decentralization, integration and the post-bureaucratic organization: the case of R & D'. *Journal of Management Studies*. 37/4; 563–85.

Hochschild, A. R. (1983). *The Managed Heart: Commercialization of Human Feeling*. Berkeley, CA: University of California Press.

Institute of Management (1994). *The 1994 National Management Salary Survey*. London: Institute of Management.

Jackall, R. (1988). *Moral Mazes*. New York: Oxford University Press.

Jackson, P. (ed.) (1999). *Virtual Working: Social and Organizational Dynamics*. London: Routledge.

Jaques, E. (1976). *A General Theory of Bureaucracy*. Aldershot: Gregg Revivals.

Jaques, E. (1990). 'In praise of hierarchy'. *Harvard Business Review*. 68/1; 127–33.

Kallinikos, J. (2004). 'The social foundations of the bureaucratic order'. *Organization*. 11/1; 13–36.

Knell, J. (2000). *Most Wanted: The Quiet Birth of the Free Worker*. London: The Industrial Society.

Korczynski, M. (2002). *Human Resource Management and Service Work: The Fragile Social Order*. London: Palgrave.

Kunda, G. (1992). *Engineering Culture*. Philadelphia: Temple University Press.

Littler, C. (1982). *The Development of the Labour Process in Capitalist Societies: A Comparative Analysis of the Labour Process in Britain, the USA and Japan*. London: Heinemann.

Marchington, M., Grimshaw, D., Rubery, J., and Willmott, H. (eds), (2004). *Fragmenting Work: Blurring Organizational Boundaries and Disordering Hierarchies*. Oxford: Oxford University Press.

Marsden, P. V., Cook, C. R., and Knoke, D. (1996). 'American organizations in their environments: a descriptive overview', in A. L. Kalleberg, D. Knoke, P. V. Marsden, and J. L. Spaeth (eds), *Organizations in America: Analyzing Their Structures and Human Resource Practices*. Thousand Oaks: Sage, 45–66.

Martin, P. (1993). 'Feminist practice in organizations', E. Fagenson (ed.), *Women in Management: Trends, Issues and Challenges in Management Diversity*. Newbury Park, CA: Sage.

McKinlay, A. (1999). 'The bearable lightness of control: organizational reflexivity and the politics of knowledge management', in C. Prichard, R. Hull, M. Chumer, and H. Willmott (eds), *Managing Knowledge: Critical Investigations of Work and Learning*. London: Macmillan.

Merton, R. K. (1949). *Social Theory and Social Structure*, Glencoe, IL: Free Press.

Meyer, J. W. and Rowan, B. (1977). 'Institutionalized organizations: formal structure as myth and ceremony', in M. Zey-Ferrell and M. Aiken (eds), *Complex Organizations: Critical Perspectives*. Glenview, IL: Scott Foresman.

Miles, R. et al. (1997), 'Organizing in the knowledge age: anticipating the cellular form'. *Academy of Management Executive*. 11/4; 7–19.

Mintzberg, H. (1983). *Structure in Fives: Designing Effective Organizations*. Englewood Cliffs, NJ: Prentice-Hall.

Nohria, N. (1992). 'Is a network perspective a useful way of studying organizations?', in N. Nohria and R. G. Eccles (eds), *Networks and Organizations*. Boston, MA: Harvard Business School Press.

Parker, R. and Bradley, L. (2000). 'Organizational culture in the public sector: evidence from six organizations'. *International Journal of Public Sector Management*. 3/2; 124–41.

Perrow, C. (1979). *Complex Organizations: A Critical Essay*. Glenview, IL: Scott Foresman.

Perrow, C. (1992). 'Small firm networks', in N. Nohria and R. G. Eccles (eds), *Networks and Organizations*. Boston, MA: Harvard Business School Press.

Pugh, D. S. et al. (1969). 'An empirical taxonomy of structures of work organizations'. *Administrative Science Quarterly*. 14; 115–26.

Pulignano, V. (2001). 'Bureaucratic Processes at the Contemporary Workplace: Evidence from Restructured Working Practices in Motor Manufacturing', Paper to International Labour Process Conference.

Ritzer, G. (1993). *The MacDonaldization of Society*. London: Pine Forge Press.

Rubery, J. (1978). 'Structured labour markets, worker organization and low pay'. *Cambridge Journal of Economics*. 2/1; 17–36.

Ruigrok, W. et al. (1999). 'Corporate restructuring and new forms of organizing: evidence from Europe'. *Management International Review*. 39/2; 41–64.

Scarborough, H. and Burrell, G. (1996). 'The axeman cometh: the changing roles and knowledges of middle managers', in S. Clegg. and G. Palmer (eds), *The Politics of Management Knowledge*. London: Sage.

Schofield, J. (2001). 'The old ways are the best? The durability and usefulness of bureaucracy in public sector management'. *Organization*. 8/1; 77–96.

Scott, P. and Falcone, S. (1998). 'Comparing public and private organizations: an exploratory analysis of three frameworks'. *American Review of Public Administration*. 28/2; 126–45.

Sennett, R. (1998). *The Corrosion of Character: The Personal Consequences of Work in the New Capitalism*. New York: Norton.

Slaughter, J. (1987). 'The Team Concept in the US Auto Industry: Implications for Unions', Paper Presented at Conference on Japanization, UWIST.

Solvell, O. and Zander, I. (1995). 'Organization of the dynamic multinational enterprise: the home-based and the heterarchical MNE'. *International Studies of Management and Organization*. 25/1–2; 17–38.

Swan, J., Newell, S., Scarbrough, H. and Hislop, D. (1999). 'Knowledge management and innovation: networks and networking'. *Journal of Knowledge Management*, 3/4; 262–75.

Taylor, P. and Bain, P. (1998). 'An assembly line in the head: the call centre labour process'. *Industrial Relations Journal*. 30/2; 101–17.

Thompson, P. (1993). 'Fatal distraction: postmodernism and organization theory', in J. Hassard and M. Parker (eds), *Postmodernism and Organizations*. London: Sage.

Van Maanen, J. (1991). 'The smile factory: work at Disneyland reframing organizational culture', in P. Frost et al. (eds), *Reframing Organizational Culture*, Sage: Newbury Park, CA: 58–76.

Von Krogh, G. (1998). 'Care in knowledge creation'. *California Management Review*. 40/31; 33–153.

Warhurst, C. and Thompson, P. (1998). 'Hands, hearts and minds: changing work and workers at the end of the century', in P. Thompson and C. Warhurst (eds), *Workplaces of the Future*. London: Macmillan: 1–24.

Wilkinson, A. and Willmott, H. (1994). 'Introduction', in A. Wilkinson and H. Willmott (eds), *Making Quality Critical*. London: Routledge.

Williams, K., Haslam, C., Williams J., Cutler, T., Adcroft, A., and Juhal, S. (1992). 'Against lean production'. *Economy and Society*. 21/3; 321–54.

Wright, C. and Lund, J. (1998). ' "Under the clock": trade union responses to computerised control in US and Australian grocery warehousing'. *New Technology, Work and Employment*. 13/1; 3–15.

5

Beyond the Iron Cage? Bureaucracy and Democracy in the Knowledge Economy and Society

Michael Reed

Introduction

The imminent collapse of bureaucracy has been anticipated many times throughout the history of modern social and political theory. On both the right and the left of the ideological and intellectual spectrum, bureaucratic organization has been generally viewed as, at best, a necessary evil that will inevitably fade away as the 'progressive democratic dynamic' inherent in historical change imposes itself on the logic and trajectory of socio-economic development. Thus, a neo-liberal management theorist such as Bennis, a neo-liberalist economist such as Schumpeter, a social democrat such as Schumacher, a neo-corporatist such as Elias, a technological determinist such as Bell or Castells, and a theorist of radical participatory democracy such as Illich, can all agree that the underlying currents of history will, eventually, make bureaucracy an obsolete form of administrative power and organization. Ultimately, they all can agree on at least one thing; that bureaucracy is incompatible with the democratizing forces unleashed by modernization and their corrosive impact on unaccountable hierarchical power and centralized administrative control.

Whatever their ideological and epistemological differences, they can all see that history is on the side of those progressive economic, technological, social, and cultural forces that put political democratization and administrative de-bureaucratization at the core of 'institution building' in the modern world. Political maturity and institutional change necessarily entail a 'de-bureaucratizing dynamic' that will inexorably lead to the dismantling of both the administrative patina and material core of the central organizational elements that have defined rational bureaucracy as the dominant organizational form in the twentieth century. Max Weber was simply wrong; bureaucratic rationalization and domination is not the collective fate of men and women alive at the turn of the twenty-first century. Indeed, there are complex economic, technological, cultural, political, and social forces at work in the world today that are radically undermining the whole basis of his pessimistic prognosis.

In this respect, the latest wave of 'post-bureaucratic' theorizing— exemplified in the various forms of 'network theory and analysis' that currently dominate contemporary organization and management studies—is simply the most recent articulation of a long line of sociopolitical thinking that has repeatedly challenged the 'bureaucratic metaphysical pathos' that Gouldner and others have identified as hanging long over modern social science. Both the explanatory logic and substantive content of contemporary network theory and analysis suggest, indeed insist, that a complex, interactive multi-causal chain of economic, technological, social, and cultural change is at work that is fundamentally undermining the material, ideological, cognitive, and moral foundations of vertically integrated bureaucratic corporations. This substantive diagnosis and prognosis is overlain by a normative theory of change in which the demise of bureaucracy and the rise of network is deemed to entail an irreversible shift towards 'high-trust' social relations based on the 'empowering capabilities' of participatory democracy, as exemplified in the decentralized decision-making forms and practices typical of 'knowledge organizations'. Not only is Weber now seen as an unreliable theorist of the dynamics of organizational change and development but his prognosis for the 'bureaucratic iron cage' becomes equally suspect as a guide to our collective organizational fate. No longer can we possibly view contemporary organization theory and analysis as a 'series of footnotes to Weber' in an ideological, intellectual, and historical context where his work has been fatally undermined by events and the ideas and discourses through which they are represented. His bleak vision of an organizational future in which rational bureaucratic forms remain the critical cultural, political, and administrative mechanisms through which institutionalized power and control are generated and maintained (Clegg 1990) is swept away by a 'new Zeitgeist' in which mobility, flexibility, and 're-enchantment' emerge as the dominant iconography of social transformation (Sennett 1998). The 'Weberian vision' of a future in which purposive-rational or instrumental action—and the organizational forms through which it is articulated and legitimated—becomes even more pervasive and dominant (Scaff 1989; Ray and Reed 1994) is challenged and overturned by alternative futuristic scenarios in which substantively rational or emotional action becomes the key driver of social and organizational change (Albrow 1992; Casey 2002). The latter creates new 'epistemic or knowledge cultures' that reflect and shape the increasingly fragmented—culturally, cognitively, and politically—structures of contemporary Western societies 'ruled by knowledge and expertise' (Knorr Cetina 1999: 5). Thus, 'reflexive modernization' is deemed to be incompatible with bureaucratic organization because the former depends on inherently flexible and reflexive forms of social engineering that the latter is incapable of supplying (Giddens 1994; Lash and Urry 1994). The organizational exemplar for understanding the fabrication and framing of collective agency in the twenty first century becomes the research laboratory, rather than the factory or the office. It embodies and symbolizes the new modes of complex, expert-knowledge-based self-organization and 'object-centred management' that are coming to define the essence of collective collaboration and coordination now and in the future (Knorr Cetina 1999: 241–60).

However, 'metaphysical hubris' may be as, if not more, dangerous than 'metaphysical pathos' in relation to a *realistic*—in all the various interpretations and meanings attached to that word—analysis and assessment of the complex interaction between bureaucracy, socio-economic change, and democracy. As Weber and many of his followers recognize, bureaucratic organization and administration provide many of the structural, procedural, and ethical preconditions necessary to the creation and sustaining of the, admittedly limited but nonetheless crucial, indirect or 'stakeholder democracy' that has come to dominate Western societies (Selznick 1992). Indeed, there is some evidence to suggest that these necessary 'organizational supports' for the theory and practice of indirect or interest group democracy—particularly, but not exclusively, within the workplace—and the more extensive development of 'social capital' that they can and do facilitate are drastically weakened within the post-bureaucratic/network model of organization (Putnam 2000). This is true to the extent that the latter is predicated on a highly fragmented and individualized corporate culture combined with internalized forms of surveillance and control—or 'self-policing'—that dissolves collective relations and identities into a smorgasbord of consumption choices in which self-image is the overriding priority (Heckscher and Donnellon 1994). The politics of production organization and class conflict, and the structures of class power from which they were generated, are superseded by the politics of identity choice and the consumption processes in which they are grounded. The 'new paternalism' and the 'new managerialism' come together to form a powerful cultural and ideological coalition in which conventional class and occupational divisions are absorbed and then dissolved within 'strong corporate cultures' based on unitary models of the firm and society (Casey 1995; Thrift 2002). But before we are all swept away, if not overboard, by the seductive rhetoric and persuasive logic of the 'post-bureaucratic or network thesis', we need to stand back and assess the cogency and viability of the case that it develops.

Building the Iron Cage

If, as Wolin (1961) contends, the twentieth century was the 'age of organization', then bureaucracy—or what Weber called bureaucracy in its most 'rational or pure form'—became its cultural icon and institutional embodiment. For Weber (1946, 1978, 1989), modern bureaucracy exhibited certain structural, political, and cultural features that set it apart from other forms of administrative coordination and control. First, it established an administrative structure and system that was functionally indispensable to the operation of the modern capitalist state and enterprise. Second, it provided an institutional mechanism for generating, concentrating, and distributing power that facilitated the continuous monitoring and control of social action in all spheres of social, economic, political, and cultural life. Third, it elevated and legitimated instrumental or functional rationality as *the* cognitive mode and cultural framework through which a 'means-ends' decision-making calculus was to be ruthlessly and systematically imposed in all walks of modern life. Taken together, the combination of these three core elements created a virtually indestructible organizational mechanism that expressed the underlying dynamic and drive of the modern world in which the search for the power to control all aspects of 'our' natural and human environment dominated over all other, emotional, traditional, and moral considerations. Bureaucratic organization, in Weber's view, provided the essential social instrument through which this 'quest for ultimate control' could be pursued. It meant, above all else, '*the exercise of control on the basis of knowledge*'. This control dynamic, in turn, entailed a progressive dismantling of the communal social ties and relations that had once held traditional societies together and their eventual replacement with more instrumental, competitive, individualistic, and non-inclusive forms of social organization and political culture (Nisbet 1967; Freund 1968).

Weber argued that bureaucratic organization had come to achieve such a dominant position and role in modern societies for three strategic reasons. First, its technical superiority over all other forms of administrative organization and management gave it an overwhelming advantage in fulfilling the functional needs and operational requirements of a modern economy and polity. Second, its cultural power and ubiquity as an overarching cognitive framework informing all forms of social action in which rational deliberation and calculation were preconditions for successful intervention provided a degree of unrivalled legitimacy and acceptability. Third—and most crucially for Weber—its in-built capacity to *integrate* administrative, cultural, and political power in one organizational form and mechanism guaranteed its indispensability to those status groups and social classes engaged in a never-ending 'struggle to control' the means and modes through which modern capitalist life is regulated. As Kallinikos (2004) argues, for Weber, *bureaucracy is the organizational form of modernity*. By imposing an abstract conception of work and a formalized structure of *non-inclusive, specialized roles* on its members and clients, modern bureaucracy regulates the relationship between the individual and the organization through a highly complex and disciplined form of functional and structural differentiation. This provides bureaucracy with the essential organizational mechanisms and capabilities required to respond to the incessant and constantly changing demands of a modern economy and society. It also creates a highly concentrated and flexible form of administrative power and control that would be fought over by social groups in their struggle to position themselves advantageously within the structures of social and economic inequality emerging in the modern capitalist world.

Weber's extreme ambivalence about the, seemingly inevitable, advance of the 'iron cage' of bureaucratic control and domination is clearly established and has been extensively discussed elsewhere (du Gay 2000). The widespread diffusion of bureaucracy in modern capitalist societies and political economies, Weber argued, produced considerable long-term material and social benefits—such as its high level of technical effectiveness compared to other administrative systems, its essential contribution to the development of a meritocracy, and the diffusion of an ethic of 'public service' in a vibrant and robust civil society based on democratic party politics. But these are consistently contrasted with the unavoidable social and moral costs of bureaucratization in a modern world in which 'alternative organizational futures' are extremely difficult, if not impossible, to project with any degree of coherence or conviction. Thus, in Weber's terms, bureaucratization necessarily entailed a 'disenchantment with the world'; the deadening and secretive hand of bureaucratic power and control seriously threatened the political and civic liberties and socioeconomic dynamism that capitalist-led modernization had encouraged. But most of the citizens of the modern capitalist democracies seemed prepared, if not happy, to engage in a 'Faustian pact' with bureaucracy as long as it continued to deliver the material gains and social progress that it promised. The sacrifice of individual liberty that this 'Faustian pact', in Weber's view, necessarily entailed was a price worth paying, if the precarious accommodation that it achieved between bureaucratization and democratization could be sustained in such a way that contained the powerful, and potentially uncontrollable, contending forces that are always liable to tear an outwardly strong but inwardly fragile social order apart.

Weber had fashioned an agenda for research, analysis, and debate that was to dominate social science in general, and organizational analysis in particular, for most of the twentieth century. As Ritzer (1993) has commented, a 'Weberian's' nightmare vision of modern society as nothing more than a seamless web of rationalized and formalized bureaucratic structures, from which there is no escape, has irrevocably framed the conversation in which social scientists have been engaged for much of the preceding century. However, this pessimistic and dismal vision of the iron cage of bureaucratic rationalization and control also had a much wider influence beyond the somewhat narrow and esoteric confines of academic social science. In literature, art, film, music, and politics, this dystopian vision of modern life being subordinated to the ruthless, unemotional, and disciplined rationality of efficiency and control captured the imaginations of poets, artists, filmmakers, and politicians as they struggled to come to terms with the rise of an industrialized, urbanized, and rationalized society. Dickens, Kafka, and Chaplin—to name but a few amongst an expanding community of artistic critics and cultural commentators— brilliantly communicate this pervasive sense of individual powerlessness, alienation, and isolation in the face of faceless and hidden bureaucratic power and control. Thus, by the early decades of the twentieth century there was a clear and growing collective perception amongst intellectuals, artists, and politicians of spreading disquiet concerning the social and political costs of economic, scientific, cultural, and administrative rationalization (Wolin 1961; Stuart-Hughes 1958).

In this way, both the social scientific and artistic communities of Western capitalist societies began to ask some pivotal questions about the *endemic tendency* of bureaucratic organizations to exceed their instrumental or technical role and to acquire unaccountable political power and influence. How can we better understand and explain the dynamics of bureaucratic power so as to control it more effectively? What are the conditions in which bureaucratization is strengthened and how might other social groups and movements or 'democratic forces' be mobilized in order to counteract its 'power concentrating and centralizing' tendencies? Can we, in Weber's terms at least, 'think the unthinkable'—that is, can we imagine a situation in which the bureaucratic iron cage will eventually become fatally damaged by countervailing socio-technical and political forces that irretrievably fracture its social foundations and terminally corrode its overarching administrative structure? Indeed, can we envisage a future in which the iron cage of bureaucratic domination and control is dismantled or, at the very least, implodes under the combined pressure of its endemic internal contradictions and irreparable external failings?

Dismantling the Iron Cage

The theme of de-bureaucratization is well established in social and political theory and contemporary organizational analysis and research (Bendix 1958; Eisenstadt 1958; Beetham 1984; Powell and DiMaggio 1991). However, it is worth pausing to reconsider this research and analysis on de-bureaucratization in a little more depth and detail before moving on to assess the more recent theorizing and research on the 'post-bureaucratic or network' organization. The former will provide a useful prelude to or context for the latter.

As we have already seen, for Weber, the distinctive source of modern bureaucracy's power and control lay in its specialized knowledge and expertise. By monopolizing the latter through 'official secrecy', prac-tised at all levels of the bureaucratic hierarchy, modern bureaucratic organizations and their appointed officials were able to become an independent social and political force within modern capitalist political economies and societies. As Beetham (1984: 75) puts it:

It was knowledge then, protected by secrecy, which made bureaucracy not only an effective administrative instrument, but also a potent force in the promotion of its own interests and outlook... There was an *inevitable tendency* for the apparatus to exceed its advisory and executive functions and come to control the determination of policy as well... In this sense, the rule of bureaucracy is co-extensive with the development of bureaucratic organization.

This inherent tendency for bureaucratic organizations and bureaucrats (as a status group or 'administrative class') to exceed their technical role and function was further reinforced, Beetham argues, by the close association developed by senior administrative and political elites and powerful social class interests in capitalist business enterprises and the capitalist economy more generally. The relative technical superiority of bureaucratic organization made its advance irresistible but the powerful machinery of surveillance and control that it makes available cements its location and position within a capitalist social class structure and political economy that are dominated by the requirements of a property owning class and its managerial agents. Thus, an understanding of the dynamics of bureaucratic power and control and the organizational mechanisms through which they are generated and sustained becomes central to an explanation of 'bureaucratization' as the growing acquisition of *unregulated* social and political power within a modern capitalist political economy that is producing unprecedented levels of material and social advance (Eisenstadt 1958).

Of course, for Weber and many of his followers, a strong pluralistic democracy—producing and sustaining dynamic political leadership (at all levels of political activity and organization) as an antidote to increasingly concentrated economic power and centralized administrative control—was the major protection against the development of bureaucratic organizations into independent and unregulated centres of power and control. In turn, this stimulated the development of the 'dysfunctionalist' research tradition in the sociology of organizations with its focus on the *internal* power and control struggles between businessmen, managers, bureaucrats, professionals, technocrats, politicians, and workers as they all jostled for position within an increasingly *hybridized form of 'private/public' corporate governance* (Selznick 1945; Gouldner 1954; Blau 1963; Crozier 1964). Within the latter, the identities of, and boundaries between, private economic interests and public political values would become increasingly complex and blurred as corporate and bureaucratic power within the modern capitalist enterprise and economy also became more closely intertwined and potentially inseparable. Eventually, these two streams of research and theorizing on, respectively, the inter-organizational and intra-organizational dynamics of bureaucratic power and control would be brought together in the neo-institutional school of organizational theory and research (DiMaggio and Powell 1983; Powell and DiMaggio 1991). This work would focus on bureaucratic organization as a 'rationalizing myth' and institutional form that was primarily driven by the political problem of legitimating potentially unregulated bureaucratic power and control through the promulgation and maintenance of various cultural myths obscuring or rationalizing the existence and expansion of the latter. In this context, various forms of 'institutional isomorphism' would become central to an understanding of and explanation for longer-term modifications to bureaucratic organizations and the power and control interests that they protected and enhanced. The 'iron cage' became less a matter of technical expertise and economic efficiency and much more an issue of cultural legitimation and political stabilization.

Underlying all this work on de-bureaucratization and re-bureaucratization, conducted over a period covering most of the second half of the twentieth century, there is a central recurring theme or 'leitmotif'; that is, bureaucratic organization and power are highly resistant to challenge from opposing social, economic, political, and cultural forces. Bureaucratic organization has a natural flexibility, tenacity, and adaptability which puts it in a strong position to absorb, accommodate, and manipulate opposing social groups and movements, as well as performing a wide, and changing, repertoire of technical tasks (Adler and Borys 1996). The 'other face' of the bureaucratic Janus gradually begins to reveal itself in its innate capacity to cope with incessant uncertainty and ambiguity by continually re-aligning itself with the shifting balances of power occurring in its wider institutional environment. This process of continuous re-alignment is made possible by the deft combination of specialized knowledge, practical political expertise, and technical effectiveness on which long-term bureaucratic survival has always been dependent. Above all else, this neo-Weberian tradition of research and analysis tells us, to paraphrase Schumpeter, that 'bureaucratic structures are coins that do not readily melt'. This work provides the background intellectual and historical context in which contemporary theories of the post-bureaucratic/ network organization need to be located and evaluated. But it is this pivotal background context that is often ignored by those who are most vocal and strident in their clamour for the 'creative destruction' being wrought by the 'network-based logic' of the, now putatively dominant, 'network society'.

As already indicated, the imminent demise and total collapse of bureaucratic organization has been confidently anticipated, if not predicted, many times before. In the 1960s there was an outpouring of critical writing and comment directed at the stultifying influence of 'modernity'—in all its multi-faceted institutional forms and cultural guises. Schumacher's (1995) contention that 'small is beautiful' and that 'intermediate technology' was always preferable to the necessarily alienating effects of large-scale mass production systems, and Illich's (1968) critique of professional power and his demand for the de-institutionalization of education, health, and welfare provision, were just two prominent examples of this growing disaffection with bureaucracy. In organization studies, Bennis (1966) was but one of a growing band of critics who called for, and indeed predicted with eager anticipation, the removal of bureaucratic organization as 'prosthetic device', no longer practically efficacious or morally defensible in a brave new world of fast-moving technologies, markets, and values.

However, by the mid-1980s this critique of the core institutions and values of modern bureaucratic industrial society had transformed itself into something more far-reaching and potentially destructive. Piecemeal social engineering and institutional reform simply was not enough to stem the rising tide of economic, technological, cultural, and political change overwhelming both capitalist and socialist societies. Instead, a much more apocalyptic vision and discourse of 'endings' began to dominate contemporary intellectual and political debate. Revolutionary or 'disjunctive' change, sweeping away out-moded values and obsolete institutional forms, rather than piecemeal and incremental reform, became the defining feature of our time and condition. A veritable maelstrom of change seems to have engulfed established institutional forms and their supporting 'organizing logics' in a way that generates seemingly uncontrollable instability, uncertainty, insecurity, and confusion. As Gray (1999) has argued, 'we live amid the ruins of the projects of the modern age and at a historical moment when the dissolution of modern society's most distinctive beliefs and practices is *immutably* under way'. The 'post-bureaucratic' or 'network organization' thesis is a core component of this 'discourse of endings'. This is true to the extent that it envisages a, if not *the*, central institutional form and organizing logic of modernity—that is, modern bureaucratic organization—imploding under the combined pressure of its internal contradictions and the cumulative force of external transformations entailed in globalization, 'informationalism', marketization, and individualism.

Three, relatively recent, publications can be taken as representative of the post-bureaucratic/network thesis and its location within a wider 'discourse of endings'—Heckscher and Donnellon's (1994) reader on the post-bureaucratic organization, van Dijk's (1999) overview of the key features of the network society, and Castells' (1996, 2000) magisterial three volume study of the rise of the network society.

Heckscher and Donnellon assign explanatory primacy to the destructive impact of new information and communication technologies upon the central structural features and cultural supports of bureaucratic organization. Contemporary capitalism, they contend, employs new technologies of coordination and control to ensure that evermore complex orchestrations of knowledge and power occur increasingly behind the scenes and beyond the purview of the 'public gaze'. This generates *extreme and continuous instability* in older bureaucratic structures of command and control so that they implode under a simultaneous miniaturization, concentration, and dispersion of central control systems that make them less visible and more flexible. Van Dijk attempts to convince us that the 'virtualization' of bureaucratic organization removes the spatial, temporal, and social 'anchorage' in which it was contained, while simultaneously stripping out the administrative superstructure on which it previously depended and replacing the latter with much more flexible and mobile interconnecting networks. Again, this does not lead to the destruction of centralized control systems but to their relocation within considerably streamlined and interconnected 'circuits of control' that facilitate swift and flexible reactions to changes in the wider environment. Castells identifies the emergence of a network society, based on a networking logic of its core social structure, as an outcome of the intersection between the globalization of capital accumulation, the IT revolution, and the increasing dominance of a highly individualistic and consumerist culture. He (Castells 2000: 501–2, emphasis added) is worth quoting at some length:

The inclusion/exclusion in networks, and the architecture of relationships between networks, enacted by light-speed-operating information systems, configure dominant processes and functions in our societies. Networks are open structures, able to expand without limits, integrating new nodes as long as they are able to communicate within the network, namely as long as they share the same communication codes (for example, values or performance goals). A network-based social structure is a highly dynamic, open system, susceptible to innovating without threatening its balance. Networks are appropriate instruments for a capitalist economy based on innovation, globalization and centralized concentration; for work, workers and firms based on flexibility and adaptability; for a culture of endless destruction and reconstruction; for a polity geared to the instant processing of new values and public moods; and for social organization aiming at the supersession of space and the annihilation of time. Yet the network morphology is also a source of dramatic reorganization of power relationships. Switches connecting the networks (for example, financial flows taking control of media empires that influence political processes) are the privileged instruments of power. Thus, the switchers are the power-holders. Since networks are multiple, the inter-operating codes and switches between networks become the fundamental sources in shaping, guiding and misguiding societies . . . the new economy is organized around global networks of capital, management, and information, whose access to technological know-how is at the roots of productivity and competitiveness. Business firms and, increasingly, organizations and institutions, are organized in networks of *variable geometry* whose intertwining supersedes the traditional distinction between corporations and small business, cutting across sectors, and spreading along different geographical clusters of economic units. Accordingly, the work process is increasingly individualized, labour is disaggregated in its performance, and re-integrated in its outcome through a multiplicity of interconnected tasks in different sites, ushering in a new division of labour based on the attributes/capacities of each worker rather than on the organization of the task.

However, Castells *is* quite clear that we are *not* talking about the demise of capitalism with the rise of the network society and organization. But this is, in his view, a profoundly different form and brand of capitalism based on an entirely different set of organizing principles, codes, and structures to those that underpinned the form(s) of industrial capitalism that dominated the Western world for most of the twentieth century. The variable geometry on which informational capitalism is based revolves around globalized financial flows and a process and dynamic of continuous capital accumulation in the 'sphere of circulation', rather than in the 'sphere of production', as under industrial capitalism. This network-based variable geometry of interconnected circuits of coordination and control, operating simultaneously at a number of different levels of economic, social, political, and cultural organization, is loosely held together by a 'meta-framework of financial flows, where all capital is equalized in the commodified democracy of profit-making' (Castells 2000: 503).

But he is equally convinced that we *are* talking about a terminal crisis in the vertically integrated and bureaucratically coordinated corporation, in both the private and (what's left of) public sectors. He is also convinced that the former is being forced to transform itself, as a result of its endemic limitations and failures, into a virtualized network of multifunctional decision-making centres to form a highly decentralized and extremely flexible structure. The 'horizontal or network corporation becomes a dynamic and strategically planned network of self-programmed, self-directed units based on decentralization, participation and coordination' (Castells 2000: 178). The basic operating organizational unit within the 'network corporation' is the business project enacted by a network—not 'the department' or 'the division', or 'the company'. Thus, the 'fixed geometry' of the traditional bureaucratic corporation is superseded by a 'variable geometry' of network organization that is inherently more dynamic, unstable, and complex than the former but is ideally suited to the conditions and needs of globalized, finance-led capital accumulation, and the flexibility that it demands. The network 'controls the uncontrollable' by developing a cybernetic system that continuously monitors, anticipates, and reshapes the work flows and activities through which 'organization' is accomplished.

From Fixed to Variable Geometry?

In many respects, the post-bureaucratic/network organization thesis offers us a highly optimistic scenario of the developmental trajectory that social and organizational change will follow over the coming decades. It presumes that a complex conjunction of economic, technological, cultural, and political 'restructurings' will, of necessity, bring about the demise of bureaucratic organization and replace it with an organizing logic and system based on fundamentally different principles. It insists that most, if not all, of the core structural features (specialized divisions of labour; extended authority hierarchies; exclusive organizational domains and boundaries) and operating principles (non-inclusivity, differentiation, standardization, formalization) characteristic of bureaucratic organization will disappear in the fluid and mobile world of the network organization. Indeed, the latter is an essentially 'structureless' and 'boundary-less' unit or process. This is so to the extent that its functioning is dependent on the spontaneous, self-organizing and self-renewing logic of an immanent transformational process that overcomes the conventional spatial, temporal, political, and cultural obstacles to radical de-bureaucratization. Network organizing is dependent on a highly complex circuitry of informational codes and flows in which a 'variable geometry' of constant movement and fluctuation defies the 'fixed geometry' of division, standardization and formalization characteristic of bureaucratic coordination and control.

In turn, the 'switches' and 'switchers' interconnecting different network systems and codes emerge as the new centres of power and control within a social structure that is much more fragmented and disconnected than its bureaucratic predecessor. We are living in a new era in which managers 'do not control, and do not even know about, the actual, systemic movements of capital in the networks of financial flows, of knowledge in the information networks, of strategies in the multi-faceted set of network enterprises' (Castells 2000: 504). This, for Castells, is the new historical and structural reality that we now confront and will continue to confront in the foreseeable future. It

leads to the concentration and globalization of capital, precisely by using the decentralizing power of networks. Labour is disaggregated in its performance, fragmented in its organization, diversified in its existence, divided in its collective action. Networks converge toward a meta-network of capital that integrates capitalist interests at the global level and across sectors and realms of activity: not without conflict, but under the same overarching logic. Labour loses its collective identity, becomes increasingly individualized in its capacities, in its working conditions, and in its interests and projects. Who are the owners, who the producers, who the managers, and who the servants becomes increasingly blurred in a production system of variable geometry, of teamworking, of networking, outsourcing, and sub-contracting (Castells 2000: 506).

It is quite clear that Castells and other theorists of the post-bureaucratic/network organization are sensitive to the fact that long-term outcomes will be dependent, as always, on power relations and power struggles between contending social groups. Yet, these power struggles are now relocated and re-embedded within a power structure in which 'labour' is permanently disadvantaged at a collective level relative to 'capital'. At the level of the individual 'labourer' a much more limited form of democratic participation (say, in work teams) and 'empowerment' (say, through job enrichment) in 'high performance work systems' is possible. But the traditional administrative codes and forms on which bureaucratic coordination and control relied cannot survive at a time or in a 'culture of "creative destruction" accelerated to the speed of the opto-electronic circuits that process its signals'. *'Schumpeter meets Weber in the cyberspace of the network enterprise'* (Castells 2000: 215 emphasis added).

However, Castells and other network theorists may be guilty of drastically underestimating the structural constraints that limit the underlying logic of network organizing and its capacity to sustain a 'variable geometry' in which social relationships and cultural forms become radically disconnected from each other and from their material base. As Paul Thompson (2003) has recently argued, 'disconnected capitalism' is generating fundamental contradictions and tensions between destructive economic, technological, and political restructuring on the one hand and the continuing need for creative, participative, and reasonably stable work systems on the other. The latter depend on the continuous renewal of social capital and the stabilizing of work relations through firm-level and workplace-level systems of democratic governance that formally guarantee a sufficient degree of equity and justice to enable 'high trust' organizational cultures to develop. But the former must remove these governance structures because they stand in the way of a dynamic of capital accumulation that demands continuing work deregulation, intensification, and exploitation through rationalization and marketization. This puts both managers and workers in a situation where radical uncertainty, insecurity, and conflict are simply contained by 'hegemonic' control regimes that construct a façade of empowerment and trust around a reality of constant threat, fear, and isolation. In the long term, this makes effective firm-level governance and workplace-level management even more difficult. It cuts the material and political ground from underneath any control strategy that requires much more than instrumental compliance from all types and grades of employees if it is to stand any chance of realizing 'high-trust' and 'high-performance' work systems and organizations (see Thompson and Alvesson, Chapter 4, this volume).

In short, network organization is not a panacea for the 'compliance/commitment' and 'control/trust' dilemmas that have confronted the organization and management of the capitalist labour process from the second half of the nineteenth century onwards (Hyman 1987). Indeed, the former exacerbates the latter to the extent that it drastically reduces the levels of job security and employment stability available to the majority of the employed labour force—including increasing numbers of professional, managerial, and technical employees (Heckscher 1995)—and maintains relatively high levels of unemployment as a permanent reminder of and threat to those lucky enough to remain in current employment. Working life in the network organization is no joy, even for the core workforce of 'knowledge workers' who retain the vestiges of employment security and stability once enjoyed by the majority of employees in the form of bureaucratic organization. Internal labour markets, strong trade unions, planned career structures, collective bargaining, and workplace participation were legitimate core components of the post-war industrial and political social democratic-cum-corporatist settlement.

These concerns are echoed, and taken further, by Jessop (2002) in his critique of network theory and its promotion of 'heterarchy' as a permanent solution to the governance problems that have bedevilled both market-based and bureaucratic-based modes of coordination and control. Castells, Jessop argues, is guilty, as are other network theorists, of presuming that networks are naturally superior to forms of imperative coordination through bureaucratic organization. This is based on three, highly questionable assumptions. First, that vertically integrated and bureaucratically controlled forms of imperative coordination have *all but disappeared* under the cumulative impact of informationalism, globalization, and postmodern individualism. Second, that network forms of governance are *necessarily* (procedurally and substantively) more efficient than markets or bureaucracies because of their in-built capacity to cope more effectively with higher levels of complexity and uncertainty. Third, that markets and bureaucracies are *endemically incapable* of fully exploiting both the technical and political advantages of new information and communication technologies. Consequently, they inevitably experience fundamental coordination and control failures that automatically exert a negative impact on their capacity to deliver the outcomes that dominant power interests and groups demand.

Each of these propositions or presumptions, Jessop argues, can be regarded as highly questionable for a number of reasons. First, they underplay the strategic role that vertical 'command and control' structures continue to play in a globalized capitalist system in which nation states remain significant 'movers and shakers' in an internationalized political economy. Second, they overplay the ability of self-organizing networks to cope with the increasingly contradictory demands of a kaleidoscopic array of national and international collective corporate actors including nation states/governments, transnational corporations, international NGO's, trade unions, consumer interest groups, ethnic representative groups, and social movements—to name but a few! Third, they too easily assume that the inherent anarchy of the market and the endemic rigidity of bureaucracy can both be overcome by horizontal, self-organizing, and self-renewing networks that necessarily lack the 'response mechanisms' built into the former and the 'steering mechanisms' interpolated within the latter. In conclusion, Jessop contends that network theorists tend to see horizontal self-organization amongst mutually interdependent collective actors (i.e. 'heterarchical' forms of governance) as something of a 'technological miracle cure' that can reconnect the radically disconnected forms of governance, at all levels, symptomatic of 'informational capitalism'. This 'network elixir' only works, however, if one wishes away the inherent resilience of both market- and bureaucratic-based forms of economic and political coordination and control. It also can only work its 'magical spell' if the powerful obstacles to, or at least constraints on, de-bureaucratization are forgotten or marginalized.

The 'variable geometry' of network organizing logic and forms may be seen to exist alongside a 'fixed geometry' of imperatively coordinated structures and the underlying coordinating, integrating, and stabilizing mechanisms that they provide. Rather than 'Schumpeter meeting Weber in the cyberspace of the network enterprise', it may be more a case of 'Marx meeting Weber in the real space of the imperatively coordinated transnational corporation'. Indeed, as Harvey (2003) has recently demonstrated, the endemic economic, technological, and political volatility of international capitalism, even in its network form, remains as powerful as ever. The latter generates a complex series of temporary 'spatio-temporal fixes' that are doomed to fail as permanent solutions to the incurable problem of over-accumulation and the inevitable economic and political crises that it reproduces. Within this radically unstable and crisis-prone environment, the political and business elites, nominally 'in charge' of 'informational capitalism', will need to call on a complex combination of organizational mechanisms to secure 'spatio-temporal fixes' that contain the endemic crises to which the latter is unavoidably exposed.

Conclusion: Beyond the Iron Cage?

Marx, and before him Saint-Simon, argued that no social order can change without the lineaments of the new already being latently present within the existing state of affairs. In realist terms (Reed 2002a), the embryonic social structures that provide the underlying 'generative mechanisms' through which radical social change—that is, a fundamental restructuring of the institutional configurations and organizational forms through which power and control are reproduced—occurs must be sufficiently advanced in their growth and strength before they can begin to exert a determining influence on future development. There must be enough of 'the new' in 'the old' and the former must have the potential to stop the latter from 'strangling it at birth'.

Post-bureaucratic/network theory tries to convince us that we have reached a period in human history and development where the 'variable geometry' of network organizing is strong and powerful enough to displace, marginalize, and eventually replace the 'fixed geometry' of bureaucratic organization. This process of displacement, marginalization, and replacement may be far from complete but, the network theorists contend, the trajectory of change is perfectly clear and it drives inexorably in the direction of a post-bureaucratic future. Schumpeter triumphs over Weber insofar as the underlying dynamic or logic of 'creative destruction' inherent in all forms of capitalist production and market exchange reaches its apogee in finance-led, globalized capitalism and the virtual technologies on which it depends. Bureaucratic forms of imperatively coordinated and controlled organization cannot hope to survive in this kind of environment because they are 'congenitally lacking' in the right kind of social and cultural 'genes' that can facilitate the appropriate internal adaptation to a radically changed environment. Indeed, Schumpeter may be as guilty as Weber in substantially *underestimating* the uncontrollable power of globalized market and technological forces and *overestimating* the organizational capability of bureaucracy to contain, even tame, their more destructive and dynamic consequences.

Yet, more recent analysis, evidence, and argument, as developed by Thompson, Jessop, and others, seems to indicate that *'hybridization'* rather than 'paradigm shift' may be a more accurate description and interpretation of what is currently occurring and where it might lead (Frenkel et al. 1995). Recent empirical reach on public sector organizational restructuring (Deem et al. 2001; Reed 2002*b*, *c*; Farrell and Morris 2003) suggests that a 'neo-bureaucratic state' may be emerging that, in many crucial respects, *increases our dependence* on bureaucratic logics and forms of organizing but in rather different ways from those typical of the classic 'Weberian idea-type' of 'bureaucracy in its most rational form'. Instead of the 'fixed geometry' characteristic of bureaucratic organizational forms defined by extended hierarchies, bloated technocracies, and intransigent autarkies, the process of hybridization—in which elements of markets, hierarchies, communities, and networks are loosely combined—may produce a situation in which far more complex regimes of coordination and control will be required to hold them together in some way or another. But these 'neo-bureaucracies' are unlikely to exhibit the fully-developed variable geometry of 'heterarchy' anticipated by Castells and other network theorists because they require and secure a far higher degree of continuity and stability than the latter envisages. Castells is right to identify 'the switches connecting the networks' as 'the privileged instruments of power and control'. But these switches are much more likely to be provided, maintained, and operated by those individuals and groups occupying key positions in the, relatively permanent and stable, institutionalized power structures that define globalized capitalism and the neo-bureaucratic state. As such, these are exactly the kind of power structures that have been identified through and analysed by research on de-bureaucratization and re-bureaucratization conducted over the post-1945 period.

Doubts over the substantive diagnosis and prognosis that network theory offers in relation to long-term 'organizational futures' also raises questions about the normative theory of change and the participatory theory of organizational democracy that emerge from the former. It raises fundamental questions about the values that indelibly shape the organizational logics and forms through which socio-economic life is coordinated and controlled. More specifically, the normative debate which network/post-bureaucratic theory has generated, opens up the distinct possibility of re-interpreting bureaucratic organization as a necessary precondition for and protector of civic values associated with the 'public domain' (du Gay 2000; Marquand 2004. See also Chapters 1 and 2 by Goodsell and du Gay, respectively, this volume).

In many respects, network theory seems to offer a very 'thin' conception of participatory democracy within the workplace. It presumes that network forms will generate an irreversible trend towards 'high trust' organizational cultures and 'empowering' organizational systems as the necessary prerequisites for the development and operation of 'high performance work systems' (Murray et al. 2002). But nowhere does this normative theory of 'participatory democracy' within the workplace connect and engage with the wider structures of class-based power and control that frame intra-organizational forms and relations. By rejecting, or at the very least 'sidelining', the class-based occupational and organizational power structures and bureaucratic systems that shape and legitimate interest group democracy within the workplace and the wider political economy (Taylor 2002), network theory and its promoters de-legitimate the micro-, meso-, and macro-level collective conflicts that defined class-based politics in the social democratic state. They trade, intellectually and ideologically, on a unitary model of the post-bureaucratic/network organization in which legitimate political activity and conflict is considerably narrowed to include only those issues that pertain to the negotiation and protection of sustainable 'organizational identities' through a consumption-based politics. Stokes and Clegg (2002: 22) are correct in their argument that 'sedimented bureaucratic principles and innovative "enterprising" freedoms produce new power games around contradictory and unresolved dualisms'. But the contemporary experience of 'organizational reform as a process of unresolved and contradictory dualisms—between an enterprising promise and a rationally accountable past' (Stokes and Clegg 2002: 226) has to be positioned within the wider ideological and organizational changes that network-theory inspired reforms have generated. There is a 'meta-narrative' of institutional change within which a chain of loosely coupled 'micro-narratives' of organizational change are located; the latter cannot be understood, much less explained, unless they are embedded within the former. Programmes of radical, organizational, and political reform have been driven by a network theory and ideology of change that may leave much undone but they have undoubtedly left deep and lasting scars on the institutional and ethical *status quo*.

The theory and practice of workplace interest group democracy may be inherently restrictive in its value range and practical aspirations when judged against the demands of 'participatory democracy or empowerment'. But at least the former recognizes and attempts to accommodate—by supporting and legitimating trade unions and collective bargaining, for instance—the inevitable conflicts of interests and values that define the world of work in a modern society. There seems to be little interest in, much less concern for, the vital bureaucratic scaffolding on which pluralistic or stakeholder models of workplace democracy are constructed and maintained within much of the contemporary thinking and writing on the post-bureaucratic/ network organization. An incipient and all-pervasive unitary ideology, combining selected elements of neo-liberal economic theory, communitarian political theory, and postmodern cultural theory seems to be emerging in an intellectual form that is conveniently forgetful of the pluralistic value conflicts that lay at the heart of Weber's social ontology and epistemology. Amongst all the hype about the virtual, post-bureaucratic, or networked organization, there is a very real need to re-assert the fundamental technical, political, and ethical virtues of Weberian-style bureaucratic organization that is in danger of being washed away in a naïve and disingenuous technological romanticism and historical determinism.

Amongst the virtues of bureaucratic organization, as identified by Philip Selznick in his book, *The Moral Commonwealth* (1992), are loyalty to assigned responsibilities, accountability to the institution and its sponsors, consultation as a requirement of the diffusion of authority, and mitigation of arbitrariness through self-restrained, rule-governed action. As he also suggests, the major lesson of the Watergate crisis under President Nixon between 1972 and 1974 was that bureaucratic prerogatives and restraints are, in important respects, wholesome and even indispensable. They provide the crucial checks and balances necessary to curtail the unfettered exercise of executive power and to sustain the organizational conditions in which democratic pluralism can be developed. This would seem to be even more critical in relation to the recent war in Iraq and the fundamental issues that are surfacing, virtually on a daily basis, about unrestrained and unaccountable state power bereft of any kind of effective 'checks and balances' from a cowed public bureaucracy.

All organizations, including the post-bureaucratic/network organizations characteristic of the 'knowledge economy and society', need strong values, rules, and mechanisms that restrain their innate authoritarian tendencies. We need to be eternally vigilant about all forms of organization. Rules and mechanisms of accountability are essential to the exercise and protection of individual and collective choice. Bureaucratic organization constitutes a distinctive and substantive, if theoretically limited and practically flawed, ethical domain and administrative form in its own right. It is a necessary organizational and ethical precondition for defending and sustaining pluralistic/interest group democracy within the workplace and beyond. This is particularly the case in extreme political and social conditions. As recent historical research on the holocaust demonstrates (Aly and Hein 2002), the aggressive ideology of transformation that drove the radical projects—such as mass extermination masquerading as a programme of population management—of the Third Reich required and secured a powerful and ferociously ambitious technocracy to make them feasible. But this 'radically empowered' technocracy found itself continually at odds with a well-entrenched public bureaucracy that attempted to maintain whatever little was left of procedural rationality and integrity. Indeed, within the first five years of the Third Reich, this technocracy constituted the youngest and most flexible technical and academic elite that had virtually swept away what it deemed to be 'outmoded' bureaucratic structures and systems built around accepted norms of 'due process' and 'equity of treatment'. The German state's, severely weakened, bureaucratic machine was all that was left to defend the ethic of 'accountability' and to try to limit this emerging technocratic power elite's increasing domination and control.

As Selznick (1992: 288) has argued, it seems clear that 'if there is a post-bureaucratic world, it will not be one in which bureaucracy is eliminated. The positive functions and moral worth of bureaucracy cannot be ignored. Rather the new, non-bureaucratic forms will be essential leaven in the bureaucratic dough'. This will certainly continue to be the case in a world where 'values and interests inevitably collide' and where endemic power struggles will shape the organizational forms and practices through which we live our lives.

References

Adler, P. and Borys, B. (1996). 'Two types of bureaucracy: enabling and coercive'. *Administrative Science Quarterly*, 41; 61–89

Albrow, M. (1992). 'Sine ira et studio—or do organizations have feelings?'. *Organization Studies*, 13/3; 313–29

Aly, G. and Heim, S. (2002). *Architects of Annihilation: Auschwitz and the Logic of Destruction*. London: Weidenfield and Nicholson.

Beetham, D. (1984). *Max Weber and the Theory of Modern Politics*. London: Allen and Unwin.

Bendix, R. (1958). 'Bureaucracy and the problem of power', in R. Merton (ed.), *Reader on Bureaucracy*. New York: Free Press.

Bennis, W. (1966). *Changing Organizations*. New York: McGraw Hill.

Blau, P. (1963). *The Dynamics of Bureaucracy*, 2nd edn. Chicago, IL: University of Chicago Press.

Casey, C. (1995). *Work, Self and Society: After Industrialism*. London: Routledge.

Casey, C. (2002). *Critical Analysis of Organizations: Theory, Practice, Revitalisation*. London: Sage.

Castells, M. (1996). *The Rise of the Network Society*. Oxford: Basil Blackwell.

Castells, M. (2000). *The Rise of the Network Society*, 2nd edn. Oxford: Basil Blackwell.

Clegg, S. (1990). *Modern Organizations: Organization Studies in the Postmodern World*. London: Sage.

Crozier, M. (1964). *The Bureaucratic Phenomenon*. Chicago, IL: University of Chicago Press.

Deem, R., Fulton O., Reed, M., and Watson, S., (2001), '*New Managerialism and the Management of UK Universities*', ESRC Report (unpublished).

DiMaggio, P. and Powell, W. (1983). 'The iron cage revisited: institutional isomorphism and collective rationality in organizations'. *American Sociological Review.* 48; 147–60.

du Gay, P. (2000). *In Praise of Bureaucracy*. London: Sage.

Eisenstadt, S. N. (1958). 'Bureaucracy and bureaucratization', in R. Merton (ed.), *Reader on Bureaucracy*. New York: Free Press.

Farrell, C. and Morris, J. (2003). 'The neo-bureaucratic state: professionals and professional managers in schools, general practices and social work'. *Organization.* 10/1; 129–56.

Frenkel, S., Korczynski M., Donoghue L., and Shire K. (1995). 'Reconstituting work: trends towards knowledge work and info-normative control', *Work, Employment and Society.* 9/4; 773–96.

Freund, J. (1968). *The Sociology of Max Weber*. Harmondsworth: Allen Lane.

Giddens, A. (1994). 'Living in a Post-Traditional society', in U. Beck, A. Giddens and S. Lash (eds), *Reflexive Modernization: Politics, Tradition and Aesthetics in the Modern Social Order*. Cambridge: Polity Press, 56–109.

Gouldner, A. (1954). *Patterns of Industrial Bureaucracy*. New York: Collier Macmillan.

Gray, J. (1999). *Endgame*. Cambridge: Polity Press.

Harvey, D. (2003). *The New Imperialism*. Oxford: Oxford University Press.

Heckscher, C. (1995). *White-Collar Blues: Management Loyalists in the Age of Corporate Restructuring*. New York: Basic Books.

Hecksher, C. and Donnellon, A. (eds) (1994). *The Post-Bureaucratic Organization*. London: Sage.

Hyman, R. (1987). 'Strategy or structure?: capital, labour and control'. *Work, Employment and Society*. 1/1; 25–55.

Illich, I. (1968). *De-Schooling Society*. Harmondsworth: Penguin.

Jessop, B. (2002). *The Future of the Capitalist State*. Cambridge: Polity.

Kallinikos, J. (2004). 'The social foundations of the bureaucratic order'. *Organization* (Special Issue on 'Bureaucracy in the Age of Enterprise'). 11/1; 13–36.

Knorr Cetina, K. (1999). *Epistemic Cultures: How the Sciences Make Knowledge*. Cambridge, MA: Harvard University Press.

Lash, S. and Urry, J. (1994). *Economies of Signs and Space*. London: Sage.

Marquand, D. (2004). *Decline of the Public*. Cambridge: Polity.

Murray, G., Belanger, J. Antony, G., and Lapointe, P.-A. (2002). *Work and Employment in the High Performance Workplace*. London: Continuum.

Nisbet, R. (1967). *The Sociological Tradition*. London: Heinemann.

Powell, W. and DiMaggio, P. (1991). *The New Institutionalism in Organizational Analysis*. Chicago, IL: University of Chicago Press.

Putman, R. (2000). *Bowling Alone; The Collapse and Revival of American Community*. New York: Touchstone.

Ray, L. and Reed, M. (1994). *Organizing Modernity*. London: Routledge.

Reed, M. (2002*a*). 'The realist turn in organization and management studies', Unpublished Conference Paper, Employment Relations Research Unit Conference, Cardiff Business School, UK.

Reed, M. (2002b). 'New managerialism, professional power and organizational governance in UK universities: a review and assessment'; in A. Amarel, G. A. Jones, and B. Karseth (eds), *Governing Higher Education: National Perspectives on Institutional Governance*. Dordrecht: Netherlands.

Reed, M. (2002c). 'New managerialism and the management of UK universities', in M. Dewatripoint, F. Thys-Clément, and L. Wilkin (eds), *European Universities: Change and Convergence*. Brussels: University of Brussels Press.

Ritzer, G. (1993). *The McDonaldization of Society*. London: Sage.

Schumacher, E. F. (1995). *A Guide for the Perplexed*. London: Vintage.

Scaff, L. (1989). *Fleeing the Iron Cage: Culture, Politics and Modernity in the Thought of Max Weber*. Berkeley, CA: University of California Press.

Selznick, P. (1945). *TVA and the Grass Roots*. Berkeley, CA: University of California Press.

Selznick, P. (1992). *The Moral Commonwealth*. Berkeley, CA: University of California Press.

Sennett, R. (1998). *The Corrosion of Character: The Personal Consequences of Work in the New Capitalism*. London: Norton and Company.

Stokes, J. and Clegg, S. (2002). 'Once upon a time in bureaucracy: power and public sector management'. *Organization*. 9/2; 225–47.

Stuart-Hughes, H. (1958). *Consciousness and Society*. Harmondsworth: Penguin.

Taylor, R. (2002). *Britain's World of Work: Myths and Realities*. Swindon: Economic and Social Research Council.

Thompson, P. (2003). 'Disconnected capitalism: or why employers can't keep their side of the bargain'. *Work, Employment and Society*. 17/2; 359–78.

Thrift, N. (2002). 'Performing cultures in the new economy', in P. du Gay and M. Pryke (eds), *Cultural Economy*. London: Sage.

van Dijk, J. (1999). *The Network Society: Social Aspects of New Media*. London: Sage.

Weber, M. (1946). *From Max Weber: Essays in Sociology*. Edited by H. Gerth and C. Wright-Mills. Oxford: Oxford University Press.

Weber, M. (1978). *Economy and Society*. Edited by G. Roth and C. Wittich. California: University of California Press.

Weber, M. (1989). *Weber: Selections in Translation*. Edited by W. G. Runciman. Cambridge: Cambridge University Press.

Wolin, S. (1961). *Politics and Vision*. London: Allen and Unwin.

6

Bureaucracy and Beyond: Managers and Leaders in the 'Post-Bureaucratic' Organization

Graeme Salaman

An insistence on the limitations of and alternatives to bureaucracy is fundamental to current approaches to the analysis of organization and business in two ways. Ideologically the notion of the market dominates thinking on organizations. An emphasis on market principles, forms and relationships, widely prevalent and pervasive within political approaches to the role of government and the necessary structure and functioning of public organizations, underpins much current consultancy and expert prescription and exhortation which impacts on public and private organizations alike. This overwhelming and largely unquestioned (at least at governmental levels) regime of truth supplies the necessary legitimation for a wide variety of organizational initiatives (or, revealingly, 'reforms').

On the academic front, the twin pillars of business school analysis of business organizations—the notions of business strategy and of human resource (HR) strategy (or capability)—would not be possible without the conviction that bureaucracy can and should be supplanted. For the notion of strategy suggests that organizational forms and purposes can be chosen. Organizational executives can make choices about organizational direction (what products to make at what price with what features for what markets) that influence organizational success and which need to be supported by 'appropriate' organizational structures and processes. Of course the search for the weaknesses—or dysfunctions—of bureaucracy has delighted organizational analysts since Merton; but it now has new urgency and significance, for the possibility that organizations can take a number of forms and that these can be chosen to support organizational strategies underpins the fundamental idea of strategic contingency or 'fit'. Without the possibility of variation in organizational structure and functioning business schools would be out of business: there would be nothing to talk about.

So the critique of bureaucracy has been redefined, restructured, and hijacked by new authorities with new purposes. Once the safe but limited concern of the academy, the critique of bureaucracy has been absorbed by wider ideological discourses of organization, economy, and government. The analysis of the weaknesses of bureaucracy has not only shifted from a critique based on analysis of the principles of bureaucracy to a critique based on the inappropriateness or lack of 'fit' of bureaucracy with new requirements and exigencies (see Thompson and Alvesson, Chapter 4, this volume), it has also been invested with new authority, organized for new and larger purposes, legitimated by new logics and values, and mounted with new energy by new champions.

Work by the author and Paul du Gay identifies the key elements of a recent, widely prevalent discourse of management which centres around a critique of and an attempt to define a replacement for, bureaucracy. This is a view of what organizations must be like, of how they work (or should work) and what they should do, and what employees need to be like to work effectively within them to promote their objectives. Within its own terms this is a well-defined and internally coherent view of organizations. It operates at and focuses on three levels: the individual, organizational, and societal and crucially insists on linkages between each. At a societal level, prevailing over-arching discourses of organization and government define market structures, relationships, and principles as moral standards essential for the achievement of organizational effectiveness and efficiency (du Gay, Salaman, and Rees 1996). Work by David Guest (1992) and Brad Jackson (1996) among others charts how the appeal of various forms of management thought derives from the way these ideas claim connections with prevailing core values, logics, and assumptions.

At the organizational level this discourse of organization stresses the critical role of enterprise, strategic thinking, concern for improvement, customer-focus, and commerciality. It comprises a series of initiatives—usually consultant-driven—which seek to redefine the organization as an enterprise within which relationships are restructured or re-engineered in terms of contractual relations and transactions. At the individual level this anti-bureaucratic approach emphasizes how individual employees must be constituted—'made-up'—in terms of their willingness and ability to define and present themselves in terms of the qualities and values required to work in the newly 'reformed' organization. All this has been thoroughly analysed and dissected by a number of researchers, (Miller and Rose 1988, 1990, 1993; Guest 1990; Rose 1990; du Gay 1991; du Gay and Salaman, 1992). This view of organizations consists of a set of key principles which are then articulated in terms of recommended types of relationships, structures, and practices. The anti-bureaucratic discourse simultaneously critiques bureaucracy while advocating its antithesis—flexibility, empowerment, and responsiveness.

Its main principle is advocated not simply as effective but as virtuous. The critique of bureaucracy appropriates morality in its analysis of the limitations of bureaucracy and its advocacy of the virtues of its alternatives. It advocates the imposition and installation of market principles, forces, relationships, and structures and defines and celebrates these as inevitable and moral. Within bureaucracy activities are defined and constrained by specification—by rule or by role. Relations and transactions between individuals or between departments or between individual and organization or department and organization are defined by formalized definition specifying what each party is expected to supply to the other. Within the new approach to employee, organization, and society, relations are defined in terms of the same relations that exist between the business and the customer (an iconic role within this approach)—see du Gay and Salaman (1992)—that is, as market relations—as buyers and sellers or services and products.

This principle is articulated through a number of recommended and popular organizational changes. The move to decentralization for example is justified by the moral critique of the role and contribution of head office within a bureaucratic system which questions the value-adding contribution of the centre while simultaneously insisting that the 'business units'—previously divisions or departments—must be free (empowered) to be able to devise and achieve their own objectives in the face of market and customer pressures and requirements rather than head office directives. Similarly organizational de-layering not only promises the benefits of cost reductions, it also requires a reduction in management-based supervision (which can now be achieved through information and communication technology (ICT)) and an emphasis on staff empowerment with staff controlled less by regulation ('inputs') and more by market and customer measures. The widespread installation of management competences—the focus of this chapter—represents another common initiative which seeks to redefine the nature of management and managers in terms of the qualities required to support the new, customer-focused empowered responsive organization.

As Thompson and Alvesson (Chapter 4, this volume) noted, there are a number of different ways in which the principle of the new approach to organization—anti-bureaucracy, and pro-market—are articulated and manifested but in essence they can be reduced to one—the various structural, cultural, and process-based ways in which hierarchical and rule-based controls are replaced by control exercised through market-type transactions, which can of course be through direct market transactions and negotiations or through a variety of market surrogates: a variety of market-type mechanisms: benchmarking, targets, levels of contribution, profit margins, service level agreements, etc.

This approach to organizational restructuring not only includes prescription and morality, it also comprises a claimed analysis. The advocated organizational changes are defined as necessary indeed inevitable consequences of identified environmental changes—powerful external factors which according to this approach 'drive' the advocated organizational changes—the pace of change, increasing consumer demands for quality and choice, innovation, globalization, hyper-competition, etc. (see Thompson and Alvesson, Chapter 4, this volume).

Internal organizational changes away from bureaucratic structures and principles and towards market structures and relationships are defined as necessary in the face of these identified external pressures.

This chapter explores this connection through an analysis of the reasons for and consequences of the installation of management competences—a common feature of the move against bureaucracy.

In the face of this massive and strident consultant attack on bureaucracy, researchers have predictably analysed the degree to which these admonitions have resulted in or are reflected by, changes in practice. Has the discourse of enterprise, and the celebration of the new market-centred organization, actually affected what organizations are like? These questions have been addressed on a number of levels.

First, researchers have justifiably and usefully pointed out the survival of bureaucracy as a major organizational form, and true to the tenets of contingency theory have argued the appropriateness of bureaucracy for certain sorts of tasks where predictability is necessary and possible, where tasks and operations can and should be systematized and mechanized, and where judgement, knowledge, and discretion can be situated in technology, system, machine, or training. But despite the claims of the consultants that we live in new times which demand new forms of organization, researchers note that bureaucratic forms of organization survive and succeed: ' . . . throughout the world the largest organizations are still essentially bureaucracies' (Mabey, Salaman, and Storey 1998: 238).

Second, authors note that new forms of organization which employ the new anti-bureaucratic, market- and enterprise-focused structures, values, and relationships of organization, and non-bureaucratic forms of control, do not necessarily involve the liberation of the employee from the iron cage of control but simply the imposition of new more insidious forms of control: 'government at a distance' (Miller and Rose 1993). This form of analysis which has certainly enriched our understanding of the subtle realities of the management of people in organizations which seek to reject bureaucratic forms, is in essence not new but is a new version of a traditional distinction in organizational and industrial analysis between direct and indirect or insidious control.

Third, researchers have looked carefully at the separate elements of the anti-bureaucratic proposition and assessed the empirical validity of these claims. Authors such as Thompson and Warhurst (1998) have identified the key claims of these advocates and assessed the extent to which these can be seen in practice, or the degree to which if they do occur they occur in the form and achieve the effects claimed by their proponents. Thompson and Alvesson (Chapter 4, this volume) rehearse a number of arguments that have advised caution in accepting too readily the more outspoken claims and predictions of those who insist that the post-bureaucratic form of organization is now pervasive, and they refers to the work of researchers who have shown that when some elements of this form of organization do occur they tend to display a combination of new and traditional features (e.g. Armstrong et al. 1994; Ruigrok et al. 1999; Hill, Martin, and Harris 2000).

This chapter contributes to this tradition of analysis which focuses on the nature, scope, and implications of the attack on bureaucracy and the advocacy of non-bureaucratic, market-type structures and relationships. It does this not by undermining or questioning the critique of bureaucracy or the advocated alternative, but by problematizing the polarity (bureaucracy/non-bureaucracy) itself. An objective of the chapter is to illustrate the complexity of the relationship in practice between bureaucracy and its claimed opposite; the enterprising non-bureaucratic form of organization.

By stressing this complexity I am not referring here simply to the simultaneous and deliberately designed coexistence of both forms of organization. Over recent years and to an increasing degree, the UK Government for example has pursued a twin track approach to organizations in the public sector, and to privatized utilities. While insisting on the primacy of market structures, relationships, and forces, it has simultaneously relied on imposed targets, benchmarks, quality assurance standards, 'value for money', 'regulators' and their requirements, and other devices. All of which involve the imposition of rule-type mechanisms on ostensibly liberated organizations and employees while at the same time (to add to the confusion) insisting on the importance and role of leadership as a way of resolving the resultant tension.

This is an interesting and important area for analysis (see Miller, Chapter 10, this volume) but in this chapter I am referring to something else: to the paradox that organizational attempts to move away from bureaucracy towards enterprise forms of organizations characterized by the dominance of market values and relationships may well be associated with and supported by bureaucratic mechanisms and structures. The chapter points to a new and relatively unnoticed paradox: that apparent and claimed attempts to move away from the much maligned bureaucratic forms of organization towards the necessary and virtuous market form of organization actually rely on bureaucratic mechanisms.

The analysis begins with some general comments on bureaucracy. The chapter then explores one of the major ways in which attempts have been made to build non-bureaucratic types of organization—the installation of management competences and associated 'architectures' of training and development, assessment and performance management which are used to create new, market-responsive, empowered output-focused organizations (the elements defined as the polar opposites of bureaucracies).

Modern critics of bureaucracy accept many of the elements of Weber's definition and regard many of these as good practice for any sort of modern organization. But two elements are identified as central to their critique of bureaucracy. First, that within bureaucracies a variety of procedures (rules, guidelines, procedures, etc.) exist which prescribe and limit how people behave; second, these controlling regulations are centrally determined. Modifications to both these core principles, through increasing flexibility of tasks and roles at the level of the job (or group of jobs) plus decentralization of decision-making authority at the organizational level are central to the new form of organization.

These twin core features of bureaucracy which result in the dominance of centrally designed and enforced regulations mean that obedience and compliance become synonymous with efficiency. A number of pathological consequences are seen to follow: input measures (compliance) are emphasized instead of output measures; predictability and standardization supersede flexibility; and individual discretion in the face of the customer requirements is sacrificed to compliance with centrally determined procedures and processes.

Despite the pervasiveness and power of the onslaught on bureaucracy and the passionate advocacy of the necessity for the virtues of anti-bureaucratic enterprise forms of organization, it is not obvious how these two forms actually differ from each other or coexist in practice. As noted earlier a number of researchers have shown empirically not only that the new form organization is less pervasive than claimed, but more significantly that elements of the new form of organization coexist with traditional forms of control—what Warhurst and Thompson have called 'dual structures'—that is organizations which combine elements of the new with elements of traditional forms (Warhurst and Thompson 1998).

It is therefore far from obvious or necessary that new forms of organization or organizations which seek to install elements of the non-bureaucratic type of organization will necessarily escape or differ from all features of the maligned bureaucratic form. How far do attempts to escape from bureaucracy through the installation of core elements of the new type of organization actually require and assume bureaucratic forms and elements?

In what follows I discuss the detailed empirical implications of the design and installation of management competences—which is fundamental to the attempt to move from the bureaucratic form to the enterprising form of organization and to create a market-based enterprising form of organization (and which is seen as such by its advocates). Management competences offer a particularly interesting way of exploring attempts to design new forms of anti-bureaucratic types of organization since they represent an attempt to construct and constitute a new type of manager—a manager who is aligned with and reflective of the values (enterprise, autonomy, etc.) of the enterprise form of organization. The new manager is the corner stone of the new organization being the final stage in the process of *translation* from business strategy, to organization, and to individual manager.

In this project I draw on work I conducted with Paul du Gay into the nature and implications of recent interest in identifying and installing management competences. The main cases consisted of a health trust (HealthCo), a cosmetics retailer (CosmeticsCo), a university (EducationCo), and a publicly owned communications organization (CommunicationsCo).

The New Enterprising Organization and the New Manager

Our respondents—senior managers and human resources (HR) specialists and middle level managers—were clear that the achievement of the new organization depended on the creation of new managers, with distinctive qualities which mirrored the defining features of the new non-bureaucratic organization: flexibility, customer-responsiveness, and enterprise. Senior managers' interest in identifying and implementing management competences within their organizations was closely and directly linked to their ambitions fundamentally to change their organizations, to make them more competitive, more efficient, and more market-focused.

Furthermore, they insisted that the need for managers with new qualities (which could only be achieved through the installation of management competences) was a central element of their attempt to move away from hierarchy and bureaucracy and towards more responsive, client-centred, commercially focused forms of organization which they saw as radically opposed to the previous emphasis on bureaucratic values of standardization, central control, and uniformity. Central to the achievement of this new form of organization was the need to redefine the nature of management and the attitudes and behaviour of managers through the installation of novel management competences.

The development of management competences by the central HR function of CommunicationsCo was explicitly and directly connected to the achievement of the newly defined strategic objectives of the business. Business targets were established within the business planning cycle to support the overall objectives through key 'metrics': the allocation of profit targets, cost ratios, business volumes and incomes, and customer and staff satisfaction levels. But business targets needed to be translated into appropriate management action, and the new management competences were seen as the major way of connecting individual behaviour to the achievement of these targets by defining and encouraging appropriate sorts of behaviour. Four key defining criteria were used to ensure the value and relevance of each of the new competences, and these criteria reveal the purposes and nature of these attempts to redefine management within the new organization:

(1) that they enable the business to develop timely and appropriate training to support business objectives;
(2) that they encourage managers to develop a sense of 'ownership' of their own (appropriate) development;
(3) that they ensured the effectiveness of training and development initiatives to be measured and assessed; and
(4) that they make available to staff a set of standards that enable them to 'know what they are there to do', as well as how to do it.

At the point of privatization, we inherited an organization built on technical excellence—engineers, predominantly. Now the pressure is on because we have introduced performance related pay which demands a lot of interaction. For people who in the past would have little or no contact on that basis, it is challenging. We had a totally new range of skills to acquire that we never needed before, we had a new management style. Managers were also involved in 'getting people out' and counselling, and again new skills were needed. There have been massive changes, and some managers are struggling to change. Hopefully the ones that are left won't find it too difficult. (Senior manager, CommunicationsCo)

Within this organization the new competences were also seen as a key support of the newly established strategic business units (SBUs). These had been devised as a way of breaking the power of the (bureaucratic) centre—as a means of ensuring that the separate product businesses responded not to central dictat but to the demands of the markets they served. Relations with the centre were reduced to those established within the business planning agreements specifying performance levels and targets. The SBUs were necessarily allocated a degree of autonomy. However the establishment of SBUs (a common feature of the move to a non-bureaucratic form of organization as noted earlier) was recognized as a potential source of divisiveness ('silo thinking'), so the competency framework was intended to reduce this danger of loss of central control and common standards through the development and imposition of a single set of generic competences as 'a strong unifying factor' to establish a shared 'understanding' of standards and expectations. But a 'strong unifying factor' could be seen as another way of describing centrally defined and imposed expectations and norms.

At HealthCo, senior managers were under pressure to respond positively to the development of an internal market in health care provision. Governmental policy changes in the early 1990s brought devolved budgets and required a higher degree of management involvement in organizations previously characterized by centralized planning and budgeting. At the operational level, employees were formed into independent multidisciplinary teams, and the new chief executive aspired to change the Health Trust into an organization where, 'people moved faster, were more flexible and less expensive'. He wanted the management competences to 'break down traditional demarcations, destroy bureaucracy and change the culture'.

The competences framework was connected to the achievement of a fundamental change of strategic focus—'from a professionally-driven service to a customer-driven service' (as the chief executive put it). Competences were presented as a means to encourage managers to focus on customers' needs, and to develop new more flexible ways of working within reduced budgets. The 'new manager'—*pace* the competences—was someone who understood the vision of HealthCo, and who could achieve high performance through the people s/he managed. The new values operationalized through the competences were seen as quite distinct from traditional, professional health care sector values:

The aim of implementing competences is to ensure that everyone within the trust is giving an effective contribution to the business of the trust, to change the culture of the organization from one of public body to a culture which is more business like and more customer orientated. If we don't provide the service, then somebody else will and we will be out of business. (HR manager, HealthCo)

Once again competences were used not simply to ensure managers and staff behaved in accordance with the new form of organization (flexible, enterprising, etc.) but also simultaneously to ensure that despite the loss of central control and the requirement that managers acted with greater freedom and authority—inherent elements of the new form of organization—they still abided by centrally defined standards. The CEO stressed that the competences would help achieve the organization's goals by developing a 'basic guiding structure' to align the organization's objectives with individuals' behaviours.

The development of competences at EducationCo was explicitly linked to wider changes, among which were increased competition for students, new technological developments, and increased cost pressures. Changes in the higher education market [*sic*] required a speed of organizational response and greater flexibility and customer-responsiveness which in turn made the link between senior management capability and sustained organizational performance all the more critical. Senior management insisted that management competences would enable the institution to make this key transition to a market-centric commercially focused organization. But here again, senior management were not confident that managers and business (or academic) units would be able to manage themselves appropriately within this decentralized and empowered structure without the centre setting standards and ensuring their achievement. The stated purposes of the competences were: to identify the qualities necessary for current and future university needs; to ensure that these formed the basis of assessment and development of senior managers; and to ensure 'the continuing capability and readiness of the university and its individual units and managers to manage effectively in a rapidly changing environment'.

At CosmeticsCo, the primary rationale for the introduction of competences was to build a coherent and equitable structure for a rapidly growing business. The competences were seen as a way of building a HR strategy, providing a unifying logic for the first time. The competency framework was presented as a way of increasing overall organizational effectiveness by supplying a basis for the systematization of the organization's previously ad hoc recruitment, selection, assessment, and appraisal. Again, as in all four of our case study organizations, the competent manager was defined through character. And 'character' was defined in terms of accepting and taking responsibility for self-regulation within a competency framework:

We have got 'Personal Quality' as one category; people talk about the need to be enthusiastic, if you want to be highly effective in your job, you need to take the initiative and be self-confident. (HR manager, CosmeticsCo)

In all the research organizations where management competences were being introduced, the competences were seen as a major means of achieving the desired shift towards the new, anti-bureaucratic, decentralized, enterprise form of organization. We will discuss how this was achieved in more detail below. But the competences were more than this. They were also a means of ensuring that despite the necessary loss of central control inevitably associated with a move away from bureaucracy and towards more empowered, decentralized, market-centric organizational units (where strategy and behaviour were driven by market pressures and customer requirements), nevertheless central control was not lost but retained through centrally designed and installed competences aimed at ensuring predictable and standardized behaviour within the decentralized business units even when rules and procedures were apparently abandoned to individual initiative—hence the emphasis on a 'basic guiding structure', or a 'strong unifying factor'.

How the Competences were Used

Competences and competency frameworks were used to define all the key processes which impact on how managers behave: to define roles—which were specified carefully in terms of the level or standard expected against each competence—to assess performance in roles—against these behavioural statements of required level of performance—to select and assess the potential incumbents of roles—in terms of their demonstration of their achievement of defined standards of behaviour against competences or potential to develop them—and to train and develop managers for the new roles. They were used to establish job descriptions, define performance standards, to create route maps for career planning—to establish the generic standards by which jobs could be defined and compared, performance could be assessed, personal development organized, training designed, and promotion decided.

Furthermore, competences, it was argued, would achieve a major impact on managers' behaviour and performance not through externally imposed rules—not by insisting on obedience to inflexible rules—but by self regulation, control from *inside*. Competences, we were told, did not specify what managers should do—for who could or should say in advance what managers should do in all and every changing circumstance—instead they specified what managers should *achieve*. The competences would be used to assist each individual's self-assessment, initially alone, then with the manager. This process would lead to what one senior manager called the 'Holy Grail' of management—a way of achieving '*organizational* capabilities through the definition of *individual* capabilities'—a mechanism to shape the conduct and attitudes of individual line managers and to ensure they are consistent with and supportive of the priorities of senior managers while preserving the managers' apparent autonomy and discretion.

At HealthCo, all management roles were profiled in terms of the necessary level of competence required in defined fields. This framework then provided the basis for integration of all aspects of the organization's HR activities: recruitment, selection, appraisal, training and development, career planning, and job evaluation. Each competency had an associated development strategy, and this process was thought to provide a 'tool' for people to identify their job requirements and development needs. All managers were assessed against the competence profile of their jobs, and each had a competence-based development plan.

The chief executive's intentions were clear: 'The whole process is to make the organization move forward to meet the business objectives of the Trust . . . the (competences) will be used to ensure that people meet those objectives'.

The CEO insisted that the competences were intended to integrate what the organization was trying to achieve through the development of a basic competence structure which ensured that managers' behaviour is in line with organizational objectives. The competences were seen as fundamental to the achievement of a basic change of focus (or change of culture)—from a 'professionally driven service' to a 'customer driven service'—this change was seen as necessary in order to succeed competitively, and to achieve the business plan.

(HealthCo) was totally resistant to change—dinosaurs, left wing and elitist— but demarcations are slowly blurring and we are challenging their (clinicians') practices so that people are beginning to think differently. The type of manager that the competences encourage is someone who understands the vision of the business, and the strategies of the business and who achieves these through the people s/he manages. This isn't how managers behave at the moment. The competences are a major element in the attempt to control and shift power from, the professionals and to place emphasis on new organizational values.

At HealthCo, competences redefined and clarified management roles, enabling managers to assess their development within the new framework. The benefits for the organization were that management roles were now more 'aligned' with the new business objectives, standards, and values. Managerial performance could be tracked against these new and explicit output standards through the language of the competences. Competences provided a link between business objectives, role requirements and individual development.

The competences are about the behaviour that we believe will enable us to succeed—the commercial behaviours, the marketing behaviours, the team building behaviours. (Chief Executive, HealthCo)

The actual competences developed within HealthCo are typical. A total of thirty-four competences were 'identified' and organized under four headings: 'Marketing', 'Team effectiveness', 'Personal effectiveness', and 'Service implementation'. These are subdivided into sets of specific constituent competences. For example, 'Marketing' consists of nine specifics, including 'Living the aims and values', 'Building credibility', and 'Meeting agreed service requirements'. Each competence is presented at six graduated levels, all of which are specified in concrete, behavioural terms. For example 'Living the aims and values', level one, is: 'shows sincerity, demonstrates loyalty to others, gets involved, behaves consistently, engenders trust'. This list of competences, classified into a set of 'families', with each competence organized into a series of levels, and each level very precisely defined in terms of the behaviours which indicate achievement, was typical of each research organization.

At EducationCo, the competences were identified in four clusters, each subdivided into constituent competences in the usual way:

- Interpersonal: leadership, communication skills, and team membership
- Visionary: strategic vision, flexibility and adaptability, and managing change
- Information: analytical skills, external focus, and student client and customer orientation
- Results Orientation: motivation and drive, business awareness, and technological awareness.

Each competence was associated with a list of positive and negative behaviours, to make assessment easier. These competences supplied a basis for discussion of organizational objectives and the necessary managerial qualities and requirements and how these inter-related. They were also used to understand and make explicit and manageable the implications of potentially radical organizational change for senior management roles and skills.

At EducationCo, competences were used to guide selection for senior management posts. The competence-based assessment of senior managers conditioned their development and training, allowed assessments for career planning, and the identification of a pool of selected managers for succession planning. They enabled the design of what was described by personnel professionals as an 'integrated competence architecture':

It is embedded in a whole process of change, where things are building on each other, and gradually making the whole thing more systematic, rational, and describable. (Vice-Chancellor, EducationCo)

At CosmeticsCo, competences were launched as an integral aspect of a new appraisal system. At workshops, participants were informed of the required competences for each role, and asked to consider their relevance and application to the organizational mission statement, departmental objectives, and key tasks in order to forge a connection between role content, the behaviours or competences of each role, and organizational objectives. Although initially used as a way of making performance appraisal more 'systematic' and better 'aligned' with corporate goals, it was expected that the competences would soon be incorporated into guidelines for selection and succession planning:

People are very excited about it, the ability to tie it in with the values process. How do we train all the values, how do you integrate it into daily life? There was a very favourable reaction to the possibility of integrating that initiative into the competence programme. It is almost a very subtle, imperceptible change. It is imperceptible from day to day, but you would expect some of that kind of level of values and social changes. Whether it would be worth the investment, or the training process involved, I don't know, but then again it is about how you change people's fundamental nature. (Head of corporate services, CosmeticsCo)

Senior managers insisted that management competences were central to the move away from bureaucracy—by articulating and supporting the new enterprising customer-focused form of organization. So it would be reasonable to assume that the ways in which they are used and the purposes for which they are used would also be clearly and fundamentally different from the forms of control employed in traditional organizations. But this is less clear.

Advocates of competences insist that they represent a new way of conceptualizing and achieving the competent manager. Traditional ways of thinking about and controlling management performance focused on input measures (qualifications, experience, personality, etc.) as the means of predicting potential capability, and regulation and task definition as the way of controlling performance. But, these advocates insist, neither of these is appropriate to decentralized, empowered customer-focused organizations. Now performance is ensured by the clear precise and operational identification of the sorts of consequences and achievements for which managers are responsible—as measured by their managers or by 360 degree feedback—the performance outputs which competent managers have been shown to display. These achievements are defined in terms of the implications and consequences of behaviour, not simply by behaviour alone. Success is defined not by how managers behave but by how they are judged by others to have behaved.

Despite the frequently claimed differences between competences and traditional forms of control—the former identifying the *consequences* of managers' behaviour ('outputs'), the latter prescribing how managers should behave ('inputs')—it is not obvious that this difference represents a significant alternative to central control, and possible that it represents little more than another form of it. It is true that competences do not specify in detail what managers should do in various circumstances as bureaucratic regulation does; but this difference may be more apparent than real and may in fact not so much offer an alternative to bureaucratic control as a replacement of it by a control based on the definition of outputs which differs from traditional forms of regulation in two ways.

First, by prescribing identified consequences rather than specifying how to behave, competences deliberately introduce ambiguity where previously there was clarity. Rules are clearly followed or broken; but there are now no rules governing how managers should behave, just clearly defined expectations they must meet: how they do this is up to them (see du Gay, Chapter 2, this volume). Second, whereas rules externalize the institution of control and authority (written specific behavioural rules) and so retain authority and crucially responsibility with the rule-maker (for if following a rule leads to poor performance the responsibility lies with those who designed the rule not with those who followed it) competences insist that authority for achieving defined standards rests not with those who designed the competence framework but with the manager. Hence the constant emphasis on empowerment, commitment, and involvement. So, while rules are intended to require *obedience*, competences, which depend on managers' willingness to achieve defined levels of performance, require *commitment*. Competences thus engage purposively and strategically with the subjectivity of their managers.

We'll be explaining the model in terms of the importance of behaviour, and how it is important to consider the way you do things, as opposed to just doing them. (Senior Manager, HealthCo)

So competences require that managers internalize control and responsibility, practise self control, and develop commitment—the willingness to control themselves in unspecified ways which if successful will achieve the desired effects specified by the competence standard which will then be measured: self regulation in the service of organizational purpose. Thus managers become responsible for translating the specified desired and ultimately measured effect into their own modes of behaviour—they become responsible for ensuring their compliance with the competences. It seems that 'becoming a competent manager is equated with becoming a better, more autonomous, accountable self' (du Gay, Salaman, and Rees.1996: 275).

But what does this mean in practice? It means that managers were clearly and formally informed that they were expected to behave in ways which were consistent with centrally defined, installed, monitored, explicit, detailed, and finely specified standards of behaviour defined in terms of specified effects and consequences covering a number of qualities at a variety of clearly described levels. But they were not told (as in bureaucratic forms of control) precisely how to respond to specific and particular situations; their decisions on how to behave were theirs alone. But how they behaved—which was their decision—must in all situations be consistent with clearly specified explicit standards. They now are responsible for working back from identified ends rather than for using clearly identified means (rule-based) to achieve ambiguous ends.

So in some respects competences differ fundamentally from conventional forms of regulation—they are opaque with respect to how managers should behave to achieve the specified effects, but very clear on the effects they have to achieve; they shift responsibility for the achievement of these effects from the institution to the manager. But neither of these differences can be seen as liberating the manager from centralized control: in fact in many respects they intensify this control and make it more burdensome by making the manager responsible for what was hitherto an organizational responsibility. Rules allow both managers and their appraisers to assess compliance with the rule. Competences allow no such certainty. It is the manager's responsibility to ensure that s/he behaves in a way so as to produce the outcomes which show compliance with the competence standards— still set however by the centre. But the burden of translating competence into behaviour in any instance is the manager's. It's true the modern manager is not subject to detailed manuals and procedures: it is true s/he is free to exercise personal discretion in the pursuit of organizational goals; but rules can be a safeguard: they tell you what to do, they make success simple: obedience, compliance.

There are now fewer rules to guide action but there are still standards—or competences—which retrospectively are applied by others to assess managers' compliance with expected behaviour, and which are applied by the manager if s/he wishes to display compliance with new expectations. The difference is less to do with a move away from rules per se and more to do with a move towards a new form of rule—which determines and specifies the outcome of actions while refusing to specify what actions should be taken. And the new type of rule by delegating authority for action requires self-regulation.

I am looking to use competences as a means of having a much clearer idea about what we expect of people. Organizations generally are nowhere near specific enough . . . [we need] to be for more specific about what we are looking for and targeting, so that it can be assessed. (Senior Manager, CosmeticsCo)

Another feature of competences which allows the achievement of a complex structure of inter-related and centrally controlled elements occurred in many of the research organizations: the development of a complex integrated infrastructure of the processes and frameworks which determine, assess, develop, measure, reward, and organize managers' behaviour. An attraction of competences to senior managers and HR professionals is that they supply a way in which these core processes, which define roles and structure assessment and recruitment, and thus establish the training and development curriculum, can be discussed and integrated within a single and unifying language.

This language allows the redefinition of the nature of management through a series of integrated processes ('architectures'), which reshape selection, appraisal, training and performance management in ways that are aligned with the image of the 'new organization' and its redefined purposes. Competence permits the apparent integration and consistency of key HR frameworks and processes. A competence architecture is an example of the type of complex mechanism, 'through which it becomes possible to link calculations at one place with action at another, not through the direct imposition of a form of conduct by force, but through a delicate affiliation of a loose assemblage of agents and agencies into a functioning network' (Miller and Rose 1993: 83).

These architectures are also important for the opportunity they offer to senior management and HR professionals to achieve a type of central monitoring of and control over key processes impacting on management behaviour to a degree never achieved within the traditional bureaucracy. Because they now share a 'common language'—the language of competences and families of competences and of different levels and different standards—they permit highly detailed measurement of job performance, of job content, of assessment standards, and critically the use of competences allows the integration of these various processes. All roles are described in terms of competences. Different types of role—technical, sales, managerial, require different combinations of competences. All managers are routinely assessed—often by 360 degree appraisal—against their job competences. Promotions are based on formal assessment of a candidate's ability to display the competence standards of the role. Succession planning employs data on candidates' competence achievements. And training and development targets the competences associated with different job levels.

We have a paradox here. The new enterprise form of organization, according to its advocates, is built on devolution, empowerment, customer focus, market orientation, flexibility, and responsiveness. The old bureaucratic form of organization was built on central control and the imposition of inflexible rules which destroyed commitment and demanded mere obedience. The development of competence architectures seeks to ensure that managers behave in ways which are customer-focused, commercially aware, flexible, responsive, etc.—that is non-bureaucratically. They define and tightly control standards, collect data, define key organizational and personal processes (promotion, succession) control key decisions. Yet these architectures display many of the features and intentions of conventional centralized bureaucratic forms of control. Indeed they allow the extension of such control through integrated centrally designed processes which exceeds what was possible in a rule-based regime where the processes of manager selection, appraisal and assessment, were conducted by different sets of criteria. The language—the content of the control—may be different but the mechanisms are similar. They differ only in their greater comprehensiveness, scope, and consistency.

Finally as well as defining the qualities of the 'new manager', competences emphasize improvement in the performance of the manager. In every organization the competences were centrally associated with the *intensification* of management work through clearer 'stretch' targets, personal development, assessment, and monitoring of improvement. Competences once again supply a framework and process for the management of improvement: explicit standards, dimensions, measurement, monitoring, and development support.

The New Manager: Conclusion

The attempt within the new organization to 'make up' a new manager, in many ways represents a radical break with traditional ways of controlling managers' behaviour, most importantly in that one of the key assumptions and purposes of competences is the move from compliance to commitment, from control from the outside to control from the inside, from detailed prescriptions on actions to detailed description of outputs. With competences, it becomes the manager's responsibility to manage herself, to accept the good sense of the approach and accept responsibility for ensuring that she achieves the defined output standards and her development in terms of the requirements ('standards') of her management role. Competences become part of the government of the organization through becoming part of the government of the individual: external requirements become personal issues and priorities. Competences allow the translation of organizational priorities into the preferences and priorities of individual managers in their professional lives and careers. To the extent that managers see themselves as responsible for ensuring their continuing marketability in terms of their employers' aspirations, then competences become part of managers' 'self-steering' mechanisms, an element in their own self-regulation. Thus free and autonomous individuals can be managed while preserving their formal autonomy (Miller and Rose 1993: 92)

Competences thus redefine the relationship between the manager and the employer. Previous models of the employment relationship placed emphasis on '. . . the psychological contract of security for long term-commitment and loyalty along with an infrastructure of training and development' (Mabey, Salaman, and Storey 1999: 270). Now the managers' employment and security are dependent on them taking personal responsibility for identifying their own development needs (through feedback against job profile requirements) and successfully developing themselves (and others) in terms of the organization's requirements. In short, job and career security now comes not only from displaying the competences essential to the organization's new strategy but also from managers being able to relate to their employer in terms of these qualities. Managers are only secure as long as they manage their relationship with their employer in broadly the same way that the employer seeks to relate to its clients: through marketing, client management, customer-focus, and continuous improvement. The application of competences embodies the conversion of the employer/manager relationship into one of purchaser/supplier. The competent manager not only must be prepared to display the sorts of behaviours required for the achievement of the new business strategy, but must also adopt an attitude towards herself as if she was a micro-cosmic business—marketing herself, developing her assets, investing in herself, designing an improvement plan, developing a strategy to ensure career and job security.

Nevertheless despite these significant differences there are also ways in which the break or contrast with bureaucracy can be over-stated. The competent manager, like the bureaucratic manager, is exposed to rules. It is true they are different sorts of rules: output not input, internal not external, post-action not pre-action; descriptive not prescriptive. But they remain rules nevertheless—rules which are clearly, precisely, and formally specified; rules which may be more insidious in that they hold the manager responsible for designing and managing her own behaviour in order to achieve outcomes consistent with the organization's purposes. If it is the existence of rules, centrally determined behaviour-controlling rules which is the essence of bureaucracy, then the new organization may be less non-bureaucratic than its advocates claim. And in insisting on the key rule: that managers regulate themselves towards the achievement of defined standards—the new organization may not have superseded bureaucracy but have found its fullest expression. The same can be said for the ways competences are used to establish architectures of interrelated and integrated frameworks, standards, and processes governing every aspect of managers' work and development. These architectures offer senior management, and their HR professionals, unprecedented opportunities to monitor and structure what managers do and how managers are managed and processed by supplying integrated HR systems and a common language and standards of assessment. It is true that the content of these systems consists of outputs and values which derive from the new model organization; but the mechanisms of monitoring, definition, assessment, and control although enhanced by the new levels of integration and coherence, and by IT support, do not represent a move away from or a negation of, bureaucratic control but its final and perhaps most complete achievement.

References

Armstrong, P., Marginson, P., Edwards, P., and Pucell, J. (1994). Divisionalization, Trade Unionism and Corporate Control: Findings from the Second Company Level Industrial Relations Survey, Paper at 12th Annual International Labour Process conference, Aston.

du Gay, P. (1991). 'Enterprise culture and the ideology of excellence', *New Formations.* 13; 45–62.

du Gay, P. (1996). *Consumption and Identity at Work.* London: Sage.

du Gay, P., and Salaman, G. (1992). 'The cult(ure) of the customer'. *Journal of Management Studies;* 29/5. 615–33.

du Gay P., Salaman, G., and Rees B. (1996). 'The conduct of management and the management of conduct: contemporary managerial discourse and the constitution of the "competent" manager'. *Journal of Management Studies.* 33/3; 263–82.

Foucault, M. (1980). *Power/Knowledge.* Harvester: Brighton.

Guest, D. (1990). 'Human resource management and the American dream', *Journal of Management Studies.* 27; 377–97.

Guest, D. (1992). 'Right enough to be dangerously wrong', in G. Salaman, (ed.), *Human Resource Strategies.* London: Sage, 5–19.

Hill, S., Martin, R., and Harris, M. (2000). 'Decentralization, integration and the post-bureaucratic form of organization: the case of R&D'. *Journal of Management Studies.* 37/4; 563–85.

Jackson, B. (1996). 'Re-engineering the sense of Self'. *Journal of Management Studies.* 33; 571–90.

Mabey, C., Salaman, G., and Storey, J. (1998). *Human Resource Management.* Oxford: Blackwell.

Miller, P. and Rose, N. (1988). 'The Tavistock programme, the government of subjectivity and social life'. *Sociology*. 22; 171–93.

Miller, P. and Rose, N. (1990). 'Governing economic life', *Economy and Society*. 19; 1–31.

Miller, P. and Rose, N. (1993). 'Governing economic life', in M. Gane and T. Johnson (eds), *Foucault's New Domains*. London: Routledge, 75–106.

Rose, N. (1990). *Governing The Soul*. London: Routledge.

Ruigrok, W., Pettigrew, A., Peck, S., and Whittington, R. (1999). 'Corporate restructuring and new forms of organizing: evidence from Europe'. *Management International Review*. 39/2; 41–64.

Warhurst, C. and Thompson, P. (1998). 'Hands, hearts and minds: changing work and workers at the end of the century', in P. Thompson and C. Warhurst (eds), *Workplaces of the Future*. Basingstoke: Macmillan.

PART 3

Bureaucracy and Public Management

7

A Service to the Public: The Containment of Ethical and Moral Conflicts by Public Bureaucracies

Paul Hoggett

The Poverty of Pragmatism

The rhetoric of pragmatism has become a defining characteristic of public service reform under Britain's (New) Labour government. Exemplified in policies such as the Private Finance Initiative and Best Value, it construes choice between public and private as essentially a matter of efficacy—what works is what's best, or so the rhetoric goes (on 'Best Value' see Miller, Chapter 10, this volume). This rhetoric has been subject to sustained critique from several directions. Some (Pollock, Shaoul, and Rowland 2001) have argued that it is simply a camouflage for the further penetration of global market forces into public life, a continuation of Thatcherism but in a more publicly acceptable clothing. Others have focused more upon pragmatism as the cloak beneath which a bland and homogenizing managerialism has spread its tentacles across public life (Clarke and Newman 1997).

In this chapter, I want to pursue a slightly different critique. I wish to examine how this rhetoric of pragmatism denudes the very notions of 'public' and 'publicness' of much of their complexity and richness and, as a consequence, radically devalues the work of those engaged in what was traditionally known as 'public service'. I believe the 'what works' perspective is part of a discourse which is dangerously misleading, one which insists that there is nothing unique about the public sphere, that it is simply a particular way of organizing the delivery of goods and services for consumers. The problem is, so the story goes, that advocates of the 'public is best' position are wedded to outmoded, bureaucratic approaches to this task which are currently being swept away by processes of modernization. The private sector, because of the discipline of the market and competition, has been quicker to abandon such approaches in favour of more flexible and therefore more efficient and responsive ones.

The managerialist inflection in Labour's pragmatism has also been responsible for an almost wilful confusion between 'bureaucracy', the noun, describing a particular form of organization designed for a particular purpose, and 'bureaucratic', the adjective, describing a style of organizing that any organization might adopt irrespective of its purpose. Paul du Gay (2000) draws our attention to the way in which the first meaning, that is, bureaucracy as a unique kind of moral institution for the organization of public affairs, which is committed to norms of impersonality, neutrality, and objectivity, has been largely lost. Many for-profit organizations are bureaucratic but, if we are to preserve the distinction we seek to make, they are not actual bureaucracies any more than some militaristically organized firms constitute a militia. In this chapter, I want to build upon some of du Gay's arguments about bureaucracy's particular purposes—what is it about the requirements for effective government in contemporary society that make bureaucracy necessary? I will argue that modern government and the state apparatus that supports it has, among other things, two unique characteristics. It is the site for the continuous contestation of public purposes and a means of containing the moral ambivalence of citizens. Such characteristics, in addition to those mentioned at the beginning of this section, serve to remind us that government, and the public sector, which supports it, is primarily a site for the enactment of particular kinds of social relations rather than a site for the delivery of goods and services. To reduce it to the latter is to commodify such relationships, to strip them of their moral and ethical meaning and potential.

Bureaucracy Misconstrued

The Fetishization of Service Delivery

Building on Hood's classic examination of the universalizing claims of the New Public Management (Hood 1991), I suggest that there are four distinct sets of administrative values underlying effective bureaucracy—keep it visible and accountable, keep it lean and purposeful, keep it honest and fair, keep it robust and resilient (see also Chapters 1 and 3 by Goodsell and Armbrüster, respectively, this volume). Each set of core values has its own standard of failure— imperviousness (avoidance of responsibility, opacity of authority), waste, malversation (unfairness, bias, corruption), and catastrophe (risk, breakdown, collapse). By concentrating virtually all of its fire on the second set of values, public service reform in the United Kingdom has conducted itself as if the government were little different from running Marks and Spencer, that is, simply a means of delivering goods and services. The necessary proceduralism of bureaucracy in allocating scarce resources (to support health, subsistence, spatial mobility, etc.) by using consistent, fair, and therefore legitimate means is obscured. Furthermore by reducing the question of 'what works' to the question of comparative organizational performance, the systemic and diachronic dimensions of 'publicness' are stripped away (Maile and Hoggett 2001). A service such as a bus service or parks maintenance does not exist in some kind of contextual vacuum rather it is situated within a matrix of spatial and non-spatial communities, developing over time, and which constitute the self-governing fabric of any society. Government policies and programmes can make or break this fabric (contributing directly to risk and social breakdown) and the effectiveness (as opposed to efficiency) of government stands or falls on the kinds of relationships which are fostered or undermined here.[1]

This inability to distinguish between bureaucracy (noun) as a method of organizing public affairs and bureaucratic (adjective) as a style of organizing that dominated the middle decades of the twentieth century has sown some confusion among critics of organizational and cultural life. In his discussion of writers like MacIntyre and Bauman, du Gay (2000) notes their trenchant criticisms of that bureaucratic state of mind which, they argue, embodies an instrumental rationality through which technical questions become split from ethical and aesthetic ones. Although du Gay does not make this point, one of the weaknesses of such writers' position is that it obscures what is becoming only too clear in our emerging global economy. It is not bureaucracy per se which is responsible for instrumentalism or hierarchy. So-called 'post-bureaucratic firms' (e.g. network based, contractual, and inter-organizational rather than hierarchical) actually constitute a more subtle and thoroughgoing expression of this very same rationality precisely because of the way in which the further extension of centralized command in a firm like Benetton is *concealed* by the new forms of operational decentralization (Clegg 1990). In other words, the new forms of decentralized organization actually correspond to a reassertion of hierarchy.[2]

The problem, therefore, is not bureaucracy per se, indeed, and here I see my argument complementing and possibly extending du Gay's analysis. I see public bureaucracies as potentially the epitome of a substantive rather than instrumental rationality; the one place perhaps where questions of technique ('what works') and questions of value stand a chance of being integrated.

Bureaucracy and Contested Purpose

Varieties of Bureaucracy

Bureaucracy is the particular form of organization assumed by the state. But the state can assume many forms and can serve very different purposes. The bureaucracy of the Bismarkian state was not the same as the bureaucracy of the post-war German welfare state. There can be as many different kinds of bureaucracy as there are different kinds of state. Indeed, it follows that there are forms of bureaucracy, which we have barely yet imagined, particularly bureaucracies which have been subject to extended forms of democratization.[3]

The post-war welfare state also assumed distinctive forms and had distinctive purposes. Claus Offe (1984) argued that the welfare state was an essentially contradictory formation which, unlike previous state formations, had to meet the requirements not only of capital but also of labour. On the one hand, it stood as the crowning achievement of the labour movement, but on the other it played a key role in sustaining the post-war economic system by producing an educated, disciplined, and healthy workforce, by sustaining the existing gendered division of labour, and so on. More so than any of its predecessors, the post-war welfare state needed to continuously work to sustain its legitimacy and it did this in two ways. First, it had to be seen to be committed to social justice via redistribution; second, it had to offer a modicum of democratic accountability primarily through the development of forms of local and regional government.

The welfarist commitment to social justice strengthened the existing constitutional liberal emphasis upon impartiality; to the avoidance of nepotism, cronyism, and patronage was added the demand to treat all citizens the same and to avoid judgement contaminated by prejudice. In reality, this imperative often rubbed up against the disciplinary function of the welfare state, one which encouraged distinctions to be made by housing officials, social workers, and many others between, for example, the 'deserving' and 'undeserving' poor (Henderson and Karn 1987). Nevertheless for many years the welfare state, in Britain through institutions such as the National Health Service, was referred to unselfconsciously as a system which embodied universalistic principles.

Much has changed over the last two decades. Not only has social policy become increasingly subordinate to economic policy (Levitas 1999) as the balance of power between capital and labour has shifted decisively towards the former, but new social identities accompanying the development of an increasingly plural and cosmopolitan society, have encouraged the development of new forms of 'recognition' politics alongside the old forms of 'redistributive' politics (for a discussion of this in relation to changing regimes of public management, see Clarke, Chapter 9, this volume). This in turn has meant that the universalist claims of the welfare state have became increasingly subject to critique by feminists, among others, both in the realm of political theory (Young 1996) and social policy (Williams 1989). Such writers have argued that a 'false universalism' has actually acted as a cover for a set of masculinist, colonialist, and other assumptions. More recently still the universalism of the welfare state has been subject to critique by advocates of 'particularism', particularly forms of cultural particularism built upon ethnic or religious identities (Spicker 1993). From this perspective the state should be able to respond to the needs of particular groups, otherwise their economic and social rights remain formal rights only. So, for example, it is argued that an educational system which does not allow for denominational schools is universalistic in name only as it denies whole sections of society the education they want.

I have argued that the tension between universalism and particularism is inherent and irresolvable (Thompson and Hoggett 1996) but, as such, it is just one instance of the conflictual nature of public purpose. A radically pluralist position argues for the existence of a set of core human values (such as liberty and equality) which cannot be wholly reconciled with one another. Conventional liberal political theory both recognizes such plurality and obscures it. It obscures it via a rationality which assumes that, through processes of argumentation, a common will or higher truth will eventually emerge so long as people are capable of being non-partisan and judge solely from the viewpoint of reason. In practice, this has led liberal political philosophers to be sceptical of the value of impassioned argument. In opposing such an approach Chantal Mouffe (1993) insists that 'politics in a modern democracy must accept division and conflict as unavoidable, and the reconciliation of rival claims and conflicting interests can only be partial and provisional' (p. 113). This 'agonistic' concept of politics as struggle is also present in the work of Hannah Arendt. Speaking of Arendt, Bonnie Honig notes 'she theorizes a practice that is disruptive, agonistic, and, most importantly, never over' (Honig 1993: 9). I hardly need to point out that this is *not* a view of democracy particularly close to the heart of the New Labour project.

Conflict, impassioned and ongoing, is an essential condition for vitality in public life. But, and this is crucial for our thinking about bureaucracy, it also follows that the public sphere (which includes the organized apparatus of government) is the necessary embodiment of such conflictual purposes. And whilst different political projects emphasize different values, those that they suppress inevitably return to haunt the political system, typically returning at the level at which policy is implemented. As Lipsky noted, 'a typical mechanism for legislative conflict resolution is to pass on intractable conflicts for resolution (or continued irresolution) at the administrative level' (Lipsky 1980: 41). As a consequence, it is often at the level of 'operations' that unresolved value conflicts are most sharply enacted, public officials and local representatives finding themselves 'living out' rather than 'acting upon' the contradictions of the complex and diverse society in which they live.

Impartiality and Responsiveness

We are always told that Weber's model of bureaucracy is an ideal-type. It is said that the model he provides us with is a theoretical abstraction the purpose of which is to provide an exemplification rather than an empirical description. It follows, the argument continues, that we must keep this in mind when talking about the actual behaviour of such organizations and the actors within them, for the actual behaviour necessarily departs from the ideal type.

du Gay (p. 29) argues that for Weber 'the ethical attributes of the "good bureaucrat"—strict adherence to procedure, acceptance of hierarchical sub- and super-ordination, abnegation of personal moral enthusiasms, commitment to the purposes of the office—are the product of definite ethical practices and techniques . . .'. At first reading this sounds like a recipe for means-oriented action in which questions of purpose, of value, have disappeared from the bureaucrat's horizon—is not this the realm of the amoral technical expert criticized by MacIntyre and others (du Gay 2000: 28). du Gay, however, seeks to come to the defence of Weber. He argues that the value attached to impersonality by Weber must be understood as itself being an expression of democratic equalization and therefore a more ethically advanced form of authority than that based on personal considerations ('grace and favour', nepotism, cronyism, etc.) which characterized organizational life in public and private spheres before the quickening of modernization in the early twentieth century. In other words, the impartiality of the bureaucrat entails 'a trained capacity to treat people as "individual" cases, that is, apart from status and ascription' (du Gay 2000: 42).

Far from being an instrument for the realization of a set of unproblematized ends, du Gay, following Weber, insists that it is precisely because of the problematic nature of the rhetoric of 'ultimate ends' in a radically plural society that bureaucracy is necessary. The 'irreducible plurality of and frequent incommensurability between passionately held "ultimate" moral ends' (du Gay 2000: 31) implies that the state bureaucracy cannot simply be an instrument for the realization of a prescribed set of ends. The bureaucrat, unlike the politician, must cultivate a 'trained indifference' to the discourse of 'ultimate ends' because of an awareness of 'the possible heavy cost of pursuing one of them at the expense of the others' (p. 31). Interestingly enough, du Gay's position here also seems implied in Jessop's (2000) notion of 'requisite variety'. This is what a liberal-pluralist 'ethics of responsibility' is all about. Part of the duty of office of the bureaucrat is to be free, not only of ties to kith, kin, and class but also of 'conscience'. In other words, the bureaucrat must set aside her/his own particular values because of a commitment to the higher purposes of the office. In this sense the apparatus of the state (whether national or local) is not reducible to the particularities of government (which is necessarily dedicated to the pursuit of specific 'party political' ends). In contrast to the totalitarian state, within a pluralist democracy the state must retain a capacity for independence, it is not just the tool of government.

But I think that by this point du Gay finds himself chaffing at the constraints of Weber's rationality. In reality, I suggest, the ideal of 'trained indifference' is simply not possible. Indeed Jessop (2000) prefers a different attitude, one which combines reflexivity and irony, and I will return to this later. Paradoxically our experience of modern bureaucracies over the last several decades suggest that it is an inherently contradictory and unstable phenomenon—segmentalism (i.e. the proliferation of partially autonomous divisional forms of organization referred to these days as 'silos') and informalization (informal strategies for making the system work including, crucially, the use of discretion) are actually constituted by bureaucracy, inherent to its nature rather than an aberrant 'dysfunction' which can be controlled and remedied (Hoggett 1991). Far from being a problem which can be removed these inherent contradictions ensure that bureaucracy remains a dynamic system.

For the public bureaucracy, particularly one subject to increasing forms of professionalization, this has vital consequences. For it means that *the system can only work if actors within it use judgement and discretion*. Thus I would argue that the real art of the bureaucrat lies not so much in practices such as 'declaration of personal interest' or the subordination of one's own wilfulness to procedurality (du Gay 2000: 32) but in the exercise of discretion and the use of judgement in the application of policies to particular cases, or the implementation of policies where there are no precedents, or the operationalization of rule-governed systems in full knowledge that no system can ever provide guidance for every eventuality. Rather than slavish adherence to rule-governed procedures the objectivity of bureaucracy is founded upon the use of judgement in complex, ambiguous, and contested environments that constitute the everyday lived reality of the civil servant, health service professional, or local government official (Vickers 1965).

In other words, I do not think du Gay's analysis gives full due to the radically pluralistic and agonistic nature of modern democracies where one of the 'arts' of government is to pass on to the 'administrative realm' the goal conflicts that it cannot manage. Lipsky, who gave more emphasis to class conflict and social control than to multiculturalism and other forms of social diversity, was nevertheless acutely aware of the way in which street level bureaucrats were left to reconcile such social contradictions. In contrast to the ideal of impartiality, he noted, 'there is often considerable disagreement about what street level bureaucrats should primarily do' (Lipsky 1980: 46). As Hill (1983: 89) once noted, discretion is enhanced because 'policy makers are far from clear what they really want'. In reality, rather than the ideal-typical world, all public bureaucracies operate in this kind of environment— complex, indeterminate, ambiguous, contested, shifting, and so on. If this seems a far cry from the calm and reasoned world of the Bismarkian state bureaucracy this may be because of the comparative absence of fiercely competitive, media-savvy political pluralism and the total absence of a combative, rights-oriented, self-confident citizenship from the picture that Weber surveyed. But, as Jessop (2000) notes, it is also due to the fact that governments are increasingly faced with problems that are beyond their means to resolve.

There are other value contradictions which the public official is required to enact every day. Besides the tension between universalism and particularism, perhaps the most crucial of these concerns is the inherent tension between an ethic of care and an ethic of justice (Mendus 1993). On the one hand a compassionate concern for the individual and his or her plight, and on the other a realization that whatever the merits of this particular case the public official also has a responsibility towards all those potentially equally worthy cases whose claims, because not immediately and physically present, can only be brought to mind abstractly.

New Public Management: Rolling Back the Frontier of Politics

So far I have argued that bureaucracy is necessarily a contested, value saturated institutional space in which ends are constantly being problematized. But, say some, we can agree with you here, but this does not in any way undermine our commitment to Private Finance Initiative, contractorization, agencyism, etc. We agree that the government is the proper site for the contestation of public purpose, but in fact the government will do its job better if it sticks to what it was designed for—making policy—and let others, conversant in the latest management techniques, get on with the operationalization of it. On the face of it this seems unobjectionable. But it obscures just how deeply 'government' has become synonymous with Whitehall. Multi-level government in much of the United Kingdom[4] has been effectively destroyed by two decades of neo-Liberal attrition. Local government has been discarded, bereft of vitality, lacking any strong independent voice, no longer a power in the land; along with the ever expanding quasi-governmental sector in areas such as housing, further education, and health it has been reduced to the status of an operational arm of central government.

In contrast, the idea of multi-level accountability is based on the assumption that matters of policy, strategy, and operations are not located at different levels of government (operations at the 'lowest' level, policy at the 'highest') but that each occurs at all levels of government (on the symbiotic relationship of rule and response in public bureaux; see Goodsell, Chapter 1, this volume). The 'dogma' (Stewart 1996) of separating policy from execution must be challenged; each level of government (including the very local) needs to be able to make decisions about policy, strategy, and operations which are appropriate for that level. In reality, policy issues exist at all levels, even the management of a swimming pool poses complex policy questions—are there reserved sessions for older users or for Asian women, how much time should be allocated to club use as opposed to general use, etc.? To term these 'detail' as if somehow they were unrelated to questions of public values and purposes is to mislead. The management of a swimming pool, a park, a health centre, a hospital, a school, etc. involves complex value questions. These everyday questions of politics are elided by managerialist discourses which frame such questions purely in business terms (so questions of value become interred in the swimming pool's business plan). The problem is that by adopting this particular set of managerialist approaches successive Conservative and Labour governments have permitted 'a widespread practice of the administration of services to develop that destroys the very idea that the providing organizations could be matters of public concern' (Hirst 1997: 108). Moreover, it is an approach which simply flies in the face of how policy and strategy is routinely made. This top-down and mechanistic model of the policy process was challenged years ago both in the field of policy research (Barrett and Fudge 1981) and business management (Mintzberg and Waters 1985).

In contrast, if we see policy questions affecting all levels of government then it is right that all levels of government should be permeated by political argument about the public purposes of the institution(s) in question. At the institutional level this implies extended forms of decentralization and democratization particularly within the ever-growing quasi-governmental sector. Current accountability arrangements are still based upon the assumption that in a sector such as schools education, all policy questions can be determined by central government, strategy can be enacted by public executives and governing bodies, and detailed operations can be delegated to local managers and professional staff. This three-way split (policy/strategy/detail) now dominates thinking about the policy process in contemporary Britain. In a previous article, we examined the rise of 'strategy speak' within public and 'quasi-public' organizations, construing it as a specifically instrumental discourse concerned with courses of action which are a 'means towards the organization's survival and/or growth' (Greer and Hoggett 1999). As a consequence of the policy–execution split, the 'autonomy' of public organizations becomes reconfigured in terms of the space to devise their own means of implementing government policy by acting strategically within their own quasi-markets. Like any organization in the private sector, questions of value, which might otherwise have found expression in locally articulated policy, become suppressed by the over-riding need to avoid failure and ensure survival in an environment preoccupied with short-term performativity (see Miller, Chapter 10, this volume). Unless things change, this is the future awaiting Foundation Hospitals, the latest Blairite policy innovation.

In contrast to this concerted attempt to depoliticize the public sector, value pluralism requires effective government to welcome rather than fear conflict. It requires recognition that value conflicts run right throughout the public realm, particularly at the operational level where it finds expression in the 'dilemmatic space' of the public official. From this perspective the New Labour project, by (among other things) its insistent separation of policy from operations or 'delivery' and its conviction that efficiency is the only criterion by which to choose between public and private, can be seen as fundamentally anti-conflict and therefore anti-democratic.

Bureaucracy and Ambivalence

Ambivalence and the Non-unitary Self

I have argued that bureaucracy, as a crucial mechanism for the organization of public affairs, is the site for the contestation of public purposes. Now I wish to examine a second unique characteristic. I suggest that the state, and particularly that part of it which is concerned with the welfare and security of its citizens, is required to contain much of that which the public seeks to alienate from itself. I argue that this finds expression in a range of social anxieties which have both existential, historical, and cultural dimensions. These anxieties are an expression of our moral ambivalence or, more accurately, of our inability to come to terms with this moral ambivalence.

Ambivalence, the coexistence in the mind of opposing feelings, gives expression to the fractured nature of the human subject. But if this is a fractured self, much of contemporary psychoanalysis insists that it is also one nevertheless capable of a degree of reconciliation and integration. And if this is an alienated subject it is also one capable, in a facilitating environment, of overcoming this alienation to some extent—in Jessica Benjamin's words, 'so that the stranger outside is no longer identical with the strange within us' (Benjamin 1998: 108). A facilitating environment is one which can contain our fears, resentments, and hatreds, help us face them and come to terms with them whilst never completely abolishing them. Parents, friends, teachers, doctors, public officials, and politicians,[5] among many others, can contribute to this 'social architecture of a more benign world' (Rustin and Rustin 1984). The key term is 'containment', a concept developed by Bion (1962) to refer to the way in which, from the outset of life, we seek to find another (person, group, institution) which can be a temporary repository for experiences that threaten to overwhelm us. Elsewhere (Hoggett 2000) I have described this role of the other as providing a 'place for experience' which is safe, strong, benign, and thoughtful.

Bion describes such forms of containment as 'symbiotic', a term he gives to a relationship in which each party develops as a result of the encounter. But he also notes that containment may assume parasitic forms, where the other 'feeds off' the self's fear and destructiveness.

The Nature of Social Anxieties

To recapitulate, what I have in mind is a subject in flight from itself but also one, in a facilitating environment, capable of returning to itself. Anxiety is the expression of this flight, of our alienation, and to an extent an aspect of our existential condition. This is the material that society gets to work on, the reservoir from which a variety of more culturally and historically specific anxieties originate. The concept of social anxiety draws attention to the existence of relatively enduring collective sentiments in society. This idea has only recently been taken up in the social sciences, for example, in Raymond Williams' notion of 'structures of feeling' (Williams 1977) and in James Jasper's notion of 'abiding affects' (Jasper 1998). The concept of social anxiety draws our attention to something which is partly existential, anxiety about the fate of self and intimates, and partly cultural, a consequence of the intense ambivalence of Western democracies towards vulnerability, destructiveness, and dependency. Such 'social anxieties' have featured sociologically in research on 'moral panics' (Glassner 1999) and in psychoanalytic explorations of organizational life, particularly life within the institutions of the welfare state (Obholzer and Roberts 1994).

I do not feel that public institutions are unique in containing unconscious aspects of citizens' emotional lives, nor that anxiety is the only affect involved. However, I do feel that such institutions, and the apparatus of government as a whole, for better or worse, play a vital role in 'containing' undigested affective conflicts within citizens' lives. I also feel that anxiety seems to be the most powerful of these affects.

I consider that the concept of 'social anxiety' refers to the anxiety that the western citizen has about a range of intimate fates which could befall him or her—as we say—'there but for the grace of god go I'. These intimate fates exist as tangible fears which connect to primitive anxieties, existential in form, and in this way become loaded with affect, which is potentially unbearable. I list the following: fear of death; fear of physical and mental degeneration; fear of pain and sudden incapacity; fear of madness (Bott Spillius 1990); fear of enduring and chronic mental turmoil; fear of indigence and destitution; fear of violation of bodily integrity (Williams 2000); fear of helplessness and loneliness; fear of failure (Sennett 1998). I could go on. Clearly we can see how the intensity, if not the initial basis, of many such fears is influenced by our culture, a culture in flight from dependency and the acceptance of human limits (Lash 1978). As a consequence of the conjoining of the cultural and the existential we find ourselves unable to think easily about such fates, and find it difficult to talk about them openly even to trusted intimates.

Containing Social Anxieties in Public Bureaucracies

Psychoanalytically informed studies of public institutions have thrown a fascinating light on how such unaddressed social anxieties influence the structure and culture of the organizations themselves. The classic study here is Isabel Menzies Lyth's examination of nursing in a London teaching hospital (Menzies Lyth 1960). Menzies Lyth argued that in the face of unaddressed anxieties aroused by illness, bodily decay and dying, the organization of nursing took on characteristics of a 'social defence system'. Menzies Lyth listed several of these socially organized defences—splitting up contact with the patient so that no nurse became 'too involved', depersonalization processes (e.g. patients, would be described as 'the liver in bed number 10'), detachment, ritualized behaviour, 'purposeful obscurity' in the allocation of responsibility, and so on. These organized defences against the experience of emotion by nursing staff constituted a particular form of 'emotion work' (Hochschild 1983).

Several of the social defence mechanisms that Menzies Lyth outlined find an echo in Lipsky's work on street level bureaucrats. Distancing and depersonalization, for example, were also used by many of Lipsky's respondents and this was often linked to labelling processes (Menzies Lyth uses the term 'categorization'). In a study that a colleague and I undertook on the housing allocations process (Jeffers and Hoggett 1995) we found similar labelling processes at work in terms of distinctions drawn between 'demanding' applicants and others. Such categories strip users of public services of some of their humanity and many officials are acutely aware of their own involvement in such processes, processes which nevertheless help to protect them against the 'assaults on the ego which the structure of street level work normally delivers' (Lipsky 1980: 152).

So far I have focused on social anxieties which relate to the passive dimension of selfhood, where self is the victim either of fate, misfortune, or the depredations of others. But there is another set of social anxieties which relate to the active dimension of selfhood and specifically to those parts of self which are potentially destructive or perverse. These social anxieties draw from the reservoir of guilt and shame upon which civilization depends for its survival (Freud 1930). Again the self is presented with a range of outcomes which are also pretty unthinkable—for example, the loss of self-control involved in violence towards one's child or partner, surrender to addiction or perversion, wishing evil to others—but this time the self is potentially the culpable agent rather than innocent object.

But, and here is the particular twist that psychoanalysis provides us with, to the extent that we cannot individually and collectively contain such anxieties about ourselves we externalize them into the other. 'I fear' becomes 'I am frightened of', the danger within becomes the danger without—the 'schizo', the child abuser, the smack-head, the dirty old man, the black youths on the corner, the pregnant schoolgirl, the kids out on the street, and so on.

Government and Ambivalence

Social anxieties are complex in form. They originate in our undeveloped capacity to contain what is strange within us—the mad, destructive, perverse, vulnerable, helpless, and frightened parts of the self. We alienate ourselves from these dimensions of our subjectivity by locating them in the other, so that what is strange within us becomes the stranger outside us. This is the basis of our ambivalence towards the subjects of welfare—the old, the sick, the bad, etc. We both identify with them and refuse to recognize ourselves in them. As subjects of welfare ourselves—when we visit our doctor because of anxiety about a nagging internal pain—we suffer the anxiety which accompanies all such experiences of helplessness and we look to the other to meet both our material and psychological needs. But when constituted as citizen and taxpayer the self so easily sees the 'subject of welfare' as the stranger, the other, somebody else's problem, somebody towards whom the invulnerable self is capable of callous indifference.

To the extent that the 'subject of welfare' is constituted as someone 'other' to ourselves, part of the foundation underlying social solidarity is destroyed. As Baldwin (1990: 34) noted, what fosters solidarity is a common experience of vulnerability, 'a sense of community is encouraged, most simply, in the face of universally shared risk'. In contrast, in the United Kingdom at least, for several decades this notion of 'shared fate' has been eclipsed by a collusion between governments and citizens which says 'they' (i.e. the government) must do something about this—child sexual abuse, the neglect of people with chronic mental health problems, the old and alone, the containment of uncontained children, etc. The systemic and relational dimensions of such social problems become obscured. Public officials get caught up in the bad faith which surrounds such issues, a bad faith which, for instance, wills the ends without willing the means, professes compassion but appears quite unconcerned by the pitiful wages of the army of care workers (from home care assistants to hospital porters) upon which the system depends. For professionally trained public officials, this bad faith is manifest in a different fashion. In his classic study of 'street level bureaucracies' Lipsky (1980: 29) noted that public professionals typically could not fulfil their mandated responsibilities because of the caseloads that they carried. In twenty years of consulting to and researching public sector workers in the United Kingdom, I would say that Lipsky's observations are more relevant now than they were even in his day. Much of the work of Cooper and others over the last decade on stress in the public sector workforce reveals that it is impossible workloads and experienced powerlessness, rather than remuneration, which is the chief source of distress (Cooper and Kelly 1993; Bogg and Cooper 1995).

When governments collude with the self-alienation of their citizens they take upon themselves a series of impossible tasks (such as the protection of vulnerable people from abuse) in which failure is inevitable. The collusion is based upon an implicit contract, one with echoes of the 'contract of mutual indifference' that Norman Geras has described (Geras 1998). Through this contract government enhances its legitimacy by not confronting citizens with issues they would prefer not to think about (e.g. citizens' contempt for their own vulnerability, a contempt which fuels a willingness to exploit or neglect vulnerable others, of which child or elder abuse is just one manifestation). Again it is often the hapless public official who becomes the whipping horse, the person who can be blamed for things that neither citizens nor governments will properly address.

To summarize, ambivalence is an inherent dimension of the social relations of welfare and, to the extent that this remains culturally unaccepted and unassimilated, we become alienated from the shadow side of our shared subjectivity. One of the functions of public bureaucracies is to 'contain' these disowned aspects of our subjectivity (Evans 2003). This occurs literally and concretely in the physical institutions that many children and elderly people end up in, and symbolically and psychologically, through the projected social anxieties that become part of the emotional labour of health workers, teachers, probation officers, and other street level bureaucrats. So long as this contract of mutual indifference prevails, the form of containment offered by welfare bureaucracies will be predominantly parasitic—the social imagination of citizens and governments will remain impoverished, and unsupported street level bureaucrats will continue to face high levels of stress.

The Ethical Bureaucrat

My argument has been that it is the fate of the public official, broadly conceived to include all those whose job involves some degree of discretion within the welfare state, to have to contain the unresolved (and often suppressed) value conflicts and moral ambivalence of society. Far from the picture of the rule-bound bureaucrat who slavishly follows procedure, the public official lives out the contradictions of the complex and diverse society in which she/he lives on a day-to-day basis and, as a consequence, is pulled this way and that in what Bonnie Honig calls 'dilemmatic space' (Honig 1996).

Honig draws on the work of the moral philosopher Bernard Williams (1973, 1981) who is keenly aware of the incommensurable nature of human values. Things just do not fit together as we would like them to, values rub up against each other, the moral agent has to live with conflicts that cannot easily be resolved and simply have to be lived with. You have to end up disappointing someone. Williams argues that in such situations there is often no right thing to do, the best that we can do is 'act for the best' (Williams 1973: 173). I think this is exemplified by the working lives of public officials and corresponds to what Lipsky described as 'the assaults on the ego which the structure of street level work normally delivers'.

There are two categories of dilemma which correspond to my two characterizations of government—as the embodiment of an inherently conflictual and a morally ambivalent public. In the first, the public official seeks to act as impartially as possible ('acting for the best') in the face of competing claims (care versus justice, the individual case versus the greater good, consistency versus responsiveness, and so on). Susan Mendus (2000) notes that we are in the terrain not just of pluralism but also of the impossibility of harmonious reconciliation, in which the moral agent is not exempt from the authority of the claim she chooses to neglect. As she puts it, such situations are characterized by 'pluralism, plus conflict, plus loss' (Mendus 2000: 117). For the public officials, it is loss which is experienced as failure. It is as if they internalize the flaws and faults of reality and make them their own, thereby taking on responsibility for what is irreconcilable in the wider world.

The second category of dilemma is the consequence of moral ambivalence, and specifically the inability of citizens to recognize and deal with vulnerability and destructiveness in self and others. Michael Feldman (1989) suggests that where X deals with ambivalence by projecting it into Y, the consequence is that Y is put in a 'no win' or 'damned if you do and damned if you don't' situation. It follows that it is in the nature of some public organizations that they will be seen to fail, indeed it is necessary for them to fail if the 'contract of mutual indifference' between government and citizens is to be sustained.

Fail Better: Agency Within Public Bureaucracies

The necessary role that failure plays in governance has recently surfaced as a significant focus of debate (Malpas and Wickham 1995; Jessop 2000; Curtis 2002). According to Jessop, 'given the growing structural complexity and opacity of the social world, failure is the most likely outcome of most attempts to govern it' (Jessop 2000: 5).

Drawing on Rorty (1989), Jessop contrasts three responses to the experience of failure. He contrasts the 'romantic ironist' with both the cynic and what one might call the 'ideologue', that is, the unreflexive champion of either markets, or the state or informal networks. I am suspicious of what seems to me to be the return of an enlightened pragmatism (a kind of 'reflexive what works is, at least for the time being, what's best') at the heart of his analysis. Nevertheless Jessop's argument is helpful because it converges towards the same point as my own thinking in the section above—that is, what kind of agency is possible and desirable within dilemmatic space? Jessop's answer to this question lies in his depiction of the ironist, someone who 'recognizes the likelihood of failure but proceeds as if success were possible' (Jessop 2000: 7). In contrast to those whose despair reduces them to the cynical forms of impression management, buck passing or 'going through the motions' the ironist willingly chooses her own form of failure, seeking 'creative solutions whilst acknowledging the limits to any such solution . . . she accepts incompleteness and failure as essential features of social life but continues to act as if completeness and success were possible' (p. 8).

Jessop's prescription of a dose of ironic detachment has much to be said for it but my own research experience[6] suggests that for all but an elite of civil service mandarins such a position cannot be sustained except on a fleeting basis. In my experience the problem [sic] for most public officials is that they care too much about what they are doing. No amount of reflexive detachment can free a general practitioner, service director, head teacher, probation officer, youth worker or 'urban manager' from the pain of the choices that they have to make, often on a daily basis. In contrast to much of contemporary management discourse with its 'heroic' picture of the change embracing, transformational leader in search of excellence, I suggest a 'tragic' perspective better describes the position of the public official for whom resilience in the face of frustration is perhaps the primary attribute. Instead of the chimerical pursuit of fail-safe procedures and 'total quality', public bureaucracies would be better advised to seek 'good enough' solutions which are satisficing rather than maximizing. The effective public manager would therefore be the 'good enough manager' (Hoggett 1992) working towards a 'good enough' set of principles of public welfare (Williams 2000).

Some Implications

By way of conclusion, what are some of the implications of the perspective that I have developed? First, recognition of the conflictual nature of public purposes and of the way in which such value conflicts saturate all levels of the public sector, from the management of a local park to the organization of transport in a capital city, runs directly counter to most of the tenets of the so-called 'new public management'. But this is not a call for the return of hierarchy, rather it is a call for the democratic renewal of all levels of government, particularly the new generation of so-called 'provider organizations' in health, further and higher education, social and public housing and transport. Effective government would, according to Fred Alford (Alford 1994), equate statecraft with soulcraft by seeking to engage citizens in ethical and moral dialogues at all levels, starting from the local upwards. This would require a revaluation of the role and function of the public official, one which would recognize the position of the public official as a fulcrum for the conflicts and contradictions of the wider society. It would also necessitate realization that the 'art of judgement' lies at the very heart of the public official's task.[7] If we take this seriously then it follows that what is called for is the 'reflexive redesign' (to use a phrase of Jessop's) of public bureaucracies to equip them to respond to the ethical tasks that confront them. This would have major implications for the training and continuous professional development of public officials; for the creation of organizational cultures in which the emotional needs of street level bureaucrats are given due recognition; for rethinking the nature and role of accountable and reflexive authority involved in the exercise of discretion; and for the development of a new discourse of public management predicated upon a tragic rather than heroic model of agency.

As I stated earlier, public bureaucracies are the one place where questions of technique ('what works') and questions of value stand a chance of being integrated. Arguably Britain has embraced the new public management more than any other western-type democracy. As a consequence, the ethical and moral foundation of public service has been suppressed more completely than in any equivalent state. Efficacy rules, and the de-moralization of public office have brought about a deep-seated demoralization of the public service workforce.

Notes

1. This is something which has been recognized by some of the very best Labour initiatives such as Surestart but which is sadly absent from many other strands of government policy making.
2. Oliver Williamson's (1985) famous 'markets' and 'hierarchies' distinction ill serves the examination of the organization of government, not only because of the way in which it has led to an all too easy equation between hierarchy and 'bureaucracy' but also because it has provided no space within which to conceptualize what is distinctive about a public bureaucracy—that is, its potential to combine two distinctive modes of coordination, hierarchy, and democracy, the latter of which is almost entirely absent from the paradigm which has emerged from Williamson's work.
3. Radical attempts to both decentralize and democratize local government bureaucracy were pursued by both local Labour and Liberal politicians in the United Kingdom in the 1980s, partly in an attempt to demonstrate that there was an ideological alternative to the neo-Liberal dismantling of local government that Thatcherism had inaugurated. Our ESRC funded study of these innovations was published in 1994 (Burns, Hambleton, and Hoggett 1994).
4. Much of the destruction of the power of local government and the creation of an extended but non-accountable local state was accomplished by successive Conservative administrations. Contrary to the expectations accompanying the Labour victory in 1997, with the significant exception of political devolution in Scotland and Wales, Blair's government has done virtually nothing to reverse this trend. Quite the contrary, Blair's has been such a dirigiste administration that by 2003 even the Conservatives were able to position themselves as the party of 'local democracy'. At the time of writing there are a number of indications that, should it achieve a third term of office, Labour will put democratic renewal at the heart of its public service reform programme. But will this involve the re-empowerment rather than the further bypassing of local government?
5. See Alford (1994), for example, on the role of what he calls 'interpretive' political leadership.
6. Along with colleagues I am currently engaged in the early stages of an ESRC funded project (Ref no. RES-000-23-0127) entitled 'Negotiating Ethical Dilemmas in Contested Communities', a detailed study of the way in which those engaged in 'regeneration work' deal with the ethical dilemmas of the job.
7. If follows that the development of the 'moral imagination' of public officials should be integral to their training and socialisation (see Whitebook 2002).

References

Alford, C. F. (1994). *Group Psychology and Political Theory*. New Haven, CT: Yale University Press.

Baldwin, P. (1990). *The Politics of Social Solidarity*. Cambridge: Cambridge University Press.

Barrett, S. and Fudge, C. (eds) (1981). *Policy and Action*. London: Methuen.

Benjamin, J. (1998). *The Shadow of the Other*. New York: Routledge.

Bion, W. (1962). *Learning from Experience*. London: Heinemman.

Bogg, J. and Cooper, C. (1995). 'Job satisfaction, mental health, and occupational stress among senior civil servants'. *Human Relations*. 48/3; 327–41.

Bott Spillius, E. (1990) 'Asylum and society', in E. Trist and H. Murray (eds), *The Social Engagement of Social Science*, Vol. 1. London: Free Association Books.

Burns, D., Hambleton, R., and Hoggett, P. (1994). *The Politics of Decentralization*. Basingstoke: Macmillan.

Clarke, J. and Newman, J. (1997) *The Managerial State*. London: Sage.

Clegg, S. (1990). *Modern Organization*. London: Sage.

Cooper, C. and Kelly, M. (1993). 'Occupational stress in headteachers: a national UK study'. *British Journal of Educational Psychology*. 63; 130–43.

Curtis, D. (2002). 'What kind of imperfection gives you Best Value?' *Local Governance*. 28/4; 287–97.

du Gay, P. (2000). *In Praise of Bureaucracy*. London: Sage.

Evans, J. (2003). 'Vigilance and vigilantes: thinking psychoanalytically about anti-paedophile action'. *Theoretical Criminology*. 7/2; 163–89.

Feldman, M. (1989). 'The Oedipal Complex: manifestations in the inner world and the therapeutic situation', in R. Britton, M. Feldman and E. O'Shaugnessy (eds), *The Oedipal Complex Today*. London: Karnac Books.

Freud, S. (1930). *Civilization and it Discontents. SE XXI*. London: Hogarth.

Geras, N. (1998). *The Contract of Mutual Indifference: Political Philosophy After the Holocaust*. London: Verso.

Glassner, B. (1999). *The Culture of Fear*. New York: Basic Books.

Greer, A. and Hoggett, P. (1999). 'Public policies, private strategies and local public spending bodies'. *Public Administration*. 77/2; 235–56.

Henderson, G. and Karn, V. (1987). *Race, Class and State Housing: Inequality and the Allocation of Public Housing in Britain*. Aldershot: Gower.

Hill, M. (1983). *Understanding Social Policy*. Oxford: Basil Blackwell.

Hirst, P. (1997). 'Democracy and civil society', in P. Hirst and S. Khilnani (eds), *Reinventing Democracy*. Oxford: Blackwell.

Hochschild, A. (1983). *The Managed Heart: The Commercialization of Human Feeling*. Berkeley, CA: University of California Press.

Hoggett, P. (1991). 'A new management in the public sector?' *Policy and Politics*. 19/4; 243–56.

Hoggett, P. (1992). 'Why being 'good enough' is good enough', in *Working and Learning Together: Papers of the 2nd Public Service Conference*. London: AMED.

Hoggett, P. (2000). *Emotional Life and the Politics of Welfare*. Basingstoke: Macmillan.

Honig, B. (1993). *Political Theory and the Displacement of Politics*. Ithaca, NY: Cornell University Press.

Honig, B. (1996). 'Difference, dilemmas and the politics of home', in S. Benhabib (ed.), *Democracy and Difference: Contesting the Boundaries of the Political*. Princeton, NJ: Princeton University Press.

Hood, C. (1991). 'A public management for all seasons', *Public Administration*, 69/1; 3–19.

Jasper, J. (1998). 'The emotions of protest: affective and reactive emotions in and around social movements'. *Sociological Forum*, 13/3; 397–424.

Jeffers, S. and Hoggett, P. (1995). 'Like counting deckchairs on the Titanic: a study of institutional racism and housing allocations in Haringey and Lambeth'. *Housing Studies*; 10/3. 325–44.

Jessop, B. (2000). 'Governance and metagovernance: on reflexivity, requisite variety and requisite irony'. Lancaster University: Department of Sociology, Online: http://www.comp.lancs.ac.uk/sociology/soc108rj.htm.

Lash, C. (1978). *The Culture of Narcissism*. New York: Norton.

Levitas, R. (1999). *The Inclusive Society? Social Exclusion and New Labour*. Basingstoke: Macmillan.

Lipsky, M. (1980). *Street-Level Bureaucracy: Dilemmas of the Individual in Public Service*. Russell Sage Foundation.

Maile, S. and Hoggett, P., (2001). 'Best value and the politics of pragmatism'. *Policy and Politics*. 29/4; 509–19.

Malpas, J. and Wickham, G. (1995). 'Governance and failure: on the limits of sociology'. *Australia and New Zealand Journal of Sociology*. 31/3; 37–50.

Mendus, S. (1993). 'Different voices, still lives: problems in the ethics of care'. *Journal of Applied Philosophy*. 10/1; 17–27.

Mendus, S. (2000). *Feminism and Emotion*. Basingstoke: Macmillan.

Menzies Lyth, I. (1960). 'A case study in the functioning of social systems as a defence against anxiety'. *Human Relations*. 13; 95–121.

Mintzberg, H. and Waters, J. (1985). 'Of strategies, deliberate and emergent'. *Strategic Management Journal*. 26; 257–72.

Mouffe, C. (1993). *The Return of the Political*. London: Verso.

Obholzer, A. and Roberts, V. (1994). *The Unconscious at Work: Individual and Organizational Stress in the Human Services*. London: Routledge.

Offe, C. (1984). *Contradictions of the Welfare State*. London: Hutchinson.

Pollock, A., Shaoul, J., and Rowland, D. (2001). *Public Services and the Private Sector: A Response to IPPR*. London: Catalyst Trust.

Rorty, R. (1989). *Contingency, Irony and Solidarity*. Cambridge: Cambridge University Press.

Rustin, M. and Rustin, M. (1984). 'Relational preconditions of socialism', in B. Richards (ed.), *Capitalism and Infancy*. London: Free Association Books.

Sennett, R. (1998). *The Corrosion of Character*. New York: Norton.

Spicker, P. (1993). 'Understanding particularism'. *Critical Social Policy.* 39; 5–20.

Stewart, J. (1996), 'A dogma of our times: the separation of policy making and implementation'. *Public Money and Management.* July–Sept: 33–40.

Thompson, S. and Hoggett, P. (1996). 'Universalism, selectivism and particularism: towards a postmodern social policy'. *Critical Social Policy.* 46; 21–43.

Vickers, G. (1965). *The Art of Judgement.* London: Methuen.

Whitebrook, M. (2002). 'Compassion as a political virtue'. *Politial Studies.* 50; 529–44.

Williams, B. (1973). *Problems of the Self.* Cambridge: Cambridge University Press.

Williams, B. (1981). *Moral Luck.* Cambridge: Cambridge University Press.

Williams, F. (1989). *Social Policy: A Critical Introduction.* Cambridge: Polity Press.

Williams, F. (2000). *New Principles for Welfare.* Cambridge: Polity Press.

Williams, R. (1977). *Marxism and Literature.* Oxford: Oxford University Press.

Williamson, O. (1985). *The Economic Institutions of Capitalism: Firms, Markets and Relational Contracting.* New York: Free Press.

Young, I. M. (1996). 'Communication and the other: beyond deliberative democracy', in S. Benhabib (ed.), *Democracy and Difference.* Princeton, NJ: Princeton University Press.

8

Bending Bureaucracy: Leadership and Multi-Level Governance

Janet Newman

Bureaucracy has come to take on a symbolic role in discussions of the reform or modernization of public services. Viewed as the source of waste and inefficiency, rules and 'red tape', and a barrier to the flexibility and entrepreneurialism required in a modern world, successive waves of reform have taken place in the name of its eradication. At the same time concern about accountability and probity have produced a series of debates about the governance of public services in a supposedly post-bureaucratic era. In each case bureaucracy is viewed as a coherent 'ideal type' representing both benefits (an ethos of office based on impartiality and probity) and disbenefits (inflexibility, rule boundedness, and departmentalism[1]). However few 'pure' bureaucracies have ever existed in public services: most organizations combine features of bureaucracy and professionalism, of bureaucracy and managerialism, or even bureaucracy and entrepreneurship. Bureaucracy, then, can be viewed as a set of principles and practices that may be articulated with others in particular organizational settings. These articulations can be loose or tight, and lead to more or less discomfort for those living with the tensions they produce. But the idea of articulation provides us with a helpful framework for examining the process of public service 'modernization'.

In particular it suggests ways in which the agency of the public service worker can be understood. The dispersal of power across multiple tiers and spheres of governance raises significant questions about the power of such service workers, especially in the context of the new emphasis on the importance of 'transformational leadership' (see Salaman, Chapter 6, this volume). This chapter explores the values and principles that shape the ways in which senior managers approach the task of delivering policy reforms in the context of public service modernization in the United Kingdom. Such managers are increasingly required to work through networks of actors across organizations and sectors, and to negotiate different tiers of governance (Reed, Chapter 5, this volume). The first section, 'Beyond the "Street Level Bureaucrat" ' reviews the re-conceptualization of agency in the context of network governance. The second section, 'From Managerialism to Transformational Leadership' highlights the significance of a new cadre of 'public service leaders' and their positioning as agents of change in delivering the agenda of the New Labour government. In the third section, 'Bending Bureaucracy', I examine their portrayal of their ethos of office, examining in particular how key features of bureaucracy may be inflected and re-articulated in their accounts; and then go on to discuss in what ways such an ethos might be viewed as bending, rather than breaking, bureaucracy.

Beyond the 'Street Level Bureaucrat': Network Governance, Agency, and Identity

Where policy studies have attempted to theorize the possibility of agency or negotiation in the process of implementation, the dominant focus has been on the role of the 'street level bureaucrat' exercising discretion at the 'front line' (Lipsky 1980). Such work has contributed new ways of thinking about the relationship between policy and practice by raising questions about where, and under what conditions and constraints, decision-making takes place. It has opened up a field of empirical work about how the relative autonomy of front line staff is exercised in different services, together with discussion about whether such discretion presents an implementation problem or has a functional value in the implementation process (Hill and Hupe 2002). It has also raised questions about the role of professional expertise in the exercise of discretion (see Hoggett, Chapter 7, this volume).

The idea of the street level bureaucrat is of continuing salience in empirical analyses of state–citizen interactions.[2] However developments in governance theory suggest the need to explore multiple sites of discretion in a complex, multi-level, and dispersed field of agency and power, rather than focusing exclusively on the front line or street level. There are many different perspectives embraced—somewhat uncomfortably—in this body of theory, but the dominant tradition in the United Kingdom is based on a narrative of the hollowing out of the nation state as power flows both upwards (to transnational political and economic institutions), outwards (through economic processes of globalization), and downwards (through the fragmentation of government institutions, and the contracting out, or privatization, of government functions and services). The result, the story goes, has been a shift from government through hierarchy (bureaucratic channels of direct control through rule-making and upwards accountability) to governance through networks (Rhodes 1994, 1997, 2000; Pierre 2000; Pierre and Peters 2000). The state, it is argued, can no longer assume a monopoly of either expertise or of the resources necessary to govern but must rely on a plurality of interdependent institutions and actors drawn from within and beyond government. Networks represent a departure from the traditional forms of governance through state hierarchies or through self-regulating markets, being based on indirect processes of influence across plural sites of action that traverse old organizational and sectoral boundaries. Rather than government acting alone it is depicted as engaged in co-regulation, co-steering, co-production, cooperative management, public–private partnerships, and other forms of governing that cross the boundaries between government and society as well as between public and private sectors (Kooiman 1993, 2003).

There is much debate about the extent and consequences of such shifts, and challenges to the idea that the power of the nation state has been eroded (Jessop 2000; Pierre and Peters 2000). I have argued elsewhere that rather than a simple story of a shift from the old to the new, the governance of the United Kingdom is characterized by an overlay of different governance regimes that produce tensions and contradictions for those delivering services and implementing policy (Newman 2001). Nevertheless governance theory is relevant to the analysis of contemporary governance in the United Kingdom. One of the distinguishing features of the Labour administrations has been the relatively high emphasis on policy innovation. Such innovation has largely been concerned with objectives that governments do not really know how to achieve—finding long-term solutions to complex, or 'wicked', problems that cut across organizational and departmental boundaries. Here managers are charged, not only with delivering specified policy outputs (e.g. cutting hospital waiting lists, improving detection rates) but also with developing local strategies in partnership with others to deliver policy outcomes (preventing ill health, reducing the public's fear of crime). But the more a government is oriented towards policy outcomes, rather than organizational outputs, the less it is able to exercise control through hierarchical channels flowing down through bureaucratic organizations. Complex policies necessarily involve more room for agency on the part of policy and managerial actors operating across organizational and departmental boundaries and building alliances between different tiers of governance. Such actors confront a field of plural goals, multiple stakeholders, and conflicting values and aspirations.

Such network and collaborative forms of governance challenge basic principles of bureaucracy in a number of respects. First, the increasing significance of 'policy networks' (Marsh 1998) challenges the view that policy formulation and implementation are distinct elements in a policy cycle. Second, the emphasis on collaboration and involvement undermines the idea that an overarching ethos of office can isolate individual actors from the social and cultural contexts within which their decisions are made. Third, the managerial shifts of the late twentieth century—in which managerialism becomes a coordinating device in a fragmented field of dispersed and devolved state power—challenges the bureaucratic principle of individual discretion being delimited by organizational rules and norms institutionalized within hierarchical chains of control (Clarke and Newman 1997). In the next section, I suggest some of the consequences of this dispersal of power for our understanding of agency and ethos in a post-bureaucratic public service.

From Managerialism to Transformational Leadership

The late twentieth century witnessed the transformation of the public sector in the United Kingdom and beyond around a managerial logic, captured in the language of the New Public Management. This managerial logic had a number of characteristics, of which two are significant for my analysis here. The first was the dispersal of power beyond the institutions of the bureaucratic state and the 'empowerment' of managers to exert new forms of control. A second, related, characteristic was the superimposition of new logics of appropriateness based on calculations of efficiency and value for money over older rationalities based on bureaucratic accountability and a distinctive public service ethos. As such the New Public Management tended to strip public services of an ethical rationality. The dispersal of power coupled with a managerialist logic meant that the dominant focus of action shifted to the organization (newly framed in a competitive environment) rather than the wider fields of professional practice or public service. As public accountability became institutionally stripped from the ethos of office of the individual bureaucrat it became enshrined in a host of audit and inspection regimes supposedly representing a wider public interest (see Clarke, Chapter 9, this volume). Similarly, the weakening of professional power was accompanied by a proliferation of standards and service frameworks set by quasi-state bodies. The task of the manager, then, tended to be stripped of the ethical dimensions that were embodied in older conception of public service associated with bureaucracy or professionalism. The emphasis was on technical rationality. Questions of value were confined to the organizational sphere, delimited by notions of organizational culture and the problem of gaining staff commitment to an organizational mission. I do not want to suggest that public service workers did not have a personal sense of wider public mission or purpose. But I do want to emphasize the importance of studying the institutional logics and managerial discourses within which identity is shaped and agency constrained.

The New Labour government of 1997 entered this rather impoverished field with a stronger emphasis on the importance of public services and a programme of reform and modernization. Partnerships and 'joined up' working were key themes in this programme, implying a shift to network governance and the consequent emphasis on open and flexible organizations, and on the need for enhanced skills of negotiation and reflexivity on the part of managers. While not abandoning managerialism—indeed Labour's whole style and approach has been strongly managerial—the government promoted a parallel discourse of public service leadership as a means of fostering the kinds of system wide transformation it envisaged, as well as promoting organizational success. The late 1990s and early 2000s saw a number of policy documents calling for a strengthening of public leadership (e.g. Performance and Innovation Unit 2000; Office of Public Service Reform 2002, OFSTED 2002). The analysis of these documents surfaces a discourse of leadership constructed in and through a number of binary divisions:

- between the 'forces of conservatism' and proactive, committed leadership
- between 'failing' and 'successful' organizations
- between stasis and transformation
- between the notions of an old 'uniform' and a new 'diverse' management cadre.[3]

The notion of 'transformative' leadership, in particular, assumed an authoritative status because of its twin associations with the United States (from which most of the literature derives) and with the business world. These associations invoke images of individual dynamism, risk taking and entrepreneurship that had strong affinities with Labour's espoused values, fitting well with its social as well as economic goals (see du Gay and Armbrüster, Chapters 2 and 3 respectively, this volume).

The discourse of leadership was readily incorporated into the modernization programme for public services (e.g. in its Fresh Start and New Start schemes predicated on the supposed power of an individual leader to 'transform' failing organizations). The period also saw a proliferation of public service leadership programmes (sponsored by the Cabinet Office, the National Health Service (NHS) and other parts of government as well as by Higher Education (HE) institutions and independent providers), all based around the idea of building a cadre of transformational leaders that might invigorate public service change. Such leaders were viewed as key agents in Labour's struggle to deliver on their targets and electoral pledges ('delivery' being a more proactive reworking of bureaucratic notions of 'implementation'). The position of these actors is significant for a number of reasons. First, they are both the carriers of state power (as agents for the delivery of government policy) and powerful actors in their own right (by virtue of the status of managerial knowledge and claims to truth in neo-liberal regimes). Second, many play roles in policy networks and communities that transcend the policy/delivery divide. Third, they are actors who have to improvise as they negotiate tensions in the modernizing programme of New Labour produced by the structural contradictions of the 'Third Way' (Fairclough 2000; Newman 2001).

But how can the agency of these supposedly 'empowered' actors be understood? There is comparatively little work exploring the meanings they attribute to their roles and actions, or how they take on particular forms of identity. The traditional conception of senior bureaucrats in policy theory views them as engaged in bureau-shaping activities in order to enlarge their spheres of power and influence (Dunleavy 1991). Assumptions about intention and agency are based on data about bureau growth or restructuring. In the governance literature the concept of agency is based on a model of 'resource dependency' that emphasizes instrumental rationality, exchange, and interest bargaining. This produces a 'thin' conception of the person: a conception that views the individual as subject to pressures to conform to rules, norms, and expectations implicated in the structural forces to which they are subject. Identity, in such conceptions, is little more than the internalization of structural requirements. To counter this, Woods draws on Weber's concept of 'inner distance':

Inner distance consists of a self conscious adherence to certain ethical values in the face of the immense daily pressures to conform to a rationalized and disenchanted world, and a degree of self mastery that resists loss of 'personality' under the relentless pressure of the demands of routine. (Woods 2003: 151)

Such inner distance enables the individual to draw on a diverse range of identity resources. These can be social as well as personal:

The symbolization of alternative orientations enables practical social engagement—collective and individual—capable, in principle, of countering or opposing instrumental rationalities. (Woods 2003: 151–2)

This suggests the possibility of an 'ethical rationality' that might transcend the institutional bounds of bureaucratic norms, rules, and organizational forms. It is a particularly significant concept in the context of any discussion of leadership. The bureaucratic principle of the separation of office from personal preference calls for an absence of personal enthusiasms. This is the very antithesis of leadership discourse, a discourse that is predicated on the visibility of the leader's embodiment of characteristics such as integrity, vision, charisma. Strong values are viewed as a key asset that transformational leaders deploy in fostering cultural change. Rather than a separation between the person and the office, the individual is integral to, and a key resource in, the office itself: he/she is its very material and spiritual embodiment.

The transfer of the concept of transformational leadership from private to public sector raises important questions. For example, how far might organizational mission and personal values be aligned with the political goals of the party in office, and what happens when there are conflicts between them? What happens when the idea of the public service manager as a 'servant' of the state, or of the wider public good, meets the idea of organizational and personal 'mastery' found in the leadership literature (e.g. Senge 1990). More prosaically, how can public service leaders set out to engage in long-term programmes of 'transformative' cultural change in the context of the frequent policy shifts associated with the relatively short life cycles of Ministerial office? Given these difficulties it is perhaps somewhat surprising that any government should seize on the idea of transformational leadership quite so emphatically as has New Labour; yet symbolically the idea is entirely consonant with the style of Blair himself. The accomplishment of the shift from Labour to 'New' Labour has much symbolic resonance with the business literature's depiction of the transformation of old, ossified, bureaucratic companies into mission-driven, customer-focused, flexible enterprises.

Transformational Leadership and the Ethos of Office

So how are public service managers, newly interpellated as transformational leaders, taking on this novel role in the context of dispersed and fragmented fields of governance? Partly freed from the norms and rules of bureaucracy, what principles do they follow? How are they reconciling being both the 'servants' of the government in power and the 'masters' of organizational and personal change? To examine the patterns of identification and agency among this new cadre of leaders (and would be leaders) I draw on a number of accounts of their experience of delivering 'modernizing' policy reforms (see also Newman 2002). These accounts are based on group discussions with senior managers attending, or contributing to, leadership programmes and action learning sets during 2002–4, together with a series of in-depth interviews with delegates to, and practitioner speakers at, such programmes.[4] These were, then, not a representative sample of senior public service managers, but a sample likely to identify with, or at least be sympathetic to, the new leadership discourse. My respondents included senior staff from government offices of the regions; assistant chief executives, departmental directors, and policy officers from local government; directors of partnership bodies and zonal initiatives; chief executives and senior managers of voluntary sector bodies, housing associations and charities; senior managers in health authorities, hospital trusts and primary care trusts; police superintendents; chief and assistant chief probation officers; and senior civil servants, the latter usually linked to some form of policy innovation or partnership initiative that involved collaboration with local agencies. I am not assuming that my respondents had necessarily taken on the new identities and enthusiasms espoused by transformational leadership programmes. However, they were examples of a cadre of senior staff newly positioned in a discursive field in which transformational leadership was valorized and bureaucratic management viewed as insufficient to meet the challenges of modernization.

The analysis is based on a discursive reading of interview transcripts and written reports of group discussions. In examining their accounts I not only explore the ways in which their accounts are framed within, but also adapt and appropriate, policy discourse. Ball (1990, 1993) argues that it is necessary to study policy as discourse as well as policy as text. *Policy as text*, Ball argues, is practical and real; the emphasis is on agency and notions of influence. Actors are viewed as agents engaged in making sense of policy and responding to it. *Policy as discourse*, in contrast, focuses on the frameworks of possibility within which policy is thought. The discourses within which policy is produced carry meanings that both enable and circumscribe agency. My emphasis, then, is not what actors do, but on the process of meaning making that they are engaged with as they negotiate the discursive field of New Labour's policy and management systems.

Continuities with a Bureaucratic Ethos of Office

In their accounts, my interviewees replicated the dominant framing of bureaucracy as a term of abuse, signifying a multitude of centralizing sins: inflexibility in the policy system, the proliferation of guidelines from the centre, the requirements of audit and inspection regimes, the multiplication of overlapping plans they were required to produce, and so on. But while feeling free to criticize these policy measures, they were reluctant to highlight defects in policies themselves. If asked directly about their relationship to the political/policy process their accounts suggested a classic view of the administrative/political boundary: my respondents had quite clear conceptions of themselves as public servants rather than policy advocates. One key episode, repeated over three occasions with different groups, illustrates the strength of this belief. Groups were confronted by a speaker—a leading national journalist—who argued that there was a leadership vacuum in the higher echelons of the public sector, and that senior managers across the sector should develop a common voice through which to contest areas of policy that were ineffective or counter-productive. But on each occasion the recipients of this message were deeply resistant to it, responding that as managers their role was not to interfere in policy-making but to try to deliver it as best they could (though see Goodsell, Chapter 1, this volume). They were aware of various formal channels through which the voice of professional associations could be heard in government but the idea of a unified public sector voice was antithetical to their beliefs about the role of public servants.

The Reassertion of Value

But their accounts of how they went about interpreting and enacting policy told a rather different story. My respondents clearly experienced themselves as the agents rather than the subjects of change—they were, in managerial language, 'empowered' or enabled by the new agenda. This did not mean that they had not been change agents under previous governments, but there was something qualitatively different arising from the alignment between Labour's espoused goals and my respondents' perceptions of the goals of public service.

The leadership literature emphasizes the importance of the person—their integrity and authenticity—in shaping the transformation of the enterprise, and we can see some collapse of the distinction between the values of the person and the values of the office in their accounts. My respondents did indeed talk a great deal about values, but, rather than using the language of organizational mission statements, tended to speak about their personal and professional beliefs or goals:

Why do I do what I do?—I suppose I want our cities back—I am working to help create cities with a strong sense of identity, outward looking and confident. (Registered Social Landlord (Housing Association) Manager)

My job involves leading for the health system—acute hospital providers, community trust providers, primary care and linkages with colleagues in social care, housing and the police. My aim is to bring all these together to try to develop strategic plans for the whole population of the area. (Senior Manager, Health Authority)

I am coming out of the silo—I feel quite humble going around—I am on a journey of discovery. In my new [corporate] role I end up in all sorts of different places—but there is something fundamental about working more with communities and trying to deliver what they tell us. In a few years' time the landscape will be completely different. (Local Authority Policy Officer)

These quotes are interesting not only for their content, and the kinds of identifications they suggest, but also for the way in which they draw on dominant policy and management discourses (working across boundaries, working with communities, overcoming old 'silo' mentalities, strategic plans) to tell what is, in each case, a very personal story. The imagery is of journeys of discovery, of working to achieve personal aims, of transforming the landscape. These actors can be seen as actively shaping and adapting policy by articulating dominant political and policy discourses ('working with communities', 'overcoming social exclusion') with local and professional goals. Often this was a positive, mutually reinforcing alignment. But it was based on a partial and selective appropriation of Labour's own policy discourse in which 'social' goals and values were pre-eminent and other values subordinated. A key feature of many of the narratives was sense of movement underpinned by a quest for social and organizational transformation:

In some ways it is quite exciting grappling with all this—is the voluntary sector an agent of the state or is it trying to bring about change? I feel that I am involved in a struggle for the future of the sector. (Chief Executive, voluntary sector)

This sense of personal mission is the very antithesis of bureaucratic discourse.

The analysis of the accounts revealed a frequent repetition of phrases such as *'empowering' users, working with communities, building social capital, enhancing public involvement* in service design and delivery, using resources to *deliver outcomes* that *promote the prevention* of crime, ill health, and other problems (rather than trying to patch things up afterwards). Here we can see the language of Labour's stated policy goals being picked up and selectively amplified at local level, but also articulated with other discursive resources. In the quotation above from the local authority policy officer 'working with communities' is directly derived from Labour's own discourse, but 'trying to deliver what they (communities) tell us' is rather different, perhaps signalling an alternative political agenda (this interviewee did indeed have a background in community politics). Many of my respondents had lived through the social changes of the 1960s–1980s, and some had participated actively in the women's movement, community politics, and struggles to transform the professions around user-centred and anti-discriminatory principles. All had a strong sense of *public* values and an active engagement with Labour's *social* agenda. That is, they were engaged in selectively drawing on and amplifying Labour's own discourses in order to pursue goals that they viewed as benefiting the communities and users they served. Many leaders were involved in a process of appropriating the language of social inclusion, preventing ill health and other themes in Labour's policy agenda in order to legitimize new ways of working across organizations and new forms of relationship with communities.

Labour's own policy rhetoric was, then, frequently used as a discursive resource. However, we can trace a process of re-articulation in which respondents used the language of 'outcomes' or 'what works'—key resources in Labour's policy lexicon—to legitimate actions that were not necessarily consonant with what were perceived to be overly narrow, output-based, or politically driven targets. The accounts illustrate the multiple ways in which government discourses—on public participation, joined up government, social inclusion, regeneration, and a host of others—were articulated with the values and goals of practitioners, values and goals perceived to have been sidelined during the Conservative years of office, but as gaining a new legitimacy under Labour.

The 'Local' as a Contested Site in Multi-Level Governance

In the United Kingdom 'the local' has a particular significance in Labour's policy programme in at least three senses. First, many of Labour's policy innovations involve bringing different actors into 'partnership' to address cross-cutting policy issues—health action zones, sure start, neighbourhood renewal, and so on. This involves an expanded spatial sense of the local within public policy as the site of policy innovation and of collaboration with 'communities' in finding solutions to locally defined problems (often termed 'community governance': see Sullivan, 2001). Second, however, the locality in a spatial sense is being subordinated in the government's attempt to ensure that national standards are met. Many managers/leaders in mainstream services—health, education, local government—complain about being increasingly constrained, viewed by government as little more than local administrators of centrally determined policy. Third, the possibility of new 'freedoms' and 'flexibilities' for high performing organizations (local authorities, schools, foundation hospitals) offer an enlarged area of potential local discretion. This is already the case as a result of changes in education and is likely to have even greater implications when foundation hospitals are established. This means that the 'ethos of office' of public service managers shaping local services is particularly significant.

However rather than a simple story of the progressive empower-ment of 'local' managers, the data highlights the 'local' as a site of major tension between conflicting regimes of governance: those based on 'top-down' and 'bottom-up' policy-making, between managerial and hierarchical governance, between network-based collaboration and bureaucratically legitimated authority. This interface is primarily negotiated by senior managers, newly constituted as transformational leaders. Despite the centralizing thrust of Labour's policies and politics, they have considerable room for manoeuvre as they interpret and enact policies and negotiate the spaces that arise in the forms and prac-tices of 'dispersed' governance. They also have an expanded sense of agency, buttressed by their discursive constitution as transformational leaders. In the accounts I studied, there were many examples of selected elements of government discourse being re-articulated with discourses of 'the local'. As one respondent commented,

There are a lot of conflicts between what you know and believe will make things different for patients from a local perspective and what you are being told. We are looking for the spaces within government priorities to legitimize issues that will make a difference to local populations. (Senior Manager, health service)

Many respondents spoke about policies being adapted 'around the needs of the users and communities we serve'. The local was used to symbolize a range of meanings, meanings not generated within a specific locality but drawn from a repertoire of widely circulating social, political, and professional discourses. But in each case they were used to legitimate the importance of local agency in the face of the strongly centralizing thrust of government policy.

Bending Bureaucracy?

The accounts suggest the importance of tracing the ways in which public service managers, newly interpellated as transformational leaders, construct an ethos of office appropriate to the social and political values of the day while retaining elements of older, bureaucratic principles. This ethos is emergent rather than fixed, diverse rather than unitary. However, I want to suggest that the actors on whose accounts I have drawn were involved in bending, rather than breaking, bureaucracy as they navigated the uncertain world of network governance and were managing the tensions highlighted in the interface between top-down imperatives and 'local' goals and aspirations. Their accounts in this chapter suggest ways in which actors were— and continue to be—selectively co-opting 'official' discourses, and articulating them with a range of social and political discourses that reflect wider allegiances and identifications and sometimes alternative moral, ethical, or political ends.

These ends rarely directly counter the espoused goals of the Labour government. The accounts suggested a frequent alignment between Labour's own discourses and those of the respondents. Many suggested a positive engagement with the agenda, and, rather than contravening its intentions, were simply pushing the limits of stated policy or antici-pating the policy intentions of ministers. They were—albeit partially and selectively—following the spirit of Labour's political project for social renewal, bending the bureaucratic rules associated with hierarchical governance in order to promote outcomes in line with this agenda. We can see, here, how political discourses create new policy imperatives that guide action, but also new possibilities of thought and thus of resistance: 'discourse can be both an instrument and effect of power, but also a hindrance, a stumbling block, a point of resistance and a starting point for an opposing strategy' (Foucault 1981: 101). So my respondents were sometimes appropriat-ing policy/political discourses—on social exclusion, joined up working, public participation, accountability for outcomes, health prevention, community involvement, regeneration and so on— but suturing them into alternative frameworks of meaning that often prioritized 'local' goals. Such processes cannot be reduced to a quasi-functionalist account of actors pursuing their self-interest—they are better understood as processes of cultural positioning and attachment.

As such the accounts of some of my respondents suggest a more proactive *social* role for public service managers than the traditional image of the public servant as neutral administrator suggests. Their partisanship on the part of users/citizens/communities challenges the separation of powers central to Weber's classic conception of bureaucracy. Such partisanship is not of course new. The idea of the 'public servant' involves several different kinds of alignment between personal, professional, and policy objectives. The civil servant may retreat to institutionalized norms to resist policy initiatives that might undermine them. The social worker might act as an advocate for particular client groups in the face of policies that would affect ser-vices adversely. The street level bureaucrat might use her discretion to 'bend the rules' in favour of an individual citizen. What is different here, however, is the particular alignment between the constitution of managerial leaders as powerful change agents and the development of dispersed, multi-level governance. This is not (just) a case of policy being adapted on the ground, but of policy being developed out of practice across multiple sites in a dispersed field of governance. Many of my respondents were actively struggling to manage the resulting tensions, but at the same time exploiting those same tensions to enlarge the space for what they termed 'local' agendas.

In doing so, they deployed a range of resources to influence others and to legitimate their own actions. Some were based on managerial power (acting in the name of pragmatism in order to 'secure quick wins' or developing the systems/procedures to meet the performance criteria that would secure them relative freedom from government intervention). Others however were based on affective, value-based claims that apparently disrupted the surface rationality of moderniz-ing discourse. This is the very stuff of leadership. Each 'bends bureau-cracy' but in a different way. The former subordinates bureaucratic rules and norms to those of managerialism. The latter disrupts the separation between the person and the office, bringing the cultural attachments and identifications of the person or the profession into the office as resources to be deployed in bringing about change.

However bending bureaucracy is not the same as transcending it. While my respondents felt free to criticize the centralizing thrust of the policy process, they were reluctant to engage in criticism of policies themselves. They continued to view themselves as public servants rather than policy entrepreneurs, and did not view themselves as crossing the policy/delivery divide. And in emphasizing agency, I do not wish to suggest that they were free from controls. These are both discursive and material. The person brought into the office is a *constituted* person. Managerial leaders operate within a discursive environment that demarcates the boundaries of legitimacy and through which identity and attachment—as well as possible forms of resistance—are constituted. The possibilities for meaning are limited by the social and institutional positions from which a discourse derives. Policy as discourse not only creates certain possibilities for thought but also constitutes actors in a field of power in which differ-ent claims to knowledge and truth collide or are enmeshed. This field of power is one in which the state struggles for dominance in promot-ing particular definitions of 'truth', for example over the effectiveness of targets, inspection, and audit as drivers of change.

It also, crucially, controls the material environment of resources, structures, incentives, and rewards in which 'empowered' public service managers operate. The experience of the last few years suggests that where freedoms are exercised to some effect, additional controls are quickly imposed. du Gay suggests that 'Those at the centre do not relinquish their overall powers by constituting newly autonomous subjects as long as they retain control over the environment in which actors act autonomously' (2000: 101). The environment is increasingly one in which the discourses of success and failure open up new freedoms for some while subjecting others to increasing constraints or even closure. Through such strategies Labour can be viewed as attempting to close off the possibilities created by a dispersed field of action through the imposition of ever tightening systems of controls. Rather than a shift to network governance, many practitioners experience themselves as undergoing a resurgence of bureaucratic modes of (hierarchical) governing. This is not, perhaps an accurate usage of the term bureaucracy. These actors are constrained not by organizational hierarchies, formal rules, and rigid demarcations (though there are plenty of these still around) but by disciplinary strategies designed to constitute the subject as a self-governing actor. As we noted in *The Managerial State*, the dispersal of power enables and empowers actors but at the same time subjects them to new strategies of surveillance and control. 'The capacity of these actors to act or make choices is not their intrinsic property but an effect of their relationship with the state in which they are both empowered and disciplined' (Clarke and Newman 1997: 29). The offer of new freedoms and flexibilities to those who can demonstrate their capacity to deliver what government wants is just the latest in a long sequence of strategies of simultaneous empowerment and discipline.

But the existence of such strategies does not mean that they are effective. In a supposedly post-bureaucratic, network-based public service the twin processes of empowerment and discipline are played out in multiple sites and at different scalar levels of governance. The study of interactions in this field of power must take account not only of patterns of resource dependency and network structuring (the classic focus of political science) but also of the cultural attachments and patterns of identification of managerial leaders. As a contribution to such an approach, this chapter has highlighted the significance of 'the local' as symbolically condensing a range of different attachments and identifications. It has also suggested ways in which managerial actors adapt, appropriate, and re-articulate policy discourse in the process of negotiating tensions between different scalar levels of governance. In doing so it offers a framework for exploring how far key features of the old, social democratic public policy system strongly associated with bureaucracy (accountability, democracy, equity) may be subordinated within new governance regimes, but also how they are being discursively articulated with other meaning systems (leadership, entrepreneurship) in new logics of legitimation that bend, rather than break, the bureaucratic ethos.

Notes

1. Departmentalism here signifies a wider issue of the breaking up and categorization of problems, producing what the public management literature often terms 'silo mentality', the antithesis of the much vaunted 'joined up thinking'.
2. For example Sharon Wright's (2002) work on the implementation of unemployment policy in job centres highlights the process of negotiation between front line workers and clients and notes the continued significance of 'discretion' at the front line in the process of interpretation and recreation of policy within agencies (see also Kingfisher 1998).
3. This meant the civil service, for example, being opened up to staff from 'outside', and the creation of more 'interchange' between staff in the public and private sectors.
4. These included the Public Service Leaders Scheme run by the Cabinet Office in partnership with Bramshill, the Civil Service College and the University of Birmingham; The Public Leadership Programme and Malvern Programmes based at the School of Public Policy at Birmingham; and Birmingham's Public Service MBA.

References

Ball, S. J. (1990). *Politics and Policy Making in Education*. London: Routledge.

Ball, S. J. (1993). 'What is policy? Texts, trajectories and toolboxes'. *Discourse*. 13/2; 10–17.

Clarke, J. and Newman, J. (1997). *The Managerial State: Power, Politics and Ideology in the Remaking of Social Welfare*. London: Sage.

du Gay, P. (2000). *In Praise of Bureaucracy*. London: Sage.

Dunleavy, P. (1991). *Democracy, Bureaucracy and Public Choice*. New York: Prentice-Hall.

Fairclough, N. (2000). *New Labour, New Language*. London: Routledge.

Foucault, M. (1991). 'The order of discourse', in R. Young (ed.), *Untying the Text*. London: Routledge.

Hill, M. and Hupe, P. (2002). *Implementing Public Policy*. London: Sage.

Jessop, B. (2000). 'Governance failure', in G. Stoker (ed.), *The New Politics of British Urban Governance*. Basingstoke: Macmillan.

Kingfisher, C. (1998). 'How providers make policy: an analysis of everyday conversation in a welfare office'. *Journal of Community and Applied Social Psychology*. 8; 119–36.

Kooiman, J. (ed.) (1993). *Modern Governance: Government–Society Interactions*. London: Sage.

Kooiman, J. (2003). *Governing as Governance*. London: Sage.

Lipsky, M. (1980). *Street-level Bureaucracy: Dilemmas of the Individual in Public Services*. New York: Russell Sage Foundation.

Marsh, D. (ed.) (1998). *Comparing Policy Networks*. Buckingham: Open University Press.

Newman, J. (2001). *Modernizing Governance: New Labour, Policy and Society*. London: Sage.

Newman, J. (2002). 'Cutting Edges or Blunt Instruments? Modernizing Discourses and Leadership Narratives in United Kingdom Public Services', Paper to the 5th International Conference on Organizational Discourse, University of London, July.

Office of Public Service Reform (2002). *Reforming our Public Service*. London: The Cabinet Office, www.pm.gov.uk/opsr.

OFSTED (2002). *Local Education Authorities and School Improvement 1996–2001*. London: Ofsted.

Performance and Innovation Unit (2001). *Strengthening Leadership in the Public Sector*. London: The Stationery Office.

Pierre, J. (ed.) (2000). *Debating Governance: Authority, Steering and Democracy*. Oxford: Oxford University Press.

Pierre, J. and Peters, G. (2000). *Governance, Politics and the State*. Basingstsoke: Macmillan.

Rhodes, R. A. W. (1994). 'The hollowing out of the state'. *Political Quarterly*. 65; 138–51.

Rhodes, R. A. W. (1997). *Understanding Governance*. Buckingham: Open University Press.

Rhodes, R. A. W. (2000). *Transforming British Government*, Vols. 1 and 2. Basingstoke: Macmillan.

Senge, P. (1990). *The Fifth Discipline*. New York: Doubleday.

Sullivan, H. (2001). 'Modernization, democratization and community governance'. *Local Government Studies*. 27/3 (Autumn); 1–24.

Woods, P. (2003). 'Building on Weber to understand governance: exploring the links between identity, democracy and 'inner distance'. *Sociology*. 37/1; 139–59.

Wright, S. (2002). 'Confronting Unemployment: policy implementation as a two-way process'. Paper to the Social Policy Association Conference: Localities, Regeneration and Welfare, University of Teeside, July.

9

Performing for the Public: Doubt, Desire, and the Evaluation of Public Services

John Clarke

Public services have been the setting for persistent and complex arguments about bureaucracy. From the 1980s onwards, they have been criticized as bureaucratic monoliths, ill-suited to the demands of modern market societies. When broken-up into marketized or contractualized forms, others saw the rise of management as the reappearance of bureaucracy, particularly in the National Health Service. More recently the growth of evaluative processes and systems—inspection, audit, performance measurement, and so on—has also been linked to complaints about bureaucracy. The apparatus of targets, measurement, and 'bureaucratic tick-boxes' is seen as a cumbersome and intrusive bureaucratization of relationships between the public, the government, and public services.

This could be the basis for a bleak story about how 'things never change', or how bureaucracy always triumphs over reform initiatives. Such stories abound, of course, but they rely on a simplified and universalized idea of bureaucracy, and on a strange disconnection between forms of bureaucratic governance and political projects intended to transform or reform states.

Here, though, I am less concerned with the persistent use of 'bureaucratic' as an adjective of criticism and disdain than with the conditions that have shaped the rise of evaluation as a central element in the new governance of public services and the displacement of traditional public bureaucracies that this process has engendered. Establishing, assessing, and improving the performance of public services has become an increasing obsession of governments—and institutions of evaluation have been adapted and invented to embody this obsession. Inspection, audit, comparative performance measurement and more have become the means by which governments seek to manage public services 'at arm's length'. Britain has been a leading force in developing this approach that simultaneously builds on and transforms well-established approaches to audit and inspection.

I will be arguing that this rise of evaluation as a mode of governance attempts to resolve two different sorts of problems. First, it addresses a governmental problem: the difficulties of managing fragmented or dispersed forms of public service provision that have emerged from the break-up of integrated bureaucratic systems. Second, evaluation responds to a political problem: the challenge of demonstrating commitment to, and improvement in, public services to a sceptical public. However, evaluation as a means of managing the performance of public services has some distinctive instabilities that call into question its capacity to resolve either the governmental or political problems.

Performance Brought to Life?

There are problems about how to account for the rise of evaluation and the management of performance. It is clearly an international trend— part of the remaking of the governance of public services (Pollitt and Summa 1999). But explanations pitched at that level, whether they deal with the New Public Management, new modes of governmentality, or changing forms of economic and political regulation, have too little to say about specific forms of national political–cultural formation (Clarke 2004a). Here, I want to argue that the United Kingdom has shaped—and been shaped by—international trends around evaluation and that looking to the specificities of UK governance and politics makes a difference to the analysis. Social phenomena are evoked and infused with meaning in specific social contexts. So the contemporary concern with evaluating public services takes place in a particular set of contexts: a particular historical conjuncture. The range of methodologies, techniques, technologies, and practices are brought to life and made to matter in this set of political–cultural contexts. They are put into play within particular sets of social and political relationships— and are institutionalized in particular forms within particular social formations. These contexts include:

1. *Corporate globalization and market populism.* The economic, political, and cultural realignments of the world are dominated, though not exhausted, by the structures and flows of a US-centred corporate capitalism, whose public face is what Thomas Frank has called 'market populism':

that in addition to being mediums of exchange, markets were mediums of consent. Markets expressed the popular will more articulately and more meaningfully than did mere elections. Markets conferred democratic legitimacy; markets were a friend of the little guy; markets brought down the pompous and the snooty; markets gave us what we wanted; markets looked out for our interests. (2000: xiv)

2. *Neo-liberalism and public choice as the economics of mistrust.* Corporate globalization is intimately connected to the rise of neo-liberalism as an ideological and political project. It has had particularly deep impacts in the United States and the United Kindom, shaping a strong anti-statist, anti-bureaucracy, and anti-welfarist politics (Clarke 2004*a*). One central strand has been the role of public choice theory in challenging conceptions of public interest, public goods, and public services. Public choice theory 'demonstrated' that public institutions were driven by venal, self-interested and self-seeking motivations (just like markets), rather than altruism, public service goals, or professional ethics. It was, as a result, a defining force in the construction of a moral economy of mistrust.

3. *The fiscal crisis of the state and the fiscalization of policy discourses.* The break-up of the post-war welfare settlements involved a sustained attack on the economic basis and relationships of the state in advanced capitalist economies, inducing what O'Connor (1973)

described as the 'fiscal crisis' of the state. But it is important to note how the 'crisis of the state' was also *defined and constructed* as a eco-nomic/fiscal problem which has enabled specific forms of politi-cal–cultural alliances and a framing of policy discourses: fiscal responsibility; what the economy needs, making work pay, etc. (Prince 2001). Economy and efficiency have been twinned in the resulting challenges to public services. Stein, for example, has argued that public services have been subjected to a drive towards efficiency in an 'attack on the sclerotic, unresponsive, and anachronistic state' that is 'branded as wasteful' (2001: 7).

4. *The problem of control in the disintegrated/dispersed state.* Processes of state reform in this period have emphasized disintegration through various means: privatization, internal markets; outsourcing, delega-tion, decentralization and devolution, competition between multiple providers, principal–agent contractualization, etc. All of these have produced a 'dispersed state' (Clarke and Newman 1997) or a system of 'control at a distance' (Hoggett 1996). 'Performance' is one way of naming the problems of control at a distance and the proposed solutions to them. Scrutiny, inspection, evaluation, and audit emerge as potential solutions to the problems of 'arm's length control' (Clarke et al. 2000).

5. *Inequalities, differences and the public realm.* Other forces have also challenged the forms and limitations of welfare states—especially around the subordinations, marginalizations, and exclusions of the nominal universalism of welfare citizenship. Struggles over wel-fare citizenship—around axes of age, gender, race and ethnicity, sexuality, and dis/ability—have been diverse, but have been increas-ingly 'spoken for' in the language and imagery of consumerism and consumer choice—a particular variant of how diversity might be construed and mobilized (Williams 1996; Clarke 1997; Stein 2001; Needham 2003):

The challenges and demands on today's public services are very different from those of the post-war years. The rationing culture which survived after the war, in treating everyone the same, often overlooked individuals' differ-ent needs and aspirations. Rising standards, a more diverse society, and a steadily stronger consumer culture have increased the demand for good qual-ity schools, hospitals, and other public services, and at the same time brought expectations of greater choice, responsiveness, accessibility, and flexibility. (The Office of Public Services Reform 2002: 8)

6. *The decline of deference and the rise of scepticism/cynicism.*
Consumerism may be located in a wider field of cultural changes in
relationships of power, authority, and knowledge. In different conceptions of social and cultural change (traditional to modern societies;
modernity to post-modernity; modern to late-modern), there is a common concern with 'dis-belief' as the emergent cultural orientation
towards 'authority'. The specific focus may be on detachment from
'traditional values and norms'; or on established and would-be
authoritative institutions; or on the knowledge–power nexus of
'expertise'; or even on the crisis of 'meta-narratives'—but they are tied
together in processes of popular disenchantment and detachment
(Lyotard 1984; Giddens 1990). Frank terms this the problem of 'public
doubt' (2001: 21)—the sceptical/cynical response to dominant truth
claims.

Together these tendencies have contributed to a complex crisis of
the 'public realm'. They call into question the value, purpose, and
organization of public services, the possibility and character of a 'public
interest'. They make problematic a variety of institutional structures
and processes through which the public—and their interests—can be
represented. For governments, they intersect in a series of problems to
be resolved. The new forms of public service delivery pose new problems of control and coordination. The public interest is complex and
contradictory—combining desire for high-quality public services with
doubts about the capacity of government to provide them. The public
expect governments to perform like governments—fulfilling promises,
meeting demands, and improving standards—while being increasingly
sceptical about their claims to have done so. These conditions constitute the possibilities for the rise of 'performance' as a governmental
and a political project.

The Rise of Performance

It is in these political and organizational contexts that 'performance
management' has come to be a central theme. In the United Kingdom,
it reveals continuities with, and developments of, the state reform
projects of the Conservatives in the last two decades of the twentieth

century. As such it is marked by many of the discourses discussed above. It sustains the focal concerns of the fiscal discourse with the economic and efficient use of resources, albeit tempered by an increased concern with 'quality' and 'standards'. The performance focus is reflected in New Labour's concern that the public should see the improvements in services that the government was both resourcing and directing (if at arm's length). It sustains the managerial discourse—emphasizing the value, authority, and autonomy of managers (and transferring responsibility from the political to the managerial locus). It continues the 'competitive' framing of public services—not just contractually, but in the form of performance comparison (league tables, benchmarking, the distinctions between success and failure, the melodramatic commitment to 'naming and shaming' and so on). Finally, it has underpinned the expansion (in number and scope) of scrutiny agencies. These have performed several interlocking functions—evaluating performance, constructing comparisons, and functioning as both policy enforcers and management consultants (Clarke et al. 2000; Davis, Downe, and Martin 2002; Humphrey 2002a;). Performance, then, emerges at the intersection of these tendencies and institutional arrangements. It emerges as something that can be managed and evaluated in the public interest.

I will deal mainly with the United Kingdom—partly because it is what I know, and partly because what I know suggests this may be the most highly developed system of performance management (offering a distinctive combination of constitutional/governance arrangements, the politics of organizational design, and the politics of public service reform). It includes audit (both narrow and enlarged: Power 1997; Pollitt et al. 1999), inspection (old and new from Her Majesty's Inspectorates to OFSTED—the Office for Standards in Education: Hughes, Mears, and Winch 1996), evaluation (Henkel 1991), and some of what may be called regulation (Hood et al. 1998; Cope and Goodship 1999). But as a loosely coupled ensemble, it also includes the emergence of evidence based policy and practice (Davies, Nutley, and Smith 2000; Trinder and Reynolds 2000). For convenience, I am going to talk about the performance/evaluation nexus to refer to the coexistence of these different elements.

So, what political contradictions and tensions can the performance/ evaluation nexus resolve? First, it attempts to address public anxiety and alarm about quality and standards of public services. This is itself partially the effect of 'fiscal constraint' since the mid-1970s (see Stein 2001: 97ff). During the second Labour government, there seemed to be a distinctive shift in language used to designate the approach to public services from 'modernization' to 'invest and reform' (as well as the emphasis on 'delivery').

Second, as I have suggested already, the performance/evaluation nexus represents a solution to the problems of managing a dispersed and fragmented system 'at arm's length'. Withdrawing from the direct—and bureaucratic—provision of services, and from the direct control of the organizations involved in provision, created new problems about how control might be exercised through other means than an integrated, hierarchical bureaucracy. A rich diversity of mechanisms has emerged—contracts, commissioning, internal trading, market dynamics, partnerships, targets, outcome measurement, and, of course, 'more and better management'. But the growth in scale and scope of evaluative systems suggests that governments find them a useful means of managing 'at a distance' (Power 1997; see also Pollitt and Summa 1999).

Third, the performance/evaluation nexus offers the latest version of how to take 'politics' out of policy choices. New Labour has claimed pragmatic decision-making ('what counts is what works') as a distinctive virtue, transcending the 'dogmatic' or 'ideological' politics of Old Left and New Right (e.g., see Blair 1998). Rational, pragmatic, evidence-based decisions can supplant 'ideologically driven' policy-making, preventing education, health-care, or other welfare provision becoming a 'political football'. Since even politicians seem to think that 'politics' is a dirty word, corrupting rational decision-making, there is a recurrent search for the 'technical fix' that will insulate policy choices from the passions, dangers, and seductions of politics. From scientific-professional 'expertise' to 'business-like' managers, policy-making has passed through a variety of such technical fixes. In turn each 'fix' has proved vulnerable to destabilizing processes. On the one hand, politics tends to rear its ugly head recurrently (since governments are also political—as are the 'hard choices' of policy). On the other hand, the 'above the fray' technical fix is vulnerable to social, political, and cultural challenges to its mode of authority—whether this be social scepticism about how trustworthy the 'experts' are; or the competence of managers. Claims to authority are always only claims and are intrinsically susceptible to challenge.

Finally, the performance/evaluation nexus offers one way of solving the (party) political problem of 'public doubt'. Governments need (politically) to demonstrate that they are taking public services seriously (since the public continue to want services) and that they can 'deliver' services, standards, quality, or improvement (promises may vary), while trying not to be directly responsible. New Labour has had to operate in a field characterized by high expectations, rising demand, the repressed energies of social, political, and cultural movements, and an increasingly consumerist discourse and at the same time has been confronted by varieties of mistrust, doubt, scepticism, and cynicism. New Labour's response has been to emphasize standards, performance management, evaluative scrutiny and a commitment to pragmatic, evidence-based policy-making. These elements are both marked by continuities (especially with the Major governments) and intensification: New Labour does it more and more often.

Performing Performance

Conventionally, discussions of performance management have addressed the problems and solutions of evaluation at a number of different levels: epistemological, methodological, technical, and organizational. Here, however, I want to explore a different dimension, starting by taking seriously the other sense of performance— the process of 'putting on a show'—as a way of thinking about the performance/evaluation nexus. There are three reasons for doing so. First, it builds on the social constructionist or constructivist perspective on organizations, evaluation, and audit that provides an alternative epistemological and analytical starting point to the positivist view of evaluation and performance (Power 1997; Paton 2003). Second, it opens up questions about performances, performers, and audiences that are obscured—or too readily closed off—within the evaluation framework. Third, it corresponds with at least some aspects of organizational and popular common sense about performance evaluation—those elements that are sceptical about the politics, process, and outcomes of evaluation. That is to say, I think a constructionist perspective is not simply an 'academic' matter, but also exists in practical forms in knowledges and beliefs about the ways in which organizational and social life are collectively constructed (and are contested).

What difference does it make to think about performance being performed? To start with the concern with performance in public services is itself a performance. It is performed by states which need to demonstrate that they can perform like states. Hansen and Stepputat (2001), for instance, have pointed to the general tensions between the thinning of the state's capacities and the increasing range of demands being made on states. States have to perform like states for a range of audiences, located in different settings and formed in different relationships to the specific state. States have to look like states—they have to demonstrate their competence and capacity to ensure that they are taken seriously as states. They must perform for domestic/electoral audiences—the 'people' in their more or less complex and inclusive forms. They must perform for audiences drawn from other states: the field of international and intergovernmental relations (of conflict, collaboration, and competition). States have to perform for an increasing array of regional and supranational organizations and agencies (from the European Union to the World Trade Organization); and for national and transnational formations of capital (who do not necessarily share a point of view on the performance). Finally, they have to perform for diverse forms of mobile and 'transnational' people (Ong 1999). These range from the transnational corporate 'business class', through tourists, to flows of migrants (who may evaluate the performances of several states on their trajectories).

So, states need to perform like states—but this does not necessarily mean performing 'performance'. 'Performance'—as something to be measured, managed, and evaluated—is one current version of what a state should look like: it is addressed to both national and transnational audiences. To mix metaphors, performance is an international currency (allowing competitive comparison between states), but it can also be spent in the local markets (particularly the electoral ones). Nevertheless, the question of performance as electoral currency is a reminder that states are not monolithic blocks, particularly in the context of dispersed state formations. They are ensembles of structures and relationships, processes and practices. So to dismember the state a little: governments also need to perform like governments and one contemporary genre of governmental performance is the 'management of the performance of public services'.

Confronted by the sceptical public, governments have to find ways of demonstrating their commitment to 'delivery', their competence in policy-making and implementation, and their capacity to achieve improvement in services. 'Performance' thus becomes a vehicle for putting on a governmental show—setting standards, showing evidence of quality and improvement, celebrating success and 'naming and shaming' the back-sliders. In the dispersed state, service-providing organizations also have to 'put on a show'. They have to present themselves as 'high-performing organizations' for multiple audiences: the users/consumers/beneficiaries of their services; other competitors or collaborating organizations; and central government and its scrutineers. This is the field of audit, inspection, scrutiny, and evaluation. It is framed by a structuring narrative about 'service providers' that starts from the neo-liberal critique of bureaucratic 'producer power'. Neo-liberalism has naturalized this narrative, with its distinctive economic agents: producers and consumers; its economic motivational system (self-interest); its rhetorical juxtaposition of markets and monopolies; and its liberation theology of choice and competition. This discourse provides the dominant conception of the interrelationship of the public, public services, and government.

In particular, it informs how the performance/evaluation nexus has worked out in the regulation of public services in the United Kingdom. Although we have seen direct forms of marketization and privatization, the dominant tendency has been towards the creation of a dispersed and organizationally fragmented system of providers that is managed through quasi-competitive processes, subjected to state funding, state targets, and state evaluation. Evaluative agencies—the scrutineers of performance—occupy a central role in this system. They audit performance, provide comparative evaluations, define success and failure, and provide information for 'consumers' of services (in the absence of market information). This system combines vertical and horizontal relationships in a distinctive field of tensions. Evaluation is centrally driven—a 'top-down' set of scrutiny processes. They are reinforced by a claim to be in the interests of the public, users and consumers of services (implying a 'bottom-up' set of pressures—though they are rarely directly embodied, except as 'cases' or 'vignettes', see Humphrey 2002a). The horizontal relations are primarily competitive or quasi-competitive between organizations—reflected in rankings, league tables, and so on. This competitive conception of performance persists despite an increasing emphasis on partnership, collaboration, and joined-up working (Newman 2001; Glendinning, Powell, and Rummery 2002).

In these ways, the dispersed state form multiplies the levels and sites at which performance needs to be performed:

- the state level (displaying state capacity);
- the government level (displaying governmental competence and managing political calculation);
- the service level (displaying delivery or measuring up to targets);
- the organizational level (displaying efficiency and achievement), sometimes modulated by partnership (displaying 'joined-upness');
- the intra-organizational level (performing like successful departments, managers, and staff).

Each of these levels involves different, if overlapping, potential audiences (many of whom are also inside the state) and variations on what it means to perform. In this context, the performance of performance is a central organizational objective. It is impossible to stand aloof from the evaluative/competitive nexus, since it has resource and reputational consequences. As Paton argues, the concern with performance places extra demands on organizations and their managers:

[Managers] cannot rely on performance in terms of self-evident operating results to secure the confidence of government agencies or other key stakeholders. Performance in the other sense—that of acting to convey a particular impression and evoke particular responses—becomes important. In other words, managers have to give increasing time and attention to securing the confidence of key audiences by building relationships with them and projecting favourable accounts of necessarily ambiguous activities and figures. (2003: 29)

Organizations are preoccupied with performance management in two senses: first, how to manage the organization to achieve the targets, goals, standards, or elements of performance that are expected, demanded, or contracted; and second, how to manage the presentation of the organization's performance in ways that testify to its achievements and effectiveness. Of course, 'failure' may be the result of either or both forms of management—the failure to achieve and the failure to represent achievement effectively may both result in poor evaluation results. Performance—as Paton argues—is constructed in specific social circumstances:

Performance is not some underlying attribute that exists and can be known independently of the people centrally involved in and concerned about that organization. Performance is what those people more or less agree, implicitly or explicitly, to be performance, what they have in mind when they use the term. Hence to say an organization is (or is not) performing is to say that one has (or does not have) confidence in the accounts offered for what it has been achieving. (2003: 5–6)

This points to the construction of more or less agreed forms of accounting for performance among participants. Such agreed forms or conventions may be arrived at through different routes. Paton's discussion of social enterprise stresses the production of consensus among 'stakeholders' within and beyond the organization, in which a shared understanding or the constructed character of conventions is part, and result, of the process. Nevertheless, conventions may also be constructed and imposed externally—the authoritative, rather than the consensual, construction of the conventional criteria, calculation and evaluation (e.g. see Humphrey 2002b). Paton later argues that the 'language of performance' typically overrides any sense of the contingent and constructed character of 'what counts' as performance:

The problem is that the language of performance takes no prisoners. Through its lenses, the world is straightforward, situations are or should be controlled, the issues are clear the criteria unambiguous—and results have either been achieved or they have not. Uncertainty, patchiness, ambiguity, riders and qualifications—all these can be read as excuses, signs of weakness. 'Performance' is categorical—that is precisely its attraction. (2003: 29)

So, evaluation is a practice that requires the cooperation or compliance of the evaluated. As Power (1997) has argued, for audit to work, organizations must make themselves auditable. To be evaluated, organizations must engage in the co-production of evaluation: the preparation of evidence; the construction of narratives; the selection of a cast (where evaluation involves a 'visit' of some kind that requires a local team to meet the visitors). Anxieties about evaluation are widespread. To some extent they are internally focused (how are we doing; do we do the right things; will they recognize what is distinctive about us?). But attention is also intensely focused on anticipating the evaluators: concerns range from the technical (who and what will they want to see; what will they already know?) to questions about process and politics (who are they; what is their approach; how sound is it; do they have an agenda?).

These issues are known to both evaluators and those being evaluated. Evaluators know that the methodology of evaluation is imperfect (though they may argue that it is, in principle, perfectible). Evaluators also know that they will have agendas (though they may think these are legitimate); and that they will be suspected of having agendas by those whom they are evaluating. Those being evaluated know that methodologies are imperfect (and cannot capture the 'reality' of their organizational practice) and may be imperfectly applied (what the evaluators missed/ignored is a recurrent feature of evaluation aftermath talk). Those being evaluated know that evaluators have agendas (visible and invisible) and become experts at decoding questions to tease out their hidden or underlying concerns. There are, then, parallel organizational worlds in which reservations about the practices of evaluation are part of the common stock of knowledge. They are also organizational worlds in which particular groups engage in simultaneous processes concerned with the practice of evaluation: preparing, performing, and reflecting (Humphrey 2002b). The evaluation of organizational performance is itself a process that typically involves a performance (in a dramaturgical sense). But it is a performance that involves bringing together two different casts who have rehearsed separately. As a result, it is a performance fraught with possibilities for disaster (which has something to do with the levels of stress and anxiety regularly reported as associated with evaluation).

The evaluation process is adversarial because of contested views of evaluative judgement and its consequences and because of the different interests that have to be mobilized in and through evaluation regimes (concealed in the benign claim that 'we all have an interest in improved public services'). These differences of interest and perspective make for adversarial encounters as evaluators demonstrate their forensic skills of investigation, while the evaluated struggle to establish the 'truth' of their organization. Humphrey argues that her study revealed that 'Joint Reviewers and local authorities approached the entire (self-) review and (self-) reform process from diametrically opposed assumptions, irrespective of the end result of the review' (2002b: 470). As such, evaluation is both a grand drama (putting public providers to the test) and a micro-drama, playing out in the interactions of particular actors within the confines of their roles:

The Joint Review team conceptualizes itself primarily as an improvement agency, as it aspires to work hand-in-hand with senior managers to the benefit of all stakeholders, and reviewers make frequent reference to their 'free consultancy services', pointing out that it is central government which shells out £55,000 per review. Local authority staff treat Joint Reviews as an inspection agency sent to deliver a public judgement which could make or break individual careers and organizational reputations, so that the position statement becomes a written examination, the interview session becomes a staff appraisal, and the entire process can be pervaded by the stage-management of performance. (Humphrey 2002b: 470)

But the process is also collusive (see also Wedel 2001: 74, 75). It requires that all parties accept the legitimacy of each other's roles. It requires that all collude in the representation of the process as non-conflictual. All actors have an interest in a well-conducted process with good outcomes, and as several studies have indicated, evaluators may advise and prompt the evaluated on how to achieve 'quick wins' or present success in the pursuit of legitimation (Humphrey 2002a,b; Paton 2003: 47, 48). More generally, though, evaluation requires that all collude in the representations of objectivity, independence, and transparency, denying the constructed character of the process, the evidence, and the judgement.

Public Doubt: Where Success and Scepticism Meet

I turn now to the place of 'success' in the performance/evaluation nexus. Success is both an effect of, and a dynamic in, the process of evaluation. The dominant regime of evaluation is comparative-competitive. It is a process that evaluates performances against 'success criteria' (targets, standards, benchmarks etc.). The construction of evaluation as a process of coordinating a dispersed state has a number of distinctive consequences that centre on 'success'. First, it is a process that is about the production of success (and failure): the comparative-competitive model of performance evaluation is intended to rank 'winners and losers'. Second, the process predisposes people to attempt to be 'successful'—and organizational analysts have long known that 'what gets measured is what gets done', focusing organizational performance on the criteria of evaluation. Third, the process creates a lot of different actors with an interest in 'success'.

In such a success-oriented field, the discourse of success is likely to be widely deployed. Scrutiny agencies also have an interest in success in two ways. They need to demonstrate that scrutiny 'works'—improving the performance of the service. Paradoxically, scrutiny agencies need to both promote success and look 'tough' by identifying 'failure' (so as to resist charges of 'producer capture', see, for example, arguments over how to compare and represent police performance: Dean, 'Figures of fun or real ratings?', *Guardian Society*, 26 February 2003: 7). Scrutiny agencies need to demonstrate their 'independence' in order to acquire credibility. This involves complicated triangulations of the relationships between such agencies and 'interests', and may involve narratives of 'standing up to' such interests, especially central government (Humphrey 2002a; see Clarke, forthcoming).

Finally, as Schram and Soss (2002) argue, 'success' is a political resource. It is a resource that matters to organizations, managers, and political representatives in a variety of ways, especially in competitive or marketized systems of service provision. 'Success' provides a competitive edge—in relation to resources, political access, and 'consumers' (directly and indirectly). The 'success' reputation of educational institutions (schools or universities) has significant 'business' effects—and institutions expend effort on being 'successful' and on managing their *reputation* for success. Organizations must tell 'success stories' (and suppress or defeat non-success stories) as a condition of organizational reproduction and development. The effect is a 'success spiral' in which all participants to the process have an inflationary interest in producing 'success'. But in such an inflationary context, there are potential problems about how audiences suspend disbelief in the performance of performance. The 'success spiral' accentuates the potential for de-stabilization. It tends to expand the 'credibility gap' in which the language of claims becomes perceived as 'rhetoric' detached from 'reality'. There are a number of potential disjunctures between performers and audiences that emerge in this process.

Scrutiny agencies publish their reports, commentaries, and evaluations, but these are little read by the general public. There remains a persistent gap between the imagined 'active citizen-consumer' and the everyday practices of citizens in terms of the value attached to, and use made of, evaluation reports. A survey for the Office of Public Service Reform revealed very low public recognition of inspectorates, with OFSTED achieving the highest score of 17 per cent of those surveyed (OPSR 2003a). Rather, these documents circulate primarily in political and policy networks. However, they do come to the attention of citizens in mediated forms. The evaluation of public services performance is reported through the mass media in a context of journalistic ambivalence and scepticism. Media treatment of the reports of scrutiny agencies range from celebrating their 'watchdoggery' to cynicism about their subjection to governmental or producer interests. In the former, 'independent scrutiny' is celebrated as a means of keeping a check on both service providers and governmental achievement/ failure. In the latter, scepticism about the 'burying of bad news', the celebration of 'massaged' good news; or the effects of producer capture in producing obfuscatory comparison is the dominant tenor. In an echo of Hackett's analysis of the media as 'watch dogs, mad dogs and lap dogs' (2001), the media have an ambivalent view of the 'independence' of scrutiny agencies. Mass media that are characterized by a combination of political–economic antagonism towards public services and journalistic cynicism about politics form a difficult setting for the publication and celebration of 'success stories'.

But it would be wrong to think that such mediated reports determine citizen responses directly. Rather, they intersect in complicated ways with forms of personal experience, knowledge, and belief. Evaluative reports—and the ways in which they may be reported—have to coexist with particularized experiences of public services (National Consumer Council 2003). This disjuncture is unpredictable: people may be concerned about the state of schools, but think theirs is fine; they may read about health-care problems, but have good experiences; they may read about policing improvements, but be a multiple victim of crime. What it does mean, though, is that people rarely read 'evaluations' from the standpoint of the abstracted taxpayer/consumer. Forms of social difference and inequality may also affect both experience and the ways in which evaluations are 'read'.

The question of 'trust' has become an increasingly significant issue in public discourse and one that has been accentuated in the acrimonious encounters between 'spinning' politicians and 'cynical' journalists (neither of whom score very highly in surveys of which occupational groups are trusted by the public, see Audit Commission/MORI 2003). Politicians complain of media cynicism and public de-politicization; journalists bewail cynical attempts to manipulate the public (and themselves). 'Spin' has become a defining term in media representations of New Labour, for example (see Finlayson 2003). As a result, evaluations of public services are always made public in an unstable field of public political discourse. They are vulnerable to media or public cynicism ('they would say that, wouldn't they?'). But they may also be subject to media and public scepticism: a more active questioning about how the evaluation was produced, what interests shaped it, how and when it is being deployed, and what its consequences might be. In the current period, I think it can be argued that both cynicism and scepticism discipline relations between the public, public services, and government, in the process forming Frank's problem of 'public doubt'.

But it would be a mistake to take 'public doubt' as the only—or even the dominant—orientation of publics to public services. Public doubt coexists with public demand (for services and for their improvement) and public commitment (to 'public' ideals of service). This, too, is a political pressure on governments and service providers and takes a specific conjunctural form in the United Kingdom in the hope (aspiration? expectation?) that 'New Labour' would restore or revive public services after eighteen years of Conservative degradation. But this coexistence of commitment and cynicism is, it seems, unstable and unpredictable—posing difficult challenges of political calculation and address. How do governments persuade people that they have invested in, modernized and reformed public services (and improved their standards) when people do not believe what governments tell them?

It is not clear that the current evaluation/performance nexus has provided an effective or compelling solution to the governmental or political problems that I identified earlier. As a *governmental project* for enhancing control at a distance, it has been structured around a centralizing, consumerist and objectivist model of organizational control. These characteristics generate several distinctive instabilities (see also Harrison 2002). Its centralism produces tensions around local responsiveness and innovation. Its consumerism produces difficulties from its antagonism towards 'producer interests'. This perceived hostility brings to the fore issues of professional autonomy and judgement, and contributes to wider problems about the recruitment, retention, and motivation of staff in public services. Its objectivism runs into organizational and public scepticism about the construction of evidence and judgements. Finally, its organization-centredness creates tension around the promotion and evaluation of collaboration and partnership working.

As a *political project*, the evaluation/performance nexus has trouble resolving the problem of public doubt (and its unstable combination with public desire). In part, this is the result of internal instabilities (the constructed nature of evidence; the problematic character of independence; and the success spiral). But it is also a matter of this form of political representation trying to work in the field of contemporary public discourse—and its mediating processes. Governmental statements do not arrive at the public directly, nor is the public predisposed to accept the truth claims of political statements. Finally, there is a problem of the gap between political rhetoric and practice. Conviction politics, faith, and evangelism (from the Third Way down to specific policies) run counter to, or at least ahead of, the evidence. For example, several New Labour policies have seemed to run counter to both existing and emergent evidence: the relationship between money and poverty; the expanding prison population, or the Private Finance Initiative as a way of funding public services. While I do not think politics, policy, and practice can—or should—be run on the basis of pragmatic adaptation to 'evidence', it does seem to me to contribute to the 'credibility gap' when evangelism, conviction, and policy 'hyperactivity' (Dunleavy 1995) are central to the mode of governing.

What we see in the performance/evaluation nexus is, above all, the unstable intersection of governmental and political projects. Evaluation must, as the Office of Public Service Reform insists, be 'independent of the service providers' (2003b: 3), but that does not make it independent of government—and it is governments that are the primary focus of public doubt. As a result the evaluation/performance nexus is doubly vulnerable—to being seen as an 'enforcement' arm of government and as the provider of 'policy based evidence' needed for political success. These instabilities emerge in the intersection of long historical trends and more particular conjunctural formations. On the one hand, the mediated rise of scepticism and the decline of deference coincided with struggles to move beyond the false universalism of welfare states towards the emergence of a more differentiated and more mobile set of publics. On the other, we have specific conjunctural features of the post-Thatcherite construction of a 'modern Britain'. In this project, a Third Way route to governing in the 'modern world' is being directed from a profoundly centralist state structure and profoundly centralizing party formation. The inherited features of the British state enable a 'central command system', and centralized command has been a unifying thread of New Labour's approach to party discipline, political management, and governmental power (on the significance of state constitution, see Taylor-Gooby, 2001a,b). In the rise of the performance/evaluation nexus we may be seeing the generic crisis of modern governmentality, but it is profoundly mediated through the instabilities of a particular strategy of governing in this specific political–cultural conjuncture. These instabilities—forged at the intersection of governmental and political projects—have inhibited the construction of a new settlement of relationships between the public, the state, and public services. Such a settlement is a primary objective of New Labour politics—and is embodied in the performance/evaluation nexus.

One critical element in this unstable and unfinished transition is how conceptions of the public and the public interest are institutionalized in governmental apparatuses. The old bureau-professional systems of collectivist public provision have been traduced as monolithic, 'one size fits all', producer-dominated, and paternalist institutions. In the process, of course, their institutionalization of a social-democratic conception of a public and a public interest (with all of its limitations and contradictions) was dissolved. But there are serious problems about how a 'public service ethos' is to be constructed or sustained in a fragmented and dispersed system of public provision. In particular, it is open to question whether the multiple apparatuses and agencies of the performance/evaluation nexus can be the setting for such conceptions. For all their apparently bureaucratic forms and processes, they are more vulnerable to capture by dominant political–policy agendas. At the same time, they are constructed around new—and narrower—conceptions of the public and its interests: a more economized, individualized, and consumerist view of a fragmented and diverse population. Nevertheless, this view of the public and its interests is itself contested by other imaginings of the public, their interests, and of how they might be served.

Note

This chapter has been shaped by thoughts and comments from many people. In addition to the participants at the original workshop, I am grateful to Jean and John Comaroff, Gavin Drewry, Rob Paton, and those involved in the Audit research project (Sharon Gewirtz, Gordon Hughes, and Jill Humphrey) at The Open University.

References

Audit Commission/MORI (2003). *Trust in Public Institutions*. London: The Audit Commission.

Blair, T. (1998). *The Third Way*. London: The Fabian Society.

Clarke, J. (1997). 'Capturing the customer? Consumerism and social welfare'. *Self, Agency and Society*. 1/1; 55–73.

Clarke, J. (2004a). *Changing Welfare, Changing States: New Directions in Social Policy*. London: Sage.

Clarke, J. (2004b). 'Dissolving the public realm? The logics and limits of neo-liberalism'. *Journal of Social Policy*. 33/1; 27–48.

Clarke, J. (forthcoming). 'The production of transparency: evaluation and the governance of public services', in G. Drewry and C. Greive (eds), *Contractualisation and Public Services*. EGPA.

Clarke, J. and Newman, J. (1997). *The Managerial State: Power, Politics and Ideology in the Remaking of Social Welfare*. London: Sage.

Clarke, J. and Newman, J. (2004). 'Governing in the modern world.', in R. Johnson and D. Steinberg (eds), *Labour's Passive Revolution*. London: Lawrence and Wishart.

Clarke, J., Gewirtz, S., Hughes, G., and Humphrey, J. (2000). 'Guarding the public interest? auditing public services', in J. Clarke, S. Gewirtz, and E. McLaughlin (eds), *New Managerialism, New Welfare?* London: Sage.

Cope, S. and Goodship, J. (1999). 'Regulating collaborative government: towards joined-up government?' *Public Policy and Administration*. 14/2; 3–16.

Davies, H., Nutley, S., and Smith, P. (eds) (2000). *What Works? Evidence-based Policy and Practice in Public Services*. Bristol: The Policy Press.

Davis, H., Downe, J., and Martin, S. (2002). *External Inspection of Local Government: Driving Improvement or Drowning in Detail*. York: Joseph Rowntree Foundation/York Publishing Services.

Dunleavy, P. (1995). 'Policy disasters: explaining the UK's record'. *Public Policy and Administration*. 10/2; 52–70.

Finlayson, A. (2003). *Making Sense of New Labour*. London: Lawrence and Wishart.

Frank, T. (2000). *One Market Under God: Extreme Capitalism, Market Populism and the End of Economic Democracy*. New York: Anchor Books.

Giddens, A. (1990). *The Consequences of Modernity*. Cambridge: Polity Press.

Glendinning, C., Powell, M., and Rummery, K. (eds) (2002). *Partnerships, New Labour and the Governance of Welfare*. Bristol: The Policy Press.

Hackett, R. (2001). 'News media and civic equality: watch dogs, mad dogs, or lap dogs?' in E. Broadbent (ed.), *Democratic Equality: What Went Wrong?* Toronto: University of Toronto Press.

Hansen, T. B. and Stepputat, F. (eds) (2001). *States of Imagination: Ethnographic Explorations of the Postcolonial State*. Durham, NC: Duke University Press.

Harrison, S. (2002) 'New labour, modernisation and the medical labour process'. *Journal of Social Policy*. 31; 465–85.

Henkel, M. (1991). *Government, Evaluation and Change*. London: Jessica Kingsley.

Hood, C., Scott, C., James, O., Jones, G., and Travers, T. (1998). *Regulation inside Government: Waste-watchers, Quality Police and Sleaze Busters*. Oxford: Oxford University Press.

Hoggett, P. (1996). 'New modes of control in the public service'. *Public Administration*. 74; 23–34.

Hughes, G., Mears, R., and Winch, C. (1996). 'An inspector calls? regulation and accountability in three public services'. *Policy and Politics*. 25/3; 299–313.

Humphrey, J. (2002*a*). 'A scientific approach to politics? On the trail of the audit commission'. *Critical Perspectives on Accounting*. 13; 39–62.

Humphrey, J. (2002*b*). 'Joint reviews: retracing the trajectory, decoding the terms'. *British Journal of Social Work*. 32; 463–76.

Lyotard, J.F. (1984). *The Postmodern Condition: A Report on Knowledge*. Manchester: Manchester University Press.

National Consumer Council (2003). *Expectations of Public Services: Consumer Concerns 2003*. London: National Consumer Council.

Needham, C. (2003). *Citizen-consumers: New Labour's Marketplace Democracy*. London: The Catalyst Forum.

Newman, J. (2001). *Modernising Governance*. London: Sage.

O'Connor, J. (1973). *The Fiscal Crisis of the State*. New York: St. Martin's Press.

Office of Public Services Reform (2002). *Reforming Our Public Services*. London: Office of Public Services Reform.

Office of Public Services Reform (2003*a*). *Inspecting for Improvement: Developing a Customer Focused Approach*. London: Office for Public Services Reform.

Office for Public Services Reform (2003*b*). *The Government's Policy on Inspection of Public Service*. London: Office of Public Services Reform.

Ong, A. (1999). *Flexible Citizenship*. Durham, NC: Duke University Press.

Paton, R. (2003). *Managing and Measuring Social Enterprises*. London: Sage.

Pollitt, C. and Summa, H. (1999). 'Performance audit and public management reform', in C. Pollitt, X. Girre, J. Lonsdale, R. Mul, H. Summa, and M. Waerness (eds), *Performance or Compliance? Performance Audit and Public Management in Five Countries*. Oxford: Oxford University Press.

Pollitt, C., Girre, X., Lonsdale, J., Mul, R., Summa, H., and Waerness, M. (1999). *Performance or Compliance? Performance Audit and Public Management in Five Countries*. Oxford: Oxford University Press.

Power, M. (1997). *The Audit Society*. Oxford: Oxford University Press.

Prince, M. (2001). 'How social is social policy? Fiscal and market discourse in North American welfare states'. *Social Policy and Administration*. 35/1; 2–13.

Schram, S. and Soss, J. (2002). 'Success stories: welfare reform, policy discourse and the politics of research', in S. Schram (ed.), *Praxis for the Poor*. New York: New York University Press.

Stein, J. G. (2001). *The Cult of Efficiency*. Toronto: House of Anansi Press.

Taylor-Gooby, P. (ed.) (2001a). *Welfare States Under Pressure*. London: Sage.

Taylor-Gooby, P. (2001b). 'Welfare reform in the UK', in P. Taylor-Gooby (ed.), *Welfare States Under Pressure*. London: Sage.

Trinder, L. and Reynolds, S. (eds) (2000). *Evidence-based Practice: A Critical Appraisal*. Oxford: Blackwell.

Wedel, J. (2001). *Collision and Collusion: The Strange Case of Western Aid to Eastern Europe*. New York: Palgrave.

Williams, F. (1996). 'Postmodernism, feminism and the question of difference', in N. Parton (ed.), *Social Theory, Social Change and Social Work*. London: Routledge.

10

What is Best 'Value'? Bureaucracy, Virtualism, and Local Governance

Daniel Miller

Virtualism—The Larger Context

In preparing you for reading this chapter it is perhaps worth starting with the admission that I am not a student of bureaucracy or indeed of government. Rather this chapter is a by-product of a much larger study that is concerned with the concept of value and its centrality to activities ranging from commerce and finance, to morality and government. As an anthropologist committed to using ethnography I am carrying out a series of studies that include, where possible, an element of participant observation. This chapter is based upon my first case study which took as its subject the 'Best Value' (from here on BV) audit of local government in England and Wales (Audit Commission 1999, 2001). My primary concern was the role of value in the transformation of public funds back into public services, but for the purpose of this chapter I will be concerned more with the issues that were encountered in the tensions between the BV inspection and the people and practices observed within local government. I will also refer to the one publication that has already emerged from this study (Miller 2003) which was directed at a different issue, that which I elsewhere call 'virtualism' (Miller 1998). By this last term, I refer to the problem of increasing abstraction in modern institutions and the way this acts to produce effects that are the opposite of intentions.

Best Value (BV), which was established in 1999, is a colossal operation, said by Martin (2001) to cost £600 million a year. It is based on a statutory requirement that every service provided by every council in England and Wales must provide a BV report and be subject to a BV inspection once every five years. At the time I finished my fieldwork there were already about 1600 of these reports published ranging from cleaning buildings and security services; maintaining playgrounds, highways, or libraries; through to planning and environmental controls—in short every aspect of what local government does (for reviews of BV see Boyne 1999; Martin 2000, 2002; Raine 2000; Snape 2000). I had some precedent for an anthropological perspective in that there have been some anthropological works on audit collected in Strathern (2000), as well on bureaucracy (e.g. Herzfeld 1992; Riles 2001). My study was equally influenced by my sense that Power (1997) and du Gay (2000) had in different ways made clear what had been my largely uninformed hunches as to what might be going on.

In conducting this study of BV, I was fortunate to be granted excellent access by the Audit Commission. I was able to accompany the pairs of inspectors in every aspect of their inspection, including the discussions that took place at Millbank Tower (the headquarters of the Audit Commission) before and after inspections. I could sit in and record all meetings with local council officials, and accompany inspectors on their 'reality checks' of actual instances of these services. I participated fully in three inspections (which I will keep anonymous) and in addition discussed BV with council officers whose departments had been inspected or were preparing for inspections. My research both as participant and interviewer took place in and around London during 2001. Although I suspect my presence was sometimes felt to be 'the third that makes a crowd', given the intimate nature of the interview process, I do not think I had a significant impact on any of the results or procedures. I did not speak during interviews but usually discussed the interviews with the inspectors after the interviewee had left.

Although my aim was to relate this inspection to issues of value, which I attempt to do later in this chapter, my reason for using audit as a case study arose from an earlier theoretical project. In what I called 'a theory of virtualism' (Miller 2003), I argued that there has been a major shift in recent times that affects a wide range of institutions we may not otherwise think of as connected. The starting point was the rise of consumption as an increasingly important source of political authority (Keat 1994). The consumer was becoming the ultimate arbiter of what should exist in the world. I argue that just as actual consumers seemed about to be, in some sense, empowered by being accredited this authority, it was in effect taken away from them by a whole series of institutions that usurped this authority. This leads to what might be called a fetishism of the consumer parallel to Marx's argument about the fetishism of the commodity as hiding its source in labour. Obvious examples of this seemed to me to include: first the power accrued to lawyers standing on behalf of consumer rights, second the power of the modern economist asserting academic models such as that of the free market that governments are supposed to conform to based on the claim that this is the best way the economy can serve consumers; third the huge increase in management consultancy and its claims to deliver clients and customers to those it advises. Also, the rise of a theory of postmodernism in the social sciences based on claims about consumer societies but often backed up with precious little research on actual consumers. Within this larger picture the rise of audit is not simply something that emerges from the internal development of government but part of a much wider series of changes over the last thirty years.

This logic seemed quite explicit and clear in the development of recent audits that seek to justify themselves as being carried out on behalf of 'patients as consumers' or 'students as consumers' or consumers more generally. As Power (1997) has argued the effect of these audits is actually to turn the attention of the institution in question from the actual clients of their services to auditors who stand in as 'virtual' consumers in the stead of users. Audits and inspections increasingly take up the time and resources of institutions that might otherwise have been directed to real users and consumers. This is precisely what I would argue happens in all these other cases of management consultants, economists, lawyers, social scientists, and others who have appropriated the mantle of consumer authority. In each case they are legitimated by the authority of the consumer but in effect end up paying less rather than more attention to actual consumers. The point of this theory of virtualism is to argue that it is no coincidence that all of these forces have grown considerably over much the same period following much the same logic.

This was my starting point, but I intended to use the study to initiate an investigation into a complementary area, which was the concept of value. This is why out of all the audits available, I chose to study BV. Even this very brief introduction should hopefully demonstrate that to talk only of government emulating the private sector is too simple. The trends that are identified here are much broader than either government or commerce, which is why at some point it is worth trying to go back to a broader theory that the term virtualism, or the concept of value are trying to address. This would, however, take us far from the immediate concern with the values of bureaucracy, and so this chapter having taken note of this larger context will now move towards the more particular issue though first stopping to examine the concept of value itself a little more closely.

The Paradox of Value

Until recently the term value has not had quite the sense of 'bedrock' associated with its use in government as one would find with 'added value' or 'shareholder value' in commerce, and where used, had a slightly different connotation. Under the Conservative government the development of Compulsory Competitive Tendering (CCT) or Office for Standards in Education (OFSTED) and many other inspection and audit regimes, represented a concern dominated by two factors—price and failure. The underpinnings of most audits and inspections were a belief in tax-cuts and thus cost-cutting and the need to justify an increase of private sector involvement through demonstrating the failures of the public sector. Yet in many ways the failure of this relatively single minded strategy has everything to do with this little word 'value'. The problem is that the word value does what might otherwise be regarded as an outrageously broad amount of work. On the one hand it can be used as almost synonymous with the word price, as in, 'what is the value of this house or antique in today's market?'. On the other hand, it pulls us close to the various meanings of the term values, which could be defined as everything in this world that we regard as irreducible to price and, more generally, money.

So the word value seems to insist upon the connection between things which the same word shows to be quite incompatible—that which cannot be priced and that which must be. This paradox was brilliantly explored by the sociologist Viviana Zelizer (1987) in her history of the insurance industry's concern with children, *Pricing the Priceless Child*. With regard to the Conservative government, it was clear in the rhetoric and focus of the last two general elections that the ideal of cost-cutting faced considerable, if not insurmountable, problems when confronted with the public's generally sentimental sense of the welfare state as one of the most valued contributions of Britain to the modern world. The problem could be said to be that the welfare state was now experienced as a valued possession that could not be reduced easily to mere value. Where the term values includes a quality that transcends that which can be reduced to price, cost-cutting was seen as something that demolished rather than, as intended, created value.

So when the Labour party came into power in 1997 the word value was at something of a high point in its ability to point to both apparent political problems and also apparent political solutions. The political problem—in a highly generalized form—is that the Conservative government was viewed as better at retaining posses-sion of value in the sense of low price, while the Labour government was better at retaining possession of value in the sense of values that transcend price. The future seemed to be with whichever party could seize upon the potential clearly expressed in the word value itself which was its ability to simultaneously occupy both ends of this apparent polarity, value as price and value as priceless.

This is of course quite typical of the kind of problem and solution with which the Labour party associated itself through the adoption of the term 'New Labour' and its doctrine of a 'Third Way'. From the perspective of this repositioning in the hallowed middle ground of politics, the word value can be located as the bridging point that potentially delivers the overcoming of all such polarities. While CCT under the Conservative government was generally regarded as subjecting local government to evaluation in terms of price and competition, value under New Labour has come back in line, in part, at least, with the sense of public service as a highly valued outcome of government. The term now implies that the bottom line of local government is the quality of the services it provides as experienced by users of those services, in balance with the obligation to those same people to keep taxes low by ensuring that the services are provided at the lowest cost commensurable with that improvement in quality. The trick here is to turn the contradiction inherent in the term value from a fault into a virtue. To simplify this chapter I will from now on use the word value to mean forces used in evaluation such as money, and the word values for the heterogeneous, incommensurable concerns that transcend such reduction to evaluation.

It is not at all unreasonable to consider local government services as situated within the paradox occupied by the term value, since one way of defining the work of local government is that it occupies the position of turning value in its homogenized form of money into values in the heterogeneous form of the many services which benefit the public. Local government transforms money as a quantifiable measure into services which have to reach a heterogeneous population with a diversity of needs. The public themselves go through many quite similar exercises in their own lives and have no difficulty in identifying institutions that they feel satisfy this ability to resolve contradictions in value. To give just one example, I recently undertook a study of the retail sector from the point of view of shoppers. In the retail sector we can see a polarity between discount stores that are good value in the sense that they offer the cheapest products, and quality stores that are seen as good value in offering products of high quality, which will last, or work effectively for some purpose or other. Sometimes, however, a store succeeds in reconciling these differences. In our study of shoppers (Miller et al. 1998: 135–58) it became quite clear that the department store John Lewis was understood by most shoppers as far and away the most effective retail outlet in exemplifying the concept of value that is based upon this reconciliation. It was not seen as anything like the cheapest store, nor was it seen as necessarily possessing the highest quality produce available. It was seen, however, as having already undertaken a good deal of the work of shoppers in seeking to balance price and quality. I would argue that one part of the aspiration behind New Labour was to become a kind of 'John Lewis' of politics and the use of the term value could have been an effective instrument in realizing this ambition. This seems to allow the possibility of cost-cutting while still preserving the sense of welfare as something valued or even 'treasured'. So it seems entirely reasonable that the inspection of local government should proceed under the auspices of the word value.

Unfortunately, however, the inspection regime in question is not called simply value, but 'Best Value'. The term 'best' immediately brings out the contradictory nature of value itself. It qualifies the word value by relativizing it, that is, by suggesting that there are multiple instances or forms of value. This itself contradicts the increasing use of value as a single 'bottom line' criteria of adjudication as implied in phrases such as 'added value'. The word 'best' adds something else. It seems to imply a sense of competition, to be won by the best. It implies a kind of free market logic whereby the BV is found through competition between different sources of value. In practice, I will try and show this is very much the case. The potential for a kind of 'John Lewis' adjudication of value between costs and quality of services becomes lost by the more market orientation towards competition that is represented by the term best.

Before turning to the results of my investigations, I want to briefly restate the above argument in the terms in which I think it was experienced and understood by those actually involved in the BV process. The first actor in this drama is the government. Those who developed BV seem to have understood it as a kind of Copernican revolution in the self-conception of local government. Up to the present, local government is viewed as something that grew up almost organically as a provider of services. It is seen as naturally developing its own self-interests and vision of its task as a provider of services but also its concerns with its own rights, and its own continuity. This led to a perception of the world where the public came to be seen as that which circled around and provided the legitimacy for the shining star of local government in and of itself. BV is intended to reverse this history. It is a strident declaration that the public does not exist to legitimate local government, but local government exists only to the degree that it serves the public. In the future everything that local government is and does must be the direct and logical result of the aspirations and desires of the public, in particular, it should concentrate on whatever the public most appreciates having done for it. In this vision, shining in the centre of the universe is the public itself and in the future local government must bask in the reflected glory of that celestial presence. This is another version of the ideal that in the future local government will be consumer led.

All of this fits neatly in to the larger ideology of New Labour.

The 'Best Value' initiative combines several strands of New Labour's approach to performance: an emphasis on what counts is what works ... There is no presumption that private or public provision is superior ... This puts local stakeholders in a stronger position to influence services, moving the focus from cost-effectiveness to community-effectiveness. (Rouse: 1999: 90)

In places such as the New Labour in-house magazine *Renewal* these positionings become quite explicit. Davis and Martin (2000) are clear that BV is intended to chart a course between cost savings and quality improvement as also between central and local government. For Martin, who leads the largest current academic audit of BV, the primary question is whether or not external inspection is an effective instrument for improving government services. The downside is pointed out in the same issue by Goss (2000). While her title 'Can New Labour make a difference?' clearly starts from a similar concern she takes note of the burden being created by so many new systems of audit and accountability. Also at issue is this tension between being a neutral adjudicator and using BV to promote a model from the private sector. Although BV officers take pains to deny any continuities with CCT, and the government claims to be 'simply agnostic' about who delivers services (Martin 2002: 132), others see New Labour as actually being more zealous in promoting performance management and expecting more involvement of private organizations in the delivery of public services than its Conservative predecessors (Horton and Farnham 1999: 255).

Underneath all this discussion is a clear political agenda. This concerns the need to find ways to get the public in their capacity as voters to acknowledge that the money being spent upon local government is well spent (see Clarke, Chapter 9, this volume). It is assumed that the means to achieve this is to have the public involved in prioritizing such services so they directly reflect that which the public cares about. So the other way of seeing this Copernican revolution is that in future, local government will revolve around the results of its own surveys of what the public is telling it it ought to be. The government wants to judge the service from a consumer perspective. Since actual consumers are too broad and amorphous a body, the government has to create 'virtual consumers' which is where the BV inspection comes in. The inspector's job is to try and assess the government service from the point of view of consumers (i.e. voters). One of the ways in which this constitutes an assault upon traditional public bureaucracy is that it undermines other responsibilities. Local government includes many tasks that are not obvious to the public. It finds itself in the invidious position that central government on the one hand knows this perfectly well, but at the same time through the BV regime is taking on a kind of disingenuous self-representation as though it is not really government but the public or consumers of services whose concern is only with what becomes apparent at the moment of consumption.

The other key part is played by the local council itself. For them the Copernican revolution represents a significant threat. They start from the position that they are the real group who are concerned with local public services and it is they who already have the interests of the consumers of those services at heart. Their immediate response is to assume that BV will be largely a continuation of CCT, and a cover for another round of cost-cutting and privatization aimed at lowering the costs of public services by lowering the wages of public servants. Value is important to local government officers more from the sense of the protection of values against evaluation. A reduction to measurement is seen as ignoring the qualitative element that stands behind what they regard as the ethos of public service. This consists of a personal commitment by workers in this sector that in effect 'adds value' beyond that of work compensated by wages. For them BV is the replacement of this actual added value by a more managerial regime of cost cutting and efficiency savings which will destroy value in the name of increasing it. So from their point of view this assault on values will ultimately lead to a reduction rather than an addition of value.

The central argument of this chapter is that government ought to facilitate the process which transforms instruments of evaluation such as money into services for the diverse body of its consumers. Indeed the ideology of BV is based upon an assumption that present bureaucracies do not properly serve their consumers while BV does. In fact, however, institutions such as BV prevent this transformation, since they tend to keep reorienting the actions of the bureaucracy back upwards to processes of evaluation and to virtual consumers such as themselves. To demonstrate this, I will first summarize the results of my investigation (which are described in more detail in Miller 2003).

I will then look at some specific instances of the problem BV has with values precisely because they cannot be subject to a single criterion of BV. In several cases it will become evident that the term 'best' prevented the inspectorate from realizing the potential held in the term 'value'.

The Findings

It was clear from accompanying the inspectors that on the whole those involved were generally well intentioned, believed in what they were doing, and could see various benefits to local government. This was not an overly aggressive inspection in the way, for example, OFSTED is often portrayed. Most of the inspectors came from local government and were likely to return there. All my conclusions derive from what I see as structural contradictions within the process itself, they are not a reflection of the intentions of either those carrying out the survey, nor of those who designed the survey. The reason local government is being hammered, at least on this evidence, is all to do with the nature of the process rather than any deliberate assault.

I divided my analysis according to the terms used by the inspectorate itself, which follows the anthropological tradition of an empathetic approach to research. The presentation of the inspection is overwhelmingly couched in terms of the four C's which are reiterated many times throughout the process and in its accompanying literature. Councils must *Challenge* how and why their service is provided, *Compare* with others, embrace fair *Competition*, and *Consult* with taxpayers and customers. Behind the four C's lies a fifth, which is the commitment to *Continuous Improvement*. In turn all of these are supposed to be carried out according to the three E's which are to work by the most *Economic, Efficient*, and *Effective* means available. These are the bedrock terms—almost anything that happens is justified in relation to them.

Challenge. This is intended to represent a fundamental rethink of the *raison d'être* for any particular section. Technically, it must show how the service performance will reach the top quartile for all councils in terms of improvement over the next five years. It sought to create a clear, jargon free set of aims, and to reduce bureaucracy in the sense of curtailing the internal dynamics of process in favour of delivering goals. My evidence was that the effect was the opposite of these intentions. Given the overwhelming importance of BV, there was developing a new cadre of specialist BV officers whose skills lay in their knowledge of the language and expectations of BV and who taught each service in turn how to get through the process. These in turn generated a higher level literature, which becomes an additional level of jargon and performance. Unlike academic jargon which tends to perform cleverness through the use of obfuscation, this jargon is a kind of performance of the language of transparency (see Clarke, Chapter 9, this volume). It consists of endless pages of fairly trite formulas, usually with no substantive content and often almost no examples, such as—'For local government, effective performance management requires coordinated planning and review systems that enable key decision-makers, both political and managerial, to take action based on facts about performance'. So the effect of BV is to impose another layer of control over that which already exists and another level of performative language above the pre-existing structure.

Competition. This is intended to increase efficiency according to third way principles that are supposed to favour neither the public nor private sector, but simply to give control to whichever gives the best return on taxpayers' money. The concept of value is obviously central to this contention, and its instrument is supposed to be 'market testing' based upon a 'level playing field'. The results were very different, however, mainly because the appearance of a level playing field was constructed through taking a number of issues, which previously would have been internal to such adjudications, and turning them into externalities. From the point of view of local government workers, the most important of these were conditions of service, such that a private company could appear more efficient simply by paying its employees less, though this has been increasingly combated by unions and other groups. Less challenged have been issues such as finance. Public sector services are simply not allowed access to the kind of capital that allow private companies the ability to invest in the large units such as incineration plants, or fleets of vehicles, or information technology that are required for efficiency and effectiveness in the long term. The best-known inequality of this kind has been the rise of PFI (Private Finance Initiatives) which various academic studies have suggested are unfairly weighted in favour of the private sector (e.g. Gaffney et al. 1999). Perhaps the most ludicrous of these externalities is the process of inspection itself. What I found incredible was that inspectors could make reference to an advantage of the private sector being its relative freedom from 'red tape', without a trace of irony. Local government officers, by contrast, constantly pointed out that it was huge inspection processes such as BV that were the very reason they were unable to carry out other duties.

Consultation. If workers in local government knew one thing about BV it was that they were supposed to consult with the public. The main workload involved in BV was the preparation of the preliminary BVR report which was based primarily on evidence for consultation which was supposed to cascade downwards as aims, priorities, and delivery. Indeed there was a strong populist element to this central part of the Copernican revolution, which was a reorientation to users of services. The problem, however, was that often this was clearly not sustainable. Surveys and focus groups would constantly show the public's priority was more likely to be 'dog-poo' on the streets than a question of whether to be more orientated to the mayor's or to central government's strategic plan for transport. Much of what local government does is of limited interest to the public. Furthermore, when government has established a statutory priority, such as recycling, this results in the council being responsible for 'educating' the public so that the latter choose the priority that fits government policy. In addition, there is already a problem in vast amounts of resources being allocated to the potential actions of 'rogue'—in the sense of litigious—users often at the expense of the priorities of the mass. Overall, what becomes evident is that, as implied in the theory of virtualism, a huge amount of resources are being redirected to the representation of the process of consultation, where previously these resources would have been spent on actual consumers of services.

Comparison. This is intended to ensure that councils take heed of and learn from their peers, but equally it signifies the use of perform-ance indicators to make such comparisons clear and therefore the rise of quantitative over qualitative assessments. So during inspections one was constantly aware that inspectors who often had many years experience within local government were therefore able to make astute qualitative assessments of the service in question. But these could not form part of their report, being dismissed as 'subjective'. Instead the emphasis was on the performance indicators built into the system of comparison through `benchmarking'. The irony was first that such experienced inspectors in their private conversation knew full well that the quantitative data was faulty, since local factors such as the specific social and environmental composition of the area were often effectively excluded. Furthermore, the process of inspection goes from a complex and qualitative reality, reduced to quantitative performance indicators, but which then for the final adjudication are turned into one of four grades along two scales, which are so generalized as to be effectively qualitative again. Not surprisingly almost all final results end up in the middle two categories available to the inspectors.

Continuous Improvement. This is in practice the fifth C, and the one that was seen by many as the primary 'driver' behind the whole process. The problem was that on the one hand performance indicators, for all their faults, start to become more worthwhile when the same indicator is used consistently over many years. But a system committed to continuous improvement tends to lead by example. There is therefore built into everyone's expectations the assumption that there will be continuous improvements in the system of adjudication including the performance indicators themselves, with a frequency which means that one is always left with the high costs of initial implementation, and hardly ever the pay-off of consistent usage. This is quite apart from the contradiction whereby everyone is aiming to be in the top quartile which also leads to an emphasis only upon that which represents measurable improvements.

There are many other contradictions which become evident from the ethnography. To give just two, first, there is the ideal that BV would lead to an overall saving target of around 2 per cent. The effect of BV is likely to be quite the opposite. This is because BV is so time consuming, taking up the energies of the most senior officers in the service, that my straw poll of services suggested that it added at least 5 per cent to the costs of that service in the year of inspection. And this is simply one of a whole swathe of audits and inspections today. Second the effect of BV is to give each service a powerful argument for having additional money spent on it in order to fulfil all the promises made towards the goal of 'continuous improvement'.

The final contradiction lay in the idea that this would be a consumer rather than a politically led audit. Unfortunately the effect of BV is almost always to politicize the service in question. The reason for this is that ultimately the aim of BV is to find ways to get the public to acknowledge the value of the tax receipts given to pay for local government, by making that service sensitive to the priorities of the public. This means that each service in turn has to rethink itself in terms of what ultimately are the vote-winning aspects of what it performs, and then present these to the local council, which as a body of local politicians is obviously extremely interested in knowing precisely this factor about each service. My conclusion was that the overall effect of BV had little to do with the public. I have never met a member of the public who has even heard of BV if they have not some work-related reason to know of it. Rather the effect is to give each service in the five-year cycle a position from which to argue for more resources and more political clout from the council itself.

I would fully acknowledge that the contradictions I have uncovered are closely related to basic contradictions inherent in the political system. For example, BV represents both a desire for greater local accountability, but at the same time a distrust of local electorates' ability to make local government financially responsible (Weir and Beetham 1999: 248). Indeed, in an excellent survey of the more general international trends of which BV is symptomatic, Pollitt and Bouckaert (2000: 170–1) more or less end up with a list of such trade-offs and cycles, including that of the trade-off between the desire to increase audit and the desire to release government agencies from too much paperwork (2000: 164). But the argument of this chapter is that there is a deeper issue here that rests on a wider sense of abstraction than that employed in the more conventional literature on this subject. These become evident when the two theoretical issues I have introduced, those of virtualism and value, are taken into account.

The Transformation of Value into Values

The ideal of local government is to transform value in the form of money and evaluative measures so that they can articulate with and thereby be consumed by the various values represented in the population. But in order to carry out this task, government has in various respects to 'let go'. For example, in the original version of the Greater

London Council run by Ken Livingstone, the radical edge of that institution consisted of handing over funds to local community groups, sometimes orthodox religious or other groups who did not share the ideology of the council itself, but were an effective means to resource the very pluralism that London so conspicuously represents today.

By contrast, a regime such as BV, while wanting an orientation to end users, is stymied by its equal concern with accountability, which has the effect of turning the attention of officers back upwards to forms of evaluation such as performance indicators, and the common language or jargon of BV itself. Furthermore as 'best' value it also exhibits a bias towards market models and, indeed, the private sector as against the values of public service. Furthermore as BV it, paradoxically, asserts itself as the hegemonic system of value by which councils shall be appraised against other potential values. The ultimate irony is that Best Value asserts itself as the best value.

An example may clarify these points. As it happens, one of my ex-students now works for the AGENDA 21 section of a local council. AGENDA 21 is the attempt to make government responsible to environmental criteria and environmentalist values. It may well be that a transformation of energy supply to self-sustaining resources also cuts costs in which case such changes score highly under the BV regime. But where the 'good' of sustainability is obtained only through the use of more expensive methods it becomes clear that a benefit that has no cost–benefits struggles to be positively regarded within the internal and external inspections. Yet thanks to the impact of the Rio conference even BV asserted AGENDA 21 as a major performance indicator. The problem is that the 'best' in BV is orientated to market-like ideals of competition. My poor student was beside himself in trying to work out what constituted market testing of the AGENDA 21 part of the service, since there are few private firms who exist simply to persuade councils to be more environmentally friendly. AGENDA 21 can only make sense within what are emerging as a plurality of 'bottom lines' including financial bottom lines, environmental bottom lines, ethical bottom lines, etc. While the council should be fostering such plural values, the inspection tries to bring things back upwards to a more abstract 'best value'. In general BV seemed to be weakest when dealing with the diversity of populations as evident in traditional Old Labour concerns such as poverty, and ethnicity. This was the more conspicuous when one found some particular characteristic of the population such as disability, which since it was turned into a clear measurable target, was constantly cited and looked for during the evaluation procedures. Whereas because they were not present as performance targets poverty and ethnicity were largely ignored. Once again the act of representation or modelling of difference was paramount at the expense of most actual diversity. It is this same difficulty in moving from value to values that ultimately becomes the main threat against which bureaucracy seeks to defend itself. I will examine this using the language of the bureaucrats in question. How does the bureaucracy talk about defending itself?

Who Owns the Process?

It is quite common for an ethnographer to search for particular phrases or practices that seem to crop up frequently in conversation and yet are not obviously germane. These are seen to provide possible clues to a better understanding of what they have been participating in. In this case there was one such phrase that I think shed light on both the larger context of, and the effect of BV on bureaucracy. Quite often during conversations participants would speak of the issue of 'who owns the process'. I take this to be a common expression in modern management, but it was not at first obvious why it should arise so often within this particular exercise. The term ownership in the specific context of management seems intended to implicate the relationship between having responsibility for and feeling responsible for. So the phrase 'to own the process' means that a group has been given sufficient autonomy to control a particular organizational process to feel that the responsibility for carrying it out is unambiguously theirs. The implication is always, however, that only under such conditions will they feel committed to the process itself. Ownership as a concept then seems to be trying to make clear that in order to expect people to be fully engaged in what they do, one has to give them sufficient autonomy and responsibility. Why then should this term come up constantly in discussions about BV?

The irony of BV is that it addresses, as though it was an absence, that quality in which local government is probably very rich. This is the sense of being a public servant. A sense that there is a reward for this work quite apart from wages and the internal activity of work. As a service head put it, 'You know, if you think about somebody who's running a service if they're doing it properly, a public servant isn't just there because they're there. If I wanted to be like that I wouldn't come to work in the public sector. I believe I come to do a job that makes a difference in people's lives'.

This is what distinguishes all public sectors such as medicine and education from private sector employment. But while education and medicine have more immediate positive goals in the form of health and education themselves, local government officials are often dealing with less obvious benefits such as leisure facilities or planning. As a result the ethos of public service tends to be generalized around the identity of being in local government itself rather than say being a teacher or being a nurse. In short if you work in education and medicine you do not need to establish your identity as a public servant, if you work in generic public service then this is exactly what you are inclined to do. I do not want to naively suggest that all workers share this ethos any more than assuming cynically that none of them do. But what is important is that to the extent to which they do identify with public service, this is denied by a BV regime that represents its Copernican revolution as though it is only thanks to BV that a council might start to have regard to the public that it serves. As individuals, inspectors who mainly come from local government were sympathetic to the ideal of public service as inherent to bureaucracy. But this was suppressed by their formal status as inspectors. In turn, council officials seemed to acquiesce quite readily in the idea that a service should be privatized or at least castigated if it genuinely failed the public. They were surprisingly open to outsourcing on the basis of a genuine level-playing field. But they insisted that a factor that should remain inside, and not external, to such evaluation was that asset represented by the ethos of service itself, which they felt tended to be lost in privatization.

There is, however, a deeper issue here, which is that of virtualism. I have argued that virtualism often operates through a fetishism of the consumer, as opposed to that of the producer. We start with the authority that we attach to the consumer by virtue of our recognition that it is the consequence of services for them that legitimate the existence of that service (see Keat 1994). Under virtualism the mantle of this authority is then stripped from actual users and worn by those bodies that stand in the stead of the public at large. The BV inspection was created by the government to act as virtual consumers of services, that is, to stand in the direct stead of users, who would ultimately represent themselves in their other capacity as voters. Yet the job of inspection is to ensure that the service is creating improvements that would be acknowledged by the users of that service. As such the key to the authority of the inspectorate is that they possess the authority of the consumer.

There is, however, a significant difference between the service and the inspectorate. This is simply that the council is capable of providing a service to the residents as consumers, while an inspectorate cannot of itself do any such thing. It can only inspect and make recommendations. This then raises the question of 'who owns the process', since the effect of this fetishism is that responsibility to the public is being taken away from those who are responsible for carrying out this work and given instead to those who are only responsible for inspecting this work and who cannot provide a service. Furthermore this relates to the single most sensitive aspect of local government identity. That is the very ethos of public service, which gives those who carry out any such work the moral satisfaction that their work is in some way of benefit to the people whom they serve. My impression was that this was not often stated as directly as might have been expected. Instead it had been recast in the language of management that had become the 'proper' vehicle for discussing such matters, to appear frequently as the issue of 'who owns the process'.

It follows that the ideal inspector is one who realizes that the process of BV has to be carried out extremely sensitively, since the process of BV can only work well if at the end everything that BV has done is given back to the service, that is the service comes to regain and retain ownership of what they do. But there are all sorts of elements of BV that militate against this. For example, a more strident inspector can easily turn BV into an instrument of alienation, such that service workers simply feel estranged from their own work. My sense was that on the whole, not surprisingly, the more experienced inspectors tended to have developed an implicit sensitivity to this issue as the heart of the exercise they were engaged in.

Conclusion

I have argued that the issue of 'owning the process' makes clear why bureaucracy requires defending from audits such as BV. It may seem reasonable that BV should include the principle that it must remove any remnant self-interest that had taken root within the bureaucracy. The Copernican revolution that states local government exists to serve the people and not the other way around again seems reasonable. But the effect of BV is not to create an orientation to consumers of services but an orientation to BV itself. Unfortunately the BV inspectorate are not in fact the actual consumers of services but what I call virtual consumers, that is people who stand in the stead of actual consumers, and I would argue that it is typical of developments in public sector governance over the last twenty years that virtual consumers have taken over the authority of the consumer and appropriated it for themselves at the expense of actual consumers.

An emphasis upon the word value helps us see how this has happened. The use of the phrase 'best value' seems most likely an attempt to evoke the increasing use of terms such as 'added value' and 'shareholder value', in the private sector. Indeed the precise term 'best value', qualifying value with the competitive sense of 'best' exemplified this borrowing. Now this is not necessarily problematic as long as it selects the appropriate model from commerce. The trouble is that most of commerce is engaged in exactly the opposite process to that of local government. Where local government transforms money value into plural values, much of commerce seeks to take a wide variety of values in the form of desires and needs and transform this into a single value. This can be considered as money, capital, or profits. Terms such as added value or shareholder value represent attempts to create single hegemonic criteria by which ultimately to quantify the benefits that accrue to business through operating successfully. So for commerce the whole point is to lose touch with the plural source of demand, that is, with values, in order to concentrate on the singular form. Now this is not true of all of commerce—added value and shareholder value works best where the commercial field is extractive or singular such as working in manufacture or in finance. When it comes to directly serving the public, commerce starts to look more like local government, and this would be the case in some sectors of retail.

So I would argue there is a commercial model that could have suited the precise task of New Labour's 'Third Way' ideal. This is what I have called the John Lewis model. The John Lewis model is just as focused upon value as is BV but here the emphasis is on matching price as evaluation with the plurality of qualities. John Lewis, which is the largest and most successful chain of department stores in the United Kingdom, is interesting because this focus upon values in its relationship to consumers is found to be compatible with an unusual focus upon values in its relationship to itself and its workers. It may be no coincidence that this is the one major company that has no shareholder value since it has no shares. It is a cooperative that distributes all profits to its own workers. So it has the language and practice of the kind of stakeholder system that the UK government appeared at one time to be interested in. Ironically in many ways firms such as John Lewis strive to achieve something that local government bureaucracy can almost take for granted, the collective identification with and commitment to service. Local government already has the asset of the public sector ethos and its concomitant solidarity and commitment. One can see the potential for this link between consumption, work, and bureaucracy clearly in the trajectory from du Gay (1996) to du Gay (2000).

But the regime analysed in this chapter is not a value inspection but a 'best' value inspection where the emphasis is not on the market as exemplified by firms such as John Lewis, but the business school model of the market with an emphasis upon competition, and the economists' and psychologists' conception of the atomistic individualized economic agent. These have no place for the John Lewis practice of social networks and investment in sensitivity to qualitative forces both with respect to workers, products, and consumers. BV relies more on inappropriate commercial models such as 'added value'.

So the effect of a rise of inspections and audits is that local government cannot concentrate on the values it should serve, but has to remain constantly wedded to the assessment of BV with its mantra of continuous improvement as a version of added value, a commercial notion of a measurable bottom line, objectified in a host of performance indicators, point schemes, and other quantitative rather than qualitative assessments. This ignores the inherent contradiction in local government bureaucracy which must involve a constant transformation between abstract evaluation required for consistency, fairness, and accountability and the plural incommensurate values represented by populations and their needs. To overcome this contradiction bureaucracy must be allowed to directly engage with the diversity and plurality of values in real populations, and thus let go of some of the measurability required by the logic of 'virtual' accountability. The primary reason why in almost everything it does BV ends up having an effect which is the opposite of its own intentions is that it fails to recognize this contradiction. Instead it ends up forcing bureaucracy to work with models and representations of populations or institutions such as BV that stand in their stead.

References

Audit Commission (1999). *Seeing is Believing: How the Audit Commission will Carry out Best Value Inspections in England.* London: Audit Commission.

Audit Commission (2001). *Changing Gear; Best Value annual statement 2001.* London: Audit Commission.

Boyne, G. (1999). 'Introduction, processes, performance and Best Value in local government'. *Local Government Studies.* 25; 1–25.

Davis, H. and Martin, S. (2000). 'Measuring "success" in service improvement'. *Renewal.* 8/4; 32–8.

du Gay, P. (1996). *Consumption and Identity at Work.* London: Sage.

du Gay, P. (2000). *In Praise of Bureaucracy.* London: Sage.

Gaffney, D., Pollock, A., Price, D., and Shaoul. J. (1999). 'PFI in the NHS—is there an economic case?'. *British Medical Journal.* 3191/10 July; 116–19.

Goss, S. (2000). 'Public services—can new labour make a difference?' *Renewal.* 8/4; 1–8

Herzfeld, M. (1992). *The Social Production of Indifference: Exploring the Symbolic Roots of Western Bureaucracy.* Chicago IL: Chicago University Press.

Horton, S. and Farnham, D. (1999). 'New labour and the management of public service: legacies, impact and prospects', in S. Horton and D. Farnham (eds), *Public Management in Britain.* Palgrave: Basingstoke, 247–58.

Keat, R. (1994). 'Scepticism, authority and the market', in R. Keat, N. Whiteley, and N. Abercrombie (eds), *The Authority of the Consumer.* London: Routledge.

Martin, S. (2000). 'Implementing best value: local public services in transition'. *Public Administration.* 78/1; 209–27.

Martin, S. (2001). 'What Have We Created? The Impact of Inspection On Local Government'. LRGRU Discussion Papers: www.cf.ac.uk/carbs/research/lrgru/publications.html.

Martin, S. (2002). 'Best value: new public management or new direction?', in K. McLaughlin, S. Osborne, and E. Ferlie (eds), *New Public Management: Current Trends and Future Prospects*. London: Routledge, 129–40.

Miller, D. (1998). 'A theory of virtualism', in J. Carrier and D. Miller (eds), *Virtualism: A New Political Economy*. Oxford: Berg.

Miller, D. (2003). 'The virtual moment'. *Journal of the Royal Anthropological Institute*. 14; 57–75.

Miller, D., Jackson, P., Thift, N., Holbrook, B., and Rowlands, M. (1998). *Shopping, Place and Identity*. London: Routledge.

Pollitt, C. and Bouckaert, G. (2000). *Public Management Reform*. Oxford: Oxford University Press.

Power, M. (1997). *The Audit Society: Rituals of Verification*. Oxford: Oxford University Press.

Raine, J. (2000). 'Five lessons from the first year of Best Value reviews'. *Local Governance*. 26/3; 151–8.

Riles, A. (2001). *The Network Inside Out*. Ann Arbor, MI: The University of Michigan Press.

Rouse, J. (1999). 'Performance Management, Quality Management and Contracts', in S. Horton and D. Farnham (eds), *Public Management in Britain*. Palgrave: Basingstoke, 76–93.

Snape, S. (2000). 'Three years on: reviewing local government'. *Local Governance*. 26/3; 199–26.

Strathern, M. (ed.) (2000). *Audit Cultures: Anthropological Studies in Accountability, Ethics and the Academy*. London: Routledge.

Weir, S. and Beetham, D. (1999). *Political Power and Democratic Control in Britain*. London: Routledge.

Zelizer, V. (1987). *Pricing the Priceless Child: The Changing Social Value of Children*. New York: Basic Books.

PART 4

Bureaucracy and Civil Society

11

Gender Equity—A Bureaucratic Enterprise?

Yvonne Due Billing

Introduction

When people talk about lack of gender equity their considerations often have to do with the horizontal and vertical gender division of labour. A gender division of labour is not in itself a problem,[1] but as women's positions often equal lower wages and often mean less access to influential positions, this state of affairs has caused many discussions about selection principles, socialization, stereotypical expectations on behalf of the employers, theories, and ideas about discrimination, biases in evaluation etc. all which has been thoroughly discussed in the gender literature. Besides the labour market division of labour there is also a pronounced gender division of labour in the private sphere, where women's average workload is higher than men's (Frankenhaeuser 1993; Lundberg, Mardberg, and Frankenhaeuser 1994).

There is an ongoing debate about whether bureaucratic practices (rules, procedures, legislations) are effective at tackling gender inequalities—or whether non-bureaucratic approaches (e.g. influences on the culture, values) are preferable from the perspective of gender equality.

My point of departure is that we should not take for granted that all bureaucracies are essentially bad, but investigate their potential more open-mindedly and be aware that there are big empirical variations, and therefore we should discuss different aspects of bureaucracy and pay attention to those dimensions which are a problem rather than abandoning bureaucracies altogether.

First, I shall discuss the meanings of gender equality and then the meanings of bureaucracy where I shall look at and discuss different ways of understanding how inequality is created; then I will assess different suggestions of establishing gender equality through bureaucratic and non-bureaucratic means. Finally, I will suggest some possible future perspectives.

The Meanings of Gender Equality

Historically, the development of equal opportunity for the sexes has been connected to the women's movement. Inequality was a result of the prevalent social view on women. As women attained fundamental rights in Marshall's (1977) sense (political, civil, and social rights) in our part of the world, the former antagonistic relation between the sexes was transformed, so that today there is consensus about the issue. This is at least the official words from the Danish Minister of equal opportunity. On the website (www.lige.dk) it is stated: 'While equal opportunity historically started as women's fight for fundamental rights, like the right to vote, the right to education, the right to decide and the right to one's own body (free abortion rights and prevention), we have now reached a point where equal opportunity is no longer a fight between the sexes.'

The classical liberal principle is that everyone should be treated equally, and for a long time period this has implied that sex, ethnicity, religion etc. should not be salient for one's life chances.[2] This formal idea has, however, not resulted in what is believed to be equity, and hence has led to positive action in many legislations, for example, in Gender Equality Acts.[3]

The Danish Ministry defines equal opportunity (EO) as a common project for women and men: to secure for all the possibility of freedom to live the life they wish—regardless of sex—and it states that EO is understood as much as a resource question as a question of justice. The purpose of the EO law is said to further equality between men and women, meaning that they should have the same opportunities and possibilities of influence in all parts of the society. It states further that the point of departure is that women and men have equal worth. Differences and the choices of the individual should be respected, and men and women should have the same possibilities to choose. Barriers which are limiting men's and women's possibilities and free choices should be broken down. Finally, it is said that EO is an important part of democracy.

These are the official words—equality is a common project for women and men, social consensus is emphasized, equality equals democracy and men are mentioned as potentially limited in their choices and possibilities. However, very often the underlying assumption is that equality is not about men but about women.

How is equality otherwise talked about by different writers? Different feminisms hold diverse views on the matter and their strategies are based on whether women and men are primarily regarded as different or as similar. I shall just draw attention to the most commonly known, which I shall call the similarity and non-similarity approaches. I shall relate these to understandings of bureaucracy and to bureaucratic and non-bureaucratic interventions.

The Similarity Approach

The following stance (mainly liberal feminism) takes the point of departure that women and men are basically similar, and that gender inequality is thus a result of individual cases of discrimination combined with sex-role stereotyping in socialization, education, and on the labour market. Women are denied the same opportunities as men, especially with regard to attaining managerial positions. Stereotyped thinking about women and beliefs that men are better fit for management positions, the typical manager being seen as male (Schein 1975; Wahl 1996) influences recruitment and selection to particular posts and also affects ongoing career development. As the strongest argument for liberal feminists is that men and women (especially those with educational qualifications) are very similar, they would mainly explain the small number of women in management positions as a result of prejudice and conservatism. EO campaigns, affecting attitudes, gender quotas, and in the United Kingdom, initiatives like Opportunity 2000,[4] and a fair and unbiased treatment of women would make things change. EO laws seem to have contributed to getting more women to enter higher ranks (Konrad and Linnehan 1999; Maddock 1999) and Opportunity 2000 has had the effect that women in member organizations fare better than others. Fairness (justice) and the idea of rights are related to a discourse of discrimination and an idea of gender imbalance.

Lately, the justice and fairness argument has, however, often become connected to a discourse of resources—equal opportunity is supported by the argument that there is a need for access to all resources. Social justice, equality, and fairness are being linked together with a business case (Cassell 2000), meaning that EO is 'sold' as something which should be good for business. This meritocratic perspective is especially prevalent in the United States (Adler 1987). These two arguments (justice and underutilized resources) are today the two common principles behind actions to promote a gender balance. Positive actions even then rest on the belief that society/ organizations are missing something when women are not included on a par with men.

Although the similarities between women and men are most often emphasized there are liberal feminists who will stress the need for bureaucratic advances which pay some attention to the misfit that may exist between women (as a result of socialization) and top-management positions in particular.

In Western societies there is a strong belief that everyone should have a fair chance, and it certainly does not correspond with the (ideal) 'laws' of bureaucracy to let one category (men) advance just because of its sex category. The solution lies in bureaucratic ways of dealing with inequality, either initiated politically by the state and involving a broader societal involvement, including legislation, or initiated by top management. Ineffective promotion practices and biases would be counteracted by improving personnel policies. None of these approaches would question the hierarchical division of labour or processes and practices other than those that directly influence and disfavour women. However, interventions are primarily related to the labour market, not to balancing caretaking. Other oppressions and inequalities are not on the agenda.

The Non-similarity Approach

Other feminists, such as those within radical feminism, have a different view on equality. It is not individual cases but the socio-economic power relations and the macro-level which are important. The state should not be seen as a possible ally for combating irrational forces preventing equity, but rather as a supporter of the very system which sustains inequality, the patriarchal society. There is a fundamental principle of organization in (this kind of) society which is at the root of oppression. The male is privileged. And the assumption is that women have different experiences and interests than men and/or that women have radically different orientations than those characterizing patriarchal society. The solution is a new social order, where women are not subordinated to men. Power relations are the focus.

Radical feminists (e.g. Ferguson 1984) regard the existing institutional arrangements in bureaucracies as fundamentally flawed and destructive to people working in them. They should be resisted/evaded and alternative organizations developed. The non-bureaucratic organizations are separatist, social, and cultural arrangements/places which challenge the values in the male-dominated culture. Women are believed to understand the world in a different way, and in opposition to male rationality. There are ideas about the authentic feminine, and a female counterculture. This stream would advocate a separatist politics until women and men are equal, and the organizations radical feminists would want should have flattened structures and build upon equality and a negation of leadership. These should better take care of women's needs and represent spaces which are regarded as necessary to compensate for, or re-evaluate, what has been devalued in the male-stream culture.

There are other approaches within what Harding (1987) called standpoint-feminism, which may differ from the radical one. For instance, in one approach, positive values attributed to women are emphasized, such as sensitivity, emotionality, and care. But instead of abandoning bureaucracies, here women should be compensated and given the possibility of working in them. This corresponds to Pateman's (1988) suggestion that women can only be equalized in a modern democracy by an upgrading of the status of motherhood—and that it is necessary to compensate, for example, for the 'inconveniences' of having children. Biological sex is regarded as the essentialistic basis.[5]

Pateman's suggestion of valuing the essential may have the effect of reproducing the opposition between male and female and accordingly the gender division of labour. There has been critique of this tendency to universalize women's experiences and to repeat what the proponents criticized masculine research for doing, presenting a narrow and biased perspective. To overcome this problem would require a differentiated approach. But before going into this, I shall look at the meanings of bureaucracy and how they are understood as creating gender inequality.

The Meanings of Bureaucracies

Bureaucracy is a particular form of organization with a specialized division of labour, and is 'the form of organization best suited to exercise legal authority' (Weber 1968: 58). Bureaucracy is government by formalized impersonal rules, with hierarchical offices which (ideally) are filled on the basis of merit as measured by professional qualifications and exams. Career structures are predetermined and contracts specify salary (which are based on rank in the hierarchy and on seniority). There are thus rules/rights for equal treatment.

Bureaucracies are characterized by formal rationality, which is necessary for its efficient functioning.[6] Frequently, however, this means that what is believed to be associated with the private sphere has to be relegated from bureaucracy.

> ... the more the bureaucracy is 'dehumanized', the more completely it succeeds in eliminating from official business love, hatred, and all purely personal, irrational, and emotional elements which escape calculation. This is the specific nature of bureaucracy and it is appraised as its special virtue (Weber, in Martin and Knopoff 1997: 40).

Martin and Knopoff claim, however, that it is impossible to achieve this dehumanization, and that this is also already indicated by Weber as he placed the word 'dehumanization' in quotation marks, thus implying that the emotional, irrational, and personal are hard to suppress. But, as stated by du Gay (1996: 29) when Weber stressed 'the impersonal, functional and objective nature of bureaucratic norms and techniques' it does not mean that personal feelings are excluded per se but refers 'to the setting aside of pre-bureaucratic forms of patronage'. Thus relations within bureaucracy do not have to be brutally inhuman.

When discussing bureaucracy in the abstract, as a concept (an ideal-type) one should not conflate or confuse the discussion with concrete descriptions of bureaucracies. What has developed historically and has caused many bureaucracies to be gendered is not necessarily a result of the 'laws' of bureaucracy but rather of some influences from the 'surrounding' society and the prevalent social view of men and women's roles and capacities. At the dawn of modern bureaucracy, the development of hierarchical structures took place along gendered lines, as women were recruited as the cheap labour that fitted into the subordinate positions, and women's entry in subordinate jobs made possible the promotion of male clerks more quickly (Witz and Savage 1992). The predetermined career structures were at this particular historical moment 'reserved' for males. In many bureaucracies there were marriage bars, forcing women to retire when married. Historically, the bureaucratic career was equivalent with a male career. The prevailing cultural ideas of gender resulted in the social division of labour, with men primarily inhabiting the public and women the private sphere. Bureaucracies were then constructed around a public and a private world.[7]

Since the development of bureaucracies there have been major changes in many organizations and in women's social situation; modern bureaucratic career-structures have benefited many women. So if women are subordinates in bureaucracies and do not make it to the top, does this have something to do with bureaucracy or with something else? Many feminist authors seem to think that bureaucracies are inherently masculine, and thus that women qua women are losers in these organizations. One might wonder what it actually means when it is said that bureaucracies are gendered masculine (or even are patriarchal, e.g. Grant and Tancred 1992). Is it a statement based on the nominal phenomenon, because it is mainly men who dominate bureaucracies, there is then an equation between the male sex and the masculine, meaning that the dominance of men has made the bureaucracy masculine? During the Second World War, many women worked in and dominated formerly male organizations, but this did not change the symbolic gender of these (to something feminine). I believe we have to differentiate between the composition of gender and the gender type of the organization. The percentage share of the two sexes is just one element but the dominance of one sex does not make the organization automatically gendered according to this sex. It is also important what sort of work is carried out, for example, the gender aura of this activity, and the values and ideas which dominate the activity and the form in which this activity is conducted (see Alvesson and Billing 2002).

In the following sections, I shall look at different ways of understanding bureaucracies and at the gendered meanings connected to bureaucracies. What the proponents have in common is that they seem to believe that bureaucracies *qua* bureaucracies are 'producers of inequality'.

Ferguson's Attack on Bureaucracy

In 1984, Ferguson promoted what would later be called a 'magnificent feminist attack on bureaucracy', (Mills and Tancred 1992). Ferguson's argument was that bureaucracy is primarily oppressive and controlling of the lives of employees, and she argued that bureaucracies by 'nature' promote inequality.

Bureaucracy is the scientific organization of inequality . . . bureaucracies are political arenas in which struggles for power, status, personal values, and/or survival are endemic. They are oligarchical and recruitment is at least partly done by cooptation' (Ferguson, 1984: 7).

Further she states that women as well as men are subordinated in bureaucracies, though women's situation is worse than men's as they rarely make it to the top and beside that they experience a double oppression, within the bureaucracy and the family, as they are also represented as women in the family by male power (1984: 92).

Ferguson describes a process of femininization in bureaucracies, meaning that characteristics associated with the female are being developed by employees, because as members of the bureaucracy they are required to please, to sense the mood of the superiors as they need approval from above to know whether they have succeeded or not. According to Ferguson this means that subordinates need the skills of femininity to deal with their subordinate status. Being a member of bureaucracy is then equated with being (like) a woman. Femininity is equated with impression management, the desire to impress others, to present positive views of oneself to others. Femininity is a 'series of traits that accompany powerlessness and confine feminized people to the depoliticized status of reactive spectators' (Ferguson 1984: 173). It is described as subordination which must be opposed. To have the skills of femininity one might think could help women's careers but it does not, as some other (masculine) traits are needed to advance in the hierarchy.

Ferguson and other radical feminists believe that the institutional arrangements in bureaucracy are fundamentally flawed and that it is impossible to change the system. She asks 'after internalizing and acting on the rules of bureaucratic discourse for most of their adult lives, how many women (or men) will be able to change? After succeeding in the system by using those rules, how many would be willing to change?' (1984: 192). Instead Ferguson believes it is import-ant to stimulate the development of alternative organizational forms facilitating the values of care and connection.

Changes and the ground for resistance are located in the character-istic experiences of women (caretakers, nurturers etc.) which Ferguson sees as different from men's experiences. Ferguson's claim that women have common experiences is based on the belief that the socialization background of girls is different from boys', the former ideal-typed as being based on emotionality and human interaction, making women supportive, non-assertive, dependent, attentive etc. while men are regarded as analytic, independent, rational, competit-ive, and instrumental (1984: 93). This belief in essential differences between women and men is then the basis for Ferguson's suggestion for feminist organizations which should be based on supposedly feminine values.

This gender dualism with regard to traits is now often questioned as is the idealization of women which made Ferguson believe that women would agree in a unitary critique of the predominant way of organizing and to a unified preference for an alternative mode of organizing. Her project is very difficult as she wants to undermine the 'traditional' feminine and at the same time advocate and build the opposition on the common experiences of women. This dilemma was also noted by Witz and Savage (1992).

Ferguson's attack on bureaucracy resembles Marxist attacks on capitalism where whatever good capitalism brings was disregarded. For example, when she claims, 'the terror sometimes used by authoritarian regimes performs a similar function to that of the control structures of bureaucratic organization' (Ferguson 1984:17). She makes a caricature of bureaucracy, and what resembles most of what is described are military bureaucracies. She suggests that by viewing feminization as a political process one could see feminization of both sexes as the structural complement to domination. One might rhetorically ask if privates in the army are best described as feminized?

The meaning connected to bureaucracies by Ferguson is to regard them as faceless and abstract tyrants and almost everyone as their victims. Having deprived people of their possibilities of agency, it is only logical to conclude that bureaucracies should be abandoned. Although acknowledging the importance of liberal-inspired battles for equal opportunity, Ferguson's pathway to equality is separatist. The (alternative) organizations Ferguson believed would benefit women were book centres, health centres etc. These are different from bureaucracies in that they are seen as ends in themselves, decentralized, egalitarian, with collective skills and information represented as resources to be shared.

However, though alternative organizations can be good workplaces, there might also be a number of problems with them. Too much is dependent on who the people occupying them are. For instance, one might be exposed to arbitrary decisions, and to all sorts of unknown expectations. Probably standpoint-feminists would say that these provide advantages for women, as women are said to prefer web-like constructions, flattened hierarchy, and organizations that are more 'personal', and where flexible arrangements are possible. But small-scale organizations, enterprises and adhocracies do not avoid power games, conflicts, and inequalities. There is always power when people meet because of interdependency whether it is in small organizations or in bureaucracies.

Loosely structured organizations may have many other disadvantages as well. For example, it may be attractive to women that the organization provides flexibility; on the other hand this may also cause insecurity and uncertainty, about what 'counts' in the organization, and the workload may easily become unbearable. Another problem with the separatist strategy is that women will have no possibilities of influence in the powerful bureaucracies, that continue to supply most employment opportunities.

P. Y. Martin's Critique of Men's Mobilization of Masculinities in Bureaucracies

As I have suggested, on the one hand Ferguson related being a member of a bureaucracy to being a woman, while on the other she argued that masculine traits were needed to advance to the top of the hierarchy. This made me curious about what sort of masculinities are being performed in bureaucracies. P. Y. Martin (2001) has attempted to trace and differentiate between ten types of masculinity, which she says are 'mobilized' in bureaucracies.

Based on interviews with six women, holding managerial or professional positions, and their stories about men, she interprets six of the masculinities as affiliating/connecting (described as visiting, 'sucking up', protecting, supporting, deciding based on liking/disliking, expressing fondness) and four of them as contesting masculinities ('peacocking', self-promoting, dominating, expropriating others' labour). Contesting masculinities she defines as men acting 'in concert to distance—differentiate, separate—themselves from others by showing superior rank or status, obtaining control over others, or obtaining benefits from work that others do' (p. 603). Especially, when mobilization of masculinity is conflated with working it is experienced as harmful by women. Contesting masculinities she says are practices which are 'compatible with the discourses and practices of bureaucracy' (p. 608). Affiliating masculinities were mobilized when the men 'aligned—connected, linked—with others in ways that benefitted self, others or both' (p. 604). Except for two (dominating and expropriating other's labour) all masculinities were, according to Martin, directed primarily to men, as the target audience.

Martin defines masculinities as 'practices that are represented or interpreted by either actor and/or observer as masculine within a system of gender relations that give them meaning as gendered "masculine" ' (p. 588). She suggests that women interpret men's behaviour as gendered when other frames (e.g. bureaucratic) fail to explain what they see them do. It is, however, not at all obvious why these sorts of behaviour are constructed as masculine, for example, that prolonged talking (called 'peacocking') in a group about something which has nothing to do with work is masculine, or when the men talk with a woman about their personal problems. Is it masculine because men are doing it, or because it does not fit into the bureaucratic framework? Would it have been called feminine had it been women doing it and had it been acceptable if women had not felt left out? Martin builds her analysis on what she was told by women about men, and relates this to what men do when acting like men. She says this behaviour leaves women out, and I would add in her analysis women are also left out, meaning we get no idea of the interaction between men and women and when women perform masculinities or how they support/take part in hegemonic masculinities.

It is interesting that at least six of the performed masculinities (the connecting ones) may equally be called doing femininity as it is stereotypically understood. If we use a feminine metaphor instead one might make another interpretation than men mobilizing masculinities, namely that men are using what is socially constructed as feminine behaviour to keep in control and to keep their power. This shows how meaningless it sometimes is to frame everything in terms of femininity/masculinity. Or it shows that doing masculinity does not necessarily exclude what has conventionally been seen as feminine. Much more interesting is the question as to whether the behaviour is harmful or not, if it sustains inequality or not, and if the behaviour 'belongs' only to men and in what ways it 'belongs' to bureaucracy?

All the ten masculinities were interpreted as 'hurting' women, 'causing them to lose time, waste energy, lose self-confidence and self-esteem, feel frustration, become disillusioned, feel confused and question themselves to the point of considering quitting . . . '. Also when men were mobilizing affiliating masculinities, 'they communicate a message to women of irrelevance or disrespect' (2001: 609).

What is interesting about Martin's article in relation to bureaucracies and the ideal worker is the claim that men are much more concerned with each other than with formal organizational aims. 'In short, the women saw men using organizational resources in ways that reflected concern with each other and masculinity/ies, not formal organizational goals' (2001: 608). So much for the 'ideal type bureaucratic worker' and organizational efficiency.

What she also noticed was that men more than women were focusing on interpersonal social relations, whereas women were much more concerned about the instrumental tasks. It is therefore difficult to understand why men's and not women's behaviour is called masculine, if this is the case. One gets the impression from Martin's analysis that bureaucracies are mainly places for the enactment of irrational behaviour. Men seem—in her analysis—primarily to behave in ways which are in fact not consistent with the goals of bureaucracy. The question is, what are the necessary practices for bureaucracy? There seems to be no acknowledgement of the fact that some masculinities are necessary for bureaucracy to function.

What do we, in fact, gain by using the concept of masculinity in relation to the above-mentioned performances? This can only lead to the view that whatever men do in bureaucracies is bad. And certainly some problems and conflicts, biases in bureaucracies can be explained by men 'behaving badly', that is not according to (ideal) bureaucratic rules. But I am not convinced that we can say much of great value about differences in men's and women's behaviour in these generalized terms. We might as well call some of the performances 'excluding' behaviour which can be done by anybody, including in project organizations, but is it 'essentially' masculine? Martin manifests her position as a feminist standpoint position and this position often advocates itself not only in opposition to a particular position but as inherently better than another position.

Femininity/masculinity do not only relate to women/men respectively, if they did we would not need these concepts. By using these terms we refer to acts and practices which are considered to be masculine or feminine whoever is doing them. The practices of gender, masculinity/femininity, are constituted/negotiated through practices, performed by women as well as by men and vary across bureaucracies and through time. In Martin's version it is difficult to see how changes/differences can be conceptualized, even those (men) who may try to 'break down' hegemonic masculinities can be 'framed' as harming women.

Given the problems connected to the use of the concepts of masculinity/femininity caution is required when using them (see the discussion in Alvesson and Billing 1997). Maybe we should think of alternative concepts to masculinity/femininity. Using other critical vocabularies (beside the gender one) may lead to much more complex ways of understanding bureaucracies and the behaviour enacted in these.

To summarize, there seems to be much confusion with regard to what goes on in bureaucracies. First, I referred to Ferguson's construction of bureaucracies as tyrants, where everybody suffered (except the elite) and where workers were feminized (except at the top); then I found that Martin constructed bureaucracies as mainly places for men's mobilization of masculinities. So what is going on in bureaucracies? There seems to be an open arena for interpreting behaviour in bureaucracies in whatever terms one feels like deploying and there also seems to be an immanent danger of conflating bureaucracies with all forms of organization.

Discussion

When considering gender equality in bureaucracies compared with alternative organizational arrangements, we should assess them more carefully. When dealing with equality issues, there is an immanent danger of falling into the trap of an essentialism that relates masculinities only to men, seeing women as having better access to the good, democratic, caretaking, and friendly values, in ways that idealize women.

Instead of relating the problems to bureaucracy as the oppressor per se and thus treating it as a general abstraction which produces the same effects, we could focus on the work cultures and the informal norms which have developed and which are often not very supportive for persons with responsibilities for children. How is gender constructed and deconstructed in a specific bureaucracy? (And how is bureaucracy constructed?) Do gendered processes and practices, open or hidden, lead to specific gender differentiations or a particular gender division of labour? That women's progress and well being at the workplace is connected to the culture and the underlying assumptions about gender was explored in a study by Billing and Alvesson (1994) and in Wilson's study (1998) of four different bureaucracies which all had more or less 'strong' equal opportunity policies. A cultural perspective means paying attention to the values and norms in the specific organization, including the gendered substructure (Acker 1992).

The gender division of labour can be connected to cultural meanings in a particular bureaucracy, and to how the prominent values are defined (in gender terms). Informal norms, shared meanings, and values are also shaped by the cultural context in which the organization exists. When gender equality is regarded in a contextual and relational perspective it must be related to the differentiating and hierarchical forms which already exist in society.

In a bureaucracy, positions are ideally filled on the basis of merit. Standardized and uniform rules of assessment and procedures, and an emphasis on objective competence, means that biases and prejudice should be minimized. If there are unclear rules there may be much more 'space' for gender stereotypical expectations. Task rotation and task sharing with, for example, rotating formal positions of authority means that no hegemonic power structure is developed. Ideally, bureaucracy breaks down patriarchal structures, personal preconceptions, and prejudice against women. There can be calculable rules for advancement with predictable outcomes, such as career ladders and wage rates. They are not negotiable, this could be an advantage for women, as men may not be in a position to exert power in the process. Bureaucracy provides protective structures, against arbitrary decisions, patriarchal ideas, etc. and there are rules for advancement. This means that one knows what counts. It is difficult to understand why Ferguson would be against this.

It is a well-known fact that there are many irrationalities which get in the way of the ideal bureaucracy. As many have argued, one might of course question if it is really possible to 'free' bureaucratic organizations of everything which is connected to the personal. It is not gender-less beings who occupy the positions, and recruiters/ promoters may act in different biased ways, all well described, for example, in the literature which is concerned about the small number of women in higher positions (e.g. Billing and Alvesson 1994). This is also identified by Martin and Knopoff (1997) who advocate small-scale reforms in order to make better bureaucracies.

The problem holding women back, many would argue, is that the concept of career is not gender-neutral but a gendered construction, 'based on men's life experiences and needs', and conventionally built on uninterrupted service to an employer, 'and premised on a separation between the public and the private spheres' (Wajcman 1998: 28). Wilson (1998) states 'women's careers have been characterized by limited opportunities, low paid part time work, breaks of different lengths for child care and other domestic responsibilities, and unhelpful assumptions about commitment and capability' (1998: 396). Recruiting women does not guarantee that they will make a career. We have to pay attention to the private sphere as well.

Often the family is not included in the definition of equality. This is in accordance with the understanding of bureaucracy that the private and public are separate spheres, thus hindering an understanding of the family sphere as an object for political interventions, although this separation between the private and the political is a constitutive factor in the subordination of women (Pateman 1988). Haas et al. (2000) suggest that organizations adopt 'active measures' to encourage men to use their parental-leave rights. They conclude that 'companies still base their policies on the traditional gender contract that reinforces male dominance in all spheres of public and private life' (2000: 252).

Martin and Knopoff (1997) also take up the issue of work/family and say that what is happening at home will influence work, and that more than full-time work will be difficult for women unless they have a househelper and a child minder. Otherwise it is not easy to make oneself valuable for bureaucracies.

Although this issue is not exclusive to bureaucracies, it is important nonetheless. In many cases there is no understanding of private (family) problems, and bureaucracies do not assume responsibility for solving them. Family problems are regarded as something private which should not bother working life. But they do. There seems, however, to be a difference in the family–work relationship for men and women. According to a study of dual-employed couples (Tenbrunsel et al. 1995) unlike men, women had a fixed level of involvement in the family independent of work. Another study of female lawyers (Schenker et al. 1997) showed that women working more than 45 hours per week were five times as likely to report high stress as those working 35 hours per week, and a study by Frankenhaeuser (1993) showed that women spend more time on household tasks than men do. It is understandable that stress will occur and perhaps also that there are limits to women's involvement in work (when they have small children and are the primary caretakers).

Martin and Knopoff suggest that a crucial priority should be to alter requirements for more than full-time work 'the requirement that top officials give a more than full-time commitment to their work makes it extraordinarily difficult for most women to hold these positions. Instead, the majority of women work in clerical or other low-status positions that require only a full- or part-time commitment. In these ways, gender inequality is perpetuated by bureaucratic requirements for . . . and more than full-time work,' (1997: 45).

But what do requirements for more than full-time work have to do with bureaucracy? Weber stresses 'full working capacity' but does this have to be more than a normal workweek? It is not built into the structure that more than, or even full-time work, is a necessity. Martin and Knopoff (1997) suggest some, what they call minor changes, like the possibility of flexible work, part-time work and leave of absence, and the possibility of part-time training and training during normal work hours. All these already exist in many of the modern bureaucracies in the Scandinavian countries or elsewhere. Furthermore they say that these changes would alter the division of labour. This remains to be seen.[8] Martin and Knopoff (1997) seem to conflate bureaucracies with all forms of organization, and they do not take into account that it may be much easier to regulate work hours in bureaucracies than in project organizations, for example.

In a number of large bureaucracies there is now an understanding that many of their workers have children. Some of these organizations have been forced to change and acknowledge the importance of families especially when men too have demanded changes in the organization along this axis (Billing 2000). In many cases mothers (and fathers) will want part-time work and this is now more of a possibility, especially in the public bureaucracies (although there may be a problem of seeing those working part-time as less committed). Rules in bureaucracies can be family-friendly. For example, it seems to be possible to 'make' rules which give leaves of absence to families, elevating the status of the father (as in Norway where a substantial number of fathers take leave at childbirth) and not make women (only) appear not fully committed to work. Employers could be 'forced' by rules to pay extra allowances for each man and woman to a special fund, so that it did not matter who took out the leave of absence. Both would be made 'insecure' labour power.

The gender division of labour with regard to caring and housework is, however, a problem which is much harder to legislate against because the private sphere in the liberal tradition is seen as outside the scope of regulations.

Returning to the statement of the Danish government it seems that the present discourse on EO is based as much on an economic discourse (economic liberalism) as on fairness (justice). Political intervention should pay off. In the official statement men and women are understood to be of equal worth, there is no conflict. Certain restrictions, which are hindering the individual, just need to be removed (according to the liberals). The justice argument is often connected to a discourse of resources—a need for different resources. Positive actions then rest on the belief that society is missing something when women's resources are not fully included.

Then it is logical that interventions are primarily outcome-oriented (half of each sex). There have been rules and EO policies for recruitment in organizations in Scandinavia (e.g. quota systems). When two candidates are equally qualified the under-represented sex (often women) should be recruited. This intervention will meet with resistance, as giving women what will look like special treatment is not popular among men as they seem to think that when a woman is promoted this is unfair, and that women are preferred to more competent men (Billing and Alvesson 1994). Another problem is that the under-represented sex will be unsure if she/he got the job because of merit/qualifications or because of her/his sex, and this will also raise doubt in relation to the persons already hired (on their own merits) who happen to belong to the under-represented category. It devalues their position. Not surprisingly, the quota suggestion is often not supported by women who made it. Because women are still constructed as the second sex it is very easy to believe that those women who got their positions qua being women are inferior to men.

The quota argument is sometimes accompanied by a presupposition about women's utility for economy, and that lack of gender equality is a problem for the economy. This corresponds with neo-liberal thinking. It is bodies that count, and not so much social and cultural aspects associated with the meaning of gender. There is no interest in a discussion of a more critical/qualitative nature, such as what changes could be relevant in bureaucracies to make them better workplaces. Rather than change organizations, people should change, conform to the existing norms. Gender is understood as a variable, and the ideal is that women and men each hold 50 per cent of all occupations, at all levels.

The potential exists for getting more gender equality, the 'laws' of bureaucracy can be neutral and have democratic effects, but the people inhabiting the different bureaucracies have the potentiality to develop bureaucracy into 'unpleasant' structures. But this may be even more of a danger in non-bureaucracies. The non-bureaucratic advocates, such as many radical feminists, are interested in getting rid of bureaucracies altogether, or more correctly, they do not think women should work in them. The alternatives suggested for women are 'idealized' organizations where freedom, friendship, and harmony exist and these organizations are often in the human service area and mostly in non-commercial areas. 'Escaping' to these domains would, however, reproduce the gender division of labour. Women would be clustered in small and largely powerless organizations with a marginalization of women as a result (Billing 1994).

In accordance with Mouffe (1995), I suggest a position where equality is based on values. The barriers to women attaining higher positions are not only a matter of lack of the 'right' bureaucratic interventions, but rather a result of the lack of interest of many women (and some men) in adapting themselves to the demands made by corporations and bureaucracies. These persons may be carriers of some values which are needed in society and may cause bureaucracies to change more fundamentally. The paradox, however, is that whatever made these persons develop anti-career attitudes and values important for society also makes it less likely that they will ever join bureaucracies. Martin and Knopoff suggested that there should be more gratitude, exhibited grace, sympathy in bureaucracies, and one could add more of the qualitative needs that have been devalued and which as a result have fostered one particularly narrow side of rationality in bureaucracies.

We cannot, however, talk about bureaucracies as abstract entities. They are located in specific cultures, and the modus operandi differs, for example, according to how much the welfare state is willing to take over the caring role for children so that this should not be a restriction for anybody to be free to work on equal terms with persons without such responsibilities, but as long as childcare is mainly women's task, such will not be the norm. We are not equal. Politics in relation to the so-called private sphere matters.

The ideas of liberal feminism all go well in hand with bureaucracy and bureaucratic means. Whereas liberal feminism seems to have a bureaucratic case for equality, radical feminism, however, has a case against bureaucracy and then as a result a case against equality, as it is defined officially. Another interesting difference is that liberal feminism in its strategy will get rid of the values/traits which are thought to be unfitting for management, while radical feminism wishes to promote the same values as liberal feminism represents as problematic. This 'strategy' needs to be 'rethought' because of the contemporary changes in the discourse on management styles, particularly those that highlight the so-called softer or symbolic skills of management.

Conclusion

In this chapter, I have tried to argue for a more fair and balanced assessment of bureaucracies and non-bureaucracies, recognizing that bureaucracies do not have to be gendered, and that non-bureaucracies do not provide the protective structures (against arbitrariness and nepotism) that bureaucracies ideally can do. Bureaucracies can operate without regard for persons and may even have some features which promote gender equity. Bureaucracies may also benefit professional women more than low-level male bureaucrats. Women have started to advance to higher levels of the organizational hierarchy but the culture and social norms at the top may not be attractive for many women (and some men). Thus it is cultures which are important to look at and make interventions in relation to, although in some cases bureaucratic interventions, such as quota systems may also be necessary.

It is important to recognize that people have a life outside bureaucracies, and if this includes children, this will affect the working capacities of women, especially if they live in a society where day care is not provided. Thus the social context is also important when we look at what can be achieved in bureaucracies. Basically, though, bureaucratic interventions are necessary, if we wish to equalize unequal social relations.

Notes

1. As women gained higher education almost on a par with men it became more visible that there is a discrepancy between the number of women with higher education and the number of women in leadership positions.

In Denmark, 74% of (the 16–66 years) women are in the workforce, 81.4% of men. Of the 40–44 years old, 87.2% women and 89.8% men work (Danmarks Statistik (2002) *Statistisk tiårsoversigt*).

2. In this chapter, I am only concerned with the gender aspect.
3. At the European Union level solidified in the Amsterdam Treaty (1997).
4. A British government backed voluntary initiative to increase the number of women in the workplace.
5. Other standpoint feminisms, as for example, materialist (socialist) feminism, prioritize social class as the factor determining women's situation under capitalism.
6. I am not going into a debate on whether bureaucracy is efficient or not.
7. When Weber developed his theory of bureaucracy women did not have the same rights as men (civil, political, or social) and Weber, although concerned with power aspects, did not pay much attention to the prevalent patriarchal structures.
8. Flexible work-time and part-time work seem to reproduce inequalities. Often these jobs are of a lower status with lower pay and advancement possibilities.

References

Acker, J. (1992). 'Gendering organizational theory', in A. Mills and P. Tancred (eds), *Gendering Organizational Analysis*. London: Sage.

Adler, N. (1987). 'Women in management world-wide'. *International Studies of Management and Organization*. 16/3–4; 3–32.

Alvesson, M. and Billing, Y. D. (1997). *Understanding Gender and Organizations*. London: Sage.

Alvesson, M. and Billing, Y. D. (2002). 'Beyond body-counting. A discussion of the social construction of gender at work', in I. Aaltio, and A. J. Mills (eds), *Gender, Identity, and the Culture of Organizations*. London: Routledge.

Billing, Y. D. (1994). 'Gender and bureaucracies—A critique of Ferguson's "The feminist case against bureaucracy"'. *Gender, Work and Organization*. 1/4; 179–94.

Billing, Y. D. (2000). 'Organizational cultures, families, and careers in Scandinavia', in L. L. Haas, P. Hwang, and G. Russell (eds), *Organizational Change and Gender Equity*. London: Sage.

Billing, Y. D. and Alvesson, M. (1994). *Gender, Managers, Organizations*. Berlin: de Gruyter.

Cassell, C. (2000). 'The Business Case and the Management of Diversity', in M. Davidson and R. Burke (eds), *Women in Management*. London: Sage.

Davidson, M. and Burke, R. J. (1999). *Women in Management*. London: Sage.

du Gay, P. (1996). *Consumption and Identity at Work*. London: Sage.

Ferguson, K. E. (1984). *The Feminist Case Against Bureaucracy*. Philadelphia, PA: Temple University Press.

Frankenhaeuser, M. (1993). *Kvinnligt, manligt, stressigt*. Höganäs: Bra Böcker/Nike.

Grant, J. and Tancred, P. (1992). 'A feminist perspective on state bureaucracy', in A. J. Mills and P. Tancred (eds), *Gendering Organizational Analysis*. London: Sage.

Haas, L. L., Hwang, P., and Russell, G. (eds). (2000) *Organizational Change and Gender Equity*. London: Sage.

Harding, S. (1987). 'Introduction: is there a feminist method?' in S. Harding (ed.), *Feminism and Methodology*. Milton Keynes: Open University Press.

Konrad, A. M. and Linnehan, F. (1999). 'Affirmative action: history, effects, and attitudes', in G. Powell (ed.), *Gender and Work*. London: Sage.

Lundberg, U., Mardberg, B., and Frankenhaeuser, M. (1994). 'The total workload of male and female white collar workers as related to age, occupational level, and number of children' *Scandinavian Journal of Psychology*. 35; 315–27.

Maddock, S. (1999). *Challenging Women*. London: Sage.

Marshall, T. H. (1977). *Class, Citizenship and Social Development*. Chicago, IL: University of Chicago Press.

Martin, P. Y. (2001). ' "Mobilizing masculinities": women's experiences of men at work'. *Organization*. 8/4; 587–618.

Martin, P. and Knopoff, K. (1997). 'The gendered implications of apparently gender-neutral theory: rereading Max Weber', in A. Larson and R. E. Freeman (eds), *Women's Studies and Business Ethics*. New York: Oxford University Press.

Mills, A. and Tancred, P. (eds) (1992). *Gendering Organizational Analysis*. London: Sage.

Mouffe, C. (1995). 'Feminism, citizenship, and radical democratic politics', in L. Nicholson and S. Seidman (eds), *Social Postmodernism*. Cambridge: Cambridge University Press.

Pateman, C. (1988). *The Sexual Contract*. Cambridge: Polity Press.

Schein, V. E. (1975). 'Relationships between sex role stereotypes and requisite management characteristics among female managers'. *Journal of Applied Psychology*. 60/3; 340–4.

Schenker, M. B., Eaton, M., Green, R., and Samuels, S. (1997). 'Self-reported stress and reproductive health of female lawyers', *Journal of Occupational and Environmental Medicine*. 39; 556–68.

Tenbrunsel, A. E., Brett, J. M., Stroh, L. K., and Reilly, A. H. (1995). 'Dynamic and static work-family relationships', *Organization Behaviour and Human Decision Processes*. 63, 233–46.

Wajcman, J. (1998). *Managing like a Man. Women and Men in Corporate Management*. Cambridge: Polity Press.

Wahl, A. (1996). 'Företagsledning som konstruktion av manlighet'. *Kvinnovetenskaplig tidskrift*. 17/1; 15–29.

Weber, M. (1968). *Economy and Society*, 3 Vols. New York: Bedminster.

Wilson, E. (1998). 'Gendered career paths', *Personnel Review*. 27/5; 396–411.

Witz, A. and Savage, M. (1992). 'The gender of organization', in M. Savage and A. Witz (eds), *Gender and Bureaucracy*. Oxford: Blackwell.

12

Bureaucracy, Open Access, and Social Pluralism: Returning the Common to the Goose*

Antonino Palumbo and Alan Scott

> The fundamental tendency of all bureaucratic thought is to turn all problems of politics into problems of administration . . . Bureaucratic thought does not deny the possibility of a science of politics, but regards it as identical with the science of administration.
> *(Karl Mannheim, Ideology and Utopia: 105–6)*

Introduction

Bureaucracy has long been the object of fierce intellectual critique and political polemic. Over the last quarter of a century or so we have witnessed systematic attempts—influenced by public choice theory, and fuelled by popular resentment against bureaucratic power—to

---

*'Tis bad enough in man or women/To steal a goose from off a common/But surely he's without excuse/Who steals the common from the goose'. (Anon: 'On Inclosures'. *The Oxford Book of Light Verse*, 1938).

dismantle bureaucracies and replace them with organizational forms that are more 'flexible', more 'accountable', more 'responsive', more 'entrepreneurial', less 'hierarchical', and 'flatter'. However, in the meantime we also have a growing literature demonstrating that the measures designed to counter the dysfunctions of bureaucracy themselves have side effects that are highly undesirable. The tightening of mechanisms of control and evaluation designed to deliver 'accountability' have been said: (a) to corrode trust and solidarity within—and beyond—organizations (O'Neill 2002), (b) to lead to a decline of the spirit of public service and the growing subordination of procedural to political concerns (du Gay 2000), (c) are themselves not immune to those very tendencies that they were intended to counter—that is uncontrolled growth and high (especially time) costs (Power 1997), (d) encourage new and increasingly authoritarian and unconstrained styles of management (Willmott 1993). At the level of the organization, the net effect is generally taken to be a decline in employee morale and of the loss of identification with the goals of the organization. At worst, organizations are said to have been reduced to places 'where people have no settled place and no say' (Hirst 2002: 18). Where the influence of these—supposedly post-bureaucratic—organizational forms spills over into a style of governance, these implications are viewed with even greater suspicion and concern (e.g. Hirst 1996).

What unites these critics of new organizational forms and the managerial styles that accompany them is a shared concern with preserving a plurality of 'life orders' (cf. du Gay 2000: 4) and a fear of what Sheldon Wolin (in the spirit of Mannheim's epigrams) long ago identified as the 'sublimation of politics' by organization (Wolin 1960). We share this concern and this fear. However, there are two ways of defending traditional bureaucracy in this context: as an end in itself— as a *value*—or as means toward an end; that end being political and social pluralism. It is this latter option that we adopt for a number of reasons. First, in the classical sociology of bureaucracy, from Weber through to Merton and Selznick, the dominant view of bureaucracy is highly nuanced. Bureaucracy is viewed both as necessary *and* dangerous. It is that 'living machine' capable of refining subordination to degrees unimaginable under pre-modern forms of slavery (Weber 1918: 158). At the same time, the predictability of its workings and its mechanical quality are necessary for both rational capitalism and rational rule. We wish to preserve that nuance. Philistine anti-bureaucratic dogma focuses only on the former aspect, but this is not best countered by an exclusive emphasis upon the latter. Second, if the preservation of pluralism is the end, then bureaucracy is neither the only nor necessarily the best, means to this end. Indeed, in certain contexts—as we shall later argue—bureaucracy has the same homogenizing logic as those forms of organizational and political governance that have replaced it. Here we need to distinguish carefully between the *levels* of governance at which various organizational types are most appropriate. We are thus sympathetic to Christopher Hood's sceptical view that no single model is unproblematic where it is imposed across a range of plural forms (Hood 1998). Finally, those theories—and the policy recommendations that have been deduced from them—which are critical of bureaucratic organizations are no less dismissive of all alternatives forms of social and organizational arrangements, with one exception: the market. An adequate response to this perspective, we argue, must move beyond the conventional dualisms of state–market, public–private, and hierarchy–network if it is to avoid the pendulum swing between poles that ultimately define, presuppose, and reinforce each other (see Reed, Chapter 5, this volume).

We shall treat the 'commons' as the embodiment of a pluralistic life order and argue that a variety of organizational types are required of which bureaucracy—at the national level—is one. Within public choice theory (e.g. Hardin (1977) [1968]), commons are identified with inherently inefficient public assets, the neglect of which can best be remedied by further privatization. In this respect, the fate of bureaucracy is, in our view, linked to the fate of the commons. Both are the object of public choice theory's opprobrium, and a defence of the former should likewise be linked to a defence of the latter. But this necessarily takes us beyond arguments that counterpoise state and market options, and entails the search for a plurality of forms of governance that reflect the plurality of life orders. The commons identify assets, organizational forms, and managerial practices that are not only distinct from those of the market, but also from those of the state. Following Durkheim, we shall argue that they represent a resource that is necessary for both market *and* state. With respect to the former, contemporary social theory has again highlighted the explanatory relevance of pre-contractual elements in recognizing the role played by trust and social capital (see Portes 1998). With respect to the latter, we share Durkheim's view that the engagement of citizens in intermediate associations is a *sine-qua-non* for the effective governance of a complex and pluralistic society.

Globalization: Conflicting Narratives and Normative Implications

Current debates on globalization suggest the idea of an inherent conflict between the state and the market, democratic decision-making and individual choice, and bureaucratic rule and private enterprise. On a neo-liberal view, state action and welfare policies are neither effective nor desirable. These objections rest on the assumption that in pluralistic societies collective decision-making will inevitably result in vicious redistributive dynamics and/or in the production of semi-private goods forcibly charged to the whole community (Mueller 1989). Moreover, it is maintained that state intervention tends to distort economic incentives, thereby undermining the self-regulating power of the market and the competitiveness of society at large (de Jasay 1989). Finally, neo-liberals claim that the state's encroachment on the economy entails a continuous and pervasive interference with individual choice which not only hinders people's ability to react to change, but seriously limits their freedoms and rights (Rowley 1993; see du Gay, Chapter 2, this volume). Accordingly, these shortcomings can be redressed by a return to the market. The privatization schemes and pro-market policies promoted worldwide are thus presented as the only means capable of protecting individual freedom from the state's interference, while promoting 'trickle down' effects that will increase the welfare of the average citizen (Mitchell and Simmons 1994). The neo-liberal perspective has acquired not only academic preeminence but has also, paradoxically, become an orthodoxy within government. Public Choice prescriptions became the basis for the internal governmental reforms carried out in the 1980s and 1990s, and for the international trade and development policies pursued by the World Trade Organization (WTO) and the International Monetary Fund (IMF) (Stiglitz 2002).

Against this view, globalization's critics point out that the neo-liberal policies carried out since the late 1970s have reduced the ability of nation states to govern pluralist societies fairly and effectively, and worsened the North–South divide. The counter-narrative supplied by these critics is threefold. Against the idea of an inherent conflict between the state and the market, they have highlighted the existence of serious and persistent market failures that continue to legitimate states' intervention in their economy (Self 1993). Opposing the claim that the public sector is riddled by bureaucratic rigidities and inefficiencies, critics of neo-liberalism have argued for the distinctiveness of the public realm and upheld its ethics of the common good and struggle for social justice (Beetham 1996). Finally, they have endeavoured to undermine economics' faith in the mystic powers of the invisible hand by showing that hierarchies can tackle coordination problems more effectively than the decentralized decision-making of markets and networks (Reed, Chapter 5, this volume). Although valuable, these attempts to engage neo-liberal thought on its own ground display two main theoretical weaknesses. First, they give the impression of having accepted the neo-liberal frame of reference along with its pair-wise juxtapositions between state versus market, public versus private, and hierarchy versus network. Consequently, they fail to question the simplistic (and Manichean) epistemology underlying most neo-liberal analyses. Second, critics of neo-liberalism have an inadequate understanding of the reasons underlining the crisis of the welfare state and run the risk of finding themselves defending a defective, and by now discredited, system of governance. If the success of the neo-liberal agenda is connected with the shortcomings of the welfare state and with the collapse of the social coalition that supported it, any attempt to revive such a system of governance will appear either backward-looking or self-defeating.

These two opposite readings are neither the most accurate, nor do they exhaust, the possible interpretations of current trends. As for the alleged trade-off between the state and the market, Karl Polanyi has made clear that far from undermining the state's ability to govern, laissez-faire policies can represent a way of reducing government costs and making state action more effective; to wit, it is itself a form of political steering. A confirming example is the 1990s introduction of internal markets within the public sector in the United Kingdom that reinforced hierarchical control while reducing the accountability of decision-makers (Scott 1996). Indeed, there is a growing literature which demonstrates that privatization and market policies have been very effective in reducing democratic control over government action through the de-politicization of areas of decision-making and the shifting of political responsibility for daily management to the private sector.[1]

Similar observations have been made in relation to the globalization of markets and financial institutions. After analysing data on global trends, Ken Waltz concludes thus:

Many globalizers believe that the world is increasingly ruled by markets. Looking at the state among states leads to a different conclusion. The main difference between international politics now and earlier is not found in the increased interdependence of states but in their growing inequality. With the end of bipolarity, the distribution of capabilities across states has become extremely lopsided. Rather than elevating economic forces and depressing political ones, the inequalities of international politics enhance the political role of one country. Politics, as usual, prevail over economics. (Waltz 1999: 11)

Cries about the irreversible decline of the nation state seem indeed overstated, if not misleading (Hirst and Thompson 1996). Historically, states have had a pivotal role in creating and imposing markets. Moreover, with the development of market economies the regulatory power of the nation state has increased rather than decreased. We do not mean to deny the reality of the changes that have occurred since the late 1970s. However, these changes can be interpreted not as a hollowing out of the state (Rhodes 1994), but as the state's ability to transform its capacities (Weiss 1998). In other words, they can be viewed as a response to the collapse of the coalition that supported the Keynesian consensus and increased interstate competition. On this view, current changes do not call for a defence of the state per se, but demand a re-evaluation of the model of state that brought about those changes and uses them as a means for reducing democratic spaces and accountability. Similar arguments can be developed in relation to central government and its administrative branches. A sound and acceptable defence of bureaucracy needs to spell out the reasons that make the latter a suitable institutional model and/or managerial practice for the governance of complex and pluralist societies. Such a justification has to clarify three things: (a) what principles bureaucracy, as an ideal-type model of organization, is supposed to engender; (b) why it is the right organizational model to achieve this; (c) at which levels it is appropriate and at which inappropriate. In this Chapter we engage in such a principled justification by connecting the defence of bureaucracy with the support, preservation, and protection it offers to the 'commons'.

The Commons as Social Capital

Several contemporary writers have drawn a parallel between current processes of globalization and the movement of enclosures that took place in eighteenth-century Britain.[2] Like the enclosures, globalization proceeds by 'fencing' assets previously used by, or accessible to, all members of the community through the establishment of a system of private and exclusive property rights. In addition, globalization promotes the commodification and commercialization of assets that were both public and run according to non-market criteria. A further common element between enclosures and globalization is that, according to its critics, both phenomena have been the result of government interventions rather than the outcome of spontaneous social forces. As with the eighteenth-century enclosures, the current combined processes of privatization and marketization raise two main theoretical questions. The first concerns the economic efficiency of common-pool resources (CPR) vis-à-vis privately owned assets. The second is related to the issues of social justice and democratic decision-making. Generations of liberal economists have attempted to prove that private individual rights and market competition not only increase the allocative efficiency of social resources but also generate 'trickle down' effects that promote the general welfare of all (Hayek 1988). As far as democracy is concerned, liberals have also tried to show that by being able to satisfy the aggregate welfare of the greatest number of people, a private market society is capable of fostering democracy and a feasible social order (de Jasay 1997). These claims are strongly contested by critics who deny they have any empirical or theoretical validity (Haworth 1994). Rather than rehearse these criticisms of globalization, we want to clarify what the commons stands for and what their relevance for society is.

Let us start with the definition of commons supplied by Barrington Moore Jr. in his study on the *Social Origins of Dictatorship and Democracy*.

As a form of insurance against natural hazards, and in some cases also in response to methods in the collection of taxes or dues to the overlord, peasants in many parts of the world have developed systems of tenure with a built-in tendency toward the equal distribution of resources . . . In addition there is the custom of equal access for all to a segment of land held undivided, the commons ... The main idea connected with these arrangements stands out very clearly: every member of the community should have access to enough resources to be able to perform obligations to the community carrying on a collective struggle for survival. (Moore 1966: 497).

In the past the commons were an essential asset of peasant villages. They contributed to the unity of the community by guaranteeing a safety net protecting the poorest members. In turn, this safety net allowed all members of the community to discharge the obligations set upon them by external political authorities. Here the village represents a partially self-regulating socio-economic unity, whereas commons are institutions devised to *reduce* internal conflicts and *enhance* social cooperation. The commons performed this function in three ways: by promoting solidarity within the group, by redistributing the cooperative surplus according to some notion of social justice, and by relying on the self-policing power of the community.[3] Too often these arrangements have been idealized. From the Romantic Movement on, traditional societies have been described as the locus of authenticity and of the harmonious development of individual and collective identities. This romanticized picture was reinforced by the dismal conditions created by the industrial revolution, thus initiating what Hirschman (1982) calls the thesis of capitalism's self-destruction. However, the commons did not disappear with modernity. Some survived and are still operating. They are also widespread in developing countries where they are threatened by a new wave of enclosures. More importantly, as Karl Polanyi (1944) argues, modernity itself generated a vast array of social and political movements that recreated new commons, eminently represented by welfare institutions.[4]

At a highest level of abstraction, the notion of commons refers to three related elements:

- a set of resources held in common and employed for collective ends
- a set of institutional arrangements devised to foster social cooperation
- a set of managerial practices regulating access and use of common resources.

David Bollier (2002) discusses a variety of assets that fill the role played by the eighteenth-century open fields. These assets can be classified along three main dimensions. According to their physical characteristics, commons can be located along a continuum from material assets such as pastures and fishing fields to immaterial assets such as social knowledge and trust. In addition, commons can be grouped in relation to their geographical extension along another continuum from local commons such as water springs and reputation to global commons like the open seas and the Internet. Concerning the nature of the resources themselves, they can finally be classified into depletible, non-depletible, and renewable. Associated with this notion of the commons as resources is a second reading that views them as institutional arrangements underpinning social cooperation and public life. On the one hand, the commons identify a type of owner-ship legally distinct (and logically distinguishable) from both private property and Crown (state) property. They are neither the exclusive and absolute domain of the individual, nor a public entitlement of the abstract citizen. On the contrary, commons belongs to specific communities who, in turn, are called to define, regulate, and police the various entitlements of the commoners. On the other hand, the commons represent a system of relationships alternative to both the hierarchical type that characterizes bureaucratic institutions and the horizontal type proper of market exchange. To borrow Grahame Thompson's expression (2003), we can say that commons are institutional forms occupying the logical space between hierarchies and markets; that is, network forms of organization. Finally, it is the commons—rather than new types of firm—that can be viewed as managerial techniques facilitating what Charles Sabel calls 'deliberat-ive coordination': 'institutions that allow each part of a collaborative whole to reflect deliberately, and in a way accessible to the others, on the aptness of its ends and the organizational means used to prosecute them, even as those common ends are themselves continuously redefined by the cumulative, mutual adjustments of partial purposes, activities, and organizational connections' (Sabel 1995: 2). These three conceptions share the idea of commons as a crucial part of what current social theorists identify as 'social capital', whether conceived of as a micro-sociological system of personal relations (Bourdieu 1985), or as a macro-sociological phenomenon influencing social interaction and growth (Putnam 2000) (see Savage, Chapter 13, this volume).[5]

Classic political economists and neo-liberals alike have perceived the institutional and managerial arrangements identified here as commons as a Byzantine system of entitlements opposing innovation and hindering growth. Hence, their call for privatization and the establishment of exclusive property rights. By contrast, we maintain that this multiplicity is a means to assure communities the ability to adapt to changing conditions. In our view, commons are not only a crucial component of current social capital, but also a diversified investment system and the locus of managerial experimentation.[6] It follows that enclosing new commons sets in motion dynamics which will deplete the social capital accumulated by, and inherited from, past generations and endanger the ability of actual societies to reproduce themselves. The dramatic effects the neo-liberal programme of governance is having on local as well as national communities across the globe warrant a reexamination of the theoretical reasons given by classical and neoclassical political economy for preferring private ownership to collective entitlements. Moreover, they demand a reassessment of the claim that the profit-motive and a self-regulating market system can bring about a flourishing and stable social order. Similar concerns can also be expressed in relation to the statist solutions employed by the welfare state. As we shall shortly demonstrate, the dismantling of commons through nationalization and bureaucratic administration can have uncannily similar effects to those yielded by privatization. Thus, a principled opposition to the neo-liberal project and defence of the public domain requires a reassessment of the role and functions of central government and its administration in relation to the commons and the plurality of social and economic institutions they supports.

Common-Pool Resources and the Tragedy of Commons

In this section, we discuss the alleged inherent inefficiency of CPR as compared to both capitalist and statist arrangements. The starting point is, of course, Hardin's 1968 paper (reprinted as Hardin (1977) linking the tragedy of the commons to the Malthusian idea that, left unchecked, a population tends to grow beyond the ability of the ecology in which it is located to support its growth. This bleak picture was meant to cast doubts on the power of Adam Smith's invisible hand by showing that individual maximizing strategies could lead to social dis-asters. In fact, it has become one of the most oft-quoted pieces of work in support of laissez-faire policies. To understand why, let us follow Hardin's own account.

> The tragedy of the commons develop in this way. Picture a pasture open to all . . . As a rational being, each herdsman seeks to maximize his gain. Explicitly or implicitly, more or less consciously, he asks, 'What is the utility to me of adding one more animal to my herd?' . . . Adding together the component partial utilities, the rational herdsman concludes that the only sensible course for him to pursue is to add another animal to his herd. And another . . . But this is the conclusion reached by each and every rational herdsman sharing the commons. Therein is the tragedy. Each man is locked into a system that compels him to increase his herd without limit . . . Ruin is the destination toward which all men rush, each pursuing his own best interest in a society that believes in the freedom of the commons. (Hardin 1977: 20)

Here Hardin describes a collective action problem (CAP) which takes the form of a Prisoner's Dilemma game (PD). In this game, herders have a dominant strategy which tells them to maximize the number of livestock they can graze on the common. The rationality of this strat-egy is twofold: (a) by doing so they avoid finding themselves in the position of the sucker who has refrained from adding more livestock while everybody else is doing so; (b) at the same time they have the opportunity to maximize the utility they can extract from the pasture by exploiting the fact that some are refraining from doing so. Unfortunately, since the game is symmetric, and since everybody can replicate that reasoning (what game theorists call 'common know-ledge rationality'), 'the inherent logic of the commons remorselessly generates tragedy . . . Freedom in a commons brings ruin to all' (Hardin 1977: 20). Note, in Hardin's account three combined factors kick-start the PD dynamics:

- the common is open to all
- people have a inner drive to maximize their utility
- there is no external force capable of restraining them from doing so.

In a forthright naturalistic way the author explains, quoting Whitehead, that the tragedy 'resides in the solemnity of the remorse-less working of things' (Hardin 1977: 20).

Hardin's naturalistic explanation is open to three sets of criticism: historical, empirical, and logical. Historically, it is possible to show that far from an internal collapse, the commons have often been dismantled from without (Hill 1996). In her remarkable historical study of enclosures from 1700 to 1820, J. M. Neeson (1993) highlights both the social relevance of common rights throughout the eighteenth century and the widespread opposition their abolition aroused. Far from being relics of a bygone feudal age without economic values, Neeson shows that the system of open fields underpinned the economy of large areas of the country and that only the overwhelming legal and military power behind the enclosure acts was capable of dismantling it. In opposition to Hardin's cavalier attitude to historical facts, she also explains that commons were part of an integrated rural economy run according to consolidated managerial practices effectively implemented and policed by the manorial courts and vestries. As far as common pastures were concerned, she clarifies that the threat of overgrazing 'came less from the clearly defined rights of cottagers than from larger flocks and herds of richer men' (1993: 86), and that overstocking was often carried out intentionally by rich landowners in order to reduce the value of the commons before enclosing them. Finally, Neeson points out that the reasons behind enclosures parallel those for vertical integration in the manufacturing industry: the creation of a weak and dependent wage-labour workforce.

Neeson's findings receive support in empirical analyses of actually existing commons. Elinor Ostrom (1990) and Glenn Stevenson (1991) have collected a wide range of case studies showing not only the vitality of the commons as a socio-economic institution, but also that some of them have outlived even the most successful capitalist enterprises. They maintain that the evidence available indicates that the tragedy of the commons is not always due to factors *internal* to a given group, but to *external* causes upon which the community itself has no influence. On this view, Hardin's approach is not only too controversial, but also fails to clarify the reasons why 'some individuals have broken out of the trap inherent in the commons dilemma, whereas others continue remorsefully trapped into destroying their own resources' (Ostrom 1990: 21). This can be further appreciated by focusing on Hardin's explanatory framework. It has been pointed out that Hardin's account of the tragedy applies to resources that are *open to all*, rather than to CPR as such (Stevenson 1991). As a matter of fact, many commons do not grant open access to all, but are often regulated by a highly complex system of norms which establishes who, how, and when CPR can be used. Open access is always connected to membership, a normative status that is 'limited by legally recognized and practically enforceable rights' (Seabright 1993: 113). In this context, for a CAP of the type described by Hardin to arise it must be demonstrated either that the norms regulating the common are highly ineffective, or that the community lacks the necessary means to supervise and enforce them, or both.[7] Hardin not only completely fails to take into account these features, but he also collapses openness and collective ownership, thus failing to uncover what generate the CAPs related to CPR, let alone showing that the commons are inevitably prone to tragedy.

The behavioural model adopted leads Hardin to depict social interaction *as if* it is taking place in a Hobbesian state of nature. People are either part of no community, or the community they are a part of is fast disintegrating, and thus incapable of controlling free-riders. The last two assumptions draw the logical boundaries of the social space where Hardin's tragedy could take place. In a context where people act *as if* to maximize their personal utilities and where there are no social arrangements in place that can check individual self-seeking tendency, 'the inherent logic of the commons remorselessly generates tragedy' (Hardin 1977: 20). Wherever these conditions are not in place 'the remorseless working of things' could well fail to materialize, as witnessed by the many examples of commons still operating. Using Bollier's typology, we can readily identify what kind of CPR are theoretically more likely generate either under-investment or over-exploitation: those that are global and pertain to resources that are both tangible and depletible. Concerning all other types of CPR, Hardin's conclusions are simply unwarranted.

Like Hobbes, Hardin claims 'the social arrangements that produce responsibility are arrangements that create coercion, of some sort' (1977: 26). Hence, the solution to the CAPs responsible for the tragedy is demanded of external institutions that can impose themselves on the individual and change the payoffs the agents face from without.

The tragedy of the commons as a food basket is averted by private property, or something formally like it. But the air and waters surrounding us cannot readily be fenced, and so the tragedy of commons as a cesspool must be prevented by different means, by coercive laws or taxing devices that make it cheaper for the polluter to treat his pollutants than discharge them untreated. (Hardin 1977: 22)

In the next section we shall discuss whether privatization and state regulation are really efficient answers to the tragedy of commons. Here we wish to stress once again that Hardin's institutional solutions—the market and the state—entail the resolution of a parallel CAP. Hardin's compelling argument seems therefore to generate a logical paradox: for he demands the resolutions of the CAP affecting the commons from institutions whose very existence and working require the resolution of an identical CAP. Moreover, institutional solutions based on competition and the profit-motive promote behavioural responses of the type he rightly attributes to the herders. Hence, Hardin seems to be caught in a further contradiction; for he claims that the tragedy of the commons, due to the self-seeking behaviour of the herders, can be avoided by institutions that promote people's self-seeking behaviour.

Coercion, Coercion, Coercion: Market Discipline and State Action

Both classic and neoclassic political economy view the commons not only as relics of a bygone era, but as institutions that distort the efficient allocation of social resources. Accordingly, to free those resources and maximize the public good they suggest two complementary courses of action: (a) the removal of any normative impediment hindering the tradeability of social assets and (b) the development of competitive pressures that push market forces to allocate social resources according to market prices. The justification for these reforms is grounded in general equilibrium theory. Since the commons are characterized by multiple entitlements that make them unmarketable, a preliminary step to improve their management requires policies that commodify them through the creation of individual property rights. A competitive market system that deals with commodities that are easily tradeable will afterwards distribute them according to their marginal value thus causing a Pareto-optimal allocation of resources. Next, we analyse the limits of this explanation by considering the implicit and explicit assumptions upon which it is based.

As anticipated, commons represent assets and resources whose access and use is regulated by a system of norms that establishes a plurality of implicit entitlements. The rationale for such a system is both historical and economic. On the one hand, the multi-level and sedimentary nature of the entitlements is due to past attempts to solve CAPs and foster cooperation. On the other hand, entitlements are implicit rather than explicit because of the costs and difficulties involved in establishing long-term complete contracts. Crucial in this context is the role of the local authorities in tinkering with the norms regulating the commons and enforcing them against free-riders. Privatization streamlines this Byzantine system of entitlements by establishing explicit contracts that attribute to a single agent the legal right to decide how that asset can be employed and the surplus produced redistributed. Since the definition and enforcement of this type of contractual relation is demanded of political and legal institutions located above the community, privatization also entails a transfer of authority from the community to levels above it. Is this new arrangement capable of tackling the CAP that allegedly affects commons thus eliminating over-exploitation?

The first thing to note about privatization is that its effectiveness rests on the efficiency of the new contractual arrangements to (a) reduce the conflicts of interest between the agents involved in the cooperative enterprise and (b) deter potential free-riders from violating ownership rights. Concerning the first point, there are reasons to believe that privatization would indeed increase conflict. By attributing to a single agent the power to determine how to distribute the cooperative surplus, privatization provides effective incentives only to the owner while ignoring the contribution of all the other agents. This could happen either because ownership increases the relative bargaining power of the owner vis-à-vis all the others who depend upon that resource, or because transaction costs cause contractual arrangements that fail to protect the entitlements of those who previously used the resource and contributed to its maintenance (Bardhan 1993). Finally, tradeability could undermine cooperation by reducing the rationality of specific investments and the credibility of long-term contracts (Seabright 1993). In other words, privatization could create distributive side effects that would reduce the informal incentives to cooperate. In this case, the convenience of a private system of rights would rest only upon its ability to deter free-riders effectively.

Privatization can enforce compliance in either of two ways. On the one hand, owners can appeal to the law and its enforcement agencies to uphold their rights against free-riders. The validity of this type of enforcement depends on the effectiveness of the institutions set up to protect property rights: government, courts, and police. Besides the neo-liberal doubts surrounding the efficiency of these institutions, transaction costs economics shows that when contractual relations are incomplete, a recourse to external enforcers of this kind is highly problematic. First, many possible kinds of violation cannot be specified *ex ante* and are therefore unenforceable. Second, many *ex post* violations cannot be observed by either the owner or the enforcing authority and are thus unprosecutable. In short, privatization not only represents a source of additional CAPs, but it also requires external forms of enforcement the very nature of which make them defective in dealing with free-riding. On the other hand, private ownership could promote retaliatory actions that would effectively deter free-riders. This type of explanation has been attempted by game theoretical approaches to non-cooperative games. The monumental literature produced by these attempts has had the unfortunate effect of supplying too many equilibrium solution concepts, each of which rests on too many qualifications and highly controversial epistemic premises in order to supply a general and satisfactory answer.[8] Moreover, these accounts concern themselves with state of nature-like interaction and do not take into account the psychological effects privatization could have on the previous occupants who have now been excluded. If privatization unilaterally removes their informal entitlements, their reaction could lead to resistance and retaliation rather than acquiescence. This, in turn, explains why measures directed at increasing the costs of collective action on the part of the excluded often accompany privatization.

A further weakness of the market solution advocated by Hardin is the allegedly positive effects of self-seeking competition. In settings where strategic interaction takes the form of a non-cooperative game, individual attempts to maximize their own interests could create suboptimalities because pre-emptive defection turns out to be the only rational strategy. Reiteration of the basic game far from assuring the emergence of cooperation predicted by Axelrod (1984), can set in motion dynamics which could deselect the cooperative players while rewarding defectors. Indeed, by imposing a neo-liberal model of governance, central governments and international institutions like the IMF and the World Bank have actively aroused the predatory interests of corporations and financial markets alike. This has led to the exploitation of local and global commons regardless of the impact it could have on people and resources alike. Corporate management has thus caused the over-exploitation of the newly privatized assets while capital global markets have allowed them an easy way out from the depleted markets leaving to local communities the costs of replenishing them. In the process, however, either the communities disintegrated or the relations of trust that kept them together were deeply undermined making replenishing of social capital a long, uncertain, and painful process. Current calls to re-evaluate the role of the state and public bureaucracies in contributing to the public good and in fostering social integration are part of the attempt to regenerate depleted social capital. However, the leading role played by central governments in pushing the neo-liberal programme forward casts doubts on the ability of these institutions not only to regenerate social capital but protect it from new predatory attacks.

As an alternative solution to the market, Hardin invokes the intervention of the state. State action is shorthand for two distinct, though connected, things: (a) decision-making and (b) administration. The first set of institutions deals with the choice of the (kind and quantities of) public goods to be produced and allocated, a choice formally resting with the representative institutions of the liberal state. The actual administration is instead the task of the executive agencies directly responsible to the representative institutions. The overall rationale of this constitutional arrangement (often identified as the Weberian model) is twofold: to arrive at legitimate decisions and to rationalize the activities of the state. As a solution to Hardin's tragedy, state action entails (a) the transfer of both ownership and decision-making power from the local community to the central government (nationalization) and (b) the attribution of managerial functions to bureaucratic agencies directly responsible to central government. Paradoxically, such a solution could trigger side effects uncannily similar to those promoted by privatization. On the one hand, nationalization could fail to take into account the informal entitlements of those living on and off the commons thus promoting free-riding strategies rather than individual compliance. On the other hand, administrative centralization could produce bureaucratic sclerosis, spiralling managerial costs, and endemic conflict with the local community. The experience of national parks worldwide supplies many a sorry account of this state of affairs. Finally, the defence of bureaucracy must confront 'one size fits all' type objections. In turning, as we now shall, from the economic to the political aspects of the commons, we shall suggest that they supply a potential response to such objections without taking us in the direction that that criticism intends: towards a 'one size fits all' market.

State, Bureaucracy, and Governance

What, if anything, justifies state action and public bureaucracy? The arguments developed so far supply a clear-cut economic justification for state intervention and administration in those instances where we are dealing with global commons and/or depletable resources. Since the community connected to a global common is the nation state as a whole, or several national communities, only state agencies or inter-state organizations seem to have the decision-making power to raise the resources and expertise needed to run the commons properly and effectively. However, even in this case it is still a moot point whether this justification also supports the technocratic and elitist management of the old centralized bureaucracies. Would a more participative, network-based managerial approach not be more effective? From our perspective, the answer is yes, for such an approach could reduce bureaucratic costs. But we also recognize that traditional hierarchies could bring about economies of scale and a more effective form of coordination. By the same token, economic analysis does not supply a rationale for the centralized public management of local commons of non-depletable and renewable resources. As said, removing the commons from its traditional users through nationalization and shifting managerial responsibility from the local community to a centralized administrative agency often simply means increasing conflicts and promoting bureaucratic sclerosis. We would like to point out, however, that such an argument while opposing traditional bureaucratic interventions, could be consistent with a non-conventional defence of bureaucratic actions directed at supporting local commons and a multi-level system of governance.

The economic analysis carried out before was not meant to supply a blanket justification of the commons either, but to question Hardin's deterministic logic and thus unmask the specious attempts to use those arguments to legitimize 'stealing the common from the goose'. To be sure, commons are often under the threat of free-riders, or can come to express mere group egotism. The question is whether these potential weaknesses justify dismantling them rather than devising institutional arrangements that can preserve them from tragedy or avoid the logic of 'amoral familism' (Banfield 1958). Given their connection to social capital and their role in promoting pluralism and social experimentation, we believe that the preservation of the commons is a necessary precondition for having a vibrant public sphere and pluralistic civil society. This sets the ground for a non-conventional, instrumental defence of public bureaucracy. For us, public bureaucracy finds a further justification in protecting the commons from enclosure by the market and the corrosive activity of free-riders. Public bureaucracies can bring this goal about not by replacing networks with hierarchies, but by empowering local communities with the decision-making power needed to deter free-riding and foster social cooperation. At this point in the argument we need to move beyond economics. A fuller defence of non-conventional bureaucracy requires a reconsideration of some traditional questions of social and political theory, namely, the ability of the state to foster social identity and govern modern complex societies while preserving a nationwide notion of citizenship.

Historically, privatization and nationalization of common pool resources promoted those modern forms of mass democracy whose most clear-sighted analyst was, and remains, Max Weber. For Weber, modern societies are incapable of self-regulation not least due to the irresponsibility of the masses who constitute them (Baehr 1990; Bellamy 2003). In such mass societies political rule 'necessarily and inevitably lies in the hands of officialdom' (Weber 1918: 145) and is exercised via the routine management of everyday administration. Consequently, questions of political representation and democracy can only be addressed as though they were technical questions of institutional design in which, paradoxically, the control over state bureaucracy becomes one, if not the, central challenge. In Weber, this dilemma gets translated into the question of how to design institutions in such a way that political leaders can emerge to counterbalance the ever-increasing power of technical administration while at the same time tying the masses into those decision-making processes (see Palumbo and Scott 2003). This leads us to think about the nature of modern democracy in terms of (a) the proper personality and orientation of political leaders and (b) the design of institutions that facilitate both effective leadership and political legitimation. Mirroring this view, we have an analysis of secondary associations that views them largely as self-seeking *Zweckverbände* (purposive associations) which pursue monopolistic strategies in order to improve their members' market situation, distorting the market in the process. Similarly, he perceives modern welfare policies essentially as a modern form of patrimony strengthened through rationalization. This is a vision that is, for all its realism, self-confirming. Technical bureaucratic management of the affairs of the masses reinforces the very disorganization, passivity, and irresponsibility that is taken to necessitate technical administration in the first place. Moreover, this approach rests on and encourages a top-down direct relationship between the state and the citizen that weakens the political role of intermediate institutions and their ability to foster collective identities.

The irresponsibility and rootlessness of the masses must be countered by the politician as embodiment of the ethic of responsibility, and by the public-spirited values of civil servants. However, as Sheldon Wolin has pointed out, this notion of political leadership is 'cut to truly classical proportions' and the leader is a 'political hero, rising to highs of moral passion and grandeur, harried by a deep sense of responsibility' (1960: 423). 'But', he continues, 'at bottom he is a figure as futile and pathetic as his classical counterpart'. Wolin greatly admires the majesty of Weber's political vision, but is sceptical about the possibility of such virtuoso moral rectitude in a modern context, and hints that an essentially aristocratic pre-modern—and thus nostalgic—vision underlies Weber's politics. A parallel problem arises with the attempt to defend bureaucracy as a value in its own right. At least two kinds of argument have been advanced in defence of the traditional bureaucratic ethos. First, it has been argued that by subscribing, and conforming, to formal principles of universality, impartiality, and neutrality the bureaucrat fosters the stability and predictability of the political system, thus actively contributing to social and economic development. Second and more importantly, it has been claimed that 'the bureau comprises a particular ethos, or *Lebensführung*—not only an ensemble of purpose and ideals within a given code of conduct but also ways of conducting oneself within a given "life-order"' (du Gay 2000: 4). On these grounds 'the ethos of bureaucratic office' can be defended from '"unworldly" philosophical and managerial bids to "establish commandments of identical content" across plural life orders' (du Gay 2000: 8). But the danger here is that we may seem to be appealing to the aristocratic values of a society that cannot be recalled, or may never have existed in quite this form.

An alternative to the Weberian model sketched above can be derived from Durkheim's theory of professional associations. According to Durkheim,

The state, in our large-scale societies, is so removed from individual interests that it cannot take into account the special or local and other conditions in which they exist. Therefore when it does attempt to regulate them, it succeeds only at the cost of doing violence to them and distorting them. (Durkheim 1957: 63)

From the above premise, he goes on to argue that if the state 'is to be the liberator of the individual, it has itself need of some counterbalance; it must be restrained by other collective forces'. These forces—secondary associations or groups—not only 'regulate and govern the interests they are meant to serve', they also have a 'wider purpose', namely, forming 'one of the conditions essential to the emancipation of the individual'. Durkheim's point is that the state apparatus is a necessary but not sufficient condition to ensure a plurality of life forms. Pluralism requires the *Rechtsstaat* and the values of 'constitutional patriotism' that support it,[9] but it also requires intermediary associations that can reduce government costs and supply forms of political participation and public identification. Without such social pluralism, the homogenizing logic of the state would go unchecked. Without the regulation of the state, pluralism alone would degenerate into competition between interests and into group egotism; hence his quest for constitutional arrangements capable of fostering moral integration while supplying social checks and balances on the authority of the state. This is the missing middle in Weber's analysis; a general moral resource, the absence of which he seeks to fill with the kind of aristocratic values Wolin identified. Similarly, our argument is not so much that faith in traditional elite values of rectitude, proceduralism, and due procedure is misplaced, but rather that if we are to preserve pluralism against the onslaught of a homogenizing managerialism, we need an account that identifies other values and organizational forms that are neither strictly those of the state nor the market, but that exist at distinct societal levels. It is here that our argument reconnects with the discussion of the commons.

As a set of resources, the commons can assure genuine autonomy and independence to a variety of social groups and professional associations. Thus, they are critical for promoting a self-sustaining social pluralism, rather than the legalistic type of associational life lamented by Durkheim, and which is now dominating our political landscape. As a set of institutions devised to foster social cooperation, the commons guarantee the existence of a plurality of organizational types that could either complement each other or bring about beneficial forms of competition. Thus, they represent an effective counterbalance to both the Weberian nightmare of a modernity cased in steel and the neo-liberal dream of a globalized market society. Finally, as a set of managerial practices, the commons are the precipitate of the successful cooperative strategies handed down by past generations and based on a larger motivational base than that underlying hierarchies and markets. Thus, they can be powerful tools for developing alternative forms of individual compliance and promoting innovation. A non-conventional model of bureaucracy could employ this social capital in several ways. First, it could use the commons to open new democratic spaces and thus deepen the legitimacy of the political system. Second, it could rely on them to redefine the political articulation of the modern state so as to strengthen collective identities. Third, it could integrate the commons in a revised system of social checks and balances which would increase accountability while reducing the costs of government. In short, a non-conventional model of bureaucracy views the commons as a pivotal medium for bringing about a multi-level form of governance. Let the mandarin classes tremble at the commons revolution. Citizens and civil servants have nothing to lose but their red tape.

Acknowledgement

We benefited greatly from the comments made and papers given at the *Defending Bureaucracy* Workshop at St. Hugh's College, Oxford. We would like to thank the participants, and particularly the organizer, Paul du Gay, for a pleasant and stimulating event. Alan Scott's contribution to this chapter is based on work for the New Orientations for Democracy in Europe research project (www.NODE-reseach.at).

Notes

1. This is the other side of the argument made in the 1970s by Habermas (1976) and Offe (1984) that states are more prone than market to legitimation crises because it is always possible to pose the question 'who decided' about political actions.
2. The most representative contemporary writers are Bollier (2002), Klein (2002), Linebaugh (2003), Vaidhyanathan (2003). For eighteenth-century enclosures see Neeson (1993).
3. This notion of a self-regulating community is incompatible with Hayek's spontaneous order because it entails both some sort of public deliberation and a commitment to a non aggregative idea of the common good.
4. Mauss made a similar argument in *The Gift* (1925) where he argues that elements of the gift relation—particularly welfare and other rights ascribed to workers—can be found in modern market societies.
5. For a critical analysis of these two meanings of social capital see Portes (1998).
6. Philosophically, this perspective partially overlaps with J. S. Mill's (1859) advocacy of experiments of life and Michael Walzer's (1983) defence of pluralism. However, we advocate a pluralist and multilevel system of governance not because it could help in achieving some metaphysical truth (Mill) or engendering the ideas of good embodied in our traditions (Walzer), but because it could strengthen the adaptive power of society.
7. Bates and Curry (1992) take into consideration the role of the local community. However, they persist in measuring the efficiency of local arrangements against the benchmark of a perfect competitive market economy.
8. Axelrod (1984), Bicchieri (1993), Schotter (1986), Sugden (1986), and Taylor (1987) set the terms of the game theoretic debate, whereas Bianchi (1994),

Hargreaves-Heap and Varufakis (1995, chapter 7), van der Lecq (1996) and Wärneryd (1990) contain good critical surveys of this literature.

9. The term is, of course, Habermas's, but the arguments that Habermas uses to support the notion of constitutional patriotism can be found in Durkheim, particularly in his writing during the First World War. See Palumbo and Scott (2003).

References

Axelrod, R. (1984). *The Evolution of Cooperation*. New York: Basic Books.

Baehr, P. (1990). 'The "masses" in Weber's political sociology'. *Economy and Society*. 19/2; 242–65.

Banfield, E. C. (1958). *The Moral Basis of a Backward Society*. Glencoe, IL: Free Press.

Bardhan, P. (1993). 'Introduction to the symposium on management of local commons'. *Journal of Economic Perspectives*. 7/4; 87–92.

Bates, R. H. and Curry, A. F. (1992). 'Community versus market: a note on corporate villages'. *American Political Science Review*. 86/2; 457–63.

Beetham, D. (1996). *Bureaucracy*. Buckingham: Open University Press.

Bellamy, R. (2003). 'The advent of the masses and the making of the modern theory of democracy', in T. Ball and R. Bellamy (eds), *The Cambridge History of Twentieth-Century Political Thought*. Cambridge: Cambridge University Press.

Bianchi, M. (1994). 'Hayek's spontaneous order. The "correct" versus the "corrigible" society', in J. Birner and R. Zijp (eds), *Hayek, Coordination and Evolution*. London: Routledge, 232–51.

Bicchieri, C. (1993). *Rationality and Coordination*. Cambridge: Cambridge University Press.

Bollier, D. (2002). *The Silent Theft. The Private Plunder of Our Common Wealth*. London: Routledge.

Bourdieu, P. (1985). 'The forms of capital', in J. G. Richardson (ed.), *Handbook of Theory and Research for the Sociology of Education*. New York: Greenwood.

de Jasay, A. (1989). *Social Contract, Free Rider: a Study of the Public Goods Problem*. Oxford: Clarendon Press.

du Gay, P. (2000). *In Praise of Bureaucracy*. London: Sage.

Durkheim, E. (1957). *Professional Ethics and Civic Morals*. London: Routledge.

First Division Association (1972). 'Professional standards in the public service'. *Public Administration*. 50; 167–82.

Habermas, J. (1976). *Legitimation Crisis*. Cambridge: Polity Press.

Hardin, G. J. (1977) [1968]. 'The tragedy of the commons', in G. Hardin and J. Baden (eds), *Managing the Commons*. San Francisco, CA: W. H. Freeman and Company.

Hargreaves-Heap, S. and Varoufakis, Y. (1995). *Game Theory. An Introduction.* London: Routledge.

Haworth, A. (1994). *Anti-Libertarianism. Markets, Philosophy and Myth.* London: Routledge.

Hayek, F. A. (1988). *The Fatal Conceit. The Errors of Socialism.* London: Routledge.

Hill, C. (1996). *Liberty Against the Law: Some Seventeenth-Century Controversies.* London: Allen Lane, The Penguin Press.

Hirschman, A. O. (1982). 'Rival interpretations of market society: civilizing, destructive, or feeble?'. *Journal of Economic Literature.* 20; 1463–84.

Hirst, P. Q. (1996). 'Democracy and Civil Society', in P. Q. Hirst and S. Khilnani (eds), *Reinventing Democracy.* Oxford: Political Quarterly Publishing/Blackwells.

Hirst, P. Q. (2002). 'The Future of Political Studies', Paper Presented at the Annual Conference of the Danish Political Science Association, October. www.londonconsortium.com/hirst/fps.doc.

Hirst, P. Q. and Thompson, G. (1996). *Globalization in Question: The International Economy and the Possibilities of Governance.* Cambridge: Polity Press.

Hood, C. (1998). *The Art of the State: Culture, Rhetoric, and Public Management.* Oxford: Oxford University Press.

Klein, N. (2002). 'Reclaiming the Commons'. *New Left Review.* 9; 81–9.

Linebaugh, P. (2003). 'The Secret History of the Magna Carta'. *Boston Review,* Summer.

Mannheim, K. (1936). *Ideology and Utopia.* London: Routledge.

Mauss, M. (1925). *The Gift.* London: Routledge.

Mill, J. S. (1859). *On Liberty and Other Writings.* Cambridge: Cambridge University Press, 1989.

Mitchell, W. C. and Simmons, R. T. (1994). *Beyond Politics. Markets, Welfare, and the Failure of Bureaucracy.* Boulder: Westview Press.

Moore, B. Jr. (1966). *Social Origins of Dictatorship and Democracy.* Harmondsworth: Penguin.

Mueller, D. (1989). *Public Choice II.* Cambridge: Cambridge University Press.

Neeson, J. M. (1993). *Commoners: Common Right, Enclosure and Social Change in England, 1700–1820.* Cambridge: Cambridge University Press.

Offe, C. (1984). *Contradictions of the Welfare State.* London: Hutchinson.

O'Neill, O. (2002). *A Question of Trust.* Cambridge: Cambridge University Press.

Ostrom, E. (1990). *Governing the Commons.* Cambridge: Cambridge University press.

Palumbo, A. and Scott, A. (2003). 'Weber, Durkheim and the Sociology of the Modern State', in T. Ball and R. Bellamy (eds), *The Cambridge History of Twentieth-Century Political Thought.* Cambridge: Cambridge University Press.

Polanyi, K. (1957). [1944]. *The Great Transformation.* Boston: Beacon Press.

Portes, A. (1998). 'Social capital: its origins and applications in modern sociology'. *Annual Review of Sociology.* 24/1; 1–24.

Power, M. (1997). *The Audit Society: Rituals of Verification*. Oxford: Oxford University Press.

Putnam, R. (2000). *Bowling Alone. The Collapse and Revival of American Community*. New York: Simon & Schuster.

Rhodes, R. A. W. (1994). 'The hollowing out of the state: the changing nature of the public service in Britain'. *Political Quarterly*. 65; 138–51.

Rowley, C. K. (1993). *Liberty and the State*. Aldershot: Edward Elgar.

Sabel, C. S. (1995). 'Design, Deliberation, and Democracy: On the New Pragmatism of Firms and Public Institutions', Paper Presented to the Conference on Liberal Institutions, Economic Constitutional Rights, and the Role of Organizations, European University Institute, Florence, December 15–16.

Schotter, A. (1986). 'The Evolution of Rules', in R. N. Langlois (ed.), *Economics as a Process: Essays in the New Institutional Economics*. Cambridge: Cambridge University Press, 117–34.

Scott, A. (1996). 'Bureaucratic revolutions and free market utopias'. *Economy and Society*. 25/1; 89–110.

Seabright, P. (1993). 'Managing local commons: theoretical issues in incentive design'. *Journal of Economic Perspectives*. 7/4; 113–34.

Self, P. (1993). *Government by the Market? The Politics of Public Choice*. London: Macmillan.

Stevenson, G. (1991). *Common Property Economics: a General Theory of Land Use Application*. Cambridge: Cambridge University Press.

Stiglitz, J. (2002). *Globalization and Its Discontents*. London: Penguin Books.

Sugden, R. (1986). *The Economics of Rights, Cooperation and Welfare*. Oxford: Blackwell.

Taylor M. (1987). *The Possibility of Cooperation*. Cambridge: Cambridge University Press.

Thompson, G. (2003). *Between Hierarchies and Markets*. Oxford: Oxford University Press.

Vaidhyanathan, S. (2003). 'The new information ecosystem: cultures of anarchy and closure'. *OpenDemocracy*. 4–9.

van der Lecq, F. (1996). 'Conventions and institutions in coordination problems'. *De Economist*. 144; 397–428.

Waltz, K. (1999). 'Globalization and governance', The 1999 James Madison Lecture of the American Political Science Association.

Walzer, M. (1983). *Spheres of Justice. A Defence of Pluralism and Equality*. Oxford: Blackwell.

Wärneryd, K. (1990). 'Conventions: an evolutionary approach'. *Constitutional Political Economy*. 1; 83–107.

Weber, M. (1918). 'Parliament and government in Germany under a new political order', in P. Lassman and R. Speirs (eds), *Weber: Political Writings*. Cambridge: Cambridge University Press.

Weiss, L. (1998). *The Myth of the Powerless State: Governing the Economy in a Global Era*. Cambridge: Polity Press.

Willmott, H. (1993). 'Strength is ignorance; slavery is freedom: managing culture in modern organizations'. *Journal of Management Studies*. 30/4; 515–52.

Wolin, S. S. (1960). *Politics and Vision*. Boston, MA: Little, Brown and Co.

13

The Popularity of Bureaucracy: Involvement in Voluntary Associations

Mike Savage

Much of the engagement with Weber's theory of bureaucracy since the 1950s has been concerned with whether it really delivers the kind of rational and efficient administration that it purports to (Blau 1956; Crozier 1964; Albrow 1970). It is increasingly clear, however, that for Weber, such arguments miss the point. Weber developed his concept of bureaucracy to differentiate modern forms of organization from those in earlier historical periods. Although Bauman (1988) reminds us (in true Weberian manner) that the ensuing differentiation of means from ends permits bureaucracy to promote all manner of evil, it is this historical focus which explains Weber's guarded support for bureaucracy (on which see du Gay 2000). Compared with older forms of administration, bureaucratic organizations did not belong to particular social classes, groups, institutions, or entities.[1] The inherent differentiation between bureaucratic organizations and their officers allowed the potential for bureaucracies to sustain democratic modes of governance. Although this in no way guaranteed that bureaucracy would lend itself to democracy, Weber's theory insisted on posing the counter-factual. What other kind of organization is better able to administer democracy? And indeed, nearly 100 years later, no obvious candidates have persisted.

The aim of my chapter is to extend this historical treatment of bureaucracy by considering how the differentiation of bureaucracies from social groups is changing in the contemporary period. My argument is a simple one. The extensive focus on bureaucracy as a form of work organization has concentrated on bureaucratic forms of coercion and control. However, if instead we look at participation in voluntary associations located in civil society, we can see a long history of extensive engagement from a wide range of social groups in bureaucratic forms of organization. All manner of people have enthusiastically supported and nurtured bureaucracies, such as trade unions, charities, sports, or hobby clubs. Bureaucracy has historically had strong roots in popular culture. However, over the past thirty years there is increasing evidence that participation in associations such as these is becoming more socially restricted and that people outside the professional and managerial 'service class' are disengaging from bureaucracy. I also argue that involvement in formal associations remains an important means by which people pursue their interests with enthusiasm. Hence the growing social exclusiveness of formal associations indicates an increasing homology between the professional and managerial service class and bureaucracy, to the extent that we can identify an administrative habitus that is increasingly socially exclusive.

I recognize at the outset that some may question whether formal voluntary associations are bureaucracies. If so, this would invalidate my analysis. However, it is clear that such associations normally possess the formalization of procedure and a hierarchy of office that is usually seen as marker of bureaucracy. Most involve an elaborate division of labour and function. The most important way that voluntary associations differ from Weber's ideal type is in his argument that 'official activity demands the *full working capacity* of the official' (Weber 1968: 958). Many formal positions in voluntary associations (though not usually the most senior ones) are provided in people's spare time, with activists taking on roles as local chairs or secretaries or as volunteers on a part-time basis, and so on. However, this difference is not disabling. Weber qualifies his argument by saying that this requirement only applies 'when the office is fully developed', where it might be claimed that local activity by voluntary associations could be seen as insufficiently developed to warrant the full working capacity of staff. In any event, the main point of Weber's distinction is historical. He seeks to distinguish bureaucratic officers from those in earlier administrative structures who conduct their offices on a part-time basis, where the office is an extension of their social position, and can be used for private advantage, through devices such as tax farming. Studying involvement in formal voluntary associations allows us to explore empirically whether and how those active in voluntary associations differentiate their involvement from their other kinds of commitments and activities.

In developing my analysis I make reference to the now extensive debates on social capital that have revitalized the study of voluntary associations (Putnam 1993, 2000). In the next section I show that 'social capital' raises issues highly pertinent to debates on bureaucracy, and I outline a positive and critical account of associational involvement, linked to the work of Putnam and Bourdieu, respectively. Section 2 then provides context by looking at the distribution of associational membership amongst the English and Welsh population to show how there is increasing social skewing, and reports evidence of increasing social selectivity in membership. Section 3 considers differences in people's modes of involvement in leisure and social activities, to assess whether those who are more involved in bureaucratic forms of organization rather than informal groups of enthusiasts have systematically different orientations and resources at their disposal.

The conclusion draws the threads together and seeks to relate my findings to debates about bureaucracy. I argue that formal associations remain crucial forms which are essential for a democratic polity with an active civil society. Romantic views which claim that informal modes of sociability convey the kinds of opportunities and resources associated with formal associations cannot be empirically sustained (see Due Billing, Chapter 11, this volume). However, the trend for associational membership to become increasingly exclusive means that the bureaucratic habitus is more socially distinct. If this is the case, it suggests, worryingly, that the advantages of associational membership are likely to become increasingly skewed to particular groups.

Social Capital and Bureaucracy

Over the past decade the study of voluntary associations, traditionally seen as a marginal research area with relatively little theoretical significance, has been radically overhauled through emerging interests in the study of social capital (Putnam 1993, 1995, 2000). Social capital refers to the interrelationships between 'networks, norms, and trust', and involvement in formal voluntary associations has been identified as a key form of social capital. Putnam's (1993) early work on Italian politics celebrates the potential of involvement in formal associations to enhance civic virtue. We come into contact with different types of people and thereby learn to develop generalized trust, not based on particularized forms of friendship or kinship, but on the possibility of coming to trust people through their public roles. He argued that democratic political forms flourished in northern Italy due to the strong tradition of civic associations but failed to develop in southern Italy where associations were weak and more clientist, and privatized social relationships dominated. 'Good government' he writes, 'is a by-product of singing groups and soccer clubs' (cited in Rossteutscher 2002: 515).

Putnam's arguments implicitly celebrate the potential of formal association to allow trust to develop through people learning how to deal with others according to their formal responsibilities. 'Internally associations and less formal networks of civic engagement instil in their members habits of co-operation and public spiritedness as well as the practical skills to partake in public life' (Putnam 2000: 583). His case is based on a similar intellectual move to that which du Gay (2000) makes in his defence of bureaucracy, that is to say that there are distinct and beneficial modes of conduct in associations which are not found in settings more attuned to personalized and charismatic relationships.[2] There is an implicit contrast with leisure based around what Bellah et al. (1985) call 'lifestyle enclaves' where we become friendly with fellow enthusiasts and rely on informal modes of familiarity in pursuing our passions. Here, it is claimed, we never learn to trust at a deeper level which goes beyond that of the personal and context specific.

It has been argued that new kinds of informal sociability do not require such formal structures or involvements. Maffesoli (1995) argues for the power of 'neo-tribalism' as a contemporary form of sociality, whilst Hetherington (1998) explores the expressivism of new social movements such as travellers. However, such claims are empirically under-developed, and open to challenge. Stebbins (1992) and Moorhouse (1993) show that even around apparently informal 'enthusiasms', such as hot-rodding, various kinds of voluntary associations are formed, and become articulated within a wider 'amateur–professional system' where formal associations interact with a wide variety of enthusiasts and fans to provide them with information, and offer means of promoting their interests. The informal and formal are not pure alternatives, but reciprocal forms of engagement.

In some respects, Putnam's work reminds us of the arguments made forty years ago by Edward Thompson (1963) in *The Making of the English Working Class*. Thompson identified the founding moment of the working class not as a particular protest, mass movement, or episode of unrest, but as resting in the formation of the London Corresponding Society in 1793. This established the principles of 'members unlimited' in which anyone was eligible to join, on payment of a subscription. This championed a mode of organization which rejected exclusive modes of patronage and allowed the constitution of a formal organization itself to be an exercise in practical democracy. This account has close resonance with du Gay's (2000: 42) rendering of Weber's positive association between bureaucratic forms and a democratic polity.[3] Indeed, it can be argued that the (no doubt partial) democratization of British social relationships from the early nineteenth century rested on popular bureaucratization as a means of resisting and countering elite patronage. In England, bureaucratic modes of organization were pioneered not in work organizations (on which see Littler 1982; Savage and Miles 1994; Savage 1998; McIvor 2001—all of whom emphasize the general weakness of bureaucratic modes of work organization) nor in state institutions (on the informative example of the 'gentlemanly' and informalized nature of British state organization in the area of secrecy see Vincent 1999) but in trade unions and civic voluntary associations (on which see Morris 1990). They formalized their operations, specified the duties of post holders and elaborated on the relationship between branches and officers as a means of developing the solidarity and trust necessary for effective organization and mobilization.[4] Seen in this light, popular bureaucracy allowed people to develop confidence and trust in each other which enabled them to participate more effectively in social affairs and gain greater control over aspects of their lives. The making of the English working class involved the making of bureaucratic organizations. It is telling that when Brian Jackson (1968) went back to his home town of Huddersfield in the early 1960s and portrayed it as a working-class community, it was its remarkable plethora of organizations—working-men's clubs, brass bands, bowling clubs, and the like—that impressed him.

However, there is an alternative to Putnam's account of social capital. Pierre Bourdieu elaborates a critical account of social capital which sees it as linked to exclusive networks, 'of more or less institutionalized relationships of mutual acquaintance and recognition—or in other words to the membership of a group—which provides each of its members with the backing of collectively owned capital' (Bourdieu 1997: 51). The social capital of some groups can thus be used to exclude others. Although Putnam recognizes the power of social capital to be 'directed towards malevolent, anti-social purposes' (Putnam 2000: 22), he sees this not as due to the nature of social capital itself but to the possibility that it can be deployed badly ('just like any other form of capital'). Bourdieu's emphasis, however, is on the way that social capital is necessarily exclusive, because the networks it generates between people also involve non-ties with outsiders, who are therefore excluded from those particular forms of social capital.

There is a way of reconciling these two views by noting that Bourdieu does not think that social capital need be formalized and bureaucratic in form. Indeed obvious examples of his approach would be non-bureaucratic modes of social capital generated by the 'old boys club' and the 'old school tie'. The argument might then run that bureaucratized forms of social capital tend to be more transparent and thereby less exclusive, though there appear to be obvious counterfactual arguments available here. The Freemasons, for instance, are bureaucratic and highly exclusive. Nonetheless, it can still be argued that as the recent, eventually successful, campaign to open up the Marylebone Cricket Club to female members indicates, where there are formal rules the possibility of challenging them becomes open in a way that it does not when there are no formal rules to challenge in the first place.

A further feature of Bourdieu's work is significant here. He focuses on the 'habitus', the implicit dispositions people possess which lead them to act in various ways. Reay et al. (2000) develop the concept of institutional habitus and argue (in a study of students applying to, and being accepted at, different British Universities) that there are uncodified assumptions about the kind of students who will fit into different universities, and that schools help to gear students up for 'appropriate' universities. The idea of institutional habitus in part refers to the argument, familiar from the work of Crozier, Blau, and Gouldner, that there is an informal aspect to every bureaucracy, and that only people with the appropriate dispositions can 'fit' into them. However, it is also consistent with Weber's own emphasis that not everyone has the aptitude to work in a bureaucracy. He is clear that it is the educationally well-qualified professional who is the ideal bureaucrat, and the ethos of bureaucracy is appropriate for those with a habitus which encourages abstraction, the ability to separate ends and means, and so forth. There are particular kinds of people, with various forms of habitus, who are best able to inhabit, and feel at home in, formal bureaucratic modes of behaviour. Bourdieu's point here is that this group is not 'innocent' in the class relations of contemporary capitalism. Indeed it is precisely their ability to draw upon the resources of cultural capital that are crucial to their own positioning.

We thus have two different ways of evaluating the nature of social capital. For Putnam, social capital generates trust through engaging with a range of others on a formal basis. Social capital is a resource which bestows general benefits and in its bridging role makes connections between different social groups. For Bourdieu (1984, 1998), those with particular stocks of cultural and economic capital are best able to reap the rewards of social capital. The differentiation of social capital from its members, as of bureaucratic offices from its officers, is only a sham which masks deeper processes of class reproduction and privilege. In such a way, we can see how debates on social capital touch on core, long-standing themes, regarding Weber's arguments about the differentiation of bureaucracy from social orders. In the remainder of this chapter, we empirically examine the value of these two different perspectives. In Section 2 we look at the changing social selectivity of members, and in Section 3 we consider whether formal associations convey different capacities and resources compared to informal modes of sociability.

Table 13.1 Participation in voluntary associations by class (disparity ratios)

	A	B	C	D	E	F	G	H	I	J	K	L	M	N	O
Panel 1: Class distribution (from row percentages)															
1972 men															
Service class	1.00	1.00	1.94	31.77	2.47	2.38	4.61	1.56	—	—	—	—	—	—	1.89
Working class	2.08	1.95	1.00	1.00	1.00	1.00	1.00	1.00	—	—	—	—	—	—	1.00
1992 men															
Service class	1.00	1.00	1.81	—	2.96	3.06	5.24	6.03	3.02	5.01	6.35	—	—	—	3.09
Working class	1.23	1.82	1.00	—	1.00	1.00	1.00	1.00	1.00	1.00	1.00	—	—	—	1.00
1999 men															
Service class	1.00	1.00	1.80	26.72	3.35	2.62	5.38	3.13	3.21	4.79	2.44	—	1.08	1.86	1.92
Working class	1.24	1.94	1.00	1.00	1.00	1.00	1.00	1.00	1.00	1.00	1.00	—	1.00	1.00	1.00
1992 women															
Service class	1.00	1.00	3.16	—	2.61	2.69	3.27	5.38	2.55	5.30	2.45	3.29	—	—	4.54
Working class	0.41	2.02	1.00	—	1.00	1.00	1.00	1.00	1.00	1.00	1.00	1.00	—	—	1.00
1999 women															
Service class	1.00	1.00	3.00	36.04	2.84	2.23	4.09	4.47	2.60	5.86	1.82	6.96	3.38	0.86	2.97
Working class	0.46	1.92	1.00	1.00	1.00	1.00	1.00	1.00	1.00	1.00	1.00	1.00	1.00	1.00	1.00
Panel 2: Class composition (from column percentages)															
1972 men															
Service class	1.00	1.00	1.08	17.80	1.39	1.34	2.58	0.87	—	—	—	—	—	—	1.06
Working class	3.67	3.49	1.00	1.00	1.00	1.00	1.00	1.00	—	—	—	—	—	—	1.00
1992 men															
Service class	1.00	1.00	2.07	—	3.39	3.50	5.99	6.93	3.46	5.72	7.25	—	—	—	3.54
Working class	1.12	1.59	1.00	—	1.00	1.00	1.00	1.00	1.00	1.00	1.00	—	—	—	1.00

	A	B	C	D	E	F	G	H	I	J	K	L	M	N	O
1999 men															
Service class	1.00	1.00	2.31	34.21	4.30	3.66	6.92	4.03	4.14	6.14	3.13	—	1.39	2.41	2.47
Working class	0.97	1.51	1.00	—	1.00	1.00	1.00	1.00	1.00	1.00	1.00	—	1.00	1.00	1.00
1992 women															
Service class	1.00	1.00	3.45	—	2.85	2.94	3.58	5.86	2.79	5.79	2.67	3.59	—	—	4.96
Working class	0.38	1.85	1.00	—	1.00	1.00	1.00	1.00	1.00	1.00	1.00	1.00	—	—	1.00
1999 women															
Service class	1.00	1.00	4.34	52.41	4.11	3.23	5.94	6.47	3.76	8.44	2.62	10.11	4.91	0.98	4.15
Working class	0.32	1.33	1.00	1.00	1.00	1.00	1.00	1.00	1.00	1.00	1.00	1.00	1.00	1.00	1.00

Note:

1. Civic organizations:

A: Trade Unions
B: Working-men's or Social Clubs
C: Sports/Hobby Clubs
D: Professional associations
E: Church or religious organizations
F: Residents'/Tenants' Associations
G: Parent–Teacher Associations
H: Political party
I: Voluntary services group
J: Environmental group
K: Other community or civic group
L: Women's Institute, Women's Group or Feminist Organization
M: Scouts'/Guides' organization
N: Pensioners' group/organization
O: Other.

2. Only the results for the service- and the working-class contrasts are presented, with the intermediate and petty bourgeois classes omitted. Full results for all classes are available on request.

Changing Contours of Social Capital

In the introduction I argued that historically there was strong popular involvement in various kinds of formal associations. Certainly, there is a remarkable historical record of what might be termed popular bureaucracy, in the form of trade unions, friendly societies, building societies, co-ops, and the like. Even some of the earliest limited companies, for instance in the Oldham textile industry, were characterized by strong popular involvement (Farnie 1978). However, the extent to which popular engagement of this kind endures is now uncertain, and Putnam (2000) is convinced that there has been a substantial decline of involvement of this kind in the United States. Hall (1999) has argued that whilst voluntary association membership remains strong in the United Kingdom (unlike the United States, where Putnam claims it is declining), there is evidence of social skewing in associational membership, with the middle classes being the mainstays of associational involvement, and his arguments have generated considerable discussion.[5]

Recent research has examined this issue by comparing the reported involvements in voluntary associations using surveys carried out at different points in time (Li et al. 2002, 2003; Warde et al. 2003). Li, Savage, and Pickles (2003) show that there appears to have been a significant drop in membership of all organizations over time. Membership rates have fallen from an average of 1.59 types of association per person in 1972 to 0.98 in 1999 for men, and from 0.89 in 1992 to 0.85 in 1999 for women. This decline is, however, nearly entirely accounted for by the falling membership of two kinds of association, trade unions and workingmen's clubs. In 1972, trade unions were by some distance the most popular kinds of association, yet by 1999 they had been overtaken by sports and hobby clubs. For men, trade union membership fell by 17.3 per cent and workmen's clubs by 9.8 percentage points, respectively, from 1972 to 1999. However, there were some kinds of association that were increasing in popularity, especially tenants' groups (up by 3.4 per cent) and professional organizations (up by 2.6 per cent). There was also a remarkable decline in the membership of political parties. Comparing women's membership profiles with those of men, the former are less likely to be in trade unions, sports clubs, workmen's clubs, and professional associations at the corresponding time points. But women are more likely than men to join religious groups, tenants' groups, parent–teacher associations or voluntary or civic organizations.

These aggregate trends indicate that the two kinds of association, which are predominantly working class in membership, have suffered the largest loss of membership. This supports the idea that membership is becoming socially skewed. This point is elaborated in Table 13.1, which examines the propensity of people in different social classes to be involved in voluntary associations at different times. The figures in Table 13.1 are expressed as disparity ratios between two social classes, the working class and the professional—managerial 'service class'. The disparity ratio reports the extent to which one class is over-represented compared with the other. Thus, the top left-hand cell in Table 13.1 indicates that working-class men were more than two times more likely (2.08) than service class men to be in trade unions in 1972. The claim that 'the working class draws its organizational affiliations disproportionately from trade unions and working-men's clubs' (Hall 1999: 456) is amply borne out.

However, for all organizations other than trade unions and working-men's clubs, we see that the service class is much more likely than the working class to join such organizations. We can further see that for most organizations, this over-representation increases over time, with the disparity ratios for the service class over the working class rising between the 1970s and the 1990s. The only exception to this trend is for sports clubs, where the disparity ratio falls slightly from 1.94 to 1.80 for men. However, we can also see that amongst the two kinds of association where the working class were over-represented, that this over-representation fell, dramatically so in the case of trade unions. By the 1990s, it was almost as likely for professional and managerial men to be in trade unions as for working-class men, and it was much more likely for professional and managerial women to be in trade unions.

Panel 2 of Table 13.1 shows the class compositions of the different organizations. Taking the example of male trade union membership, it shows that over three quarters of those union members who were from the working and service classes in 1972 were from the working class (the disparity ratio is 3.62). But as we move to the other associations (C-O), representing sports/hobby clubs to 'Other', we find that the service class represents a clear majority and that the service and the working class ratios are again two or more in most of the cases. We can also see how this composition becomes ever more marked over time, with all the disparity ratios strengthening in favour of the service class over the period. By the 1990s, such is the disparity of membership between classes in most associations that it seems reasonable to identify them as largely one-class associations. Rather than being vehicles where the working class mix with the middle classes, they are ever more uniformly service class in membership. In loosely descending order, the most socially uniform are professional associations (disparity ratio of 34.2 for men, 52.4 for women); parent–teacher associations (6.92 for men, 5.94 for women); environmental groups (6.14/ 8.44); political parties (4.03/6.97); church or religious organizations (4.30/4.11); and residents/ tenants groups (3.66/3.23). These are all very large disparity ratios. However, what is even more remarkable is that even for organizations previously dominated by the working class, the disparity ratios move in favour of the service class by the 1990s. In 1972, trade unions were overwhelmingly dominated by working class men (compared with service class men), but by 1999 service class men were narrowly in the majority. For women, indeed, unions were overwhelmingly dominated by the service class. Only amongst working-men's clubs did working class members predominate over service class ones, yet even here the disparity had narrowed sharply since the 1970s.

Table 13.1 therefore clearly indicates that there has been a dramatic skewing of associational memberships over the past thirty years. Historically significant forms of working class formal organization—trade unions and working-men's clubs—have both lost numbers and become more 'gentrified'. Today, the most unionized sections of the workforce are not in manual occupations but are amongst professionals. Formal modelling of these relationships using logistic regression (Li, Savage, and Pickles 2003) indicate that the growing skew is not simply due to numerical shifts in the size of the respective classes, but indicates increasingly that the professional and managerial service class have a greater propensity to be members of associations.

Our basic finding, therefore, is that whilst historically we can identify different class specific forms of social capital, and that both workers and the middle classes had their own kinds of bureaucratic involvement, this has changed radically over the past thirty years. Whereas civic involvement fifty years ago did spread between different social groups, this is less the case now. Perhaps this indicates a greater tendency for formal organizations to be aligned with middle class habitus?

Contemporary Popular Involvement in Associations

In this section we report qualitative interview data to explore the significance of membership from the point of view of the public, examining the extent to which involvement conveys capacities, skills, resources, or other benefits that might not be available to those who do not join such associations, and whose interests and enthusiasms are organized in purely informal means.[6] We here examine the way that 182 residents in four different parts of Manchester[7] talked about their involvement in formal and informal social, leisure, and voluntary activity. Systematically exploring how people talked about their range of involvement, and comparing their narratives of involvement in formal associations with their narratives regarding other enthusiasms and hobbies which are not related to any kind of formal associations, a number of points emerge.

First, there is a considerable range of activity in various kinds of associations. Table 13.2 indicates the extent to which people were involved in associations. It is worth noting that our respondents report higher levels of aggregate membership than are found in national random sample surveys. The BHPS in 1998 reports 44 per cent not having any associational membership, compared with 16 per cent in our sample (Warde et al. 2003). In part this discrepancy is likely to reflect the nature of our sample (which is skewed towards the highly educated middle classes who, as we have seen above, are more likely to be members), but in part also reflects that in-depth interviews are likely to reveal higher memberships. There are several examples in our interviews of people who recalled memberships that did not come instantly to mind, or alternatively revealed memberships during the interview that they did not mention when explicitly asked about them.

Second, those who are not in formal associations tend not to compensate through informal involvement in pursuit of hobbies or enthusiasms on a private basis or with fellow enthusiasts. Rather, those who are not formally involved tend to fall into two types. (*a*) a group which is more socially withdrawn in general, with its leisure

Table 13.2 Associational membership in four areas

	Cheadle	Chorlton	Ramsbottom	Wilmslow
All Civic	2	5	11	25
Church	1	2	5	12
Parents	0	3	4	8
Charities	2	3	6	12
Educational	0	0	0	3
Residents	0	0	0	0
All Sports	12	8	7	24
Golf	1	0	3	10
Tennis	1	0	0	3
Rugby	0	0	3	0
Fishing	3	0	1	0
Darts/snooker/ bowls	4	0	0	0
Gyms	1	8	2	7
Social	11	5	5	1
All Campaigning	0	13	4	4
Women's	0	1	2	2
Environmental	1	3	2	2
Hobby clubs	5	11	8	9
Prof associations	5	9	9	8
Trade unions	3	8	6	3
Other	1	2	3	1
Total memberships	61	77	76	120
Memberships per person	1.4	1.6	1.6	2.7
Non-members	7	14	9	0

interests focusing on relatively privatized activities such as gardening, home decoration, television watching, and so forth; (b) a group of mainly middle-class professionals, nearly all graduates, living in Chorlton, a gentrifying area of inner Manchester. These groups often do have intense informal social lives, but these tend to be socially exclusive, with like-minded people with similar stocks of cultural capital. The weakness of formal associational culture tends to produce a rather insular culture.

Third, and by way of contrast, those with the most active hobbies or enthusiasms were almost all without exception those in formal associations. A few examples illustrate the point. A retired airport worker, a flying enthusiast belonged to a flying club, and had even formed a limited company to purchase a plane with his fellow enthusiasts. A mother of a teenage girl who was competing in English show jumping competitions was an active member of the Pony Club and had been asked to sit on its committee. Whereas there were many respondents who enjoyed walking and hiking, those who were the most interested, belonged to Alpine Clubs, hiking clubs, and the like. Perhaps most striking of all are a number of elderly women who had travelled to different parts of the world, and generated a strong sense of personal satisfaction and involvement, as well as numerous friends and contacts, through their activity in formal associations. Consider the case of Sarah, who spoke lovingly of her role in the Inner Wheel, which was attached to the Rotary Club:

Well their motto is 'service above self'. It was formed by an American in 1905 for business people to get together not for business reasons, but to help people who were less well off than themselves and it came abroad, it's an international organization now. After the First World War the women who had been carrying on the work for their husbands didn't want to break it up and they formed the inner wheel in 1924 in a Turkish bath in Manchester. So you had to be the wife of a Rotarian, or the mother of a single Rotarian, or the sister of a single Rotarian, or the daughter of a widowed Rotarian. I became involved in the district when there were 75 which goes from I suppose Chorley is furthest north going to Biddulph and Warrington Eastish and West to Newton-le-Willows and we were reduced to 35 in 1985.

So what sort of things were you doing?

A few charity things, we provided backup for the Rotary. We're going to do a Swimathon on the 6th March . . . . I shall be President again for the 3rd time next year.

What does that involve?

It doesn't involve anything. It involves as much or as little as you wish. . . . Well you meet all sorts of people, professional people, service people. We have a conference every year for the association which is the whole of Great Britain.

Is that something you go to?

I used always to go, one year it was in Bournemouth, one year it was in Blackpool and next year they haven't decided whether it's going to be Cardiff or Glasgow.

So what happens at the conference?

You meet all the people from the other clubs and learn what they're doing. There are also international conferences.

You say international?

Yes, the last one I went to in 1977 was in Brussels, a Dutch lady was the association President, it was a fantastic do. One was in Australia, which I obviously didn't go to, then there was one in Berlin . . . you see all these people in their national costumes and you talk to them and you find out how very similar people are from various parts of the world.

Could you put in a nut shell what you've gained from being in that?

I was an intensely shy person, I couldn't have got up and spoken in front of people, 2 or 3 let alone a house full. I couldn't walk into a room with people I didn't know without getting a panic attack, but it doesn't worry me now. I would advise anybody who has a Rotarian husband, or to get a husband to join the Rotary and become a member of the wheel because that friendship is there for life. If you move anywhere you can transfer your membership.

So you feel part of a network of women throughout the world in that respect?

Oh yes.

Here is a striking example of how associational involvement stretches and extends a person's capacities and resources, in a way that Putnam would celebrate as an example of social capital at its best. The main point here is that formal involvement is linked to informal practices. This is even true for practices of neighbourliness which may not require formal associations. Thus, the most neighbourly residents in our research were in Cheadle, where there were high levels of interaction and support between neighbours. This was also the area where local social and working-men's clubs continued to be important, and where significant numbers of respondents mentioned that they were members of, and would meet their neighbours in such venues. These findings therefore offer strong support to Stebbins' (1992) contention that informal and formal leisure are intricately connected. Formal organizations are crucial to anyone wishing to develop and nurture their interests. There are few avenues whereby people with 'serious' leisure interests can rely on informal avenues to pursue their interests and bypass associational activities.

Fourth, there are clear differences in the way respondents report their involvement in commercially and managerially run organizations, such as gyms, leisure, and sports clubs, where they pay a commercial fee, compared with those formal associations relying on voluntary effort. In the former, people adopt a more consumerist ethos, and tend to be more privatized in their engagement with other users. For many respondents, and especially women, going to clubs such as these provides a structured means of removing themselves from the demands of their family and work and hence are a means of having time to themselves. A young female actress who went to a private gym twice a week reported that 'I just do my thing and then come out again'. A female optician who went regularly to a gym but had no social contact with other users reported that 'I'm not a very clubby person, really', whilst a youth worker said that 'I just did my thing, and then went in the steam room and chatted to people but I did not go there for that, I was quite happy not to. I wanted to be in a little bubble really'. Similar findings are evident for a wide range of involvement in fee charging sports clubs which now form the most popular kinds of associations, certainly for men. Large-scale, commercially run clubs, proved very attractive. Many affluent respondents were attracted to the large sports complex, with golf course, tennis, swimming, gym facilities, as well as full catering facilities, in which (in return for a large fee) people were pampered. Commercially run activities do not stretch or extend people's capacities in the way that a large number of people reported was the case in formal associations.

Perhaps surprisingly, a similar picture applies to engagement in pressure groups, which were especially popular in gentrifying areas. Here, membership in associations without local branches such as Greenpeace, Amnesty, and Friends of the Earth was common but rarely led to sustained involvement. For these respondents, belonging to a campaigning organization was primarily a private badge of social concern, a means of indicating that they were 'concerned individuals'. Part of the reason is that some had become disenchanted with involvement in political parties and social movements, or had scaled down their commitments in recent years for practical reasons or because their energies moved elsewhere. One woman had been very active in hunt saboteur association, but had experienced something akin to burn out: 'I'm going to sound really callous now, but its not conducive to the life I lead now because its getting up at 4am and just being militant and I don't have the energy any more'. During her last year at University 'I took my finals very seriously and a change happened in the third year, I moved into this property, I moved in with a boyfriend who I thought was going to be there forever, and all of a sudden it was something that I could not really commit to and my energies were just going away with running a house and doing the course'. For another woman, this distance from involvement was explicit: 'I mean I tend to belong to things, you know, like I'm a member of Amnesty International, but my social life isn't bound up with them, I'm very much the sort of, here's my annual fee, and I might write some letters and join in a campaign, but I do it very much under my own steam, so I wouldn't really count things like that . . . '.When asked if she ever attended meetings, she replied, 'I've tended not to. I have done in the past and at the moment quite honestly I'm what I'd call a sleeping member'. She had joined because 'I completely believe in what they're doing, and I suppose it is a convenient way for me, as someone who is not going to run about and do anything about it myself, to actually support what they're doing. It's very much that sort of thing'.

Fifth, whilst 84 per cent of respondents were members of some kind of association, a much smaller proportion were active in formal roles within the associations. The exception to this is the involvement of people in social clubs, where a number of respondents were prepared to serve on committees, but elsewhere people often resisted being incorporated into active positions. An instructive example is Jane, who came from a very affluent household (her husband being an owner of a large textile wholesaling firm). She had become vice-chair of the county branch of the National Society for the Prevention of Cruelty to Children.

Well it was when I lived in Adlington, that was very much a sort of community, much more than here and you got involved and they asked you to get involved in everything and because I wanted to be part of the community I joined and of course once they have got you they don't let you go, charities never let you go.

What kind of things have you done?

All sorts. Running functions really. I had a lunch here for over 100 and a fashion show and things like that. I was Chairman of North Country.

That must have been quite a major commitment?

It was. I found it very hard really.

Why?

The politics of it all really. I realized how difficult people could be and also it worried me a lot because I don't mind helping with anything but I don't like being totally responsible because it worries me terribly. I would rather someone delegated me. I would do it for them. I don't mind working but I hate the worry. It worried me because you are under pressure to hit targets all the time. It is supposed not to be but they do, you feel bad if you go backwards. And also I don't think my husband understood this, it is not like a business, they are not employees, they are all volunteers and you have to handle them with kid gloves so it was very hard, I found it very hard.

What kind of people used to get involved in the NSPCC?

Well unfortunately there is a problem with charities. Most of the committees are old and you get new people interested and get them coming along and they just sort of say this is going to be awful and don't stay. There are some young committees but it is getting harder to attract young people and also I think they probably work a lot more now so there are quite a lot of elderly ones that we can't let retire because we would not have anyone if they retired.

What do you discuss at these meetings?

What everybody is doing. Anything that has come from London, any problems or any new projects. Just general discussions and also it gives people the chance to air any problems or grievances. Quite often we are annoyed with Head Office because London thinks very differently.

You must have pressures here.

Yes and they are very different, so there is always a clash.

This case is intriguing for a number of reasons. In many respects, Jane is a contemporary exponent of the upper class 'county' woman, where she's being involved in charities as an important aspect of her expected social role. She reports that she was asked to become active, and one can detect that the bureaucratization of charitable activity does not fit well with her expectations, experience, and habitus. The traditional association between women's domestic roles and their ability to play leading roles in civic organizations is stretched.

Another example of this point is the case of Susan, a training consultant for a leading bank and who had also been active for a Cat Charity and in the Conservative Party. She instructively relates how she had become active in these associations.

When I worked in Manchester and I was sort of based there a lot of the time I did a lot of work . . . . I was on a regional committee and so I did a lot of fund-raising with them. I was more active, I suppose, with the logistic side of it. Not the planning side, although I did a lot of the planning as well, but this is the plan, how in practise does that work and who needs to be involved . . . .

Why did you join it in the first place?

All that had happened was that when I, without going into too great a detail, I'd been seconded to work for the general manager of operations . . . . Because of the type of job I'd held, it had required somebody who didn't need any help at all. So when I actually came back to Manchester, the chap who was running the region, thought well, I think I can use this . . . . And what he wanted was to do some PR work for the region not just for one or two branches, there were twenty seven something branches in the region and that takes a lot of putting together and he wanted somebody to do this and he did-n't want to have any involvement, he wanted to just be able to hand it to somebody and say: 'Do something with this' . . . So he said to me: 'Get in touch with Macmillan', so I did, and really it took off from there. What I found was there was a lot of—because I didn't realize—a lot of solicitors and accountants that I knew very well in Manchester were involved. They were asking us what we were doing and it turned out people who had gone to school with my husband were involved, you know, knew Macmillan, the Secretary of the region was a solicitor who knew Macmillan. So I really got into it that way.

Did you feel quite attached then to other members who were involved? No?

Their words to me were: 'If we could afford to buy in your services we would love to, but we couldn't as a charity'. It's very, very much an accountal issue.

The picture from both these cases—as well as many others not reported here—indicates that those who become core members of the organization tend to be co-opted by the institution, and because the institution seeks out people with particular skills and capacities, they tend to be those in professional and managerial occupations, so helping to generate a more exclusive institutional habitus. There is an overlap between the skills and aptitudes required in professional and mana-gerial work and in organizing and participating in associations. One needs to be able to speak publicly, have a degree of confidence in one's views, know how to relate to others. We can see here a situation in which formal associations are indeed important for conveying a range of social advantages, and their activists are becoming increasingly socially selective. It is not, by and large, that such associations are being snobbish in looking to recruit socially selectively, it is more that they seek to engage people with the kinds of generic skills and aptitudes that they will find valuable.

Conclusion: Excavating the History of the Bureaucratic Habitus

Let me now draw the threads of this chapter together and relate my findings to the current debate on bureaucracy. Formal associations are a largely unexplored arena in which bureaucratic forms can be said to extend and enrich modes of popular participation and involvement in a remarkable range of avenues and areas. Although there has been recent speculation about the potential of new modes of informal association to replace more formalized modes of involvement, our evidence indicates that formally organized activities are crucial to provide a range of services, practices, and activities that would otherwise simply not be done. They remain, therefore, a key part of a pluralist, democratic culture with an active civil society. In this respect at least, my arguments support the claims of Putnam (2000) and indicate the value of bureaucratic forms in civil society.

However, I have also noted the power of a distinctive institutional habitus. This is in keeping with du Gay's concern to relate the ethos of bureaucracy to its formal structures. Here, my reflections are less optimistic. Weber recognized that bureaucracies needed to be staffed by those with the appropriate dispositions, and talked about the significance of rational specialists with office holding constructed as a vocation characterized by forms of advanced training. In the early development of bureaucratic forms, this habitus had a wide-ranging, populist appeal, in part because of its popular repudiation of patronage and elite control. It was members of the working as well as the middle class who pioneered popular bureaucratic forms, recognizing their distinctive merits over gentlemanly and status-based forms of organization. A shared recognition of the merits of bureaucracy could be seen as one of the axes which bound together elements of the organized working class and parts of the middle class, in a kind of progressive class alliance that Clarke (1971) and Stedman Jones (1983) saw as key to the success of the Labour movement in the early and middle years of the twentieth century. Bureaucratic organization could be harnessed to an ethos which celebrated a form of cross-class populism which sought to eliminate patronage and elitism through the formalization of procedure.[8]

However, as the professional and managerial classes have matured and expanded, so they increasingly colonize bureaucratic forms of organization. I have shown that there is significant fall off in working class involvement in formal organizations, with the declining membership of trade unions and working-men's clubs being especially dramatic. A vicious circle is likely to take place in which the ability to perform in bureaucratic structures is seen to reside in those with certain kinds of aptitudes and experiences. Our evidence pointing to institutional selection processes by which core members are recruited points in this direction. We need to distinguish different kinds of bureaucracy. There are a myriad possible types of bureaucracy which conform in broad terms with Weber's ideal type, each of which has a different kind of habitus and ethos. It is perhaps not the erosion of bureaucracy itself, so much as the dominance of a particular form of centralized, commercial management form, which should concern us. du Gay's defence of bureaucracy in large part involves defending the principles of public sector bureaucracy. No doubt this is important, but I would also argue the need to recognize the distinct significance of popular bureaucratic forms which are losing ground even in areas where traditionally they have been significant. One way of considering the significance of the current (New) Labour government is that (building on the previous Tory administration) it has axed any remaining links between popular bureaucratic forms and the public sector, and instead yoked public and private sector bureaucracies together. Thinking seriously about how to recharge the appeal of popular bureaucratic forms in such a situation may well be a crucial political intervention.

Does it matter if core members of voluntary associations are socially exclusive so long as they observe the ethos of office and act even-handedly in the discharge of their duties? Well, in the spirit of Weber's own ideal type methodology, we can at least point to some unexpected consequences of a situation where the ethos of office is closely aligned to particular types of middle class habitus. First, it is likely to encourage further social polarization as the middle classes able to draw upon the social capital from their associational roles will gain resources compared to those without. Second, it will tend to construct large sections of the population only as 'consumers', as people reliant on, but not actively involved in generating, services and leisure interests through associational activity. This may lead to a situation where bureaucracy may be ever more important for sustaining democratic modes of governance and civic engagement, but practically less able to deliver this precisely. Along these lines Pierre Bourdieu (1984) claims that the major division is not between left and right, but between those who have political opinions and those who are not able to claim the right to such opinions. The evidence in this chapter indicates that the alignment of bureaucracy with the institutional habitus of the professional and managerial middle class closes down one historical avenue for the advancement of more popular concerns.

Notes

1. Indeed, read in this way, Weber anticipated Foucault's much discussed arguments regarding the shift from sovereign to capillary forms of power (Foucault 1975).
2. In his later work on *Bowling Alone*, Putnam extends his interest in social capital to include informal social relationships. 'When philosophers speak in exalted tones of "civic engagement" and "democratic deliberation", we are inclined to think of community associations and public life as the higher form of social involvement, but in everyday life, friendship and other informal types of sociability provide crucial social support' (Putnam 2000: 95). Yet he is able to extend his definition of social capital only by weakening his theoretical explanation of the mechanisms which produce social capital. He uses metaphors and aphorisms, such as the idea that 'bonding' social capital is a form of superglue, and bridging social capital a form of WD40, but with relatively little precision as to how the mechanisms of social capital actually operate. See Li et al. (2003), and Blokland and Savage (2005) for an elaboration of this point.
3. And see Weber himself, 'Bureaucracy inevitably accompanies modern *mass democracy* . . . This results from its characteristic principle: the abstract regularity of the exercise of authority . . . . Hence of the horror of "privilege" and the principled rejection of doing business "from case to case" ' (Weber 1968: 983).
4. Certain forms of church organization, for instance, in the Methodist church, were also implicated in these forms of popular bureaucracy.
5. This section draws on work carried out under an ESRC project '*Social Capital: developing a measure and assessing its usefulness in empirical research*' (with Yaojun Li and Andrew Pickles), 2001–3.

6. This section draws on work carried out under an ESRC project *'Lifestyles and social integration: a study of middle class culture in Manchester* (with Gaynor Bagnall and Brian Longhurst), 1997–9. (see Savage, Bagnall and Longhurst 2001, 2004).

7. The four places we studied were each chosen to represent a different mix of habitus and capitals, as identified by Bourdieu (see Savage, Bagnall and Longhurst (2004) for more details). The four areas were

- Wilmslow, a market town twelve miles south of Manchester, which was located in the desirable north Cheshire suburban belt focusing on Macclesfield and Altrincham. We expected to find high status, affluent middle class. We interviewed in areas of detached housing, where properties were valued in 1997 at between £250,000 and £750,000. We chose Wilmslow as a location where those with unusually large amounts of economic capital were located.
- Ramsbottom, an old Lancashire mill town twelve miles north of Manchester. The area had been subject to considerable new building and had emerged as a popular commuter belt location. We interviewed in large older terraced and newer semi-detached housing which sold for between £50,000 and £150,000. We chose this as an area where we expected to find those with reasonable amounts of economic and cultural capital to be located.
- Chorlton, an area of urban gentrification close to the centre of Manchester, clustering around an area with new cafes, wine bars, restaurants, and specialist shops. We expected to find large numbers of academically well-qualified public sector workers, and interviewed in 'desirable' streets where properties ranged in price from £50,000 for small terraces to £200,000 for the largest terraced houses. We expected to find large numbers of respondents with high levels of cultural capital.
- Cheadle, an interwar suburban estate of three bedroom semi-detached housing. In 1997/98 houses were valued at between £50,000 and £65,000, and we expected to find large numbers of intermediate class white-collar workers.
- In each location we aimed to obtain fifty in-depth interviews, which were taperecorded and transcribed. We took a one in three sample from the electoral roll, using a quota to obtain similar numbers of men and women.

8. Though there were tensions between centralized forms of bureaucratic provision, which tended to be supported by professional interests, and more localized forms of mutualized control, often popular amongst workers (see Johnson 1979; Savage 1987). Many of the most powerful popular bureaucratic forms such as trade unions and cooperative societies managed to combine elements of both local and central control.

References

Albrow, M. (1970). *Bureaucracy*. Basingstoke: MacMillan.

Bauman, Z. (1988). *Modernity and the Holocaust*. Cambridge: Polity.

Bellah, R. N., Madsen, R., Sullivan, W. M., Swidler, A., and Tipton, S. A. (1985). *Habits of the Heart: Commitment in American Life*. Berkeley, CA: University of California Press.

Blau, P. (1956). *Bureaucracy in Modern Society*. New York: Random House.

Blokland, T., and Savage, M., (eds). (2005). *Social Capital on the Ground*. Oxford: Blackwells.

Bourdieu, P. (1984). *Distinction: A Social Critique of the Judgement of Taste*. London: Routledge.

Bourdieu, P. (1997). 'The forms of capital', in A. H. Halsey, H. Lauder, P. Brown, and A. S. Wells (eds), *Education: Culture, Economy, Society*. Oxford: Oxford University Press.

Bourdieu, P. (1998). *The State Nobility: Elite Schools in the Field of Power*. Cambridge: Polity.

Clarke, P. F. (1971). *Lancashire and the New Liberalism*. Cambridge: Cambridge University Press.

Croizier, M. (1964). *The Bureaucratic Phenomenon*. London: Tavistock.

du Gay, P. (2000). *In Praise of Bureaucracy*. London: Sage.

Farnie, D. (1978). *The English Cotton Industry and the World Market*. Oxford: Clarendon Press.

Foucault, M. (1975). *Discipline and Punish*. London: Penguin.

Hall, P. (1999). 'Social Capital in Britain'. *British Journal of Political Science*. 29; 417–61.

Hetherington, K. (1998). *Expressions of Identity: Space, Performance, Politics*. London: Sage.

Johnson, R. (1979). *Unpopular Education*. London: Hutchinson.

Li, Y., Savage, M., Tampubolon, G., Warde, A., and Tomlinson, M. (2002). 'Dynamics of social capital: trends and turnover in associational membership in England and Wales: 1972–1999'. *Sociological Research Online*. 7/3; U97–U132.

Li, Y., Savage M., and Pickles, A. (2003). 'Social change, friendship and civic participation'. *Sociological Research Online*. 8/4; U412–35.

Li, Y., Savage, M. and Pickles, A. (2003). 'Social capital and social exclusion in England and Wales (1972–1999).' *British Journal of Sociology*. 54/4; 497–526.

Littler, C. (1982). *The Development of the Labour Process in Capitalist Societies*. London: Hutchinson.

Mafesoli, F. (1995). *The Time of the Tribes*. London: Sage.

McIvor, A. (2001). *A History of Work in Britain, 1880–1950*. Basingtoke: Palgrave.

Moorhouse, H. (1993). *Hot-Rodding*. Manchester; Manchester University Press.

Putnam, R. 1993. *Making Democracy Work: Civic Traditions in Modern Italy*. Princeton, NJ: Princeton University Press.

Putnam, R. 1995. 'Bowling alone: America's declining social capital'. *Journal of Democracy*. 6/1; 65–78.

Putnam R. (2000). *Bowling Alone: the Collapse and Revival of American community*. New York: Touchstone.

Ray, K., Savage, M., Tampubolon, G., Warde, A., Longhurst, B. J., and Tomlinson, M. (2003). 'The exclusiveness of the political field: networks and political mobilization'. *Social Movement Studies*. 2/1; 37–60.

Reay, D., David, M., and Ball, S. (2001). 'Making a difference? institutional habituses and higher education choice'. *Sociological Research Online*. 5/4; U126–U142.

Rossteutscher, S. (2002). 'Advocate or reflection: associations and political culture'. *Political Studies*. 50/3; 514–28.

Savage, M. (1987). *The Dynamics of Working Class Politics: the Labour Movement in Preston*. Cambridge: Cambridge University Press.

Savage, M. (1998). 'Discipline and the career: the construction of internal labour markets on the Great Western Railway, 1840–1914', in A. McKinlay (ed.), *Managing Foucault*. London: Sage, 299–326.

Savage, M. and Miles, A. (1994). *The Remaking of the British Working Class*. London: Routledge.

Savage, M., Bagnall G., and Longhurst, B. J. (2001). 'Ordinary, ambivalent and defensive: class identities in the north west of England'. *Sociology*. 35/4; 875–92.

Savage M., Bagnall, G., and Longhurst, B .J. (2004). *Globalization and Belonging*. London: Sage.

Stebbins, R. A. (1992). *Amateurs, Professionals and Serious Leisure*. Montreal: McGill University Press.

Stedman-Jones, G. S. (1983). *The Language of Chartism*. Cambridge: Cambridge University Press.

Tarrow, S. (1995). 'Cycles of collective action: between moments of madness and the repertoire of contention', in M. Traugott (ed.), *Repertoires and cycles of collective action*. London: Duke University Press.

Thompson, E. P. (1963) *The Making of the English Working Class*. London: Gollancz.

Vincent, D. (1999) *The Culture of Secrecy: Britain 1832–1998*. Oxford: Clarendon Press.

Warde, A., Tampubolon, G., Longhurst, B. J., Ray, K., Savage, M., and Tomlinson M. (2003). 'Trends in social capital: membership of associations in Great Britain, 1991–1996'. *British Journal of Political Science*. 33; 515–34.

Weber, M. (1968). *Economy and Society*. Berkeley, CA: University of California Press.

Index

Printed in the United States
By Bookmasters